THE CLASH OF EMPIRES

Lydia H. Liu

The Clash of Empires
The Invention of China in
Modern World Making

HARVARD UNIVERSITY PRESS
Cambridge, Massachusetts, and London, England

First Harvard University Press paperback edition, 2006

Library of Congress Cataloging-in-Publication Data

Liu, Lydia He.
    The clash of empires : the invention of China in modern world making / Lydia H. Liu.
      p. cm.
    Includes bibliographical references and index.
    ISBN 0-674-01307-7 (cloth)
    ISBN 0-674-01995-4 (pbk.)
    1. China—History—1861–1912. 2. China—Politics and government—19th century.
  I. Title: Invention of China in modern world making. II. Title.

DS761.L58 2004
951'.034—dc22   2004042218

For Li Tuo

Contents

Illustrations

Acknowledgments

My research on this book would not have been possible without the generous support of many libraries, archives, foundations, and individuals in China, Europe, and North America. A 1997 John Simon Guggenheim Award relieved me from teaching and administrative responsibilities at UC Berkeley and greatly expedited the writing of the book. Thanks to a Lilly Fellowship in religion, I was able to spend a year's leave at the National Humanities Center at Research Triangle Park in North Carolina in 1997–98 and be part of its lively scholarly community. Mary Campbell, Elizabeth Helsinger, Dyan Elliott, Michele Longino, Kent Mullikin, the library staff, and the other residential fellows made my stay at the Center truly rewarding. I am grateful for the assistance offered by the curator, Qin Guojing, of the First Historical Archives of China and Zhu Jiajin of the National Palace Museum in Beijing, and to the American Bible Society, the Presbyterian Society, the National Archives and Records Administration of the United States (NARA), the School of Oriental and African Studies library at the University of London, Cambridge University Library, the Public Record Office, the Indian Office of the British Library, the Shanghai Library, the National Library of China, the Chinese Academy of Sciences Library, the Hoover Institution Library of Stanford University, the UC Berkeley libraries, and the University of Michigan libraries. The final revisions were completed during my transition from UC Berkeley to the University of Michigan. I thank both institutions for kindly providing me with the leave time and resources to bring this book to its final shape.

Sections of Chapter 5 and the conclusion appeared previously in an essay I wrote for the special issue of *Diacritics* in honor of Benedict Anderson that was co-edited by Pheng Cheah and Jonathan Culler. The editors' comments helped improve the conceptualization of that essay as well as some of the chapters in this book. An earlier version of Chapter 4 was included in my edited volume *Tokens of Exchange: The Problem of Translation in Global Circulations,* published by Duke University Press in 1999. I appreciate the generosity and kindness of Duke University Press and of the publisher of *Diacritics,* Johns Hopkins University Press, for permitting me to reuse the materials here. I thank the American Bible Society for letting me use photographs of two images from the Presentation New Testament in this book.

Chapter 2 was originally presented as the 2002 Renato Poggioli Memorial Lecture in Comparative Literature at Harvard University. I thank Stephen Owen, Jan Ziolkowski, Patrick Hanan, Susan Suleiman, James Engell, and Marc Shell for their astute comments and warm encouragement. Over the years, I have had many conversations with the audiences of my lectures in the United States and abroad which have greatly enriched the development of this project. I thank the following institutions for giving me those opportunities: Yale University, Stanford University, Cornell University, the University of Chicago, the University of California at Los Angeles, Duke University, Smith College, Göttingen University, the University of London, the University of Arizona, Rutgers University, Bowling Green State University, UC Berkeley, Columbia University, and the University of Michigan.

It is impossible to name all those who have helped me in the research and writing of this book. Patrick Hanan has shared some of his unpublished work and his vast knowledge with me throughout the writing process. I am deeply indebted to him in many ways and, in particular, to the model of meticulous scholarship he represents. Back in 1994, Andrew Jones helped me read and decipher many rolls of poorly shot microfilms I had purchased from the American Bible Society and wrote copious notes on them. I hope the final result will live up to the labor he and I put in working on the microfilm reader. Haun Saussy read a draft prospectus and made excellent suggestions. His work on William Dwight Whitney inspired Chapter 6 of my book. My former colleagues and graduate students at UC Berkeley shared their ideas and research projects with me and encouraged me in many other ways. I gratefully acknowledge the generosity and support of Paul Rabinow, Victoria Kahn, Caren Kaplan, Chris Berry, Aihwa Ong, Frederic Wakeman Jr., Larissa Heinrich, Alan Tansman, Stephen West, Jeffrey Riegel, and Peter Zinoman. I have had the good fortune of receiving the able research assistance of Jami Proctor-Xu, Carolyn Fitzgerald, Yang Lihua, Mark Miller, Elizabeth Veldman-Choi, and Petrus Liu at various stages. The writing of this book has benefited greatly from comments and suggestions made by Pamela

Crossley, Alexander Woodside, Benjamin Elman, Jonathan Spence, Gayatri Chakravorty Spivak, Paul Cohen, James Hevia, Leo Ou-Fan Lee, Theodore Huters, Martin Powers, Murray A. Rubinstein, Peter Bol, Emily Apter, Roger Hart, Paula Versano, Reyes Lazaro, Wang Hui, Shang Wei, Chen Yangu, Mark Elliott, Lisa Rofel, Shu-mei Shih, Zhao Gang, Barbara Fuchs, Cui Zhiyuan, Dilip Basu, Wilt Idema, John Zou, Tamara Chin, and Jody Blanco, as well as the anonymous reviewers of the manuscript. My conversations with Yopie Prins, Madhav Deshpande, William Baxter, Robert Sharf, James Lee, Miranda Brown, Jing Jiang, Hai Ren, Paul Strohm, David Porter, and James Porter led to valuable sources and insights. I am deeply grateful to Adrienne Munich for sending me her glossy print of the 1872 illustration of the Burmese envoy offering presents to Queen Victoria that is included in the book. I thank Michel Hockx, Henry Y. H. Zhao, Bonnie McDougall, J. P. McDermott, Wang Hui, Wang Xiaoming, Ni Wenjian, Bao Kun, Xu Baogeng, Luo Gang, Liu Dong, Yuefei Wang, Liu Yan, and Wang Zhongchen for kindly hosting my visits to the United Kingdom and China. The completion of this book coincided with my move to the University of Michigan, where I was given leave time and the opportunity to present some of the chapters. I am grateful to Donald Lopez, Tobin Siebers, Shuen-fu Lin, and my other colleagues and graduate students for their encouragement and intellectual support. The writing and preparation of my manuscript has taken more than a decade since its inception. I would like to thank my editor, Lindsay Waters, for his enthusiasm and patient guidance in the publication of the book. I am grateful to Amanda Heller for her careful reading and thorough editing of the manuscript and to editors at Harvard University Press for their assistance and good work.

To Li Tuo, the smart and uncompromising critic of my work, I dedicate this book. I am grateful to him and to my friends in China for drawing me into their sphere of intellectual activism and sharing their dream of a new internationalism.

THE CLASH OF EMPIRES

Civilizations Do Not Clash; Empires Do

Language has always been the perfect instrument of empire.

—Antonio de Nebrija, *Castilian Grammar* (1492)

I spent the summer of 1997 conducting archival research at the British Library and the Public Record Office in London. When I first arrived, the countdown clock was ticking away, as it was the eve of Hong Kong's historic handover to the People's Republic of China. Newspapers updated the public regularly about Prince Charles's preparations for the upcoming event and published opinion pieces predicting the future of Hong Kong. After glancing through the headlines each morning, I would get into an Underground train headed toward the Kew Gardens station and resume my research at the Public Record Office. There, I would spend most of my day going through the old diplomatic dispatches between the British Empire and the Qing government during the Opium Wars. It was the first of those wars that led to the British colonizing of Hong Kong in 1842.

The return of the British Crown Colony to China in the summer of 1997 refocused my attention on the issue of empire and sovereignty, one that had troubled Anglo-Chinese relations for over a century. The timing of it greatly affected the shape of my research project, as I had originally planned to work on the nineteenth-century missionary translations of the Bible. The strange experience of coming into physical contact with the official documents that had sealed Hong Kong's fate a hundred and fifty years before and then witnessing the moment of its return to China was enough to make me ponder the meaning of it all and rethink my book project. It struck me that the contemporary quibbling over the proper meanings of "handover," "takeover," and "return" with regard to the sovereignty of Britain or China seemed to echo a set of older concerns and anxieties. As I was to discover in the Reading Room of the Public Record Office, the argument over dignity,

1

entitlement, and the proper use of words carried just as much weight as the business of the opium trade insofar as treaty negotiations were concerned in the nineteenth century. The battle of words and translations in the official archives turned out to be central, not peripheral, to the sovereign will that had driven the Opium Wars.

Having been trained as a literary critic, I am intensely interested in archives, historical texts, artifacts, and so on because these things put me in touch with the rationale and, if I may say, the essence of the theoretical work I wish to pursue. This book is engaged with the hetero-cultural legacy of sovereign thinking in the nineteenth century, broadly defined. I emphasize the moments and forms of moral and affective investment in sovereignty that articulate effectively to the modern world of empires and nation-states. The itinerancy of signs and meanings in modern global history requires that a work like this pay close attention to the extraordinary circulation of text, object, and theory across linguistic, ethnic, cultural, and civilizational boundaries in modern times. Each chapter of the book investigates a central aspect of the problematic of sovereign thinking and makes a close examination of the texts, whether legal, diplomatic, religious, linguistic, or visual. A sustained focus on desire and sovereign thinking throughout the book enables the disparate strands of my research—on international law, semiotics, imperial gift exchange, missionary translations, grammar books, and colonial photography—to interweave in ways that I had not thought possible when I first embarked on the project.

Civilizations do not clash, but empires do. Having said this, I have the burden of proving it with this book. Chapter 1 raises the possibility of reading empire by engaging with the theory of semiotics and the notion of the sign in light of the novel military technology of telegraphic communication in the second half of the nineteenth century. I argue that reading empire entails thinking historically about the intimate connections among language, war, international law, semiotic inventions, and the idea of foreignness. The chapter provides a number of theoretical and historical grids for reading later chapters and seeks to reframe the issues of intersubjectivity, indexicality, and violence in light of the work of Charles Sanders Peirce, Michel Foucault, Georges Bataille, and other theorists.

In Chapter 2 I analyze the Anglo-Chinese Treaty of Tianjin, government archival sources, and published material to show how the translation of the written Chinese character *yi* at the time of the Opium War led to the invention of the super-sign *yi/barbarian* by the British, who believed that the use of the character was intended to insult the foreigner and thus sought to ban the word. I raise two historical questions: Why should the character have posed a threat to law and to the emergent order of international relations? And what are the sources of the anxiety that led to the ban?

In Chapter 3 I focus on the concept of *yi* in the articulation of the mandate of Heaven and in the imperial ideology of the ruling Manchus. The Yongzheng emperor's infamous literary persecution of Zeng Jing in the eighteenth century, for example, poses the intriguing issue of why, unlike the British, the Qing emperors chose not to ban the character while punishing the Chinese dissidents who opposed their alien rule but instead gave the Confucian concept a distinctly geopolitical reading in order to promote their own imperial projects.

Chapter 4 tackles the circulation of international law, in particular, the classical Chinese translation of Henry Wheaton's *Elements of International Law* in 1864. Drawing on archival sources, public records, and published works, I bring to light the role that the American missionary W. A. P. Martin played as a translator and diplomat at the close of the second Opium War. His translation of *Elements of International Law* was a major historical event that came to shape the relationship among the Qing, the Western powers, Japan, and Korea in the nineteenth century.

Chapter 5 focuses on the long, overlapping reigns of Queen Victoria and the Empress Dowager Cixi, raising new questions about gender and empire. I attempt to develop a reading that helps us understand issues such as imperial gift exchange and the sovereignty complex, as well as the colonial condition of the nineteenth-century women's suffrage movement.

Chapter 6 centers on the sovereign subject of grammar in nineteenth-century linguistic science. My analysis of the work of the American linguist William Dwight Whitney indicates that there emerged a symbiosis of international law and the laws of language that informed comparative scholarship as well as mainstream linguistic theory. Comparative grammar provided the objective ground on which positivist arguments about race, culture, and sovereign rights could be advanced and proved on behalf of the Indo-European language family. My study of Ma Jianzhong, the first Chinese comparative grammarian, shows that when he undertook the task of composing the monumental *Ma's Universal Principles of Classical Chinese* (1898), he was trying to negotiate a sovereign position for classical Chinese vis-à-vis the Indo-European languages.

In the conclusion I reflect on the implications of this study for our understanding of the new imperial order of the present. The chapter focuses specifically on the fetishizing of the throne chairs of the Qing emperors and the circulation of visual images of those chairs via photography and contemporary film, showing how the imperial unconscious continues to be haunted by the ghost of its past.

CHAPTER 1

The Semiotic Turn of International Politics

> It is not quite true, as is so often asserted, that it is the "newness" of contemporary technology that leaves us culturally unprepared. It is also the effacement of "oldness" of so many of the background assumptions and practices that lurk unexamined at the edges in these cases which contextualize the technology and frame our questions and responses.
>
> —Paul Rabinow, *Essays on the Anthropology of Reason*

It may seem a truism that a nation-state cannot imagine itself except in sovereign terms. But what is the truism saying to—or, rather, withholding from—us? Consider the contemporary makeup and breakup of national territories and identities, where the personal continues to be haunted by the sovereign and where the imperial may well appear in the guise of the national. Consider also the familiar notion of human dignity. Indeed, what is human dignity if not somehow vested with the mystique of sovereign thinking? Conversely, does the loss of sovereignty condemn to existential abjection those who experience that loss and must recuperate their dignity in the name of sovereign right?

In *Black Skin, White Masks*, Frantz Fanon provides some extraordinary insights into the formation of what he calls the "massive psychoexistential complex" brought about by the violence of colonialism.[1] The symptoms of the inferiority complex and colonial schizophrenia he diagnosed among colonized black people in the twentieth century remain potent and fascinating to this day, but they now appear to be migrating toward a different sort of problematic from that which troubled Fanon decades ago.[2] Increasingly, it seems that the critique of sovereign thinking must factor into our discussion of empire and colonial abjection, so that the psychoexistential complex of colonial and postcolonial subjects may articulate meaningfully to the general problematic of sovereign rights in our rapidly changing world.

In his reflections on the condition of sovereignty in the post–cold war era, the philosopher Jean-Luc Nancy points out that globalization may appear to displace the concept of war, along with all the politico-juridical concepts of sovereignty, but the return of war appears at the very heart of these displacements, even though some may claim that it does not appear at all. "Our anxiety also testifies . . . not to a regret, or to a nostalgia," writes Nancy, "but rather to a difficulty in doing without sovereign authority [*l'instance souveraine*], even down to its most terrible brilliance (seeing as it is also the most brilliant)."[3] As we follow the movement of diasporic populations in our time, the conflicting ways of sovereign thinking among those who migrate from one sovereign state to another, be it for political asylum or economic reasons, tend to support rather than disprove Nancy's observation about the difficulty of doing or thinking without sovereignty. For one cannot assume without a degree of philosophical naïveté that the will to sovereignty exists only among those who struggle for independent states but becomes irrelevant for diasporic communities that fight for their rights, dignity, and political recognition within an adopted sovereign state. Is political recognition not already articulated by the theory of sovereign rights? Is the personal not vested in the sovereign as one adopts the identity of an Asian American, African American, Jewish American and so on? Finally, is the argument of hybridity and multiplicity capable of grasping the ground of its own desire for sovereignty?

Inasmuch as sovereignty continues to be contested in the international as well as national realm, national and even racial identity needs to be understood and analyzed in terms of what the international is doing within the national imaginary, not just beyond its borders. This may be one of those simple lessons that dialectical reasoning can teach us; but it is not so simple when it comes to making personal choices at particular times. The choice of personal identity or bio-political belonging, of which citizenship is but part of the game, is very much constrained by the types of questions we can or cannot ask of sovereign rights in the modern world.

Such questions matter because we are dealing with a thoroughly historical, legal, and philosophical discourse of freedom. Or as Benedict Anderson rightly points out, "nations dream of being free, and, if under God, directly so. The gage and emblem of this freedom is the sovereign state."[4] Anderson's thesis is well made and seems indisputable on historical grounds. It is precisely on those grounds, however, that we need to pursue further the meaning of "freedom" beyond the established discourse of rights and to comprehend, rather than assume, the universal condition of any nation's dream of freedom when that dream must be figured a priori as a desire for the sovereign state. We should ask, for example, what renders the truth of *sovereign right as freedom* so self-evident, powerful, and inevitable? Insofar as sovereignty articulates a major mode of exchange between nation and empire in recent history, the truism of its truth needs to be unpacked carefully.

One of the ways in which we could begin the inquiry is to raise some new questions about desire, rights, and sovereign thinking, not exclusively in terms of legal discourse, but in light of what we can learn about colonial exchange and its production of difference, fetishism, identity, and the logic of reciprocity in translingual practices. As I try to demonstrate in this book, intellectual and material developments of this sort have had such significant bearing on sovereign thinking and the rise of international law that our study of the latter can no longer be confined to the self-explanatory evolution of legal discourse in Europe and North America. For sovereign thinking is one of those intellectual legacies of empire and nation building that must be reexamined, to borrow Edward Said's words, "according to a detailed logic governed not simply by empirical reality but by a battery of desires, repressions, investments, and projections."[5]

Signifying Empire: A (· ——) B (—— · · ·)

Reading empire, which is what this book essentially does, entails thinking historically about hetero-cultural and hetero-linguistic moments of sovereign thinking. It requires that we take the interactive engagements of language, war, international law, semiotic theories, and inventions among sovereign nations and empires seriously. The history of military technology demonstrates that major innovations in naval and military telecommunication systems took off in the beginning of the nineteenth century and underwent a dramatic upsurge in the latter half of the century. What it suggests to us is that the pioneers in the studies of the sign, Charles Sanders Peirce (1839–1914) and Ferdinand de Saussure (1857–1913), did not invent the meanings of the "code," "sign," "signal," and so on but already shared their usage with the engineers of the Royal Navy and the inventors of Morse code, Albert J. Myer's signal system, and other nineteenth-century systems of telegraphic communication.[6] From the start, the development of modern communication systems has been linked to military requirements and has been interwoven with the communication systems for the navy and army.[7]

The mnemonic aid for the international Morse system (1851), designed to assist rapid memorization of the code through short syllabic alphabets, throws fascinating light on the imperial ambitions of an evolving technology. One aid, reportedly developed by Samuel Morse himself, calls for the letter A (· ——) to be memorized as "Ag-ainst" and the letter B (—— · · ·) as "bar-ba-ri-an." Thus, the first two letters of the English alphabet in international Morse code are rendered as "against barbarian." The same memory aids continued to be used by the U.S. Army well into World War I.[8] Morse code was thus rendered meaningful as the master code of civilization and barbarity that came to govern the local meanings of numerous military actions taken by the British, the French, the Russians, the Americans, and their allies against the peoples of Asia, Africa, the Americas, and elsewhere in colonial warfare. As I show in Chapter 2, the super-sign *yi/barbarian* arrived at its prominent enunciatory position during the Opium Wars when the British crusade "against barbarians" encountered one of its strangest mirror images in the Chinese character *yi*. The signing of the Anglo-Chinese Treaty of Tianjin in 1858, therefore, fulfilled the destiny of the mnemonic coding of A (· ——) and B (—— · · ·) by banning the hetero-linguistic super-sign *yi/barbarian* for good.

Myer's system of "aerial telegraphy," the chief competitor of Morse code, was one of the most versatile of the signal systems invented in the nineteenth century. It involved waving a flag or torch to indicate individual letters according to a prearranged code. Developed around 1858, this system was based partly on Myer's prior work as a doctor with the deaf and the mute and partly on observations made by the U.S. Army of the signal practices of American Indians during the military campaigns against the native population. According to David Lyndon Wood, Myer served as an army doctor at various rugged frontier posts in Texas in 1854–1856 and had frequent opportunities to observe how the Native Americans signaled across vast distances.[9] Myer's *Manual of Signals* suggests that his innovative code was directly linked both to the U.S. wars on the Native Americans and to intelligence gathering.[10]

It is well known that the Swiss linguist Saussure took a deep interest in the sign language of deaf mutes and closely followed the new developments in military and maritime signaling and the telegraphic technologies of his time. The scope of his investigations included these as well as the writing systems of existing languages and artificial languages such as Esperanto.[11] Saussure recognized the importance of the novel signifying systems and treated the inventions by European naval and commercial forces as systems of visual signifiers among other signifying systems.[12] Peirce, for his part, made a legendary contribution to technological development by applying Boolean logic to electric switching circuits in 1867. Both semioticians inhabited the brave new world of signs and signals invented by their contemporaries and predecessors; in that sense, they initiated the study of the sign as much as they were initiated into it by the unprecedented innovations in military communication systems that enabled the major Western powers to advance their imperial bid for domination of the world.

The proliferation of international treaties and agreements among sovereign states has left a profound mark on our thinking about language, international politics, national histories, and modernity in general. The relationship between international politics and the study of the sign, however, is not patently obvious, nor are the disciplines of international law and linguistic science in the habit of speaking to each other in today's scholarship. Whereas treaty making and the study of language can each be dated to the centuries before the dawn of modern international relations and of modern linguistic science, the regulation of the sign and its global circulation had been unthinkable and unnecessary before the onslaught of modern colonial and global warfare. Insofar as we acknowledge the novelty of the work of Peirce and Saussure and their original contribution to the study of the sign, we must simultaneously register the novelty of the semiotic turn of international politics itself in the nineteenth century.

In recent decades a good deal of attention has been devoted to revisiting and analyzing Saussure's notion of the *conventionnel* or the *arbitraire* that was thought to characterize the relationship between the signifier and signified in a sign. Jacques Derrida argues in *Of Grammatology* that Saussure's concept of the *arbitraire* fails to account for the movement of the instituted trace central to the constitution of meaning and the objectivity of the sign within the classical system of oppositions. The instituted trace is where the relationship with the other is marked prior to the possibility of binary opposition and arbitrariness of the sign; but the movement of that trace, argues Derrida, is necessarily occulted, and "it produces itself as self-occultation. When the other announces itself as such, it presents itself in the dissimulation of itself."[13] In contrast, Derrida discovers in Peirce's multiple trichotomies the superior quality of being able to accommodate supple conceptualizations of the sign over and above Saussure's binary opposition of the signifier and signified. Peirce's notion of *symbol*, in particular, allows the movement and endless play of signs that appears to have anticipated Derrida's own critique of semiology and phenomenology.

My interpretation of the Peircian symbol differs from Derrida's endorsement of it. But before I move on to a detailed analysis of the subject, let me quickly observe that the idea of the *arbitraire* was hardly Saussure's invention and could be interrogated further with reference to the semiotic turn of international politics in the nineteenth century. As I demonstrate in Chapter 6, the American linguist William Dwight Whitney's (1827–1894) earlier elaboration of the *arbitrariness* of the sign resonated directly with the nineteenth-century vocabulary of positive law, and his appropriation of the concepts *phusei* (natural) and *thesei* (conventional) from the Greeks bears the hallmarks of contemporary legal discourse. Saussure, who was familiar with Whitney's work, joined this intellectual effort by developing his own notion of the conventionality of the sign for general linguistics. In an article titled "The Convention of Geneva: History of Linguistic Ideas and History of Communicative Practices," Daniele Gambarara draws our attention to the novel uses to which "convention" was put in Saussure's time, notably with reference to international assemblies and treaty meetings that sought to regulate semiotic projects as well as matters relating to war. The first international convention on road traffic and signals, the Geneva Convention of 1909, and the Brussels Convention of 1910 on maritime collision (and danger and distress signals) took place during the interval between the second and third courses given by Saussure on general linguistics.

The novel study of the sign, which was to exert a major impact on modern theories of language and communication, begins to acquire new meaning when approached in light of what I have called the semiotic turn of international politics in the long nineteenth century. For the first time in history, sovereign states and imperial powers convened and drew up binding treaties among themselves to regulate maritime signals, road signs, electrical codes, and other sign systems. International conventions became the venue par excellence for the standardization and adoption of various artificial sign systems. The novelty of this phenomenon is, as Gambarara puts it, that "we find men assembling in council for the purpose of establishing the meanings of signs and communication contexts by decree, and language being tested and specified by senior civil servants solemnly gathered around a table: semiotic convention at work under our eyes."[14] In 1868 a commission launched by the British and joined by representatives of other sovereign European nations succeeded in laying down an international code of signals for merchant navies, later extended into the International Code of Maritime Signals. This and other international agreements for the standardizing of codes and transportation systems such as railways and motor vehicles were only afterwards incorporated into the various national laws. Road traffic and signals were deliberated at the Geneva Convention, while danger and distress signals (maritime collisions) became unified at the Brussels Convention, and so on.[15]

What Whitney and Saussure have to say about the "conventionality" and "arbitrariness" of the sign is now common knowledge in modern semiotic discourse. All the more reason why we must reevaluate the novelty of their ideas in the context in which they emerged and, in particular, their relationship to the widespread utopia of global communication inspired by the technological innovations of their time. Particularly intriguing is the question of how and why abstract speculations about the sign mattered under those circumstances. Be it the burgeoning of new sign systems, military and otherwise, or the growing importance of international conventions that regulate semiotic practices in the international community, this course of events seems to bear meaningfully on the logic of reciprocity as practiced among sovereign nations and on the newly acquired sovereign status of the Indo-European family of languages, reigning supreme among the myriad tongues of the world. If the developments in military technologies and related legal instruments have proved indispensable to the making and consolidation of modern imperial powers, it follows that a semiotic reading of empire and a rethinking of the propositions of semiotics in light of empire are not simply unavoidable but absolutely necessary. In what follows, I explore the possibility of hetero-cultural refashioning of the notion of the sign both for the purposes of this book and for the sake of those who wish to venture beyond the Englishness of the Peircean sign or the Frenchness of the Saussurian sign.[16]

The Super-Sign: How Languages Get Thrown Together

The familiar triad of *icon*, *index*, and *symbol* in Peirce's semiotics is a subdivision of the dynamic *object*—a concept that brings to mind Saussure's signified—in its relation to the sign.[17] These trichotomous divisions are intended to demonstrate how the sign, the object, and the interpretant interact to produce meaning in complex ways.[18] Of the triad, the *iconic* sign turns on the logic of resemblance to convey ideas of the things it represents by mimicking them; interestingly, photography is cited as an example of the iconic sign. The second group of signs, called *index*, is characterized by their primary function of directing attention or pointing, such as a road sign, a pronoun, or a vocative exclamation like "Hi there!" The third, and by far the most dynamic and complex of the triad of signs, is the *symbolic* sign, which becomes associated with its meanings through convention or usage. According to Peirce, the natural language is a perfect system of symbolic signs because linguistic signs always grow out of other linguistic signs, *omne symbolum de symbolo*. And even the Greek etymology of the word "symbol" is shown literally to underscore this view of the sign. Peirce writes:

> Etymologically, it [symbol] should mean a thing thrown together, just as ἔμβολον (embolum) is a thing thrown into something, a bolt, and παράβολον (parabolum) is a thing thrown besides, collateral security, and ὑπόβολον (hypobolum) is a thing thrown underneath, an antenuptial gift. It is usually said that in the word *symbol* the throwing together is to be understood in the sense of "to conjecture"; but were that the case, we ought to find that *sometimes* at least it meant a conjecture, a meaning for which literature may be searched in vain. But the Greeks used "throw together" (συμβάλλειν) very frequently to signify the making of a contract or convention. Now, we do find symbol (σύμβολον) early and often used to mean a convention or contract.[19]

Peirce ponders and rejects one sense of the Greek word for "symbol" in favor of a translation that will lead him to the proper meaning of the original term in its literal, albeit already translated, manifestation: "throw together." But in what sense does the Greek etymology truly authorize and ground his notion of the linguistic sign as symbol? Is the English term "contract" or "convention"—one that carries the full weight of positive legal discourse as discussed earlier—not already *thrown together* (or equated) with its Greek counterpart before the ancient etymology can present itself intelligibly and authorize particular meanings in the foreign tongue? If the answer is yes, as I am suggesting, Peirce is clearly engaged in a manner of reasoning, common among those who look toward Greek or Latin roots to help secure the meanings of modern words, that requires the hand of translation to perform the etymology yet simultaneously occults the traces of that redoubled, authorizing gesture. What I mean to say is that the act of translation exemplifies the situation of "thrown-togetherness" in the quoted passage better than the particular etymology of the Greek word σύμβολον, and that same act renders the concept of the "linguistic sign" inadequate to the translated sense of "symbol." In short, we are catapulted into the realm of what I call the *super-*

sign—a linguistic monstrosity that thrives on the excess of its presumed meanings by virtue of being exposed to, or thrown together with, foreign etymologies and foreign languages. The super-sign escapes our attention because it is made to camouflage the traces of that excess through normative etymological procedures and to disavow the mutual exposure and transformation of the languages.

It is a commonplace that verbal signs are not stable and can change with time and usage; but as two, three, or multiple languages are involved and implicate one another, can we recapture the foreignness of that which has penetrated the opacity of the indigenous? Registering the influx of loanwords is not enough, because loanwords tend to gesture back toward the language(s) from which they borrow the etymologies and meanings and do not bother to hide the fact, as attested to by the existence of dictionaries such as the *OED*. There are a large number of hetero-linguistic verbal phenomena in modern languages that do not lend themselves to loanword analysis, nor can they be properly classified as indigenous elements or even words. Recognizing them as super-signs constitutes the first step toward identifying and analyzing forms of translingual speech and writing that would otherwise elude our grasp completely.

What is a super-sign? Properly speaking, a super-sign is not a word but a hetero-cultural signifying chain that crisscrosses the semantic fields of two or more languages simultaneously and makes an impact on the meaning of recognizable verbal units, whether they be indigenous words, loanwords, or any other discrete verbal phenomena that linguists can identify within particular languages or among them. The super-sign emerges out of the interstices of existing languages across the abyss of phonetic and ideographic differences. As a hetero-cultural signifying chain, it always requires more than one linguistic system to complete the process of signification for any given verbal phenomenon. The super-sign can thus be figured as a manner of metonymical thinking that induces, compels, and orders the migration and dispersion of prior signs across different languages and different semiotic media. For that reason, it offers ample insight into the workings of intellectual catachresis, of which this book offers many instances, such as the legal ban introduced by the British on the Chinese character *yi* through the super-sign *yi/barbarian* at the time of the Opium Wars (discussed in Chapters 2 and 3).

The super-sign marks the place where one might begin to analyze the instituted traces that Derrida mentioned, for example, in his critique of

Saussure but did not fully conceptualize as a hetero-linguistic and hetero-cultural movement of the signifying chain across different languages and writing systems.[20] This movement is generally occulted so that a word may appear free of the traces of the super-sign that animates it. The super-sign is good at camouflaging the foreignness and internal split of a verbal unit by adopting the unchanging face of an indigenous word, be it in written or phonetic form, and projecting an illusion of homogeneity onto the façade of concrete *wordness,* the materiality of the written script, to the unsuspecting eye of a native speaker.[21] In short, the super-sign exemplifies the semiotic operations of translingual speech and writing by acting out the verbal unit of one language and simultaneously displacing its signification onto a foreign language or languages, always in what one might call an occulted movement of thrown-togetherness.[22]

Not surprisingly, when Peirce began working on his theory of the sign, he envisioned the scene of first encounter between foreigners as a pure model of communication and invited us to "imagine two men who know no common speech, thrown together remote from the rest of the race. They must communicate; but how are they to do so?"[23] The innocuous conjuration of a first encounter presupposes, once again, a condition of *thrown-togetherness* between strangers and a certain hypothesis of communication that lead the semiotic inquiry in directions other than that of the etymological closure performed by the evocation of the Greek word for "symbol." We are driven to ask: What causes the strangers to be thrown together and removed from the rest of the human world? Whence does the theological injunction "they must communicate" originate? Peirce's originary fiction of a first encounter cannot but refer us to other originating fictions in which the primary scene had occurred before and been repeated countless times until it had blazed a trail of simulacra of first encounters since the European conquest of the New World.

Daniel Defoe had imagined just such an encounter in his novel *The Strange and Surprising Adventures of Robinson Crusoe.* The meeting of Crusoe and Friday takes place on a fictional Caribbean island and exposes them to certain risks. To what risks, one might ask, do Peirce's fictional characters expose themselves? Is it the state of being thrown together, or their removal from civilization, or the impulse to communicate? Suppose we transpose Peirce's hypothesis onto Defoe's island and imagine a European outcast and a Caribbean "savage" being thrown together in this remote place and cut off from the rest of human society. Must they communicate? If so, how? Peirce

would reply that they communicate "by imitative sounds, by imitative gestures, and by pictures. These are three kinds of likenesses. It is true that they
will also use other signs, finger-pointings, and the like. But, after all, the
likenesses will be the only means of describing the qualities of the things
and actions which they have in mind."[24] The immediate occulting of finger
pointing or the indexical sign troubles Peirce's attempt to establish the prim-
itivity of the first encounter in terms of *mimetic iconicity.* Let us pause and ask
how the possibility of finger pointing may transform the local meanings
of imitative gestures, sounds, and pictures and put them in the service of
indexicality.

The Terror of Intersubjective Communication

The transposition of Defoe's and Peirce's fictions of first encounter opens the
primary scene of first encounter to semiotic inquiries and enables us to
ground the originary fiction of communication in a new understanding of
thrown-togetherness so we may avail ourselves of other points of departure for
semiotic studies as well as employ a new set of analytical apparatus in the
reading of empire. Whereas Peirce's scientific hypothesis leaves the identity
of his strangers deliberately abstract and vague, the novel *Robinson Crusoe* is
almost painfully straightforward and unambiguous in the manner in which
it brings the British man and the Caribbean "savage" together on Defoe's
fictional island. Will Crusoe be compelled to talk to Friday in a Peircian vein
"by imitative sounds, by imitative gestures, and by pictures"? What are the
plausible semiotic conditions under which the strangers will begin their
communication? This excerpt from Crusoe's narrative account hypothesizes
the scenario very well:

> So to let Friday understand a little what I would do, I call'd him to me again,
> pointed at the Fowl which was indeed a Parrot, tho' I thought it had been a
> Hawk, I say pointing to the Parrot and to my Gun, and to the Ground under
> the Parrot, to let him see I would make it fall, I made him understand that I
> would shoot and kill that Bird; according I fir'd and bad him look, and im-
> mediately he saw the Parrot fall, he stood like one frightened again, not-
> withstanding all I had said to him; and I found he was the more amaz'd be-
> cause he did not see me put any Thing into the Gun; but thought that there
> must be some wonderful Fund of Death and Destruction in that Thing, able
> to kill Man, Beast, Bird, or any Thing near, or far off, and the Astonishment

this created in him was such, as could not wear off for a long Time; and I believe, if I would have let him, he would have worshipp'ed me and my Gun:
As for the Gun it self, he would not so much as touch it for several Days after; but would speak to it, and talk to it, as if it had answer'd him, when he
was by himself; which, as I afterwards learn'd of him, was to desire it not to
kill him.[25]

In this extraordinary moment of first encounter, Crusoe's communication
with Friday appears to employ imitative sounds and mimetic gestures, but
these mimetic acts simultaneously perform the deictic task of finger pointing. The sacrificing of the talking bird both mimics and forestalls the act of
killing Friday. The latter is invited to play the audience on condition that he
be capable of decoding the message correctly or else mimick the death of the
parrot. Crusoe's message does not seem lost on Friday: submit or be killed.

Now, the precariousness of Friday's situation goes without saying, since
he is thrown together with someone who has a gun and who intends to
shoot him should he refuse to obey. To Crusoe, the failure of communication
poses an immediate threat because it means that Friday would not *recognize*
him as the sovereign of the island or his gun as that "wonderful Fund of
Death and Destruction." His first task, then, is to terrorize Friday, to make
him comprehend the sovereign power of himself and his gun and be subjugated. Defoe anticipates Peirce's hypothesis of communicative behavior by
initiating a series of semiotic maneuvers on behalf of Crusoe. Essentially,
what the Englishman does is to point and kill vicariously. The staging of literal, deictic pointing turns Crusoe's gun into an extension of the human
finger, exposing Friday to the terror of indexicality. The gun-sign initiates
the familiar ritual of colonial subjugation and fetishism in the European
imagining of first encounter and establishes the Englishman as the master,
lord, and sovereign of the Caribbean island on the strength of his unparalleled military technology.

It should be emphasized that the power of Crusoe's gun lies not in its
physical ability to take the other's life but in its very indexicality as a sign of
terror and human intention. It would be interesting to reconsider Louis
Althusser's notion of interpellation in this light and ask whether the Althus-
serian pedestrian would indeed turn around to answer the call of the police-
man.[26] The situation can be further elucidated by the concept of deixis in
linguistic theory. According to structural linguistics, a deictic situation arises
when two or more interlocutors engage in a reciprocal exchange of the pro-

nominal "I" as each addresses or hails the other as "you." Emile Benveniste, who has theorized deixis extensively, discusses the deixis of pronominal forms:

> The importance of their function will be measured by the nature of the problem they serve to solve, which is none other than that of intersubjective communication. Language has solved this problem by creating an ensemble of "empty" signs that are nonreferential with respect to "reality." These signs are always available and become "full" as soon as a speaker introduces them into each instance of his discourse. Since they lack material references, they cannot be misused; since they do not assert anything, they are not subject to the condition of truth and escape all denial. Their role is to provide the instrument of a conversion that one could call the conversion of language into discourse. It is by identifying himself as a unique person pronouncing *I* that each speaker sets himself up in turn as the "subject."[27]

Intersubjective communication is the compulsory condition under which the deictic construction of subjectivity takes place among the speakers of a language. The ground of reciprocity in deixis allows the production of difference through the deictic exchange of person as well as a simultaneous leveling of that difference with respect to reciprocal address. Benveniste's concept of deixis escapes the conditions of truth and denial and along with them the potential risks attending the circumstances of intersubjectivity. This instrumental understanding of subjectivity, whose partial truth has been reiterated by recent poststructuralist scholarship, disavows the conceptual tie between subjectivity and sovereignty and, consequently, the possibility of raising an issue about the reciprocity of deictic address that, for all we know, may produce the relations of sovereign rule as much as it produces reciprocal subjectivity.

Benveniste's model of communication, like Peircian semiotics before him, occults the terror of intersubjective communication to which some speakers could be exposing themselves in a given deictic situation. In contrast, Defoe's candid tale of colonial domination suggests that the Englishman inaugurates his sovereign consciousness not only by occupying the position of the *I* but also by fantasizing, naming, and subjugating the other. The double act of deictic enunciation creates simultaneously a sovereign (the lord of the island) and a subject (the slave attached to the lord) as well as the phenomenological ground of intersubjective communication. I should add that such acts are often gendered if not simultaneously racialized. One of the foremost feminist thinkers of the nineteenth century, Elizabeth Cady Stanton, was given to fantasizing the self-sovereignty of liberated (white) woman in the image of "an imaginary Robinson Crusoe with her woman Friday on a solitary island."[28] Such a fantasy may be shocking to today's sensibility, but it has been part of a progressive feminist legacy that once shaped and transformed the political agendas of the imperial states of the past.[29] As my discussion of gender and empire in Chapter 5 shows, the desire to become a female Robinson Crusoe with her woman Friday not only troubles the liberal notion of political freedom by bringing it face to face with imperial desire but also suggests that the mutual constitution of sovereignty and subjectivity merits closer attention in our theoretical reflections on power and language.

Desire and the Sovereign Subject

Foucault's work on the politics of biopower has interjected a cautionary note into any subsequent attempt to take up the issue of sovereign power this way, because his theory of subjectivity is premised precisely on the idea that the archaic forms of sovereignty in the West have been superseded by the disciplinary regimes of knowledge and technologies of biopolitics which are organized around the management of life rather than the threat of death. This process of "making live and letting die" *(faire vivre et laisser mourir)* must be rigorously distinguished from the way in which sovereign powers used to exercise the right over life and death *(faire mourir et laisser vivre)*.[30] In *The History of Sexuality,* Foucault states that sovereign power was "a right of seizure: of things, time, bodies, and ultimately life itself; it culminated in the privilege to seize hold of life in order to suppress it."[31] If genocide is indeed the dream of modern powers, "this is not because of a return of the ancient right to kill; it is because power is situated and exercised at the level of life, the species, the race, and the large-scale phenomena of population."[32]

By construing an archaic notion of sovereignty within Europe's self-referential geographic boundaries, does Foucault place imperial rule outside the narrative of European bourgeois subjectivity? Ann Laura Stoler raises a good point in *Race and the Education of Desire* about Foucault's ethnocentrism proposing that "we should be pushed to ask what other desires are excluded from his account, to question how shifts in the imperial *distributions* of desiring male subjects and desired female objects might reshape that story as well."[33] Reflecting on Judith Butler's earlier work on the subject of desire,

Stoler further argues that if a desiring subject has the philosophical aim of finding within the confines of this self the entirety of the external world in the process of externalization and mimesis, the imagined and practical world of empire must be seen as one of the most strategic sites for realizing that aim. She contends:

> No political story is more relevant to the production of western desire than colonialism, itself the quintessence of a process in which the mirroring of bourgeois priorities and their mimetic subversion played a defining role. Affirmation of the bourgeois self entailed an overlapping series of discursive displacements and distinctions on which its cultivation rested. There was no bourgeois identity that was not contingent on a changing set of Others who were at once desired and repugnant, forbidden and subservient, cast as wholly different but also the same.[34]

Stoler's postcolonial intervention makes it imperative for us to reconsider Foucault's notion of *assujetissement*—subjugation and subjectivization—in light of modern imperial history.[35] We may pursue further the question whether, by assigning the idea of sovereignty to the absolutist form of rule, Foucault was not foreclosing the possibility of investigating the condition of modern subjectivity as a *reinvention of sovereignty*.[36] That foreclosure would presuppose the severance of the historical ties between subjectivity and sovereignty that have long defined the meaning of the one in terms of the other and would lead to the conviction that sovereign thinking has ceased to inhabit the realm of modern subjectivity and requires no further debate. George Steinmetz's comparative work on German colonial native policy in Asia and Africa reminds us that the colonial state as an actor and determinant of its own policies was keenly invested in the production of imperial subjectivity.[37]

My immediate concern is not whether the power of the state and its juridical system ought to continue to engage our attention but whether sovereign power is necessarily archaic and therefore irrelevant to our consideration of desire and subjectivity in this book.[38] If the answer is no, as I am trying to argue here, we may question the hypothesis that sovereign power produces only juridical subjects but not other types of desiring subjects. Judith Butler's critique of Foucault in *The Psychic Life of Power* ponders a number of scenarios that bring into question Foucault's argument of subjugation and subjectivization. She does so by making a psychoanalytical incursion into the discursive site of injury, such as a person's seemingly perverse attachment to injurious interpellations, and asks, "How do we account for *attachment* to precisely the kind of state-linked individuality that reconsolidates the juridical law?"[39] Butler tries to articulate the conditions under which the resignification of prior interpellations becomes possible and emphasizes that such resignification should be regarded not as an unconscious outside of power, but rather as "something like the unconscious of power itself, in its traumatic and productive iterability."[40]

Does the *unconscious of power* point in the direction of sovereign thinking in our future reflections on modern subjectivity? I believe so. The iterability of the emperor's empty throne, which I analyze in the concluding chapter, shows that the disenchantment of the modern world is not so thorough as to cause the fetish to lose its meaning and its power of enchantment in our own time. The throne chairs of Chinese emperors on display at the Victoria and Albert Museum and at the National Palace Museum in the Forbidden City are empty yet occupied in the sense that their emptiness is constantly filled with the dreams and fantasies of those who come upon them in museums, photographs, films, novels, and history books. The traces of sovereign thinking in the psyche of the modern subject appear to act in the manner of the *unconscious of power* even if they elude our grasp as such.

Let us consider a number of theoretical propositions that may further explain why the notion of sovereignty as an archaic power can hamper our ability to understand the process of subject formation in modern times. Georges Bataille has argued that sovereignty is not just about emperors, kings, or absolutist forms of rule but is about the production of subjectivity through social labor and can be central to a theory of general economy. In *The Accursed Share*, Bataille writes:

> The sovereign does not labor, but consumes the product of the others' labor. The share of this product that is not necessary to the subsistence of the *object* that the man who produces is for the time being, is the share of the *subject* that the sovereign is. The sovereign restores to the primacy of the present the surplus share of production, acquired to the extent that men submitted to the primacy of the future. The sovereign, epitomizing the *subject,* is the one by whom and for whom the moment, the miraculous *moment,* is the ocean into which the streams of labor disappear. The sovereign spends festively for himself and for others alike that which the labor of all has accumulated.[41]

Kings and other royalty are traditional figures of sovereign power, but Bataille is not being literal about them. The dialectic of the sovereign epitomizing the *subject* is that of Hegelian recognition *(Anerkennung)*, whereby the multitude labor for the benefit of the sovereign and recognize him insofar as they recognize themselves in him. This is how the sovereign comes to signify and epitomize subjectivity for the multitude.

Bataille's dialectic is almost certainly drawn from Hegel's analysis of *Begierde* (desire) in the *Phenomenology of Spirit*, where the philosopher shows that, in the movement of desire, self-consciousness seeks absolute self-certainty by treating all otherness as something to be negated and superseded.[42] Bataille's reworking of the dialectic of lordship and servitude turns on a Marxian understanding of surplus value and the material and symbolic expenditure of that value. The sovereign is the one who epitomizes the *subject* inasmuch as he consumes the share of the product that is not necessary for the subsistence of the multitude but is otherwise productive of a miraculous moment in which the multitude recognize the sovereign insofar as they recognize themselves in him. Why does Bataille call the process a miraculous moment? Does it have anything to do with what we might call the mystified power of recognition (or conjuration)? This is the kind of issue that Frantz Fanon set out to explore in *Black Skin, White Masks* and he echoes and revises the Hegelian narrative:

> For Hegel there is reciprocity; here the master laughs at the consciousness of the slave. What he wants from the slave is not recognition but work.
>
> In the same way, the slave here is in no way identifiable with the slave who loses himself in the object and finds in his work the source of his liberation.
>
> The Negro wants to be like the master.
>
> Therefore he is less independent than the Hegelian slave.
>
> In Hegel, the slave turns away from the master and turns toward the object.
>
> Here the slave turns toward the master and abandons the object.[43]

Fanon had thought long and hard about the situation of colonial subjectivity and black people's struggle for independence. The miraculous moment arrives when the slave turns toward the master and demands a different relationship of reciprocity. "One day the White Master, *without conflict*, recognized the Negro slave," writes Fanon. "But the former slave wants to *make himself recognized*."[44] The new meanings Fanon tries to wrestle from the Hegelian notion of *Anerkennung* lead to the contention that self-consciousness occurs when the slave demands recognition on an equal footing with the master and risks his life fighting for true reciprocity.[45] Fanon's engagement with the struggle for recognition is not just a mimicking of Hegel but derives from his reflections on the history of colonial warfare and the struggle for sovereign independence.[46] He converts the fiction of lordship and servitude into a historical narrative about the socioeconomic and psychological abjection of black people by European colonial domination. "As soon as I *desire*," writes Fanon in the guise of a slave, "I am asking to be considered. I am not merely here-and-now, sealed into thingness. I am for somewhere else and for something else. I demand that notice be taken of my negating activity insofar as I pursue something other than life; insofar as I do battle for the creation of a human world—that is, of a world of reciprocal recognition."[47]

The dialectic of reciprocal recognition did not, however, do the same job for Fanon as it did for Bataille and the other Hegelians of his time. Jean-Paul Sartre, for instance, challenged his fellow countrymen to imagine "what then did you expect when you unbound the gag that had muted those black mouths? That they would chant your praises? Did you think that when those heads that our fathers had forcibly bowed down to the ground were raised again, you would find adoration in their eyes?" Rather than greet the French intellectual on his support of the decolonization movement with open arms, Fanon balked at those rhetorical questions and gave his legendary rejoinder to Sartre: "I do not know; but I say that he who looks into my eyes for anything but a perpetual question will have to lose his sight; neither recognition nor hate."[48] If Sartre's rhetorical questions suggest that he somehow knew the subjugated people and their desires, Fanon resists that knowledge claim. His enigmatic response to Sartre causes the mirror of subjectivity to shatter momentarily by introducing an element of aporia into the Hegelian logic of reciprocal recognition. Looking fails to guarantee knowledge, at least not the type of knowledge a specter would impart to one's soul. A terrifying moment of non-seeing or self-blinding may ensue from direct contact with another looking subject whose eyes may or may not return the gaze. *Loss of sight,* therefore, becomes Fanon's primary figure of epistemic upheaval—a prognosis of the breakdown of the colonial mirror image of the sovereign subject.[49]

Violence and the Colonial Origins of Modern Sovereignty

Fanon's radical rethinking of the Hegelian struggle for recognition suggests that violence is central to the constitution of modern subjectivity. Sovereignty, far from being archaic, has a proper place in the violent structuring of the unconscious of power and the continual investment in the workings of modern subjectivity. If Foucault's conceptualization of sovereignty as the archaic "right to kill" is no longer adequate to the task of understanding the conjuration of the sovereign/subject, how do we go about analyzing the structure of violence in these processes?

Giorgio Agamben has provided some answers to the question in his investigation of the sovereign exception in the legal traditions of the West. His book *Homo Sacer* is an attempt to push Foucault's central premise about life and biopower further by examining the enigmatic character of the sovereign exception and analyzing how sovereign power relates to bare life through that exception. In the course of reassessing Carl Schmitt's and Bataille's work on sovereignty, Agamben argues that "if the exception is the structure of sovereignty, then sovereignty is not an exclusively political concept, an exclusively juridical category, a power extended to law (Schmitt), or the supreme rule of the juridical order (Hans Kelsen): it is the originary structure in which law refers to life and includes it in itself by suspending it."[50] Agamben explains the concept of sovereign exception by evoking the archaic Roman figure *Homo sacer,* a sacred figure who represents the simultaneous unpunishability of killing and exclusion from sacrifice according to Roman law. He observes a structural parallel between the sovereign exception and *sacratio* in situations where "the sovereign is the one with respect to whom all men are potentially *homines sacri,* and *homo sacer* is the one with respect to whom all men act as sovereign."[51] The political sphere of sovereignty is thus constituted through a double exclusion, an excrescence of the profane in the religious and of the religious in the profane, which takes the form of a zone of indistinction between sacrifice and homicide. Thus "the sovereign sphere is the sphere in which it is permitted to kill without committing homicide and without celebrating a sacrifice, and sacred life—that is, life that may be killed but not sacrificed—is the life that has been captured in this sphere."[52] This is the sphere of the sovereign exception.

Agamben refuses to let the sovereign exception stand as an archaic problem of the remote past and takes it all the way to the Nazi state in the twentieth century in order to explain the structure of violence in the modern state's exercise of biopower. In my view, this is an important intervention into the poststructuralist theories of subjectivity which have heretofore downplayed the problem of sovereignty and its relevance for thinking about the disciplinary regimes of power. Agamben chooses to be silent, however, on the issue of colonial violence in the discussion of violence and modernity, a subject that had centrally engaged Fanon's attention. When modern colonialism disappears from Agamben's genealogy of sovereign power, should the historical linkages between colonialism and the Holocaust be likewise disavowed? The severing of the vital connections between colonial violence and the European notions of sovereignty cannot but distort the story of how sovereign power came to mean what it means. As will be seen shortly, there is ample proof in the evolution of international law that our familiar notion of sovereignty has been a product of centuries of colonial expansion, treaty making, and reciprocal dealings rather than of intra-European conflicts; but one must shed the myopia of European exceptionalism and the universalist aspirations of Western legal discourse in order to be able to observe and document these dynamic processes.

Keeping this in mind, the intervention that Michael Hardt and Antonio Negri make in their book *Empire* deserves a brief comment here. In the course of analyzing what they call the "sovereignty machine" of the modern nation-state, the authors argue that modern sovereignty is fundamentally different from that of the ancien régime because it has been achieved through a synthesis of sovereignty and capital and through the transcendental exercise of authority. Sovereignty turns into a political machine in this process, one that rules both as a police power and as a political power against all external political powers. "Through the workings of the sovereignty machine," they write, in a Deleuzean vein, "the multitude is in every moment transformed into an ordered totality."[53] Unlike Agamben, the authors acknowledge colonialism as part of these processes and allow colonial sovereignty to be implicated dialectically by the notion of modern sovereignty, concluding that "the end of colonialism and the declining powers of the nation are indicative of a general passage from the paradigm of modern sovereignty toward the paradigm of imperial sovereignty."[54]

Does the passing of modern sovereignty to imperial sovereignty signify a historical passage from imperialism to Empire to which the reality of colonialism seems no longer relevant? Such a claim would have to rest on the assumption that our notions of sovereignty, modern or imperial, are not fundamentally grounded in coloniality, an assumption that must be scrutinized in light of the results of the new empire studies by Anthony Pagden and the other historians whom I will discuss shortly. The genealogy of modern sovereignty as traced out by postcolonial scholars is sufficiently different from the Eurocentric ones constructed by Foucault, Bataille, Agamben, and even Hardt and Negri as to merit serious consideration. The main point of the dissent, as I view it, is whether coloniality enters the big picture in the manner of a belated negative dialectic or as the originary condition of modern sovereignty.[55] The postcolonial scholar would argue that modern sovereignty is colonial sovereignty *tout court* rather than its negative mirror image, and, by extension, what Hardt and Negri identify as imperial sovereignty should be properly grasped as a response to postcolonial sovereignty. Let us ponder the matter in greater detail.

Scholars of international law have long regarded the sixteenth-century Spanish theologian Francisco de Vitoria (1492–1546) as the founder of their discipline.[56] Vitoria and his students at the University of Salamanca were responsible for elaborating the basic concepts of natural law and international relations, and these concepts were further developed and perfected by Hugo Grotius, Samuel Pufendorf, and other major figures in international law. Vitoria's two main extant lectures, *De Indis Noviter Inventis* and *De Jure Bellis Hispanorum in Barbaros,* place the imperatives of the *ius gentium,* or law of nations, unmistakably in the early years of colonial encounter. As Anthony Pagden argues in *The Fall of Natural Man,* it was the "Indian problem" during the early years of the Spanish conquest of America that raised the issue of "the nature of the relations between the different groups of men within, as Vitoria termed it, 'the republic of all the world *(respublica totius orbis).*'"[57] The central question with which Vitoria and his fellow scholastics were preoccupied was: By what right had the barbarians, namely, the American Indians, come under the rule of the Spaniards? Was it legitimate for the Spaniards to dispossess the American Indians of their land and property purely on the ground that the natives were not Christians and that they lived in what the Europeans regarded as barbarian societies? The answer to these questions, as Pagden points out, was of paramount importance at the time because the task of the theologians and jurists under Habsburg rule was to establish the ethico-political principles whereby the Castilian crown was seen to act as the guardian of universal Christendom.[58]

Vitoria organizes his lectures around a consideration of legitimate and illegitimate public titles to Indian lands which define the limits of sovereign consent and authority. He concedes that the Native Americans were "barbarians" and were guilty of mortal sins and forms of heresy but rejects the idea that the moral and religious inferiority of the natives constitutes legal ground for civilized Europeans to deny them legitimate public title to the territory: "This title, or the ability to act as a sovereign, is subject to moral order which requires sovereigns to permit free intercourse and propagation of the faith. Any attempt to violate these divinely revealed 'rights' terminates their public title and enables the Spaniards to use whatever force seems necessary to enforce the divine order."⁵⁹

Vitoria's reasoning is based on a notion of the *ius naturae* or natural rights, that could be applied to both "believers" and "nonbelievers." In the lecture *De Indis*, delivered in 1537, he argued that the "affairs of the Indies" was a question not of the limits of papal jurisdiction, nor of Roman law, but of the law of nature or of natural rights. Pagden analyzes Vitoria's complex theological arguments in his essay "Dispossessing the Barbarian: The Language of Spanish Thomism and the Debate over the Property Rights of the American Indians" and summarizes the principles of the *ius naturae* as follows:

> Under the *ius gentium*, the Spaniards possessed what [Vitoria] called the "right of society and natural communication." Seas, shores and harbours are necessary for man's survival as a civil being and they have, therefore, by the common accord of all men, been exempted from the original division of property. It had always, Vitoria claimed, been an objective right in law that no man could be forbidden to land on any stretch of beach, no matter to whom it actually belonged, which is why Aeneas had rightly described the ancient kings of Latium as "barbari" when they refused him anchorage. This right to travel, the *ius peregrinandi*, therefore, gave the Spaniards right of access to the Indies. There was also, under the headings of *communicatio*, an implied right to trade. As the Spaniards had come to America, or so Vitoria claimed, as ambassadors *(legati)* and traders, they had to be treated with respect and be permitted to trade with all those who wished to trade with them. And since this was a right under the law of nations, it could only (at least by the terms of Vitoria's present definition) be changed by the consensus of the entire human community, not the will of an individual ruler. Vitoria also claimed that *ius gentium* granted the Spaniards the right (the *ius predicandi*) to preach their religion without interference—although it did not compel anyone to accept it—and that it permitted them to wage a just war against any tyrant "in defense of the innocent."⁶⁰

Central to Vitoria's concept of sovereignty is the right to wage war. The last observation in the quoted passage stresses the circumstances under which the Spaniards could be justified in waging war on the native population in the name of the *ius gentium*. According to Vitoria, the American Indians maintained their legal rights and protection so long as they guaranteed the "safety and peace" of Spaniards journeying, trading, or preaching the Gospel on their land. The reciprocity of "natural rights" stipulates further that, if the Spaniards' right to trade with the natives and to sojourn in their lands were violated by the natives, it would constitute ground of injury. "The vindication of injuries constitutes a just war, and ultimately it was only by means of such a war that the Spaniards could legitimate their presence in America."[61] In that respect, Vitoria's allusion to Aeneas is highly significant because it claims a legal precedent for what he is proposing and raises the issue of how antiquity is generally appropriated to support present and future causes.[62]

The requirements of freedom of trade, travel, and proselytizing anticipated their later definition as part of the standard of "civilization," one that still prevails in the postcolonial international politics of our own time.[63] Indeed, the colonial refashioning of the concepts of *jus gentium*, sovereignty, and rights of war during the Spanish colonial conquest of the Americas has provided a pattern rather than an exception in the evolution of the law of nations.[64] The Europeans who entered the East Indies at this time found themselves unexpectedly in the middle of a complex network of organized Asian states. In terms of the law of nations of the sixteenth century, there was no room for the application of titles of discovery or occupation of *terra nullius* in the East Indies. Neither was this possible from the point of view of local interstate custom, which counted treaty making and cession of territory or conquest among its established legal institutions.[65] Toward the end of the sixteenth century and the beginning of the seventeenth century, the Dutch began to challenge the Portuguese monopoly on trade and navigation in the East Indies. It was at this juncture that Hugo Grotius, long regarded as the forerunner of European international law, was invited (and possibly commissioned) to intervene in the Dutch-Portuguese dispute. The archival evidence collected and analyzed by C. H. Alexandrowicz in his research on the controversy and the history of treaty making and diplomatic relations between European and Asian sovereigns speaks against the anachronistic view of sovereign rights as something that first arose as a result of intra-European conflicts and extended to non-European countries centuries later.[66] This view has continued to prevail in the contemporary scholarship on international relations and, in particular, on the status of European exceptionality that is granted by the Peace of Westphalia of 1648. Modern international society is taken to be an enlarged version of European Westphalia, as summarized in this description of the latecomers: "Others advanced to full Westphalian status—the United States in 1783, Canada in

1867, and China and Japan by the early twentieth century."[67] But, as Alexandrowicz has pointed out, "to consider the European nucleus of States as the founder group of the family of nations to the exclusion of Asian Sovereigns in the East Indies was to view the origin and development of that family in the light of positivist conceptions which were only born at the turn of the eighteenth and nineteenth centuries."[68]

In his *Introduction to the History of the Law of Nations*, Alexandrowicz has brought to light the significant fact that Grotius carried out his study of the Indian Ocean regimes in the archives of the Dutch East India Company, where he first formulated the doctrine of the freedom of the sea on the basis of what he knew of Asian maritime custom. During a time when the doctrine of *mare clausum* was more prevalent in European state practice than the freedom of the high seas, Asian maritime customs served as a legal precedent for his purpose. Grotius noted that navigation from east of the Red Sea to the Pacific had been free and that local state practice never treated the Indian Ocean as *mare clausum*, although the Islamic-Portuguese conflagration changed the whole situation, and the arrival of the Dutch made it even more precarious. Grotius composed his seminal text *Mare Liberum* when his opinion was solicited on the case of the *Santa Catharina* after a Dutch naval commander named Heemskerck had captured the Portuguese galleon loaded with valuable cargo in the Straits of Malacca in 1602 and brought it to Amsterdam to be sold as a prize, the proceeds being distributed as part of the profit of the Dutch East India Company. On this case, as Alexandrowicz shows, Grotius probably acted as a counsel for the company, and he certainly had access to company documents that revealed to him the importance of the East Indies to European trade and led him to examine the position of Asian rulers in the law of nations.[69]

In *Mare Liberum* (1608), Grotius attacked the problem of free seas from a legal point of view and defended the rights of the East Indian communities against Portuguese claims. In 1625 the Portuguese jurist Serafim de Freitas presented his rebuttal of the Dutch position, in which he brought canon law to bear on his approach to the East Indies problem. Both jurists covered a wide range of legal arguments, concentrating on the questions of classification of sovereignty and territorial rights, each concerning himself with the problem of freedom of navigation and trade in the East Indies. Grotius eliminated the possibility of conceiving the East Indies as a legal vacuum as far as the law of nations was concerned, arguing, "These islands [Java, Ceylon, and the Moluccas] of which we speak, now have and always have had their own Kings, their own government, their own laws and their own legal systems."[70] He observed that European powers coming to this part of the world could not acquire territorial or other rights by discovery, occupation of *terra nullius*, papal donation, or any other unilateral act carried out in disregard of the sovereign authorities governing the countries. They could consider themselves sovereigns only over territories acquired by cession or conquest in accordance with the rules of the law of nations. The Portuguese could not, therefore, by virtue of any fictitious right of sovereignty, prevent the Dutch from any access to the East Indies and from dealing with Asian sovereigns. In defense of Dutch interests against the Portuguese, Grotius conceded to East Indian sovereigns a defined legal status in the law of nations.[71]

The long history of treaty making between Europeans and Asian sovereigns bears him out by way of testing how the concept of sovereignty actually worked in diplomatic relations. It was not until the turn of the nineteenth century that the positivist jurists began to reimagine East Asian countries as existing outside the family of nations and in need of being (re)admitted into the international order. Alexandrowicz, who had more sympathy for natural law than for positive law, observed in *The European-African Confrontation:* "Positivism discarded some of the fundamental qualities of the classic law of nations, irrespective of creed, race, colour and continent (non-discrimination). International law shrank into an Euro-centric system which imposed on extra-European countries its own ideas including the admissibility of war and non-military pressure as a prerogative of sovereignty. It also discriminated against non-European civilizations and thus ran on parallel lines with colonialism as a political trend."[72] Of course, as Pagden's study of Vitoria has demonstrated, the classic law of nations itself had not existed outside of colonial violence and was already part of that history, but it did at least grant sovereign rights to peoples and territories that would subsequently be excluded from the family of nations by the jurists of positive law. The commonsensical narrative of East Asia's belated entry into the family of nations that we routinely encounter in modern scholarship is largely indebted to this anachronistic vein of positivism in international law in the nineteenth century.

In conclusion, the semiotic turn of international politics I suggested at the outset of this chapter shares some of the same positivist spirit of the nineteenth century as international law itself. One could arguably treat the instituting of international conventions as a formal and physical endorsement of the positive law notion of sovereign right. The novelty of this institution lies in its timely grasp of the importance of language and semiotic events for international politics dominated by Europe and North America and in the growing need to regulate the proliferation of military signals and other semiotic practices. In the chapters to follow, I identify and analyze what appears to be a transcultural semiotic, which troubled the negotiations of sovereign claims between the British and Qing empires during the Opium Wars and thereafter. Chapters 2 and 3 focus on what I call the terror of intersubjective communication among the British, Chinese, and Manchus that resulted in the banning of a written Chinese character in the Anglo-Chinese Treaty of Tianjin and in the consolidation of the Chinese-English super-sign *yi/barbarian.* As I will show, when the British and the Manchus disputed the particular meanings of a hetero-linguistic sign in translation and concluded treaties to fix some of its meanings, they were simultaneously disputing each other's sovereign claim to China and turning the diplomatic negotiations into a veritable semiotic event.

CHAPTER 2

The Birth of a Super-Sign

When the question arises of understanding why the European, the foreigner, was called *vazaha,* which means *honorable stranger;* when it is a matter of understanding why shipwrecked Europeans were welcomed with open arms; why the European, the foreigner, was never thought of as an enemy, instead of explaining these things in terms of humanity, of good will, of courtesy, basic characteristics of what Césaire calls "the old courtly civilizations," scholars tell us that it happened quite simply because, inscribed in "fateful hieroglyphics"—specifically, the unconscious—there exists something that makes the white man the awaited master.

—Frantz Fanon, *Black Skin and White Masks*

Never has a lone word among the myriad languages of humanity made so much history as the Chinese character *yi* 夷. By history I mean world history. Countless events and fantastic happenings have come to pass over the last two centuries, but none could rival the singularity of the Chinese word *yi* in its uncanny ability to arouse confusion, anxiety, and war. *Yi* is one of those monstrous creatures one must reckon with, subdue, destroy, or exile before it comes back to haunt us. What is the meaning of this all-powerful and dangerous word—"barbarian," "stranger," "foreigner," or "non-Chinese"? As soon as we engage in this sort of tautological exercise in semantic equivalences and given translations, we are already jumping ahead of ourselves and ahead of history. The question I am posing here is not what it appears to be, for I am not looking to settle on a good definition, even if it were possible to do so, or a proper translation of the word into other terms. Had it been just a matter of deciding whether the Chinese character *yi* means "barbarian" or which of the two words conveys more of a pejorative sense according to dictionary definitions, history itself would seem superfluous and would matter little. The trouble is that neither *yi* nor "barbarian" could possibly be grasped outside of the two terms' respective histories and their entangled and embattled etymologies in modern times; not even the archaic etymology of *yi* nor that of the Greek term *barbaros,* which mimics the sound of incomprehensible speech, could escape the long shadow of their modern-day usage.[1] That is why, before we too quickly allow the English word "barbarian" to take over the Chinese character *yi* as its proper, given provenance, we must ask some questions about the conditions of their reciprocal signification, their mutual intelligibility, and, above all, the jurisdictional determination of their alleged commensurability after the Opium Wars.

The Ban

The event that marked the first appearance of *yi* in an international legal document was the signing of the Anglo-Chinese Treaty of Tianjin in 1858.[2] Article 51 of that treaty issued a consummate ban on the Chinese character (Figure 1). The Qing imperial government was party to this bilateral agreement, as it had been to a string of coerced treaties in the nineteenth century that aimed to fulfill the objectives of British foreign policy in the Far East. The original English text of the treaty took care to provide the written character for the word *yi* and to insert it between the nineteenth-century romanization "i" and the English translation.[3] To ensure that the English meaning of the character *yi* and other Chinese words in Anglo-Chinese bilingual communications would be taken as original and authoritative, Article 50, which precedes the ban on *yi* in the treaty, made the following provision:

> All official communications addressed by the Diplomatic and Consular Agents of Her Majesty the Queen to the Chinese Authorities shall, henceforth, be written in English. They will for the present be accompanied by a

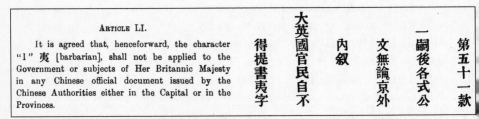

ARTICLE LI.

It is agreed that, henceforward, the character "I" 夷 [barbarian], shall not be applied to the Government or subjects of Her Britannic Majesty in any Chinese official document issued by the Chinese Authorities either in the Capital or in the Provinces.

第五十一款

一嗣後各式公

文無論京外

內叙

大英國官民自不

得提書夷字

Figure 1.   Article 51 of the Treaty of Tianjin, from *Treaties, Conventions, etc., between China and Foreign States.*

Chinese version, but, it is understood that, in the event of there being any difference of meaning between the English and Chinese text, the English Government will hold the sense as expressed in the English text to be the correct sense.

This provision is to apply to the Treaty now negotiated, the Chinese text of which has been carefully corrected by the English original.[4]

A treaty agreement can hardly be construed as an official communication from the British government to the Chinese if the document had been the result of bilateral deliberations.[5] The second paragraph of the article makes it clear, however, that the rule of the English original is to apply to treaty negotiations in general and to the languages used therein. In fact, Article 51 is so closely predicated on Article 50 in the order of British demands that the question of whether or not the Chinese word *yi* has been subjected to correction, literally, by the English word "barbarian" arises immediately. I would suggest that the extraordinary injunction in Article 51 relates to Article 50 in the manner of a call for correction, yet the correcting is accomplished precisely by appearing not to have done so. The law simply secures a three-way commensurability of the hetero-linguistic sign 夷/*i*/*barbarian* by joining the written Chinese character, the romanized pronunciation, and the English translation together into a coherent semantic unit.

What does the three-way commensurability of the hetero-linguistic sign 夷/*i*/*barbarian* mean exactly? It means that the Chinese character *yi* becomes a hetero-linguistic sign by virtue of being informed, signified, and transformed by the English word "barbarian" and must defer its correct meanings to the foreign counterpart. With an almost silent gesture, the hetero-linguistic sign gathers into itself the Chinese and English etymologies and binds their commensurability to a fantastic semantic whole. This manner of correction actively produces a hetero-linguistic super-sign whose meaning and integrity must now come under the protection of law. That is to say, whoever violates the integrity of the super-sign 夷/*i*/*barbarian* (hereafter represented as *yi/barbarian* for convenience) risks violating international law itself.

The risk, of course, was always there; so was the fascination with the exclusive signification of *yi* in terms of the English word "barbarian." The legal injunction of Article 51 catapulted what seemed at first a trifling matter of translation into the broader realm of international conflicts with major implications for our understanding of the narratives of civilizational clash, past and present. A good deal is at stake when it comes to identifying the "true barbarian" for civilization. The stakes rise higher with the scandal of the word *yi* because its enunciation issues forth from the language of a non-European society which is regarded as less than civilized by the British. In other words, the Chinese character *yi* appears to have thrown the barbarian back onto civilization itself and turned into its double and mirror image.

Granted that the character *yi* posed a credible threat to law and to the emergent order of international relations, what jurisdictional meanings pertained to the word and its application? Can we identify the sources of anxiety that had surrounded the ban at its conception? In what ways was the psychic life of *yi/barbarian* symptomatic of the psychic life of other hetero-linguistic signs in general? These questions form the basis of the analysis I undertake in this chapter. My goal is to show how the hetero-linguistic sign *yi/barbarian* articulates a particular vision of sovereignty at the meeting ground of the British and Qing empires (as the Manchus were also foreigners in the country they ruled) in what James Hevia has called the encounter between "two imperial formations, each with universalistic pretensions and complex metaphysical systems to buttress such claims."[6] We shall see how that vision led to war and to the other measures by the British and their Western allies as they tried to cope with matters of survival, transgression, anxiety, and death in a foreign land.

Who Was the Barbarian?

In my discussion of Peirce's semiotics in Chapter 1, I briefly introduced the notion of the super-sign and called it a linguistic monstrosity. The super-sign is a monstrosity because it crouches behind the "wordness" of a concept and articulates the latter without itself being articulated in any reified form. The super-sign does not seem to fit into our familiar descriptions of linguistic phenomena and almost always eludes normative etymological analysis because it never announces its positivity in terms of a discrete verbal unit. In short, the super-sign is not a word but a hetero-cultural signifying chain. As a fantastic hybrid of translated concepts, it can be technically demonstrated with a series of verbal signs connected by slashes, as in *yi/barbarian*. This analytical method has the advantage of overcoming the traditional semiotic preoccupation with positive signs and taking us instead into the realm of enchanted meanings, excesses of signification, camouflaged traces of foreign invasions, potent but disavowed forms of translingual speech and writing as well as meaning making across languages, and so on.

To be sure, a super-sign may invade a language and assume the look of a known word in that language, but it never fails to defer the meaning of that word elsewhere, toward some foreign language or languages. The Chinese character *yi* has undergone precisely this sort of transformation. The banning of *yi* by Article 51 may be said to be the banning of a strange hybrid of the Chinese word that metonymically evokes "barbarian" as its signifying other and guarantor of meaning. In fact, that ban was responsible for consolidating the super-sign and forcing the Chinese word to refer its signified (or the Peircian "object") onto the English word "barbarian" rather than relate it meaningfully to other known Chinese words such as *xiyang, xiren,* or *xiyang ren* (western ocean, westerner, a man of the western ocean) or to prior super-signs superseded by *yi/barbarian* such as the official Manchu equating of *yi* with *tulergi* (outer, outside).[7] The historical events that catalyzed this becoming, as I show in the next section, were the Opium Wars and other Anglo-Chinese diplomatic and military confrontations in the nineteenth century.

Going through the volumes of official Chinese papers from the Ming through the Qing dynasties, one finds no documentary evidence whatsoever to support the argument that *yi* was the Chinese term used *exclusively* for the foreigner. (I discuss how *yi* was used in the context of the imperial ideology of the Qing in Chapter 3.) Alternative Chinese modes of address, like the aforementioned *xiyang, xiren,* or *xiyang ren,* had always existed and often appeared side by side with *yi* in the Ming and Qing dynasties, just as the English word "foreigner" had been adopted as an alternative equivalent of *yi* by the British East India Company in the eighteenth and early nineteenth centuries.[8] Matteo Ricci, for example, was called a *xiyang ren* (a man of the western ocean); so were most of the Jesuit missionaries who visited China in the seventeenth century. In the early eighteenth century, when the imperial government appointed the Thirteen Co-Hongs, or the official Cantonese merchants, as the sole Chinese trading counterpart to foreign traders, *yi* and *yang* (ocean) began to acquire a functional distinction generated by the need to differentiate between foreign traders and Cantonese Hong merchants in foreign goods. Thus, the Qing official documents from this period on invariably refer to the merchants of other countries as *yi shang* and to the local Hong merchants as *yang shang* (also known as *guan shang,* or "official merchant"), who acted as the intermediaries between the foreign communities and the local Chinese government. (The word *yang shang* reflects symmetrically on an interesting usage of "Chinaman" in eighteenth-century English to refer to a Jewish dealer in porcelain in London or a manufacturer of porcelain.) The important distinction between *yi shang* and *yang shang* survived through the troubled years 1834–1842, when the first Anglo-Chinese military confrontations took place.[9] After *yi* was outlawed by the Anglo-Chinese Treaty of Tianjin in 1858, the word *yang* began to take on broader meanings to describe all things foreign well through the Republican years. What seems to have happened was that *yang shang* came to substitute for the function of the absent term *yi shang* to designate foreign merchants, while its earlier association with the local Hong merchants dropped out of the picture completely.[10]

Naoki Sakai's critique of the model of communication is right on target when he suggests that "only in the representation of translation can we construe the process of translation as a transfer of some message from 'this side' side to 'that' side, as a dialogue between one person and another, between one group and another, as if dialogue should necessarily take place according to the model of communication."[11] This insight leads us to ask by what intellectual mechanism the word *yi* turned into its own super-sign *yi/barbarian*. Or, more accurately, how did the Chinese character come to be signified by *yi/barbarian*? Let us ponder the logic of reciprocity for a moment since this logic seems to underlie the invention of all super-signs. If X is believed to be commensurate with Y, it is understood that Y is capable of translating X. But when that occurs, there is no guarantee that X would not be inversely affected or transformed by Y following the same logic of reciprocity. Translators generally rely on this logic of reciprocity to produce the fact of commensurability between the languages involved, and this is what happens when a motivated act of translation attempts to forge a coherent and unbreakable super-sign out of the existing repertoire of hetero-linguistic signs and prior super-signs. The new super-sign arises out of this doubling effect of translation but leaves few traces of it behind. As the camouflaging of the internal differentiations of the super-sign occurs at the very moment of its inception, not afterwards, its novelty or foreignness becomes quickly absorbed into the unchanging appearance of the material signifier or its *wordness* so the super-sign does not look anywhere different from the original term. It is misleading, therefore, for us to pursue a straightforward etymology of the word *yi* as if it were just another indigenous word, untouched and uncontaminated by English, Manchu, or other languages. Such philological pursuits could only intensify the effect of camouflage on the foreignness of the super-sign.

Until it is advisable to abolish the idea of wordness as a unit of analysis in semiotic studies, we may try lifting the screen of the reified word to investigate what the linguistic sign is doing there. The etymology of a word can hardly substitute for the semiotic analysis of its manner of signification because there is a good deal going on in a sign that the etymological evolution of the word and its presences cannot explain. For example, nothing is explained by pointing out that language is inherited and the meanings of words change over time. "Let there be no mistake about the meaning that we attach to the word 'change,'" Saussure observed a long time ago. "One might think that it deals especially with phonetic changes undergone by the signifier, or perhaps, changes in meaning which affect the signified concept. That view would be inadequate. Regardless of what the forces of change are, whether in isolation or in combination, they always result in a *shift in the relationship between the signified and the signifier.*"[12] This insight was central to Saussure's synchronic study of the linguistic sign and remains relevant to our examination of the hetero-linguistic process of signification which Saussure himself took for granted and neglected to analyze.[13] What I am proposing here is an attentive analysis of the formal attributes of the super-sign as well as a grounded historical explanation attending to both the indigenous etymology and what is foreign to it.

The novelty of the super-sign *yi/barbarian* consists in the fact that not only is it capable of dissolving the earlier Manchu interpretation of *yi* in the manner of a further hetero-linguistic shift in the relationship between the Saussurian signified and the signifier, but it also brings an end to the etymology of the word *yi*, making it disappear into the moratorium enacted by Article 51. The material signifier of the Chinese character may continue to evoke or hallucinate an uninterruptible etymology in classical Chinese; yet what it evokes or hallucinates is but the ruins of an already dead word. Article 51 summons the word *yi* to appear in the guise of "barbarian" only to banish the Chinese word from prior, alternative positions of enunciation. The act of banishing secures a sovereign position for the English word "barbarian" in a bracketed translation which cannot but institute a profound split and internal differentiation within the super-sign *yi/barbarian* and brings the commensurability of the two words into question: What does this split or internal differentiation mean? Can a verbal sign from one language become the destiny and destination of a verbal sign from another language? Can the two cross each other's threshold without appearing to have made the transgression? In this chapter I attempt to answer these questions from a number of historical and analytical angles.

When Article 51 compels the destination of the word *yi* to be "barbarian" and appoints the latter to inhabit the super-sign and become its proper signified, it requires that the word "barbarian" be sufficiently shielded from *yi* to enjoy a different destiny and a different mode of survival. This is how the law inscribes the internal differentiation within the super-sign to produce the coincidence of meaning between "barbarian" and *yi* and to disavow their apparent translatability at the same time. But the super-sign hides this monstrosity well behind a façade of perfect commensurability or "perfect equality," a positivist language of reciprocity repeatedly used by the British throughout the treaty negotiations in 1858 as well as in 1842. Should someone think of raising the issue of the aptness of that translation, the super-sign becomes the linguistic evidence of its own truth even as it dissimulates what is incongruous, uncanny, and monstrous on either side of the equation. Indeed, when the seventeenth-century theologian Samuel Pufendorf described empire as an irregular and monster-like body ("irregulare aliquod corpus et monstro simile"), he might as well have been anticipating the ways in which translingual speech and writing about the "barbarian" would do the work of empire in centuries to come. "Shapeless, huge, and horrifying," the monster of a super-sign is the offspring of empire as well as its mirror image and is bound to haunt it.[14]

This explains why the super-sign *yi/barbarian* seemed utterly unreasonable and repulsive to the British. If we read the ban carefully, Article 51 exiles the super-sign *yi/barbarian* but does not otherwise banish the English equivalent of the exiled term. It might be suggested that the English word enjoys the double advantage of being both the authoritative signified of the super-sign *yi/barbarian* and an independent English word, uncensored and safely bracketed by the treaty clause. In that light, the internal differentiation of the super-sign can be interpreted as putting into place two supplementary commands on behalf of the injunction of Article 51: (1) the Chinese character 夷 *yi* shall be signified by "barbarian" and be its super-sign; and (2) the English word "barbarian" shall refer its own signification elsewhere and be excluded (bracketed) from the same ban against the super-sign *yi/barbarian*.

So what do the supplementary commands of the ban entail? The Chinese word *yi* would be chased out of the living language in due course. But something else must happen for the coercive force of the legal provision to remain effective in *longue durée* and become the mainstay of historical wisdom and popular opinion. This is where historical writing comes into play. Article

51 provides the legal authority from which the historians of international relations have drawn their strength of positivity and professional confidence as they discourse on the universal Chinese condescension toward foreigners. With very few exceptions, the history books on nineteenth-century Anglo-Chinese relations published to date are very much given to psychologizing a universal Chinese mentality, dubbed sinocentrism. This excessively psychologized mentality characterizes much of what has been written on the subject both before and after John King Fairbank, including *The Cambridge History of China*.[15] The appendix to this book, which correlates against each other two English translations from different time periods of Imperial Commissioner Lin Zexu's famous communication to Queen Victoria, reveals some startling facts about the legacy of Article 51.

That legacy has continued to shape modern scholarship as scholars reiterate the word "barbarian" endlessly to impute the Chinese use of the term, whereas in most cases, the Chinese documents make reference only to the word *yi*. The sleight of hand in citational and translingual practices has had major consequences for people's understanding of modern history and cross-civilizational encounters. For one thing, it prevents us from interrogating the super-sign *yi/barbarian* as a legal and historical problem of the nineteenth century; for another, it severs and renders invisible the crucial historical linkage between the super-sign *yi/barbarian* and the colonial discourse of "barbarian" in English and other European languages. When the history of European colonial expansion is so intimately bound up with the narrative of Chinese xenophobia, we can hardly keep that history out of the discussion without forfeiting the idea of history altogether.

In what sense does the Chinese character *yi* provide hard linguistic evidence for the theory of Chinese xenophobia that has prevailed for so long in modern historiography? Is the theory itself not already indebted to the ban on the super-sign *yi/barbarian* at one time or another? It seems to me that the difficulty of thinking against the ban is formidable. One would have to contend with a gigantic textual edifice erected on what passes as archival scholarship—that solid foundation of international treaties, government correspondence, colonial historiography, journalistic propaganda, and colonial pedagogy. If the international relations as defined through international law are themselves "a naturalized hegemonic discourse that exists today as an artifact of European global expansion from the sixteenth century forward," what are the chances of our bringing a critical eye to this body of material and interpretations?[16] It is encouraging to know that there is a growing tendency to reflect critically on what has been written in the past and explore alternative avenues of understanding nineteenth-century Anglo-Chinese conflicts.[17] The intervention I am hoping to make in solidarity with critical historiography is for the purpose of reexamining the hetero-linguistic ground of the super-sign *yi/barbarian* that has been occluded by the glib evocation of the word "barbarian" by academic and popular writings of the past hundred and fifty–odd years in the West and elsewhere. The invention of the super-sign *yi/barbarian* and the introduction of the ban in Article 51 were among the lasting achievements of the British Empire in the sense that not only did the ban terminate the life of the Chinese character *yi*, but also it continues to cast a long shadow over our understanding of modern history. By documenting the instituted traces of the super-sign, I am attempting to show that the conflict over the meaning of this particular term is a life-and-death struggle waged between the declining Manchu Empire and the rising British Empire as each tried to determine who would have the ultimate control over the meaning of the Chinese sign, and hence the future of China.

Contesting *Yi:* 1832

The British protest of the word *yi* to the Chinese authorities can be dated to the year 1832, when Hugh Hamilton Lindsay (also known as Hu Xiami), a supercargo of the British East India Company, was instructed to sail up the coast of China to gather information and report back on the possibility of opening trade in the northern regions. The secret instructions Lindsay received from the head of the company were "to ascertain how far the northern Ports of this Empire may gradually be opened to British Commerce which would be most eligible and to what extent the disposition of the Natives and local governments would be favorable to it."[18] Among those who sailed with Lindsay was the flamboyant adventurer and independent missionary from Prussia, Karl Gützlaff (1803–1851; also known as Guo Shila and Charles Gützlaff), who was charged with the office of interpreter and surgeon. On board the *Lord Amherst* was also a draughtsman, who mapped out the key positions of Qing military defense along the coast that would prove helpful to the British Navy a few years later, as well as a Chinese man with some learning whose task was to assist Lindsay and Gützlaff in the writing of petitions and letters to Chinese officials during the voyage. Lindsay and his crew departed in early March 1832 and returned to Macao on September 4, although they had been instructed to return not later than

June 1.[19] On this voyage, the *Lord Amherst* made stops at Xiamen (Amoy), Fuzhou (Foochow), Ningbo (Ningpo), and Shanghai, and on its way back visited parts of Korea and the Loo-choo Islands.

On June 20, 1832, the *Lord Amherst* dropped anchor off the coast of Shanghai as Lindsay addressed a petition to the office of the principal magistrate with a request to open foreign trade in that area.[20] His missionary-interpreter, Gützlaff, who kept a detailed journal about the journey—the second of his three famous voyages along the coast of China before the Opium War—recounts that the Taou-tae (Admiral Wu Qitai) promptly rejected their petition and issued an order that they return to Canton without further delay.[21] The journal entry that bears on the story of the British protest against the mandarin's use of the word *yi* is dated June 24. It reads:

> We reasoned our friends out of the use the epithet *E* [*yi*], "barbarians," which they apply to all strangers indiscriminately. The idea of cunning and treachery is always attached to this name when uttered by the Chinese. As foreigners trading to China have hitherto patiently borne such an appellation, they have been treated as barbarians. It was highly necessary to object to this epithet and to shew from its use in Chinese writings that the term conveyed reproach. From this time, they abstained from the use of it, and called us foreigners, or Englishmen.[22]

This detail is highly significant because it provides an alternative translation and interpretation of the word *yi* that challenges Robert Morrison's earlier rendering of the same word, *e jin (yi ren)*, as "foreign" or "foreigner" in the *Dictionary of the Chinese Language* (Figure 2).[23] Gützlaff's translation flies in

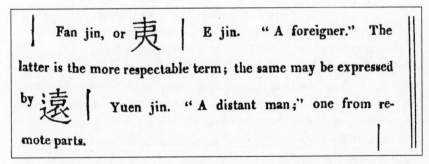

Figure 2. Morrison's 1815 translation of the character *yi* in *The Dictionary of the Chinese Language*.

the face of the interpretations of nearly all the previous translators hired by the East India Company, who had thought the same as Morrison since the beginning of the eighteenth century.[24] The factory records of the East India Company show that the use of "foreigner" persisted through the early 1830s. The English translation of the emperor's edict dated May 22, 1831, for instance, renders *yi shang* as "foreign merchant."[25] But at some point around 1832, the character *yi*, which had heretofore caused no trouble to the East India Company in the eighteenth century, became a nuisance.

Without attributing the abrupt shift simply to Gützlaff, I would note that his remarks in the journal entry quoted earlier suggest an important turning point in the interpretation of the Chinese character.[26] Gützlaff was one of the few European travelers in the early nineteenth century who had ventured into inland China and had written promptly and spontaneously in English about his firsthand experience with and close observation of the locals.[27] His works, especially the story of his first two voyages along the coast of China, published in 1833, were widely read and disseminated, affecting imperial policies as well as commercial enterprises. The manner in which Gützlaff's popular writings opened China to the colonial gaze brings to mind the extraordinary impact of that other nineteenth-century missionary David Livingstone, whose published works greatly facilitated the opening of the "Dark Continent" of Africa to imperial expansion a few decades later. If Dr. Livingstone can be regarded as the unwitting accomplice in Europe's scramble for Africa, Gützlaff never hesitated to embrace the colonial cause in Asia. In the *Journal of Two Voyages along the Coast of China*, for example, he makes an enthusiastic appeal to a general readership in language that seems to anticipate the Opium War:

> The reader of these details should remember, that what has been done is only a feeble beginning of what must ensue. We will hope and pray, that God in his mercy may, very soon, open a wider door of access; and we will work as long as the Lord grants health, strength, and opportunity. I sincerely wish that something more efficient might be done for opening *a free intercourse with China,* and would feel myself highly favoured, if I could be subservient, in a small degree, in hastening forward such an event. In the merciful providence of our God and Saviour, it may be confidently hoped, that the doors to China will be thrown open. By whom this will be done, or in what ways, is of very little importance; every well wisher and co-operator will anxiously desire, that all glory may be rendered to God, the giver of every good gift.[28]

Within ten years, Gützlaff would be working for the British plenipotentiary and assisting him in drafting the Anglo-Chinese Treaty of Nanjing. It was during one of those meetings that the character *yi* was first added to the agenda of the treaty negotiations.[29]

Gützlaff's account of the *yi* episode from his second voyage contains useful information about the supercargo's interaction with the local officials but is otherwise vague on the specifics of the altercation between Lindsay and the local head of military defense. The Chinese-language documents concerning the same incident give us a much better sense as to how the actual conversation went and what conclusions may be drawn from it.[30] When Lindsay's petition was rejected, Admiral Wu Qitai, who had reviewed the request, circulated a memo saying: "I have examined and find that there is no precedent for the *yi* vessel to trade in Shanghai. We shall not break the rules but will bring the matter to the attention of the court."[31] Taking offense at Wu's use of the character *yi*, Lindsay presented a second note to protest: "Great Britain is not a *yi* state but a *wai* state" (meaning literally "outside"). To this, Wu responded with a pedantic explanation, arguing that he was merely adopting a common usage for foreigners with no implied pejorative meaning. The ancients had used the term *man* to designate those who lived to the south of China, the word *yi* to refer to people who lived to the east, *di* to those who lived to the north, and so on. "Since time immemorial," Wu concluded, "we have always said southern *man*, northern *di*, eastern *yi*, and western *rong*. Take our own noble sages King Shun and King Wen. Mencius himself said, 'King Shun was an eastern *yi* and King Wen was a western *yi*.' How can the word be offensive? You must be overreacting."[32]

Lindsay refused to be persuaded by Wu's argument. Relying on the sinological skills of Gützlaff and the learning of the Chinese scholar on board the *Lord Amherst,* he composed a rebuttal by quoting passages from the Chinese classics as well as the Qing code to prove the contrary. Essentially, Lindsay advanced four points in the rebuttal. First, the Koreans were known to the ancient Chinese as eastern *yi*, whereas the native land of the British subjects lay to the west of the Qing empire and technically did not fit the geographic description of eastern *yi*. Second, Great Britain possessed colonial territories lying to the east, west, south, and north of the Qing empire.[33] Third, volume 11 of the *Great Qing Code* assigns the *miao, qiang, man,* and *mo* (minority peoples) to the category of *yi*. Fourth, Su Dongpo (Su Shi), the eminent Song dynasty poet and statesman, made the observation that "one must not govern the *yi* and *di* the same way one rules the Central States. As it is with beasts and animals, excessive rule almost certainly leads to excessive chaos. The ancient sages knew this well and advocated non-rule as proper rule. Non-rule is truly the most profound rule of all." From that Lindsay drew the conclusion that "when you address someone as *yi*, you are labeling that person a *man* and a *mo*. When you apply the word *yi* to the subjects of Great Britain, you are humiliating the *timian* (body/face, proper manner) of our country, offending its people, and provoking anger and retaliation."[34] Lindsay refused to obey Wu's order and would not leave the area until the disagreeable word *yi* was removed from the official language. Wu, for his part, wanted the British to depart immediately and feared the consequences should he let the trespassers linger too long off the coast of Shanghai. Eventually he gave in and substituted the word *shang* (merchant, trader) for *yi* in a new order he issued on July 6, 1832.[35]

Lindsay's mention of the eminent Song dynasty writer and official Su Shi (1037–1101) is a matter of curiosity, because there apparently were Latin as well as English translations of the same words circulating widely among the foreign community at about this time. The Jesuit scholar Joseph de Prémare (1666–1736) had rendered Su Shi's words into Latin as "Barbari haud secus ac pecora, non eodem modo regendi sunt ut reguntur Sinae. Si quis vellet eos magnis sapientiae legibus instruere, nihil aliud quam summam perturbationem induceret. Antiqui reges istud optimé callebant, et ideo barbaros non regendo regebant. Sic autem eos non regendo regere, praeclara eos optimé regendi ars est."[36] The English translation cited along with the Latin version by Sir John Francis Davis, who was to become the colonial governor of Hong Kong, in his 1836 book *The Chinese: A General Description of the Empire of China and Its Inhabitants* provided a strange reworking of Su Shi's language: "The barbarians are like beasts, and not to be ruled on the same principles as citizens. Were any one to attempt controlling them by the great maxims of reason, it would tend to nothing but confusion. The ancient kings well understood this, and accordingly ruled barbarians by misrule. Therefore to rule barbarians by misrule is the true and best way of ruling them."[37] The original Chinese phrase *bu zhi* ("non-rule" or "not to rule"), or the Latin *non regendo*, is translated as "misrule," which turns Su Shi's words into perfect gibberish, if not a verbal monstrosity.[38]

Did Lindsay and Gützlaff read their Su Shi in the Chinese original, in Latin, or in English translation? I would not rule out the possibility that Lindsay read the English version only. In any event, both sides drew on their share of the knowledge of the classics and writings by renowned Chinese literati in order to shore up their own position and undermine that of the

other. The question of *yi* as it relates to the classical scholarship and the imperial ideology of the Qing dynasty is an important one, to which I devote
the entire next chapter. In Chapter 3 I also analyze the Yongzheng emperor's
condemnation in 1730 of his enemy's subversive evocation of the same Su
Shi quotation. For now, let me observe that the Lindsay-Wu quibble anticipated much of what was to come in Anglo-Chinese communications up to
the time of the first Opium War and beyond. It created a discursive pattern
whereby the British would reason or dispute with the Chinese authorities
about the meaning of *yi,* insisting that the word was insulting, whereas the
mandarins would uniformly deny that *yi* meant what the British thought it
meant, and so on. The British defended the dignity of their empire from the
mandarins, who, for their part, believed that the dignity of the Qing empire
should be defended from the aggressive behavior of the British. Lindsay's
second point in the rebuttal is particularly revealing in this regard. By describing the massive geographic spread of the British colonial possessions as
lying to the east, west, south, and north of the Qing empire, Lindsay brings
out the true stakes of the argument, suggesting that the dispute with Wu
Qitai was as much about *yi* as about the sovereign claims of the British Empire. Insofar as the discourse of the "barbarian" had long been germane to
the processes of European colonial expansion before the arrival of the *Lord
Amherst* on the coast of China, the unexpected encounter with the Chinese
word *yi* through translation brought the familiar discourse of the other to a
crisis by forcing the enunciation of the "barbarian" to face its own caricature
in someone else's language.

The actual language of discussion between the British and the Chinese,
however, bypassed the issue of translation entirely, as if the burden of understanding devolved solely on the indigenous word and on the Chinese
classics which proved to be too polysemous and ambiguous to serve a single
purpose. But as Gützlaff's journal reveals, the English word "barbarian" had
a tangible presence already in that exchange and served as the interpretive
grid through which Lindsay and Gützlaff would grasp the meaning of *yi*.[39]
This manner of interpretation is what I call hetero-linguistic catachresis. By
this term, I refer to the act of (mis)translation that manipulates the meaning
of a super-sign by transgressing the boundaries of languages and camou-
flages the traces of that transgression at the same time. The Lindsay-Wu dispute over *yi* was carried on primarily in Chinese terms as if the English word
"barbarian" did not matter when the latter actually mattered a great deal
and was the true point of reference in that exchange. This mode of trans-

lingual interpretation anticipated the Napier affair, which took place two years after the voyage of the *Lord Amherst* and dominated nearly all subsequent diplomatic interactions between Great Britain and the Qing as each tried to impose its own terms of dignity, power, and sovereignty upon the other.

The Barbarian Eye

Lord Napier arrived in China in 1834 to be the first official representative of the British government. His appointment by the foreign secretary Lord Palmerston came in the wake of the expiration of the charter of the East India Company.[40] On July 25, 1834, Napier sailed into Guangzhou (Canton) without permission and without his credential papers and demanded to communicate with the governor-general of Guangdong and Guangxi, Lu Kun, by letter. The Chinese authorities refused to accept his letter and instructed him to go through the *yang shang*, the Hong merchants in Canton who had traditionally served as the intermediaries between foreign traders and the local government.[41] Napier's frustration with the local government turned into indignation when he discovered that the Qing official documents referred to his official title, Chief Superintendent of British Trade in China, as *yimu*.[42] Curiously, Napier's interpreter Robert Morrison translated *yimu* as "the barbarian eye," a monstrous catachresis that has since taken on a life of its own.[43]

The August 1834 number of the *Chinese Repository* concurred with the spurious translation of *yimu* by publishing an English version of the edict issued by Lu Kun. The edict begins by observing that "an English war vessel having on board a barbarian *eye*, had from the outer seas, sailed to Cabreta Point [off Macao], and there anchored." The translator or the editor italicizes the word "eye" so the reader's eye is effectively drawn to the *eye* as we continue to peruse: "The barbarian *eye* who has now come is of course for the superintendence and examination of this business. And the barbarian *eye* is not on a par with the taepans [supercargoes]. If he wishes to come to Canton, it will be necessary to make a clear report, requesting the imperial will on the subject."[44]

"The barbarian *eye*" continues to be adopted as the literal translation of *yimu* even after a parenthetical note is inserted on the next page to explain the meaning of "the barbarian eye" as "the headman" in Chinese.[45] The *Chinese Repository* printed the catachresis on page after page throughout Napier's stay in Guangzhou and after his death in Macao. Was the translator poking fun at the literalness of the Chinese word? Or was the hetero-linguistic catachresis laughing at the translator? In any case, Napier was infuriated by the disrespectful treatment of him by the governor-general, whom he called "a presumptuous savage," and vowed to punish him for committing an outrage against the British Crown.[46]

Was the Chinese character *yi* capable of that much injury?[47]

The incident of *yimu* and a number of related clashes over the proper manner of diplomatic address and protocol (see my discussion later in this chapter of the contested format of official communication) led to the first military skirmish between England and China. In his virtual declaration of war on September 8, 1834, Napier repudiated the governor-general's condescension toward England by proudly asserting that

> his majesty, the king of England, is a great and powerful monarch, that he rules over an extent of territory in the four quarters of the world more comprehensive in space, and infinitely more so in power, than the whole empire of China; that he commands armies of bold and fierce soldiers, who have conquered wherever they went; and that he is possessed of great ships of war carrying even as many as 120 guns, which pass quietly along the seas, where no native of China has ever yet dared to show his face. Let the governor then judge if such a monarch "will be reverently obedient to any one."[48]

Napier requested a guard of marines from the warships at the Bogue to come up to the city of Canton. Two British sloops, the *Imogene* and the *Andromache*, arrived and anchored at Huangpu (Whampoa) on September 11. A battle ensued. It may seem strange in retrospect that the first British military action in China was occasioned by neither opium nor trade, as British trade actually suffered during the standoff. The direct cause was instead Napier's determination to vindicate the honor of the government of His Britannic Majesty, which had been grievously injured and wronged by the governor-general's arrogant treatment of him.

To suggest that the super-sign *yi/barbarian* was one of the most tragic and costly fabrications in modern diplomatic history is by no means an exaggeration. Napier's indignation was real and led to the loss of lives on the *Imogene* and the *Andromache* as well as his own deteriorating health and death on October 11, 1834.[49] Robert Morrison died in the same year, apparently through overwork and exhaustion, with his son John Robert Morrison succeeding him as the Chinese secretary.[50] It appears that what had begun as a quibble over a word and a set of diplomatic protocols became deadly serious. As P. C. Kuo later observed: "With the commencement of the hostilities on September 7, the situation transgressed from a conflict of principles to a state of war. In the creation of this state, the guilt was on the side of the British Superintendent."[51] Whoever was to blame in that situation, Napier's unfortunate death supplied much ammunition to the war party when the British Parliament began to consider the possibility of a military showdown and later retaliation against the destruction of British property (opium) by Imperial Commissioner Lin Zexu, an action that gave rise to the Opium War.

The condemnation of Chinese arrogance toward foreigners became a counteroffensive against the imperial prohibition of the opium trade, in which people such as Gützlaff himself had a lucrative share.[52] Upon Napier's death, the sixty-four British merchants in Canton headed by the families of the major opium traders William Jardine and James Matheson drafted a petition to the king on December 9, 1834, asking for the appointment of a plenipotentiary backed by three warships and empowered to demand from the Qing court the dismissal of Lu and redress for the trade stoppage. They urged the British government to put a stop to the external and internal commerce of the Qing empire and take possession of all the armed vessels of the country. They argued, "Such measures would not only be sufficient to evince both the power and spirit of Great Britain to resent insult, but would enable your Majesty's plenipotentiary to secure indemnity for any injury that might, in the first instance, be offered to the persons or property of your Majesty's subjects."[53] The petition included many of the demands that would eventually appear in the Anglo-Chinese Treaty of Nanjing and the subsequent treaties signed by the two countries.

"The barbarian eye" did not go uncontested at the time, however. Sir George Staunton, a widely acknowledged authority on the Chinese language, remarked that *yimu* provided no legitimate ground for dispute because the Chinese translation simply meant "Foreign Principal" and that *mu* ought to be rendered as "principal," not literally as "eye."[54] How to explain such a wide margin of discrepancy between the two translations? The historian Dilip Basu calls "barbarian eye" respectable rhetoric for war, noting a vital link between the British interest in the word *yi* and Napier's misguided policy of armed expedition. Basu's research shows that Staunton and Peter Perring Thoms were among the few Britons who had voiced their disagreement with Morrison's translation and were suspicious of the policy maneuver behind it. Reflecting on P. P. Thoms's losing struggle against the rising tide of the linguistic crusade against *yi,* Basu observes:

> Thoms's contestation was of no consequence. He noted that up to the time of Napier, no one complained about the term *yi* in Qing communications. He knew why. The communications mostly addressed commercial matters; they were respectful and elegant. Yet in 1834 no less an authority than Morrison or Gützlaff was translating the concept as offensive. He suspected that Morrison must have been acting "*under authority* [Thoms's italics] and not in compliance with his usual judgment." He further noted that in the "Correspondence relating to China" presented to both Houses of Parliament in 1840, the offensive terms occurred, in not a very long document, not less than twenty-one times.[55]

Interestingly, when the duke of Wellington took Lord Palmerston's place on November 15, 1834, the new foreign secretary wanted to show a more conciliatory attitude toward the Qing. He was of the opinion that the dispute over Lord Napier's high-sounding titles was but a pretext and that the true cause was Napier's pretension in fixing himself at Guangzhou, without previous permission, and insisting on direct communication with the governor-general.[56] The new foreign secretary ordered that "the Superintendent must not go to Canton without permission. He must not depart from the accustomed mode of communication."[57] Sir John Francis Davis, who became acting first superintendent after the death of Napier and then governor of Hong Kong after the Opium War, criticized the petition of the British merchants as crude and observed that some of the most respectable houses refused to sign it. The Glasgow Chamber of Commerce, however, aggressively pressed for direct access to the Qing court and the opening of the whole coast of China to trade. At the same time, the Foreign Office received a lengthy memorandum from Hugh Hamilton Lindsay, saying, "That Lord Napier acted in some respects injudiciously I will not attempt to deny," but "that the Chinese were predetermined to insult him and that no moderation on his part would have procured for him a fitting reception." Lindsay weighed the viability of open military conflict against the need to obey the laws of a foreign country and asked on what grounds one could justify war. His answer was that obedience was owed to the laws of a foreign country, "but, on the other hand, it always presupposes that our intercourse is with a civilized nation, that the laws and regulations to which your compliance is required are clear and defined and that they give a reasonable protection to Life and Property."[58]

Lindsay's argument about civilization and its other is grounded in a theory of natural rights and a colonial discourse of injury, which I will examine in detail shortly, that had taken shape during the earlier European encounter with the "barbarians" in the New World. The role Lindsay played in the 1832 episode and in the Napier affair calls our attention to the existence of a prior European discourse of civilization that figured centrally in the British protest of the super-sign *yi/barbarian*.

And one must not forget Karl Gützlaff, the missionary interpreter, who had worked for Lindsay on the *Lord Amherst*. Gützlaff was now an interpreter and assistant to the Chinese secretary John Robert Morrison to help manage official communications between Britain and the Qing. I should mention that the office of the Chinese secretary played a pivotal role in the changing interpretation of the word *yi* during this crucial period of Anglo-Chinese relations.[59] Robert Morrison's correction of his own earlier translation of the character *yi* as "foreign" or "foreigner" in his *Dictionary of the Chinese Language* (Figure 1) is symptomatic of the new relationship between the Chinese secretary and the British Empire.[60] Before the arrival of Lord Napier, the office of the Chinese secretary had served the language needs of the East India Company and performed various translation tasks, but after 1834 it was turned into a government institution where official communications as well as secret intelligence were processed and translated.[61] The missionaries and diplomats who received formal appointment as the Chinese secretary of His (and later Her) Majesty's plenipotentiary were, indeed, expected to act under authority. The individual judgment of the Chinese secretary was not allowed to stray from the official policy of the British government, as, for example, in Lord Palmerston's silencing of a conflicting interpretation suggested by John Robert Morrison, which I discuss shortly. Between 1834 and 1860, the Chinese secretary's office was the venue where the British government managed most of its diplomatic exchanges with the Qing government. Robert Morrison, his son John Robert Morrison, Robert Thom, Karl Gützlaff, Walter Henry Medhurst, and Thomas Wade all worked in this capacity at one time or another.[62]

The chief interpreter for the Anglo-Chinese Treaty of Nanjing was John Robert Morrison, assisted by Karl Gützlaff and Robert Thom. John King Fairbank's book *Trade and Diplomacy on the China Coast* gives us a glimpse of how the interpreters worked with the languages they used to draft the trade regulations in 1843:

Morrison's first draft of the regulations, in thirteen articles, was rewritten by Thom and submitted to the Chinese authorities, who found the Chinese version "in some parts wanting in perspicuity" and sometimes incomprehensible, and so rewrote the thirteen articles with minor changes to form sixteen. This Chinese version having been translated back into English, Thom drew up a commentary either agreeing or objecting to each article, and on the basis of these papers, which Morrison and Thom brought back from Canton, Pottinger [Sir Henry Pottinger, the plenipotentiary] penned some "Remarks." On July 15 [1843] he wrote Ch'i-ying enclosing fifteen regulations as finally amended, which Ch'i-ying at once submitted to Peking.[63]

The management of Chinese-language texts was no trifling matter in these treaty negotiations. When the British won the first Opium War and lifted the ban on the opium trade, one of the first items they brought to the negotiating table was a proposal to ban the word *yi* from the official language. When Thomas Wade served as the Chinese secretary at the negotiations of the Anglo-Chinese Treaty of Tianjin, he succeeded in writing the ban into the treaty.[64] The trouble was that *yi* was not the only item of diplomatic offense the British were concerned about. There was a genre of official writing in Chinese, a mode of address equally unacceptable to the British, that had to be eliminated or brought under control.

British Honor

After Napier was succeeded by Captain Charles Elliot, the British foreign secretary Lord Palmerston instructed Elliot to remain vigilant with regard to what the Chinese officials would write or say to him and make every effort to defend the honor of Great Britain in his communications with the Chinese authorities.[65] When Elliot came into office in December 1836, he adopted an official Chinese genre of communication known as the *bing* to open formal channels of conversation with the Qing authorities. For that he was taken to task by Palmerston, who wrote on July 22, 1836, "I have to add, that His Majesty's Government do not deem it expedient that you should give to your written communications with the Chinese Government, the name of 'Petitions.'"[66] Elliot defended himself by saying that the genre was not inappropriate for someone of his rank to use in addressing the governor-general, just as the officers of the Chinese government themselves used it to report to superior officers. He further pointed out, "And having regard to the radical character under which it is classed, (*Shee*, to admonish, enjoin, or produce,) perhaps it may be rather thought to mean the respectful exhibition of information, than a distinct signification of the ideas, involved in our word 'Petitions.'" Here Elliot tries to effect a reversal of the terms in which the commensurability of *bing* and "petition" might be conceived and contested by pointing to the English word "petition," not the Chinese word *bing*, as the possible source of disrespect. To fortify his argument, Elliot solicited a memorandum from John Robert Morrison to be included in his letter to Palmerston. Here is how Morrison understood the genre *bing:*

> All officers holding subordinate jurisdiction, who are below the third rank, (of whom the highest may be regarded as corresponding in station to the prefects and sub-prefects of departments in France,) when addressing the chief authorities of the province, make use of the word "*Pin* [*bing*]," and they receive from the same authorities, documents denominated "*Yu.*" The signification of these words I subjoin, as extracted from the Chinese Dictionary of Dr. Morrison.
>
> "'*Pin.*' Commonly used to denote a clear statement of any affair made to a superior. *Pin*, is to state to a superior, whether verbally, or by writing, whether *petitioning* something, or to give *information* of; whether from the people to an officer of Government, or from an inferior officer to a superior several degrees higher . . . Commands are called "yu," which word is used by superiors in the Government to express their *orders*, given to inferiors, or to the people.
>
> These are the words which have always been used by foreigners in their correspondence with the Government; and "*Pin*" is the word which the Governor, in 1834, required Lord Napier to make use of.[67]

The mention of Napier had the dangerous implication of undermining the legitimate ground of the earlier dispute over the proper manner of diplomatic communication with the governor-general that had been dictated by Palmerston himself.[68] On this occasion Palmerston abided by his decision and forbade Elliot to use the *bing* in his communications with the Qing officials. He did so by evoking "the established usages of England, which do not admit that an officer commissioned by the King of England should so address an officer commissioned by any other Sovereign."[69]

The spirit of Palmerston's directive was duly incorporated into the Anglo-

Chinese Treaty of Nanjing in 1842 after China's defeat in the first Opium War. Article 11 stipulates:

> It is agreed that Her Britannic Majesty's Chief High Officer in China shall correspond with the Chinese High Officers, both at the Capital and in the Provinces, under the term "Communication" [*zhao hui*]. The Subordinate British Officers and Chinese High Officers in the Provinces under the terms "Statement" [*shen chen*] on the part of the former, and on the part of the latter "Declaration" [*zha xing*], and the Subordinates of both Countries on a footing of perfect equality. Merchants and others not holding official situations and, therefore, not included in the above, on both sides, to use the term "Representation" [*bing ming*] in all papers addressed to, or intended for the notice of the respective Governments.[70]

The word *bing* partially survives in the last category, *bing ming*, meaning "representation," and nowhere do we find the word "petition" as a plausible translation for either of the Chinese characters. Since this interesting reworking of the official Chinese genres is predicated on a language of "perfect equality," we need to ask what the British were trying to accomplish with this rhetoric. Was it a necessary fiction designed to "obscure the violent means through which 'China' was brought low"?[71] Let us examine the terms of the negotiation closely to get a basic understanding. On August 29, 1840, when the treaty negotiations began, the British had placed the issue of equality on the agenda as the second major item for discussion. Qishan (Ch'i-Shan), the imperial commissioner, raised the objection that the bureaucratic system of every nation had its hierarchy and Great Britain was no exception. Did the British not make distinctions between higher and lower official posts and between superiors and subordinates? Acting under the authority of Palmerston, Elliot observed that the treaty demand had nothing to do with particular bureaucratic hierarchies and that the British subjects desired equal treatment so that they could communicate with their Chinese counterparts as equals.[72] Qishan was eventually forced to expunge the *bing* genre from Anglo-Chinese communications and agreed to include Article 11 in the treaty.

It is interesting that when Qishan came under attack by Yu Qian, the governor-general of Jiangnan and Jiangxi, for succumbing to the British demand regarding the *bing*, the Daoguang emperor defended the former's decision by pointing out that the issue of genre and respectful address was merely a matter of *xiaojie* (trifling detail).[73] Commenting on the said governor-general's memorial, the emperor wrote: "Your judgment is flawed and inferior to that of Qishan in your understanding of our edicts. The original words and letters [of the British] must be conveyed to us so we may gain a clear insight into the *yi* affairs and be able to tell the truth from falsehood and make our decisions accordingly. To be overly concerned with *xiaojie* at the expense of matters of *dati* [major proportions] such as you are, it could only lead to disaster."[74] Guo Weidong's study of related Chinese documents shows that Qishan took the liberty of making a number of decisions about the format of official communications between Britain and China to conform to the British demands without memorializing the court first. When he did memorialize the court to propose permanent changes to the established usage relating to Anglo-Chinese communications in Baihe and Guangzhou, for example, the court raised no objection whatsoever. It appears that the Daoguang emperor exhibited more flexibility than his British counterpart in the matter of formal genre and respectful address. Territorial concessions and indemnity payments to the British were the uppermost concerns in his assessment of the Anglo-Chinese crisis.[75]

To the British, however, formal genres and respectful address mattered no less than the balance of profit and loss because they had to do with national pride and honor. Herman Merivale, who in 1839 published his popular *Lectures on Colonization and Colonies,* which was reissued in 1861 (both dates coinciding with the two Opium Wars), had this to say about Britain's position in its colonial empire:

> The sense of national honor, pride of blood, and the tenacious spirit of self-defence, the sympathies of kindred communities, the instincts of a dominant race, the vague but generous desire to spread our civilization and our religion over the world: these are impulses which the student in his closet may disregard, but the statesman dares not, for they will assuredly prevail, as they so often have prevailed before, and silence mere utilitarian argument whenever a crisis calls them forth.[76]

These lectures were first delivered to the students of Oxford University, where Merivale, in his late thirties, held the Drummond Professorship of Political Economy. Over twelve years beginning in 1848, Merivale occupied a senior position at the Colonial Office as the colleague and successor of Sir James Stephen and spoke with great authority on matters of British colonial policy. Merivale's lectures had such an impact on the British public in the nineteenth century that they caused a twentieth-century commentator to remark that "no serious student of the British Empire in its development can afford to neglect a work which has behind it so much good thinking, is informed by so ripe an experience, and deals with so critical and characteristic a stage in the history of Colonial Administration."[77] Merivale's observations about national honor and racial superiority were by no means empty assertions but had clear policy implications, as they derived from the day-to-day interactions with colonial subjects and foreign countries. Queen Victoria reiterated that policy in her speech to Parliament on January 26, 1841, when she stated: "Having deemed it necessary to send to the coast of China a naval and military force, to demand reparation and redress for the injuries inflicted upon some of my subjects by the officers of the Emperor of China, and for indignities offered to an Agent of my Crown, I, at the same time, appointed Plenipotentiaries to treat upon these matters with the Chinese Government."[78] The injuries and indignities to which Victoria referred include, of course, the issues of formal genre and respectful address we have been examining in this chapter.

Sir Henry Pottinger was the new Chief Plenipotentiary appointed by Queen Victoria in place of Elliot, who had been stripped of his official title for failing to defend British interests in the treaty negotiations.[79] As soon as he took office in May 1841, Pottinger began another round of Anglo-Chinese treaty negotiations in which he stood firm on the issue of equality and tried to introduce a ban on the word *yi*. According to Zhang Xi, a member of the Chinese delegation who recorded the negotiating process in his "Fuyi riji" (Journals of the pacification of the *yi*), that discussion took place on August 26, 1842, on which occasion Pottinger observed that *yi* was not a nice word and should cease to be used. Xian Songpu, one of the chief negotiators representing the Qing government, cited the sage's words "Shun was an eastern *yi* and King wen was a western *yi*" to rebut that objection. Insofar as the two sides could not agree on how to determine the meaning of this word, the negotiation came to a deadlock, and no conclusive legal provision regarding *yi* was incorporated into the treaty—not until the Treaty of Tianjin—although Pottinger did pressure the Qing officials not to use the character in the Chinese version of the Treaty of Nanjing.[80] Thus concluded the notorious unequal treaty that resulted in China's loss of sovereignty over Hong Kong and in the other major concessions to the British and other Western powers.

For an unequal treaty to insist on perfect equality within the treaty articles seems like hypocrisy or bad faith. Perhaps it was both. T. Mullet Ellis, who drew a fanciful portrait of Queen Victoria in a nineteenth-century children's book called *The Fairies' Favourite*, reveals how Britain would have *liked* to be treated by the rest of the world:

> Kings from the far East, Princes from Colconda, and Rajahs from Seringapatam, the emperor, the Emperor of Morocco, the Grand Llama of Thibet and Fee-fi-fofum, had all crawled on their bare kness [sic] to the foot of the throne with sacks of jewels on their backs, and something special in their breast-pocket for the queen. She had all these costly presents, cargoes of bar-gold from California and scores of ships chock-full of gold in its raw state from Australia—which is a very nuggetty island—Her cellars were crammed with ingots of gold, and cart-loads of precious stones were shoveled in the ton.[81]

The picture of desire that comes to life in this description and in an 1872 illustration of the Burmese envoy offering presents to the queen on his knees (Figure 3), is not one of equality but of something else. Such stories aimed

Figure 3. W. B. Wallen, "The Queen Receiving the Burmese Embassy" (1872), from Arthur Lawrence Merrill, *Life and Times of Queen Victoria* (1901).

to indoctrinate the British from childhood on to fantasize about national wealth and privilege in this manner and to expect the other races, especially their kings and emperors, to offer treasure to the British sovereign and show their respect. This also explains why the issue of *koutou* (kowtow) and other forms of humiliation during Lord Macartney's mission to the Qianlong emperor's court obsessed the British imagination for nearly two centuries, and why the nineteenth-century British officials in China were not prepared to treat the Qing officials as their equals.

On August 20, 1842, nine days before the formal conclusion of the Treaty of Nanjing, the Chinese imperial commissioner Chiying and his entourage were scheduled to visit the warship *Cornwallis* and meet with the British plenipotentiary. Chinese Secretary John Robert Morrison informed the Qing delegation that it was the British custom to greet distinguished visitors with ceremonial gun salutes. The higher the guest's rank was, the greater the number of salutes, up to a maximum, he said, of twenty-three.[82] When the British plenipotentiary Pottinger stepped on board the *Cornwallis*, he was greeted with a nineteen-gun salute. Pottinger's counterpart Chiying, who negotiated the treaties on equal footing with him, and his suite received three. They were told by Morrison that the British were following the Chinese ways. This carefully engineered spectacle of humiliation did not help the British promote their cause of equality. Four days later, the Qing officials played their own game of equality by greeting their English guests with three salutes when the two parties met on land.[83] Thus the British discourse of equality met with the Qing policy of *yishi tongren* (equal treatment) in a strange drama of imperial rivalry.

Commenting on the Qing government's readiness to extend the most-favored-nation clauses to all other foreign nations, John Fairbank suggested that "the ancient idea of equal treatment of all barbarians was applied by the Manchu negotiators of 1842–1844 of their own accord. Since the emperor was accustomed to viewing all men from afar with equal compassion, his ministers almost instinctively decided to extend the British treaty terms to the Americans. Their aim was to prevent the British themselves admitting the Americans to these privileges and so winning for Britain the gratitude which ought really to be felt by the Americans toward the emperor."[84] Fairbank's speculation as to why the emperor would desire equal treatment of foreign nations against his own best interests is somewhat off the mark. The Qing foreign policy of *yishi tongren* was less about gratitude than it was about the court's awareness of Britain's ambition to dominate the world.

When Lord Macartney's mission came to China in 1793, the Qianlong emperor had become suspicious of the true intent of the British mission with regard to China. To the British, the emperor acted like a haughty sovereign when he downplayed the importance of English merchandise, as exemplified, for example, by the emperor's letter to King George III. But often overlooked were the Qianlong emperor's secret instructions to his trusted ministers in which he expressed his apprehension that the English might try to use the opportunity to monopolize trade in Guangzhou by elbowing out the merchants of other foreign nations who had maintained enduring trade relations with China for centuries. His edict to the Grand Minister in the Council of State in 1793 asserted that "among the western ocean states, England ranks foremost in strength. It is said that the English have robbed and exploited the merchant ships of the other western ocean states so that the *yi* people along the western ocean are terrified of their brutality."[85] The emperor instructed Chang Lin to reach Canton ahead of the Macartney team on their return journey and inform the entire foreign business community there that the emperor had not granted special privileges to the English, and the latter had no right to extort revenue or profits from the other foreign merchants by claiming to represent them collectively to the Qing state.[86] The Qianlong emperor's foreboding became reality fifty years later, when the British seized control of the Maritime Customs of the imperial Qing state during the suppression of the Taiping Rebellion. In retrospect, the imperial policy of *yishi tongren,* which had been reiterated so many times in the official edicts to the foreign community from the eighteenth through the nineteenth centuries, was entirely intended to contain the influence of the British. When the British depicted the Chinese as "anti-social" and stubbornly resisting "European penetration and the public-sphere of 'reason,' while continuing to function outside a Eurocentrically imagined world," they were in fact reacting to a long-standing imperial policy that had successfully curbed British colonial ambitions when India and the countries of Southeast Asia succumbed to colonial rule.[87] Interestingly, when C. H. Alexanderowicz tries to explain the major differences between China and India during this period, he attributes them to the ideological rigidity of the Qing court as exemplified by the Qianlong emperor's treatment of the MacCartney mission in contrast to the Moghul emperor's measures of expediency in dealing with the Europeans. This observation derives from British impressions and narratives of the time and has not benefited from a cross-examination of the Qing sources. These sources suggest that the Qing court was entirely aware of the imperial ambitions of the British.[88]

The Colonial Discourse of Injury

The British plenipotentiary Pottinger would have banned the character *yi* if he could at the conclusion of the Treaty of Nanjing in 1842. And he would have done so less out of regard for equality than to vindicate the honor of Her Britannic Majesty. That the traumatic injury to the sovereign body of the British Empire should have hinged on a hetero-linguistic maneuver that required an English word to complete the meaning of a Chinese one might challenge a psychoanalyst to come up with a good explanation. Might the British have projected a masochistic self-image onto the Chinese word, just as they had fantasized about the Chinese projecting a sinocentric worldview onto the British? The possibility is there. But if these multiple projections mean anything, where do we go to search for that meaning? What are the stakes in such projections? Is injury indispensable to the ways of sovereign thinking in colonial discourse?

In *Aryans and British India*, Thomas Trautmann observes that the British crafting of the Aryan story—the claims of distant kinship and family reunion with India—turned colonial rule into a love story. The discourse of friendship that shaped colonial relations in British India during this period may help throw some interesting light on the affective economy that appears to be at play here. "A central issue for the British in their arguments over Indian policy," Trautmann writes, "was how the Indians might be made to love the British regime."[89] For William Jones, founder and first president of the Asiatic Society, the study of Sanskrit was part of an elaborate work of philological assemblage aimed at establishing that Indian culture was "Western" culture. Thus the British presence in India, in the words of Roy Harris, "could be seen not as colonialist adventurers pillaging the riches of the East, but as restoring a far-flung, ancient outpost of Aryan civilization to its rightful place within the corresponding political boundaries of the modern world."[90] Love, friendship, and emotional attachment mattered to colonial governance insofar as they matter in all dramas of psychic struggle between ruler and ruled, man and woman, the strong and the weak. When the British arrived in China, often directly from India, they had certain expectations as to how they would be treated by the Qing government and the local people. Did love figure in those expectations? Had the British officials followed Morrison's earlier translation of *yi* as "foreigner" instead of "barbarian," would they have reacted differently?

As we have seen, Frantz Fanon throws some helpful light on these questions in his reflections on the early colonial encounter between the Europeans and the people of Madagascar. In *Black Skin, White Masks,* he observes that "when the question arises of understanding why the European, the foreigner, was called *vazaha,* which means *honorable stranger;* when it is a matter of understanding why shipwrecked Europeans were welcomed with open arms; why the European, the foreigner, was never thought of as an enemy, instead of explaining these things in terms of humanity, of good will, of courtesy, basic characteristics of what Césaire calls 'the old courtly civilizations,' scholars tell us that it happened quite simply because, inscribed in 'fateful hieroglyphics—specifically, the unconscious—there .exists something that makes the white man the awaited master.'"[91] The conjuring of the European master through a translation of *vazaha* as "honorable stranger" seems to be the polar opposite of what causes *yi* to mean "barbarian." But might the opposing translations not be the two sides of the same imperial coin? To the British, the super-sign *Ying yi/English barbarian* flaunted the evidence of Chinese contempt for foreigners and contradicted the experience of the British elsewhere in their global warfare of sovereign rule. The Manchus and the mandarins, however, were uniformly taken by surprise whenever the British accused them of showing disrespect. They denied strenuously that *yi* meant what the British thought it meant. Ten years after the signing of the treaties of Nanjing, the acting imperial commissioner in Guangzhou, Bo Gui, continued to be puzzled by Sir George Bonham's protest of the character *yi* and wondered why the word was a matter for dispute.[92] Bonham, of course, was reading those communications in English translation supplied by the Chinese secretary's office in which the word *yi* was duly spelled out as "barbarian."[93] This was only a few years before the signing of the Anglo-Chinese Treaty of Tianjin, at which point the English text of any diplomatic communication would be taken as the original and correct version. In any case, an impasse of accusation and denial arose between the British, who protested vehemently against *yi,* and the Qing officials, who routinely dismissed the charge as groundless, arguing that *yi* was not an issue. But the character must have raised some kind of issue if a British subject felt that the term of address was capable of insulting a foreigner.

The issue, it seems to me, lies in the elusive status of the super-sign *yi/barbarian,* hence its ubiquity and secret power. The character *yi* eluded the Chinese as well as the British in its flight into the intermediate area of heterolinguistic catachresis, straddling two languages and turning into the monstrous super-sign of itself.[94] If we agree that the originary point of injury is the enunciation of *yi* by the Chinese toward the British, who heard "barbarian," we might as well register the fact that the deictic address of the super-sign *yi/barbarian* is already a doubling and translated address.[95] To complicate the matter further, the word "barbarian," being a loanword from Latin and Greek roots, is itself an excessively translated address that the Europeans had applied to one another and to their colonized peoples for centuries. The British colonial officials had come to China with the foreknowledge of a colonial discourse of the "barbarian" and could not but see the absurdity of being put in the position of "barbarians" themselves. David Porter has shown that the British elite began to classify the Chinese among the "barbarians" in the final quarter of the eighteenth century, if not earlier. James Boswell recorded an interesting conversation he had with Samuel Johnson in 1778:

> Johnson called the East-Indians barbarians. Boswell: "You will except the Chinese, Sir." Johnson: "No, Sir" . . . Boswell: "What do you say to the written characters of that language?" Johnson: "Sir, they have not an alphabet. They have not been able to form what all other nations have formed." Boswell: "There is more learning in their language than in any other, from the immense number of their characters." Johnson: "It is only more difficult from its rudeness; as there is more labour in hewing down a tree with a stone than with an axe."[96]

I will have more to say in Chapter 6 about language and race in connection with the rise of comparative philology. The quoted passage, whether or not it captures the actual conversation or merely reflects Boswell's own opinion, suggests a degree of ambivalence in eighteenth-century Britain with regard to the relative standing of the Chinese. But the factory records of the East India Company, which I discuss shortly, make it clear that the British had begun to apply the term "barbarian" to the Chinese as early as 1721.

Horatio Nelson Lay, the former assistant Chinese secretary at the negotiation of the Anglo-Chinese Treaty of Tianjin, certainly referred to the Chinese as "barbarians." Even after he was appointed Inspectorate General of Custom by the imperial Qing government in 1861 during the suppression of the Taiping Rebellion, Lay described his position "as that of a foreigner engaged by the Chinese government to perform certain work *for* them, not *under* them," and added, "I need scarcely observe that the notion of a gentleman acting *under* an Asiatic barbarian is preposterous."[97] As Hosea Ballou Morse shows, Lay drew Chinese pay for eight years, and Captain Sherard Osborne, who commanded the Anglo-Chinese fleet, also accepted service "under the Asiatic barbarian" and took his pay from the imperial government, although both of them were perennially troubled by the question "How shall European officers and seamen levy war for a barbarous sovereign, without being made to participate in acts which our country would repudiate?"[98]

Our assessment of this situation would suffer, however, from focusing exclusively on individual opinions and prejudices. The racializing of the Chinese in the late eighteenth century and throughout the nineteenth was accomplished by a complex organization of scientific knowledge and mobilization of public opinion through the writings of race theorists, craniologists, physical anthropologists, and novelists. Carl von Linné's *System of Nature* (1735), George Steinmetz shows us, included the Chinese within the human category of *Homo/Monstrous*, describing them as "head conic" and grouping them with the Hottentots, who were considered by the Europeans as the epitome of debasement. By the middle of the nineteenth century, when the treaties of Tianjin were being signed, the European scientists and writers had correlated the shapes of Chinese skulls, facial angles, the inner constitution of the skin, and the racially distinctive shape of the hand with arguments about the intelligence and moral failings of the Chinese, who changed from "white" to "yellow" in all European languages during this time.[99] The diaries of Elizabeth von Heyking, wife of the German consul in Beijing during Germany's annexation of Qingdao, states her view bluntly: "Whatever the Chinese might have been before, today they are nothing but dirty barbarians, who need a European master and not a European ambassador!"[100]

As I suggested in Chapter 1, naming can be a form of deictic address in the process of initiating the colonial terror of intersubjective communication. Narratives of colonial encounter abound in situations where the absolute terms of deictic address figure in the emerging relations of domination between the colonizer and the would-be colonized. The deictic conception "I am I because I am not you" underlies almost all colonial claims of universals and difference. The discourse of the "barbarian" plays into the deixis of naming a colonial other and consolidating the sovereign subject at the same time. By calling the Native Americans and other non-European races savages and barbarians, the European empires had secured the episteme of colonial otherness as well as a universal order of civilizational superiority and inferiority based on race, culture, technology, language, proprietorship, and so on. The law of exclusivity does not permit the same address to be applied to the original addresser simultaneously in reverse deictic articulation, just as the Hegelian bondsman cannot be named and addressed as lord by his previously recognized lord without contradicting the very terms of the deictic address that regulate the reflexive but hierarchical relationship between the two. This explains why the logic of colonial address does not tolerate deictic contradiction and reversal without becoming comical or absurd.

If Napier, Robinson, and Palmerston took the reversals of the colonial discourse of "barbarian" quite seriously, their contemporaries at home equally saw the absurdity but seemed to enjoy the opportunity to mock the pretentiousness of the British nobility. The popular magazine *Punch*, for example, played on the comedy of such reversals by describing the garter worn by the British peer as an article bestowed by "the Barbarian Queen" and by calling Shakespeare the national poet of the barbarian English (Figure 4). The same comedy of reversal is seen in a cartoon from *Punch*, dated November 4, 1860, in which Lord Elgin is portrayed as gesturing to the emperor of China to "come, knuckle down! No cheating this time," while holding what looks like a cannonball in his right hand (Figure 5).[101] Apparently, Lord Elgin's contemporaries grasped the comedy of reversal in its true light; that is, the Anglo-Chinese confrontation was not about the British noblemen's notion of equality but about their sovereign claims to the Qing empire and to the world. In that sense, the much maligned word *yi* figures the reversal as well as the aporetic breakdown of the logic of colonial address. Who is the true barbarian for civilization? The comic and tragic reversals of colonial address in the British experience of China in 1834–1860 were fraught with uncertainty and anxiety as to how to answer that question properly.

What does the aporia tell us about injury? Can we name the place of injury in the enunciation of "barbarian" in Western legal discourse prior to its encounter with the Chinese word *yi?* Has "barbarian" ever been part of the legal definition of injury? In Chapter 1 we saw how the Spanish Dominican Francisco de Vitoria had reflected on some of these issues as he tried to resolve the legality of the Spanish conquest of America. He and his students were centrally concerned with the question: By what right had the barbarians—the American Indians—come under the rule of the Spaniards?[102] I will not reiterate Vitoria's major arguments here except to remind the reader that, for Vitoria, the *ius gentium* granted the American Indians their legal rights so long as they guaranteed the peace and safety of the Spaniards journeying, trading, or preaching the Gospel on their land. Should the natives

EXHIBITION OF THE ENGLISH IN CHINA.

MR. FRISBY, our friend and correspondent, late Anglo-Chinese pundit of Canton, has favoured us with a most particular and lucid account of an exhibition now opened at Pekin ; a show which has attracted all the mandarins and gentry, their wives and families, of the "flowery kingdom." Little think the sagacious English public who visit Mr. DUNN's Exhibition, Hyde Park Corner, to marvel at the pigtails and little feet of the Chinese, that a DUNN from Pekin—LI LI by name—has sojourned many years in England, for the express purpose of showing to his countrymen the faces and fashions of the barbarian English. But so it is. At this moment there is open in Flying Dragon Street, Pekin, an exhibition, called "THE BARBARIAN ENGLISH IN CHINA." There we all are, from high to low ; numbered in cases as at Hyde Park-Corner, and a catalogue of our good and bad qualities illuminates the darkened mind of the curious.

Our dear friend the aforesaid pundit has translated this catalogue for *Punch* ; and has, moreover, regardless of expense on our part, caused drawings to be made of our countrymen as they are presented by LI LI to the dwellers of the Celestial Kingdom. The prominent parts of this catalogue we lay before the reader ; they will be found to beautifully harmonise with the skill which has displayed us in cases ; wherein, sooth to say, we do appear with a certain Chinese air, which proves the national prejudices of the artist. Whether he has improved our looks or otherwise for the Chinese public, we leave to the opinion of the judicious and reflecting beholder. Our simple duty is now to lay before the reader the Chinese catalogue, translated and enriched with notes, by our indefatigable and profound correspondent. The Exhibition is dedicated to the "Son

of Heaven," very vulgarly known as the Emperor. The dedication, however, we omit ; as it tells us no more than that LI LI is, in his own opinion, a reptile, a dog, a wretch, a nincompoop, a jackass, when addressing the said "Son of Heaven ;" that his "bowels turn to water" with dread, and his pigtail grows erect with amazement. It will be conceded that, allowing a little for oriental painting, the dedication in no way differs from many other such commodities of home manufacture. Leaving the preface, we begin with the

INTRODUCTION.

When your slave remembers that through the creamy compassion of the Son of Heaven, the Father of the Universe, and the Dragon of the World, the barbarian English were not, in the late war, seized, destroyed, and sawn asunder ; that their devil-ships were spared, their guns respected, their soldiers mercifully permitted to retain their swords, and their sailors allowed to return to their barbarian wives and little ones,—when your slave remembers all this, his heart is turned to honey by the contemplation of your natural sweetness, whilst, in admiration thereof, his soul drops upon its knees, and prostrate, worships.

And when your slave further remembers, that in some leisure hour, you may—with a benevolence that is as broad as the earth, and as high as heaven,—vouchsafe to reign over and to comfort the aforesaid barbarians, your slave tremblingly takes hope that the samples of the people he has gathered together, with the subjoined faithful account of their manners and their doings, may find favour in the sight of Him, who when he sneezes, arouses earthquakes ; and when he winks, eclipses the moon.

CASE I.—AN ENGLISH PEER.

He wears a garter about his leg ; an honourable mark of petticoat government bestowed by the barbarian Queen. The Garter is sometimes given for various reasons, and sometimes for none at all. It answers to the peacock's feather in the "flowery kingdom," and endows with wisdom and benevolence the fortunate possessor. The Peer is represented at a most interesting moment. He has won half-a-million of money upon a horse, the British nobility being much addicted to what is called the turf, which in England often exhibits a singular greenness. The nobleman, however, displays a confidence always characteristic of the highly born. By winning so much money, he has broken the laws of the country, by which more than his winnings may be taken from him ; but it will be seen that he has pens, ink, and paper before him, and is at the moment he is taken, making a new law for himself, by which he may, without any penalty whatever, protect his cash. It is the privilege of the nobility to have their laws, like their coats, made expressly to their own measure.

CASE II.—SHAKSPEARE.

This is the national poet, which the barbarians would, in their dreadful ignorance, compare to Confutzee. It is melancholy to perceive the devotion paid by all ranks of people to this man. He was originally a carcass butcher, and was obliged to fly from his native town because he used to slip out at nights, kill his neighbours' deer, and then sell the venison to the poor for mutton. (All this I have gathered from the last two or three authentic lives lately written.) He went to London, and made a wretched livelihood by selling beans and wisps of hay to the horses of the gentlemen who came to the playhouses. Thinking that he could not sink any lower, he took to writing plays, out of which—it is awful to relate—he made a fortune. (It is, however, but justice to the barbarians to state that they give no such wanton encouragement to playwriters at present.) SHAKSPEARE, or SHAKSPERE, or SHIKSPUR—for there have been mortal battles waged, and much blood shed, about the

Figure 4. "Exhibition of the English in China," from *Punch,* 1844. The satire is an imagined reversal of the actual "Chinese exhibition" of artifacts that took place in a building at Hyde Park Corner in London after the Opium War. The exhibition was organized by an American entrepreneur named Nathan Dunn.

NEW ELGIN MARBLES.

ELGIN TO EMPEROR. "COME, KNUCKLE DOWN! NO CHEATING THIS TIME!"

Figure 5. Lord Elgin and the Emperor of China, cartoon from *Punch*, 1860.

oppose the *communicatio* or the *ius predicandi,* their act would constitute sufficient ground of injury for having infringed on the natural rights of the
Spaniards. "The vindication of injuries constitutes a just war," writes Anthony Pagden, "and ultimately it was only by means of such a war that the
Spaniards could legitimate their presence in America."[103] Nowhere in international legal discourse, however, do we find a precedent for the enunciation of the term "barbarian" as sufficient ground for war. So, again,
what were the possible sources of the British sense of injury and justification
for war?

In his study of the notion of *barbaros* in Greek antiquity, Jonathan Hall has
suggested that the discourse of *barbaros* was a mechanism of Greek self-
definition beginning in the fifth century B.C.E. "By establishing a stereotyp-
ical, generalized image of the exotic, slavish and unintelligible barbarian,"
Hall says, "Greek identity could be defined 'from without,' through opposition with this image of alterity. To find the language, culture or rituals of the
barbarian desperately alien was to immediately to define oneself as Greek.
The construction of a sharp symbolic boundary between Greek and barbarian should theoretically no longer leave any doubt as to the Greekness of
those on its inside."[104] It turns out that the boundary was necessarily mythical. Take the Hellenic genealogy often cited as evidence of a Greek identity
which embraces, through the genealogical metaphor of Hellen and his sons,
the ethnic groups that represent its constituent elements. Hall's research
shows that the claims of Hellenic ancestry do not square with either archaeological findings or literary and linguistic evidence: "The Aitolians were considered Greek but their eponymous ancestor, Aitolos, did not derive his descent from Hellen but from Endymion. Likewise, Arkas, the eponymous
ancestor of the Arkadians, was the son of Kallisto, who was the daughter of
Lykaon and the granddaughter of Pelasgos—a lineage that finds no point
of correlation with the Hellenic genealogy."[105] If the origin of the self was
not much of an origin insofar as it had been defined in opposition to the
barbaros, what was left of the *barbaros?* Did the latter not take flight in a
chain of signifying events that have come to characterize the act of appropriation itself? In *The Fall of Natural Man,* Pagden suggests that by the time
Gregory the Great began to use *barbarus* in the sixth century, the word had
become synonymous with the term *paganus,* or pagan, as Christians were
thought to be fundamentally different from all other categories of distinction in the pagan world. So when Eusebius of Caesarea felt called upon to
persuade his readers that he and his kind were "new men," he explained,
"We do not think like Greeks, nor live like the barbarians."[106]

Michel de Certeau's perceptive reading of Montaigne's essay "Of Canni-
bals" suggests, furthermore, that the signification of "barbarian" and "savage" as a mechanism of European self-definition had reached a high degree
of semantic mobility by the sixteenth century. Montaigne's writings chase
the colonial discourse through a series of disappearances in light of the European contact with Native Americans to show that the elementary unit of
nomination ("barbarous," "savage") and its discourse "signify not the reality of which they speak, but the reality from which they depart, and which
they disguise, the place of their enunciation (élocution)."[107] The fictions of
"barbarian," which are meant to define the position of the other in language, cannot but destroy one another as soon as they touch: in Certeau's
words, "a shattering of mirrors, the defection of images, one after the
other."[108] But there is more to it. Pagden's study of Vitoria demonstrates
convincingly that there was an emergent discourse of injury that came to
ground the concept of *barbari* in the *ius gentium* for the law of nations. I
would argue that this legal sense of potential injury infused the English notion of "barbarian" with the spirit of natural rights on top of the etymological roots of a loanword that extended back to the Greek *barbaros* and the
Christian notion of *barbarus*.

The legal definition of injury articulated a condition of reciprocity and a
condition of violence that were both deeply rooted in the early colonial
thinking of civilization and barbarity with important implications for our
understanding of the enunciation of "barbarian" in later centuries. When
the freedom to trade, to travel, and to proselytize comes to rest on the rights
and principles granted by the *ius gentium*, the opposition by a native population cannot but be interpreted sui generis as an injury to the life or property
of the Europeans and therefore cause for just war. This provides us with a
historical perspective on some of the key developments in the modern discourse of international law (see Chapter 4) and allows us to situate the legal
concepts properly at the heart of European colonial history. The litigation of
cases involving the shooting and killing of the Chinese in the early eighteenth century by British subjects put the conditions of reciprocity and violence to the test.

The factory records of the East India Company recorded a number of cases
of homicide committed by Europeans against the Chinese during this period. An incident that took place on October 30, 1722, involved a British
ship from Bombay, the *King George*, arriving in Guangzhou. The gunner's
mate claimed to have been firing at a bird in a paddy field, but he shot a Chinese boy who was reaping the field.[109] The boy was seriously wounded by

the gunshot and died. Under the Penal Code of the Qing, the case would have been prosecuted according to book two, section 282. But unlike some other cases, this affair did not lead to criminal prosecution because the boy's parents and the government officials agreed to a financial settlement.[110] The factory record dated November 15, 1722, reads, "The China boy killed by Gunner's Mate of *King George*, hath not only given Messrs. Scattergood & Hill great trouble, but hath cost them already near 2,000 taels."[111] If one should marvel at the utter lack of human compassion for the boy in the English account, the explanation may be sought in the notion of injury in the theory of natural law. What constitutes injury in a colonial setting is not the killing of the natives, for such matters can always be settled by financial arrangement, or by evading the native systems of justice, or even by contemplating extraterritorial rights, a subject that comes up again and again in the records of the East India Company. Injury seems to make sense only where the natural or property rights of the Europeans are concerned in cases under litigation. When the supercargoes Scattergood and Hill were asked to pay compensation for the homicide, they complained about the parents and mandarins "who too often vilely encrease their personal estates, by such misfortunes, but all in our power shall not be wanting to prevent such practices."[112] It is as if the injured party had been not the boy and his family but the Europeans; yet this was not the only time when a reversed claim of injury was made by an Englishman or a European after one of their countrymen had committed homicide.

The factory records bear witness to an earlier incident that occurred on November 22, 1721, when the killing of a Chinese man was converted into the potential injury of the rights of Europeans: "Some of the *Bonitta*'s people had shot a Chinaman about Wampoa, in the service of the Hoppo, and that Mr. Scattergood [the *Bonitta*'s supercargo] had withdrawn himself from his own house to the United English Factory to escape (though entirely innocent) from falling into the hands of these Barbarians, who are glad of the least handle to plague people."[113] Here "barbarians" refers to the Chinese officials who had arrived to investigate the murder and made a few arrests. The British supercargoes went to the Hoppo (the superintendent of marine customs for Guangdong) to complain of the "violation of the privileges he had granted us for our Persons, Officers, Seamen, &c." with a warning that "His Majesty the King of England has several Men of War about Madras and other places in the East Indies, we cannot answer what may be the consequences of such a procedure, as the denying us that justice which we demand."[114] The procedure refers to the application of the Penal Code of the Qing, which would require that the offender be prosecuted and punished according to the degree of his crime.[115] The grounds for injury spelled out in a language of rights and privilege à la Vitoria seemed to warrant a just war in terms of natural law. What is more significant, the discourse of "barbarian" as rooted in the British experience in China had articulated the coloniality of injury many decades before its fateful encounter with the Chinese discourse of *yi* and certainly before the aporetic breakdown of the logic of colonial address in the super-sign. For when the super-sign *yi/barbarian* became reality, and when the enunciation of "barbarian" was perceived as drifting from colonial speech into the other's language, the threat of a reversal was bound to cause a jolt, a breach, a further injury, and a dangerous subversion of the episteme of the other. It is in this sense that the coloniality of injury found its fullest legal expression in the ban on *yi*, in the supplementary demands of the Anglo-Chinese Treaty of Tianjin, and in the British justification for war.

CHAPTER 3

Figuring Sovereignty

In hundreds or thousands of years, the Central States may endure
hardships caused by the Western countries from the oceans beyond.
We give our word of prediction.

—the Kangxi emperor to his Grand Secretariat and nine chief ministers,
December 9, 1716

Writers and printers in China began to subject their publications to screening and self-censorship when the British authorities intensified the effort to implement the 1858 ban on the character *yi* after the second Opium War. The character was carefully taken out of each text, to be
replaced with a multitude of terms such as *yang* (ocean) or *wai guo* (foreign
country), or with the names of individual nations. The post-ban editions of
Daoguang yangsou zhengfu ji (A history of the combat and pacification of foreign battleships in the reign of the Daoguang emperor), which is attributed
to Wei Yuan, underwent this sort of correction and self-censorship.[1] The
same thing happened to the revised editions of Xu Jiyu's *Yinghuan zhilüe*
(An outline history and geography of the world) and other late Qing publications.[2] Three months after the signing of the Anglo-Chinese Treaty of
Tianjin, Imperial Commissioner Gui Liang memorialized the Xianfeng emperor on October 9, 1858, to inform the throne of a British complaint about
the court's violation of the treaty's terms:

The British principal Elgin came to see me and accused us of violating the
treaty because he had caught the expression "*yi* vessel" in one of your imperial edicts printed in the official newspaper. Your servant checked Article
51 of the British treaty which says: "It is agreed that, henceforward, the
character 'i' 夷 [barbarian] shall not be applied to the Government or subjects of Her Britannic Majesty in any Chinese official document issued by

the Chinese Authorities either in the Capital or in the Provinces." But the language here does not clearly spell out whether the same article applies to imperial edicts. Your servant is preparing a reply [to the British] to indicate that we intend to comply with the treaty terms. As for whether it would be advisable to instruct the Council of State not to publish copies of the various documents dealing with *yi* affairs in the future to keep them confidential, I defer to your imperial judgment.[3]

Gui Liang's suggestion of imperial exceptionality is intriguing. The English version of the treaty article would seem to include the emperor's edicts among "any Chinese official document issued by the Chinese authorities," but the Chinese-language version is highly ambiguous. It mentions *geshi gong wen* (all kinds of public documents), which may or may not include the emperor's *sheng yu* (imperial edicts), and certainly not his confidential edicts to his ministers. Gui Liang's hairsplitting argument reflected the last ditch attempt to defend the sovereignty of the Qing empire, but the odds were against him because Article 50 stipulated that the interpretation of the terms of the treaty must follow the English meaning.

In the preceding chapter I examined the itinerancy and reversibility of the super-sign *yi/barbarian* and argued that the character *yi* should not be taken as positive evidence of its own etymology, much less the collective mentality of a people predisposed against foreigners. I have considered a number of analytical and historical angles from which we might comprehend the translingual conditions of deictic enunciation under which the colonial discourse of injury was able to turn a sign from one language into the destiny and destination of another. After the implementation of the ban, the super-sign *yi/barbarian* camouflaged the traces of that semiotic and hetero-linguistic migration and has succeeded for so long in deterring us from making further inquiry into its particular heterogeneity. It remains to be seen, however, where the classical Chinese discourse of *yi* stands in this discussion, that is, prior to its encounter with the English "barbarian" and prior to its being turned into the super-sign *yi/barbarian*. Can the discourse be traced to some earlier articulations of the sovereign self and to the imperial ideology of the Qing dynasty? It would be interesting to speculate, for example, whether the eighteenth-century translation of the character *yi* by the interpreters of the British East India Company as "foreigner" had been somehow related to the domestic and foreign policies of the throne in the Yongzheng and Qianlong reigns.

Yi: Naming the Boundaries of Sovereign Rule

This chapter is devoted to exploring the place and placement of *yi* in the eighteenth-century universalist ideology of the Qing empire and their implications for the "barbarian" question I analyzed in Chapter 2. The concept of *yi* as it appears in the classical sources traverses immense areas of interdisciplinary scholarship, ranging from the commentarial traditions of Confucian learning to imperial ethnology and novel official policies and projects relating to issues of identity and border crossing in the course of Qing expansion. As I highlight the centrality of this concept to the articulation and disarticulation of the mandate of Heaven and to the imperial ideology of the ruling Manchus in the Qing dynasty, the reader will see that neither the Yongzheng emperor nor the Qianlong emperor sought to ban the character when they punished the Han dissidents who opposed Manchu rule by insisting on the distinction between *hua* and *yi*. Instead, the emperors chose to appropriate the Confucian discourse of *yi* and harness the idea for the purpose of consolidating their empire. Their handling of the oppositional discourse of *hua* and *yi* seems to represent a very different political strategy from the British handling of the super-sign *yi/barbarian* in the nineteenth century. That difference, however, should not prevent us from observing how central the notions of *yi* and of the super-sign *yi/barbarian* have both been to the claims and disputed claims of sovereignty over the territory of the Central States.[4]

My chief argument is that the discourse of *yi* names the boundaries of sovereign rule and advances a classical theory of sovereignty through the millennia-long commentarial scholarship surrounding the Confucian texts and, in particular, the *Spring and Autumn Annals*. To isolate this and other related usages from the classical Chinese texts as if they were proto-racial concepts is to run the risk not only of distorting the sources themselves but also of misrepresenting the classical commentarial traditions. As we saw in Chapter 2, the sleight of hand in the translation of such concepts can pose a particular risk to Western-language scholarship if one is not careful about how one represents ancient Chinese concepts to a modern English- or European-language audience. In his book *The Chinese Discourse of Race*, Frank Dikötter claims to have discovered evidence of some degree of "racial" discrimination in early China from the ancient texts, but his evidence turns out to be a strategic misquotation of James Legge's 1872 English translation of the *Zuo Commentaries*. Whereas Legge's rendering of "Fei wo zulei qixin bi yi" is "If he be not of our kin, he is sure to have a different mind" (see the Glossary for the Chinese characters), Dikötter quotes Legge as saying, "If he is not of our race, he is sure to have a different mind," and comments that "this sentence seems to support the allegation that at least some degree of 'racial discrimination' existed during the early stage of Chinese civilization."[5] If Dikötter's statement sounds somewhat speculative, his careful retranslation of *zulei* does not hesitate to fix the meaning of the characters and aspire toward a polemical super-sign *zulei/race,* one that simultaneously misrepresents the concept of *zulei* and that of "race." The discussion of *zulei* took place in the fourth-century B.C.E. *Zuo Commentaries,* with specific reference to the state of the Lu (*not* China), their kinship views, and their diplomatic relations and warfare with the states of the Chu and the Jin. Dikötter's rendering of *zulei* as a concept of "race" boldly bypasses the millennia-long commentarial traditions surrounding the Confucian text to allow the modern speculation about the existence or nonexistence of racial discrimination in ancient China to stand as an anachronistic judgment on the classical concept.

Interpreting and translating words and texts that were written by those whose world did not resemble our own is never an unproblematic enterprise. In his study *Ancient China and Its Enemies,* Nicola di Cosmo urges us to look carefully at the ancient sources and try to comprehend what a particular text was saying and to what audience rather than jump to a blanket imputation of "barbarian" whenever one catches words like *man, yi, rong,* and *di.*[6] Indeed, if the practice of historiography allows the commonplace episteme of change and historical transformation, why should words remain more or less the same through the ages or be held hostage to modern translations in a foreign tongue? The role of super-signs in the evolution of words and their meanings makes the situation even more complicated. It seems that the evidential fallacy in the field of early modern European history that Anthony Pagden has criticized characterizes the methodologies of other areas of historical scholarship as well. "What a sixteenth-century theologian might have understood by a word or phrase and what a modern historian might understand by the same word or phrase," writes Pagden, "is assumed to be, in all significant respects, the same. This failure to perceive that words change their meaning and that issues of pressing intellectual concern for one generation may be of scant interest to the next has led to much historically irrelevant and politically tendentious discussion."[7] The evidential fallacy with respect to the claims of civilization and cultural interactions in modern scholarship has typically operated around the material evidence of words and texts, but that evidence itself is seldom given the close examination it deserves.

Approaching the idea *yi* as an evolving and contested historical concept can provide us with new interpretive possibilities so that we need not begin by assuming that the indigenous discourse is merely about one people's (true or biased) knowledge of the other as opposed to a stable notion of the self—an epistemological reductionism on the basis of which the British conceptualized their ban. There is much to be gained by looking instead at how the idea of *yi* has historically defined and redefined the boundaries of sovereign rule and fashioned the terms of political legitimacy through war and insurgency. In other words, the *yi* or the *yi-di* should be grasped as a discursive figure that traverses territorial and political boundaries and has been regarded as dangerous for that reason. The danger lies in proportion to the degree in which the enunciation of *yi*—the illocutionary force of statements about the *yi* rather than what is merely asserted—poses a threat to the legitimacy of those who rule just as much as it can provide a discursive weapon to those who oppose the rule. That the weapon is a double-edged sword goes without saying. To comprehend how it works, one must first ask: What kinds of enunciatory positions are made available or not available to the ruler and the ruled whenever the distinction between *hua* and *yi* is broached and reiterated?

The answer to that question, which is going to be worked out in the course of this chapter, will then enrich our understanding of the figuration of the boundaries of sovereign thinking between the Qing and the British in the nineteenth century. The Kangxi emperor's apprehension about the future of his empire underscores the larger global implication of that figuration and, in a sense, predicted the coming of the Opium Wars with the warning that "in hundreds or thousands of years, the Central States may endure hardships caused by the Western countries from the oceans beyond."[8] Of course, it took less than 150 years before Kangxi's nightmare turned into China's reality. The magnitude of the hardships and suffering caused by the British to the lives and livelihood of the people of the Central States provides the context in which I reexamine, in the second half of this chapter, the sudden surge of popularity of the epithet *gui zi* or *fan gui*, commonly translated as "foreign devils," during the Opium Wars.[9] One would have to be blind not to notice the obvious connection between the verbal abuse to which the British and the other Westerners were subjected on the one hand and the military violence to which the Chinese people were subjected during the Opium Wars on the other. It makes sense for us to ask what kinds of enunciatory positions were opened up by the appellations *gui zi* and *fan gui* from the south to the north in the 1840s. Do we detect a discursive linkage between *yi* and *gui zi?* Did the British try to police the colloquial expressions *gui zi* and *fan gui* with the same degree of vigilance with which they pursued the ban on the classical character *yi* on paper? Finally, did the hit-and-run encounters between the British and the people on the streets of Chinese cities and towns tell us anything about the Opium Wars that we do not already know?

The Missing Referent for Cīna, Shina, "China"

The Qing rulers were from the nomadic Manchu tribes of the North who had overthrown the Ming dynasty and imposed their imperial rule on the native population in 1644. The violence of the Manchu military conquest, such as the massacre of the population of Yangzhou, gave rise to numerous local resistance movements and acts of Ming loyalism, including suicides en masse, which have been well documented and analyzed by historians.[10] The Qing haircutting command issued in July 1645, for example, required that all Chinese males shave their foreheads and plait their hair in a tribal queue like the Manchus to signal their loyalty to the Qing regime. Those who obeyed were accepted as subjects of the Qing, but the ones who resisted were treated as outlaws under rebel command and severely punished to the point of losing their heads. As Frederic Wakeman Jr. shows in *The Great Enterprise*, the Han Chinese men regarded the order as a kind of tonsorial castration, a symbolic mutilation of one's masculinity and moral integrity. When the renowned scholar and teacher from Suzhou, Yang Tingshu, was arrested on suspicion of involvement in the 1647 Songjiang uprising, the prosecutor made it clear to Yang that he would not be arraigned for political crimes and would be treated with deference should he conform to the haircutting decree. But Yang flatly refused, saying, "To cut off my head is a small matter but to shave my hair is a grave matter." Yang was subsequently beheaded.[11]

Other renowned Ming loyalists such as Wang Fuzhi (1619–1692) and Gu Yanwu (1613–1682) responded by drawing on the Confucian commentarial tradition in the *Spring and Autumn Annals* to rework the distinction between *hua* (or *xia*) and *yi* (or *yi-di*) in order to subvert the sovereign claims of the Manchus on intellectual grounds.[12] Such distinctions have always been mobilized to make or unmake identities in times of dynastic upheaval and foreign conquest. But if we take the notion of *hua* or *xia* as suggesting some essence or identity, it embraces such a wide range of shifting geopolitical boundaries and ethnic and cultural self-descriptions that the heterogeneity of *hua* or *xia* can no more be reduced to "Chineseness" than the notion of *yi* can be settled with a single meaning. *Yi* or *yi-di* articulates *hua* or *xia* just as much as the latter articulates the former, with changing connotations through the millennia of military conquests, ethnic conflicts, and cultural and discursive practices before the arrival of the Manchus.

Still, what is the plausible referent for what we call "China" or "the Chinese"? The familiar geographical contour known as modern China has been inherited from the Qing empire, but the inheritance itself is not without intense irony. In Pamela Crossley's words, "The irony is underscored by the meticulousness with which Qing imperial ideology had objectified China as a province of the empire."[13] The Qing rulers named their state the *Da Qing Guo* (Great Qing state), whereas the official name of the dynasty they had replaced in the seventeenth century was *Da Ming Guo* (Great Ming state), never the Chinese empire.[14] Nor did the territorial boundaries of the Ming and Qing dynasties coincide, because the Qing empire greatly expanded to double the amount of territory under its sovereign rule between 1660 and 1760. Are we confronted with the possibility that the referent for "China" and "the Chinese" has always been missing from the picture?

That the referent was probably missing became a cause for alarm among late Qing nationalist intellectuals such as Huang Zunxian, Zhang Taiyan, Liang Qichao, and others. Huang wrote in 1898:

> Research indicates that the diverse countries in the world all boast of their own state names, such as England and France, the only exception being the Central States. People in the northwestern regions call us the *Han*, whereas those from the southeastern islands name us the *Tang*. The Japanese have used the name *Tang* or *Nanjing*, but the latter, referring to the Ming dynasty, is valid for one dynasty only and is by no means transhistorical. The Indians use the word *cīna* [Sanskrit], the Japanese say *Shina*, the English "China," and the French "la Chine." But "China," as variously transliterated in these languages, is a term that other people have used to name us and does not coincide with our self-identify.[15]

Huang proposed that the phrase *Hua Xia* be adopted as the formal name for the Central States.

In the spirit of that argument, the prominent intellectual Liang Qichao lamented that "there is no shame greater than our country being deprived of a name. The names that people ordinarily think of, such as *Zhu Xia*, *Han*, or

Tang, are the titles of bygone dynasties. Foreigners call our country *cīna* or "China," but that is not how we view ourselves."[16] Liang preferred to adopt *Zhongguo,* or "the Central States," as the name for his country, but it turned out that this term, too, was fraught with imprecision and misunderstanding. Zhang Taiyan was quick to point out that

> *Zhongguo* is meaningful only insofar as it refers to the four outlying boundaries. The Indians used to call their Mojiatuo [Madhyadesha] the central state, and the Japanese named Shanyang their central state. The descriptive term "Central State[s]" is by no means unique to the land of the Han. In the language of the Han dynasty, however, the Central States was defined by the ancient boundaries of the Han provinces and counties. When the Indians and the Japanese spoke of their central states, they were defining a center vis-à-vis the peripheral states. The Han usage was very different, as the term defined the territorial boundaries of the Central States against foreign countries.[17]

The uncertain candidacy of the various indigenous names for remaking the Qing empire as a kind of "China" indicates that the naming of a Chinese identity by English, French, Sanskrit, and Japanese—a significant othering of the self—was already present in the desire for modern nationhood before the indigenous intellectuals could give the object of desire a proper name. In other words, Liang Qichao's renaming of the *Da Qing Guo* as *Zhongguo* in anticipation of the birth of the new nation-state presupposed the existence of a translingual signified "China" and the fabulation of a super-sign *Zhongguo/ China.*

Where does the Sanskrit term *cīna* figure in the overall translingual making of the super-sign *Zhongguo/China?* Has the super-sign always been there, lurking in the shadows of history? The late Qing intellectuals were perfectly aware that the various modern terms for "China" originated from the Sanskrit root *cīna* and it is widely believed that the Sanskrit term itself derived from the dynastic name of the first unified China, the Qin (Ch'in) dynasty (221–206 B.C.E.).[18] Scholars have dated the earliest mention of *cīna* to the *Rāmāyana* and the *Mahābhārata* and to other Sanskrit sources such as the Hindu Laws of Manu. According to Alf Hiltebeitel, the *Mahābhārata* was probably composed between the middle of the second century B.C.E. and the millennial turn, and the *Rāmāyana* was written at about the same time. The early epics mention the *Xiongnu* Huns, who were "the great northern rivals of the Chinese, whose Sanskrit name 'Cīna' must recall the Xin/Ch'in [*sic*] dynasty founded by Shih Huang Ti, who began the great wall in 214 B.C.E. to defend against them."[19] Patrick Olivelle, in a study of the Laws of Manu, has reexamined the related evidence surrounding the Sanskrit word *cīna* and concluded:

> The reference to the Chinese with the word *cīna* is problematic. The term is not used by Patañjali or the Dharmasūtras. The word was probably derived from a central Asian language and is related to the Qin (Chin) dynasty (221–206 B.C.E.), which, although short-lived, was the first to unify China. The term itself, however, may have been older, because the Qin was a state in Northwest China prior to that time with strong trade connection with Central Asia. The term "China," like "India" itself, is not a term of self-iden-tification by the Chinese. The term came back to China probably from India via Buddhist monks and texts. When a people known as *cīna* came to be known to India is difficult to estimate. The term's absence in the earlier lit-erature, however, makes it likely that it could not have been known before the 1st century B.C.E. It was during this time or a little earlier under the Han dynasty that Chinese trade with the west began to flourish.[20]

Olivelle's evidence affirms that *cīna* is related to the Qin dynasty but leaves the precise nature of that linkage open to speculation.[21]

What complicates the matter further is that we are confronted with a re-lated ancient Chinese toponym, the *Da Qin* (Great Qin), written with the same character as the one used for the Qin (or *Chin*, in the Wade-Giles romanization system) dynasty in the same period. Between the first and fifth centuries, *Da Qin* appeared as one of the names for the Roman Empire in Chinese historiography and referred specifically to the renowned me-tropolis of Alexandria in Egypt, where the trade with Africa flourished.[22] Judging from the verbal descriptions contained in the *History of the Latter Han*, the term *Da Qin* appears to have been coined according to a logic of similarity that named the other in terms of the self, as it is recorded that "the people [of Egypt] are tall and gorgeous looking and resemble the people of the Central States, hence the name *Da Qin*."[23] Can the same ideographic character *Qin* that names the first unified dynasty be a source of *cīna* as well as the name that the people of *Cīna* applied to the Roman Empire in Egypt?

Until scholars come upon new evidence or give us new insights to help explain the enigma, it appears that the Sanskrit term *cīna*, the Persian *chīnī*, and their variants in the European languages have long been the toponyms that foreigners have applied to the topography known as "China" over the millennia. But there is a modern twist to this story, because the ideographic transcriptions 支那 (Zhina) for "China" and "the Chinese" did reach modern Mandarin via the Japanese *Shina* at the turn of the twentieth century. Although a few isolated instances of such ideographic transcription can be found in the earlier translations of Sanskrit texts by Buddhist monks, the phonetic mimicking of "China" in ideographic characters had never been adopted as an official or unofficial toponym for the country either by the Japanese or by the people of the Central States. The characters for *Shina* represent a modern Japanese *kanji* (Chinese written character) imitation of the pronunciation of the European terms for "China" that quickly evolved into a racial marker in Meiji Japan.[24] *Shina* copies the foreign sounds of "China" into the Japanese pronunciation of the written Chinese characters; its enunciation was designed to supersede the established Japanese toponyms for the Central States such as Tō (Tang), Todo (Tang tu), Chūgoku (Zhongguo), Chūdo (Zhong tu), and Chūka (Zhonghua) and to estrange the written characters—since *shi* and *na* drop their ideographic etymologies when serving as mere sound tokens for a loanword—to name a China for the purpose of Japanese colonial conquest. The renaming literally inscribed the desire of imperial Japan to mimic Western civilization by mimicking Western imperialism. The mirror of colonial mimicry captured the object of its imitation with a faithfulness that cast a sinister light back on the exemplarity of the Western powers that pursued imperialism in the name of civilization.[25]

In this light, the European terms for "China" not only authorized the phonetic structure of the Japanese loanword *Shina* but also functioned as the instituted trace within the signifying chain of the modern super-sign *Shina/China/Chine/Cina/Zhina*, the last component in the chain being the modern Mandarin pronunciation of the characters for *Shina*.[26] The Qing students who studied in Meiji Japan brought the loanword to their native land, and some even adopted it for self-identification, although *Shina* and *Shina jin* (the Chinese) were quickly caught up in the history of Japanese aggression and racism on the continent and were ultimately rejected by the "Chinese" themselves.[27] Curiously, those who found *Shina* offensive stopped short of objecting to the English and European toponyms for "China" that had been mimicked by *Shina* in the first place or being disturbed by the fact that the English terms "China" and "the Chinese" and their European equivalents were just as caught up in the history of racism and colonial conquest as the Japanese term *Shina*.[28]

Notwithstanding the etymological ties to Sanskrit, Persian, and other languages, the English terms "China" and "the Chinese" do not translate the indigenous terms *hua, xia, han,* or even *zhongguo* now or at any given point in history.[29] If people speak of themselves as *zhongguo ren* (men or women of the Central States) or *hua ren* (men or women of the Efflorescent Land) in Mandarin, where do the terms "China" or "the Chinese" fit on this translingual map?[30] Does the super-sign *Zhongguo/China* or *Zhongguo ren/the Chinese* conjure an ethnically blind but racially marked identity? The Qing official Zhang Deyi who accompanied the first official embassy to Europe found himself troubled by these sorts of questions. In May 1871 Zhang was confronted by a Frenchman in Paris who asked why the Chinese insisted on calling the Europeans *gui zi*—"foreign devils"—even after they had been acquainted with the fact that the Europeans all had individual state names, like England, France, Germany, and Russia. Zhang gave him a tongue-in-cheek reply, saying that the classical etymology of the characters *gui zi* derived from a Han dynasty compound that originally referred to a place in the *Xi Yu* (the West, i.e., Central Asia) called *qiu zi,* but the name was mispronounced by common people as *gui zi.* From this place named *qiu zi* in Central Asia, he explained, the Chinese had brought back their first grape seeds via the ancient trading route, and with the passage of time the written characters for *qiu zi* were corrupted by their popular mispronunciation and became the present compound *gui zi* that came to be represented by two different characters, and so on. Addressing the Frenchman's charge that the Chinese refused to use the actual state names to designate the Europeans, Zhang pointed out that one might consider turning the question back to the foreigners, "who, after decades of East and West diplomatic and commercial interactions, know very well that my country is called the *Da Qing Guo* or the *Zhonghua* [the Central Efflorescent States] but insist on calling it 'China,' 'la Chine,' 'la Cina," 'Shina,' etc. Over the past four thousand years, we have never used the toponym 'China' [to designate our country]. On what basis do the Westerners call my country by that name?"[31] The basis seems to be a long history of hetero-cultural interactions, trade relations, and, in modern times, European colonial expansion; and as far as nineteenth-century Britain, France, Japan, and other imperial powers were concerned, the term "China" unambiguously named an object of possession (the biggest market to capture), evangelization, aggression, and conquest.

In the effort to recover a missing referent for "China," the late Qing nationalists such as Huang Zunxian and Liang Qichao helped forge the powerful super-sign *Zhongguo/China* that masked a dubious referent even as it produced simulacra of Chineseness that came already embedded in the other's discourse. Having said so, what do we make of the indigenous naming of the self in the past? Has it been less burdened by similar sorts of conjurations and anxieties? The answer is no. For the bounded geopolitical entity variously known as *Zhonghua*, *Zhongyuan* (Central Land), *Zhongtu* (Central Terrain), or *Zhongguo* (Central States) has been subjected to "alien" rule for a good portion of its dynastic history and is never fully identical with itself. Whether we are talking about the Warring States, the Han dynasty, the Tang, the Song, the Mongol rule in the Yuan, the Ming, or the Qing dynasty, the ideas of *Zhonghua* and *Zhongguo* have never achieved a stable, definitive meaning in indigenous discourse. The leading twentieth-century scholar Qian Mu was baffled by the Chinese elite's longing for the Mongol rule at the fall of the Yuan dynasty, when one would have expected them to rejoice at the coming of the Ming, or at least be willing to serve a "Chinese" emperor. Apparently that was not the case. It took two or three generations, some eighty years into the Ming dynasty, before the Chinese elite began to revise their attitude toward the Mongols and identify with the Ming.[32] This presents a sharp contrast to the hostility that the Qing intellectuals felt toward the Manchus and to the certainty with which Zhang Taiyan and the others would embrace the Han identity in the late nineteenth century. Qian Mu's work throws the continuity of Chinese identity off kilter and bids us to read our sources more carefully rather than repeat the usual things people say about the self-positioning of "China" as the center of the universe while China looks down on everyone else as barbarians. When it comes to interpreting the dynastic histories of the past, the explanatory power of the concepts of *hua* and *yi* is limited to the extent that the latter have always been subjected to discursive appropriations. It would take a good deal of work and imagination to figure out what was truly at stake in any given moment when people decided to evoke or drop the concepts.

The Yongzheng Emperor and His Literary Persecutions

We recall from Chapter 2 that when Hugh Hamilton Lindsay quibbled with Wu Qitai about the meaning of *yi* in 1832, the latter responded by quoting a few lines from the Confucian sage Mencius (ca. 372– ca. 289 B.C.E.) and argued that the imperial paragons of the ancient Central States had themselves been of *yi* origin. In the *Mencius* we find this passage:

[King] Shun was born in Zhufeng, moved to Fuxia, and died in Mingtiao. He was a man of the eastern *yi*. King Wen was born in Qizhou and died in

Biying. He was a man of the western *yi*. Those regions were distant from one another more than a thousand *li* and the age of the one sage was posterior to that of the other more than a thousand years. But when they got their wish, and carried their principles into practice throughout the Central States, it was like uniting the two halves of a seal. When we examine those sages, both the earlier and the later, their principles are found to be the same.[33]

King Shun (ca. 2253–2205? B.C.E.) and King Wen (ca. 1184–1135? B.C.E.) were virtuous sovereigns and served as models for the future rulers of the Central States, but they were originally the *yi* and not the *xia* of the Central States. Distance mattered little when the principles of righteousness were carried out by virtuous rulers. It is curious that Wu should evoke Mencius this way if he had intended to insult the British. Was Wu being facetious in trying to pacify Lindsay? Not entirely. We will find that the Yongzheng emperor had drawn on the authority of the *Mencius* in his famous treatise *Dayi juemi lu* (Awakening to supreme justice) in 1730 when he stated his own position on the *yi* or *yi-di* issue and set forth the sovereign claims of his Manchu emperorship. The emperor's evocation of the *Mencius* was contradicted by the Ming loyalists' citations of other classical texts, notably the *Zuo Commentaries on the Spring and Autumn Annals*. Wang Fuzhi, Gu Yanwu, Lü Liuliang (1629–1683), and their followers found the line "If he be not of our kin, he is sure to have a different mind" useful for mobilizing and inciting rebellion against the ruling Manchus. These, however, were not ordinary appeals to intellectual authority, as the Confucian classics were used to support one position and refute another. The familiar gesture of classical citation notwithstanding, we must understand that the social condition of Confucian studies itself was changing in response to the consolidation of imperial ideology in the Qing dynasty, to which one can fruitfully trace the novel metamorphosis of the discourse of *hua* and *yi* in the eighteenth century.

In looking at the Qing emperors' appropriations of the Confucian classics, one often faces the temptation to fall in line with the sinicization argument. To be sure, Kangxi, Yongzheng, Qianlong, and other Qing emperors were familiar with the Confucian texts, and some of them were even erudite scholars. But that knowledge does not necessarily convert them into Han Chinese. And the Manchus were not the first foreign rulers through the dynastic histories of China who negotiated their relationship with the conquered people this way. In "Han Literati under Jurchen Rule," Peter Bol shows that the idea of the "sinicization of the barbarians" cannot explain the extraordinary social transformation undergone in each instance by Khitans, Jurchens, Mongols, and Manchus as rulers of the Han. In the case of Jurchen rule (1115–1234), the question of "how Jurchen rulers could adopt Chinese political institutions while maintaining their distinct ethnic identity for political purposes" must be addressed. Bol answers the question by examining the role of "civilization" in political rule. He writes: "Jurchen rulers recruited Han literati not as Hans but as guardians of civil ideals; if they had only needed Hans they had other options. For their part the Han literati did not think all other Hans were like them. The literati were a minority among their own, they faced the problem of 'civilizing' other Hans, whether powerful men like the Ming founder Chu Yuan-chang [Zhu Yuanzhang] or the relatively powerless people who made up local society."[34] Mark Elliott's study *The Manchu Way* demonstrates likewise that the ruling elite in the Qing dynasty maintained, with vigilance and resolution, the ethnic and social divide between Manchu and Han and were never truly absorbed into the civilization of the conquered population.[35] I would even argue that they managed to do so in part with the help of the Confucian classics, and their readings of the classical notion of *yi* were calculated to refute the teachings of some Han scholars.

One of the followers of the Ming loyalists, a man named Zeng Jing (1679–1739) from Hunan Province, got into trouble and was prosecuted on charges of high treason in Yongzheng's reign. Deeply immersed in Lü Liuliang's anti-Manchu teachings, Zeng Jing believed that the governor-general of Sichuan and Shaanxi, Yue Zhongqi (1686–1754), a descendent of the Song patriotic hero Yue Fei, was sympathetic with his cause and would lead a rebellion against the government. In 1728 Zeng Jing sent his assistant Zhang Xi to Shaanxi to contact the governor-general and transmit to him the private writings of Lü Liuliang along with his own letter and unpublished manuscripts. Yue, however, reported the incident to the imperial censors and took Zhang Xi into custody. The Yongzheng emperor presently summoned Zeng Jing as well as the former students of Lü Liuliang and other suspects to Beijing and charged them and their families with treason. A curious byproduct of this notorious case was the composition and dissemination of Yongzheng's own polemic, *Awakening to Supreme Justice*, in which the emperor rebutted the subversive views of Zeng Jing and Lü Liuliang, in particular their reading of the classical *hua/yi* distinction.[36]

From the very first day that Yongzheng inherited the throne from the

Kangxi emperor, his reign had been tainted by questions of illegitimacy, fratricide, court intrigue, and abuses of power. Distrustful and paranoid, the emperor went out of his way to persecute those who spread rumors about him or hinted at his unfitness to rule as the *jun zhu*, or sovereign of the empire.[37] Such were the circumstances under which Zeng Jing discovered the works of Lü Liuliang, a renowned Confucian scholar from the Kangxi era, who had reinterpreted the *Spring and Autumn Annals* for a secret counsel to "revere the emperorship and expel the *yi*" *(zun wang rang yi)*.[38] Lü had argued that upholding the distinction between *hua* and *yi* was more urgent than observing the righteous bond between the sovereign and his subjects, because moral reasoning began with that distinction. Zeng Jing heeded Lü's injunction. In an unpublished work, he charged the Yongzheng emperor with ten major crimes and called for the overthrow of the Manchu regime.[39]

When the Yongzheng emperor first perused Yue Zhongqi's memorial containing the charges, his reaction was one of shock and outrage: "When we read the seditious writing, we were shocked into tears. Never did we dream of anyone under the skies who would talk about us in this manner or give a hint of the magnitude of his rebelliousness."[40] Curiously, instead of executing Zeng Jing for treason, Yongzheng, in his four-chapter polemic *Awakening to Supreme Justice*, decided to cast him in the figure of a reformed offender testifying to the righteousness of the emperor's words. The emperor ordered Zeng Jing to be taken from place to place confessing his crime and praising the emperor's wisdom to the public while helping to disseminate the emperor's own writings.

One of the first things Yongzheng did when composing *Awakening to Supreme Justice* was to undermine the credibility of the *hua/yi* distinction. He opens the treatise by observing:

The seditious rebels make the suggestion that we were the sovereign of Manchuria and later entered the Central States to become its ruler. Their prejudices about the territorial division between this land and that land have led to hateful lies and fabrications. What they have failed to understand is that Machuria is to the Manchus what the *jiguan* [birthplace or ancestral place] is to the people of the Central States. Shun was a man of the eastern *yi* and King Wen was a man of the western *yi*. Did that diminish their *sheng de* [sagely virtue]?[41]

De, or virtue, rather than one's place of origin is the criterion by which subjects ought to judge their sovereign's fitness to rule. This classical Confucian idea enabled Yongzheng to shift the contested ground of his sovereign claims to moral achievement and argue that the mandate of Heaven had rightfully passed into the hands of the Manchus not because of where they came from but because of what and who they were: men of virtue.[42]

The Yongzheng emperor did not see any reason to forbid the use of the word *yi* or *yi-di*. He stated this repeatedly in *Awakening to Supreme Justice* and argued that *yi* or *yi-di* was only the archaic equivalent of the contemporary word for "birthplace." Therefore, "if the seditious rebels think that they can insult the Manchus by calling them *yi-di*, they are just like beasts and animals daydreaming about their being born or being dead."[43]

The criminal prosecution of Zeng Jing exerted an extraordinary impact on society, and the fear of punishment led authors and publishers to suppress the character *yi* and similar terms and replace them with homophonic characters. Yongzheng noted this act of self-censorship in 1733 and ordered his ministers to put a stop to it:

> We do not understand what this is supposed to mean. Our conjecture is that the authors believe that these words [*yi* and *lu*] are forbidden by our reign, so they avoid using them to show their diffidence and respect. They do not understand that in so doing they are precisely abandoning reason and righteousness and showing us little respect.
>
> The distinction between the *zhong* [center, central] and the *wai* [outer] is a line drawn on the ground but the distinction between the *shang* [high] and the *xia* [low] is made in Heaven. Our dynasty originated from the shore of the eastern ocean and has since unified the diverse states. The sovereign rules all under Heaven. The tradition that has been inherited [by our dynasty] is that of *zhongwai yijia* [the Center and the Outer being one family] which goes back to the times of King Yao and King Shun. The talents we employ, be they literary or military, join this universal family of the Center and the Outer. Our administrative policies, our rituals, and military conquests are all made for this universal family of the Center and the Outer. Our subjects, from Zhili and the other interior provinces to Mongolia and the remote tribes, and those living on the edge of the oceans and in mountain valleys, as well as tribute-bearers who travel hither by land or by sea from foreign and faraway places, all without exception show their respect

toward their parents and deference toward our sovereign rule. To trace the beginnings of our empire to its original place and regard us as the outer *yi* is merely to draw a territorial line between the Center and the Outer. I call it outrageous treachery, no matter how you avoid the word between the lines, for the only distinction in Heaven is that of the high and low.

Mencius said: Shun was a man of the eastern *yi;* and King Wen was a man of the western *yi.* Shun was a sage king from the ancient times and Mencius called him a *yi.* King Wen was the founder of the Zhou dynasty who had the mandate of Heaven and Mencius called him a *yi.* The word *yi* simply names the *fangyu* [geographic area] and none of the ancient sages attempted to outlaw its use.[44]

This statement reiterates much of what Yongzheng had said in *Awakening to Supreme Justice,* but it also condenses a number of important features of the imperial ideology of the Qing as it evolved and solidified in the eighteenth century. First, the concept of *yi* is central, not peripheral, to the Manchu notion of sovereignty as it structures the ways (territorial or heavenly) in which the mandate of Heaven may be interpreted by the conquerors and the conquered. Second, the Manchu ruler develops a notion of universalism that is uniquely suited to the Manchu vision of empire. This notion is called *zhongwai yijia,* or the universal family of the Center and the Outer, whereby all differences of ethnicity and culture appear to be miraculously suspended and the Manchu nobility, the bannermen, the Han Chinese, minority peoples, tributary states, and foreign countries are organized into the hierarchical order of universal kinship. Third, the Confucian classics are brought in to legitimate and articulate the Qing vision of empire, which would soon lead to the revival of the New Text studies of the Han dynasty in the latter half of the eighteenth century. The Yongzheng emperor read his *Mencius* to argue that the idea of *yi* merely named a local region, and therefore scholars should not make a fuss over it by censoring or avoiding its usage. Instead, one ought to attend to the mandate of Heaven and to the ways in which Heaven grants the distinction between those who are fit to rule (high) and those who are ruled (low) and be less concerned about the territorial boundaries of the Central States and its neighboring regions. If the Manchus refused to be named *yi,* it was because they considered themselves the rightful rulers of Hans and no longer foreigners.

It is significant to note that Yongzheng's geographical interpretation of *yi* agreed with the Manchu-language rendering of the Chinese terms *yi ren* (person) and *yi shang* (merchant) both as *tulergi gurun i hudai niyalma* (literally, "outer country–born person"). The Manchu translation of the Chinese phrase *yi-di* was *tulergi aiman,* or "outer tribes."[45] According to the Manchu sense, there was no need for the emperor to ban the character *yi* as the British did in the nineteenth century; instead, Yongzheng adopted the strategy of limiting the semantic scope of the concept of *yi,* taming it with the Manchu interpretation and rendering it harmless to his rule. When the Qianlong emperor inherited the throne in 1736, he disobeyed his father's order by putting Zeng Jing to death and took *Awakening to Supreme Justice* out of circulation, for it had turned out to be the vital conduit for the unintended spread of Zeng Jing's and Lü Liuliang's subversive views.[46] Like Yongzheng, however, Qianlong remained vigilant toward any seditious use of an essentialized *hua/yi* distinction and continued to gloss the meaning of *yi-di* in geographical terms.[47] The emperor issued an edict stating that it was not necessary for the editors of the Four Treasures of the Imperial Library to censor the character *yi,* and, as Benjamin Elman's research shows, "the edict was promulgated at a time when one disrespectful word uttered against a Manchu or Mongol was severely punished."[48]

The historian Zhuang Jifa's close examination of the imperial Manchu rendering of the phrase *yi-di* in Qianlong's reign in comparison with the terms adopted earlier in Kangxi's reign suggests that Qianlong's emphasis on geography rather than ethnicity was a careful decision. In fact, the seventeenth-century Manchu translations of the Confucian classics were subjected to numerous corrections and improvements in the eighteenth century, among which the rendering of *yi-di* received its share of revisionary attention. In Kangxi's reign this phrase was transcribed in Manchu to approximate the Mandarin pronunciation of the characters *yi* and *di* in the published Manchu edition of the *Zhongyong* (Doctrine of the Mean). The same phrase, however, was translated as *tulergi aiman* (outer tribes) in Qianlong's *Imperial Translation of the Four Confucian Classics;* likewise, a related phrase, *man-mo*—which was brought up by Lindsay, whom I discussed in Chapter 2—was translated in Qianlong's reign as *tulergi amargi aiman,* or "tribes of the South and North."[49] The geographic redefinition of *yi-di* or *man-mo* was intended to dissolve the subversive potential of the *hua/yi* distinction and to produce the *da yitong,* or the universal order of the Qing empire. With that distinction seemingly abolished, the alien identity of the Manchus became unimportant and incidental. Instead, the legitimacy of that regime and its subordination of the Han population were said to rest on the classical concept of *de* or virtue that the Manchus took from the Confucian rituals.

The Imperial Ideology of the *Da yi tong*

The Qianlong emperor encouraged the study of the Confucian classics and set an example by repudiating the work of the Song dynasty scholar Hu Anguo in the imperial editorial notes included in the Four Treasures of the Imperial Library.[50] Hu's well-known commentaries on the *Spring and Autumn Annals* had endorsed the distinction between *hua xia* and *yi-di* to which the emperor objected.[51] Over and against Hu's interpretation of the Confucian classic, Qianlong reiterated the idea that the Qing empire was *zhongwai yijia*, or one family uniting the Center and the Outer. It was this imperial vision that inspired the emperor's elaborate commissioning of literature, architecture, painting, portraiture, and dictionary and encyclopedia projects, as well as his patronage of the Chinese and Western scholars and artists who gathered in Beijing under the sovereign rule of "the unique son of Heaven" *(tianzi, abka i jui)*.[52] In Chapter 2, I discussed how the British, according to Thomas Trautmann, invented the Aryan story to claim distant kinship and family reunion with India. The Qing emperors had subdued China and sought to rule the Han Chinese on the basis of persecution and strict social and ethnic hierarchies, but, on the ideological front, they developed a discourse of brotherhood and familial love and practiced a universalism that embraced all. This imperial legacy was what the British officials bumped up against when their own imperial ambition and universalism brought them to the Central States. The Aryan story appears to have been mirrored back by the imperial vision of the *zhongwai yijia*, and in both cases the classics—Sanskrit and Confucian—were mined by the conquerors to legitimize sovereign rule over a foreign population.

The Manchu version of the legendary Imperial Tributaries Scrolls commissioned by Qianlong in the mid-eighteenth century translated the Chinese phrase *yi ren* into the Manchu *niyalma* (man) or *tubai niyalma*. The character *yi* was folded into the term *niyalma* or served as the deictic marker *tubai* (here). By the same token, the ethnographic description of an Englishman in the Imperial Tributaries Scrolls—*yingjili yi ren* (English *yi* male)—was translated as *ing gi lii gurun i niyalma* (a man from the English state) in the Manchu version.[53] The management of the semantic bounds of the character *yi* in the Manchu documents in this instance and in the imperial translations of the Four Confucian Classics suggests the ways in which the Manchu language represented the meaning of Chinese words to the ruling members of the Qing. As we know, Manchu and Chinese were both the official languages of the dynasty. Until the signing of Article 50 of the Anglo-Chinese Treaty of Tianjin, the Manchu, not English, interpretations of Chinese characters appeared to have dictated the terms of hetero-cultural translations.

As I have mentioned, the Qianlong emperor's universalism led to the revival of the Gongyang New Text studies of the *Spring and Autumn Annals* in the latter half of the eighteenth century.[54] The leading figures in that movement were Zhuang Cunyu, a scholar-official from a prominent Changzhou lineage, and his nephew Liu Fenglu, who enjoyed an illustrious career in the Qing officialdom. Espousing the Han scholar He Xiu's interpretation of the *Annals*, Zhuang Cunyu and Liu Fenglu discovered in the Confucian text a vision of cosmic change and dynastic transformation that was figured in the unfolding of the three epochs. That vision, they maintained, was substantiated by Confucius's own careful inclusion of the historical sources he had used in composing the *Annals*. The first epoch, called *ju luan shi*, is the age of chaos, when the distinction between one's own state (inner) and the other *xia* (outer) states has to be maintained. The second epoch, *sheng ping shi*, is the age of ascending peace, where distinction is drawn between all *xia* (inner) and *yi-di* (outer) states. The third is the epoch of *tai ping shi*, or great peace, where there is no longer the need to make any distinction between the *xia* and the *yi-di*. Thus, the Gongyang scholars argued, Confucius had encoded the *Annals* with a vision of the ascending order of *ju luan shi*, *sheng ping shi*, and *tai ping shi* that would culminate in the *da yi tong* (great unity).[55]

In what ways did the Qing empire negotiate the terms of the *da yi tong* in its practice of diplomatic relations? In his book *Classicism, Politics, and Kinship*, Benjamin Elman discusses a revealing case that was handled by the scholar-official Liu Fengliu himself at the Ministry of Rites in 1824, when Liu met with a tribute mission to the Manchu court from the recently crowned king of Vietnam, Minh Mang. The Vietnamese envoy in charge of the mission had objected to the language of the official rescript that the Daoguang emperor had prepared for transmission to the Vietnamese king. The envoy was particularly offended by the reference to the Vietnamese as "the outer *yi*" and insisted on being reclassified as "the outer *fan*." Drawing on the etymological evidence from the Later Han dictionary of paleography, *Shuowen jiezi* (Explicating texts and analyzing characters), Liu Fengliu argued that the written character *yi* consisted of the radicals "great" *(da)* and "bow" *(gong)*, indicating respect for the outer *yi*. He pointed out that in the ancient offices of the Zhou dynasty, areas outside the capital city had been divided into *jiu fu* (nine regions). The *yi fu* was located seven thousand *li* from the capital, whereas the *fanfu* was nine thousand *li* away. The former enjoyed a rank higher than the *fan* within the Zhou system of foreign relations. Liu reiterated Mencius's words to remind the Vietnamese envoy that the sage-king Shun was an eastern *yi*, King Wen, the founder of the Zhou dynasty, was a western *yi*, and so on.[56] More important, he discreetly suggested that "in the midst of strenuous efforts to weed out anti-Manchu sentiments in books and manuscripts as well as to trace the origins of the Manchus as a people, the Manchu emperor himself had found nothing disrespectful in the term *yi*."[57]

Interestingly, the 1824 incident was restaged in less than two decades when another Vietnamese envoy, Lý Văn Phú'c, found the Qing application of the term *yi* objectionable on his 1841 mission to the Qing court. He wrote an impromptu essay in elegant classical Chinese prose to emphasize the Confucian nature of Vietnamese elite culture and presented the essay to the Daoguang emperor.[58] Alexander Woodside's analysis of this episode in *Vietnam and the Chinese Model* suggests that the Vietnamese saw themselves as no more *yi* than the ruling Manchus because they, too, inhabited the Confucian civilization and were its center. One of the Vietnamese emperors proclaimed in 1835 that his capital city was the core of a geographically transposed but ideologically correct new "Central Domain" in Southeast Asia. To signify his legitimacy as the true successor of the ancient Zhou that had once presided over the primordial "nine regions," the ambitious Vienamese emperor constructed nine bronze urns—the mythical symbol of Zhou sovereignty—at his ancestral temple in Hue.[59] In light of this challenge, the irony of Liu Fenglu's exegesis of the etymology of the nine regions becomes evident, for he had assumed that the "capital city" lay within the imperial domain of the Qing, an assumption with which the Vietnamese emperor would not concur.[60] The latter's transposed capital city implied that it was the subjects of the Qing empire who were the *yi* and lived on the borders of the "Central Domain." This is by no means an expression of the whim of an ambitious Vietnamese sovereign, since, as a number of studies have demonstrated, the Koreans and Japanese likewise placed themselves at the center of the Confucian order *(hua)*, treating the Qing as the periphery *(yi)* of that core.[61]

The foregoing analysis may provide a helpful interpretive grid for further understanding the place of *yi* in the articulation and disarticulation of sovereign claims to the "Central Domain," not just within a bounded geographical area known as China but across the entirety of Confucian Asia, particularly as this drama of sovereign rivalries continued unabated through the Opium Wars. When the British began to protest the character *yi,* they, too, laid a certain claim to the Central States, albeit in the interest of free trade or colonial conquest, and insisted on "equal footing" with the Qing empire. As I demonstrated in Chapter 2, the equating of *yi* and "barbarian" within the sovereign structure of the super-sign gave the British the opportunity and satisfaction of exercising their sovereign rights by successfully inserting a coercive ban into the unequal treaties.

Imperial Commissioner Lin Zexu's (1785–1850) letter to Queen Victoria and its subsequent English translations indicate that the British conflict with the Qing over the opium trade extended to a whole range of symbolic practices beyond trade and economic matters. Representation and self-representation, reciprocity, sources of moral authority, law, and imperial responsibility had real bearings on the conflicting ways of sovereign thinking at the time of the first Opium War.[62] Lin Zexu was close to a circle of prominent Gongyang New Text scholars of the time, whose members included his friend Gong Zizhen, who had been Liu Fenglu's student. Lin and his fellow officials drafted their well-known letter to Queen Victoria to present the reasons for the Qing government's aggressive campaign and ask the British Crown to stop the opium trade. The English translation of the first draft of this letter was printed in the *Chinese Repository* as early as May 1839 after the Chinese original had been copied and circulated for about two months. The second and official version of the communication, sealed with the Daoguang emperor's approval, was issued on August 3, 1839, and its English version appeared in the *Chinese Repository* in February 1840. Co-signed by Deng Tingzhen, the viceroy of Guangdong and Guangxi, and Yi Liang, vice president of the Board of War, Commissioner Lin's letter drew on a Confucian logic of reciprocity, arguing:

> It is said that the smoking of opium is strictly forbidden in your country, the proof that you are clearly aware of its harm. Since you do not permit opium to harm your own country, you should not allow it to be passed on to other countries, certainly not the Central States! Of all the products the Central States exports to foreign countries, there is not a single item that is not beneficial to the people: they are beneficial when consumed, beneficial when used, and beneficial when resold: all are beneficial. Has any article from the Central States done any harm to the foreign countries?[63]

The articles of export mentioned here include tea, rhubarb, silk, and porcelain. Lin's argument of reciprocity would not have been lost on the British sovereign, or any Christian, and one wonders how Queen Victoria would have responded to it had the letter not been purloined and failed to reach the hands of the intended recipient.[64] The survival of this document was indebted to a mode of citation and translation in printed media that has in turn generated a fascinating history of the exchange of signs and supersigns.

The official genre of Lin's communication is called *xi,* which is a dignified statement and official declaration to the enemy in times of military conflict. The purpose of the *xi* is to admonish and warn the enemy about one's intentions, not to give verbal abuse. Thus, Lin speaks of England as *gui guo* (your honorable country) and addresses Queen Victoria as *gui guo wang* (the honorable sovereign of your nation) even as he condemns the evils of the opium trade and reiterates the strict regulations and punishments in the Qing empire. The letter employs expressions such as *jian yi* (*jian* meaning "cunning," "treacherous," or "wicked") to condemn foreign offenders, which appears to support Karl Gützlaff's allegation in his 1832 journal that "the idea of cunning and treachery is always attached to this name when uttered by the Chinese." Gützlaff did not mention that it is the character *jian,* not *yi,* that bears the weight of moral opprobrium in the phrase *jian yi.* Qing government documents routinely referred to native offenders as *jian min* (treacherous commoner) in contrast to the *liang min* (good commoner), and spoke of foreign offenders as *jian yi* (treacherous foreigner) in contrast with the *liang yi* (good foreigner).[65] As a pair, *jian min* and *jian yi* shadowed each other in the imperial edicts and memorials of the eighteenth century through the early nineteenth century. The latter was reserved for those foreign traders who disobeyed the laws of the country and the former for the local merchants who cheated foreigners or collaborated with them in the smuggling of illicit goods.[66]

In his investigation of an earlier instance of Chinese-English disputes, the Qianlong emperor had applied the phrase *jian min* to a merchant named Ni Hongwen in his 1776 edict. In that edict the emperor condemned the fraudulent behavior of Ni, who had failed to make good on his promise to pay back the money he owed his English creditor. Qianlong ordered the governor of Guangdong, Li Zhiying, to confiscate Ni's property and make up for the difference with funds from the local county government to help compensate the Englishman for his financial losses, for, as the imperial edict pointed out, "the *yi* merchant had risked a great deal by crossing the vast oceans to trade hither. Since his goal was to seek profit, we must engage in fair trade practices and let him return home with plentiful goods, for such is the highest principle of the Central States. When the *yi* merchant has been cheated by some cunning and treacherous commoner [*jian min*] in the inner land and lost both his goods and capital, we must pursue the matter by legal means."[67] Conversely, when Lin Zexu adopted words such as *jian yi* and sometimes *ni yi* (rebellious foreigner), he was condemning the foreign merchants for violating the country's law by smuggling opium into the Central States.

The character *yi* was rendered as "foreigner" in the 1839 and 1840 English versions of Lin's letter printed in the *Chinese Repository*.[68] The name of the translator is not given, although a number of sources point to Yuan Dehui, one of the four English interpreters who worked for Commissioner Lin at the time.[69] Of these four, the *Chinese Repository* printed a brief postscript in the June 1839 number that read: "The commissioner has in his service four natives, all of whom have made some progress in the English tongue. The first is a young man, educated at Penang and Malacca, and for several years employed by the Chinese government at Peking. The second is an old man, educated at Serampore. The third is a young man who was once at the school at Cornwall, Conn., U.S.A. The fourth is a young lad, educated in China, who is able to read and translate papers on common subjects, with much ease, correctness, and facility."[70] Yuan Dehui is the first young man described here. He had learned Latin at the Roman Catholic School in Penang and studied English at the missionary John Milne's Anglo-Chinese College in Malacca in 1825. After returning to China, Yuan was appointed official interpreter of the Court of Tributary Affairs in 1829. He visited Canton twice, in 1830 and in 1838, to procure foreign-language books for the Qing government. In 1839 Yuan was placed on Commissioner Lin's staff to help with the volumes of translation work generated during the anti-opium campaign.[71] Lin took a personal interest in the work of his translators and supervised Yuan's rendering of the second version of his communication to Queen Victoria. To check on the accuracy of his translation, Lin asked an American merchant named William C. Hunter to render it back into Chinese and have his translators improve the translation. With respect to Lin's request for his service in 1839, Hunter recalled:

An English translation of a communication addressed by His Excellency, soon after his arrival, jointly with the superior officers of the Canton Government, to Her Majesty the Queen of England, on the subject of the opium trade, was brought to me at the Consoo House to be translated into Chinese, as a test of the proper reading of the original, which turned out to have been made by my old schoolmate Shaow-Tih [Yuan Dehui]. He continued at Canton until the end of the year, when I learnt that he had returned to Pekin, and I never heard of him again. The coincidence of both him and me having been occupied on the communication in question, unknowingly a check upon one another, was a remarkable one.[72]

The result of this collaborative work was duly published in the February 1840 issue of the *Chinese Repository*. From this we can surmise that the decision not to render *yi* as "barbarian" was probably guided by Lin's own understanding of the character, if not from his awareness of the contentiousness of the issue since the time of the Napier affair.[73]

When Ssu-yü Teng and John King Fairbank set out to retranslate the same text in 1954, they decided to correct the *Chinese Repository* version of Lin's letter by converting all instances of the character *yi* into "barbarian." This has had the curious effect of altering the author's tone of moral persuasion because, in the new version, the courteous address "your honorable country" appears side by side with the word "barbarian," as if the commissioner would entertain the notion of an honorable barbarian and say, as Teng and Fairbank have made him say, "Having established new regulations, we presume that the ruler of your honorable country, who takes delight in our culture and whose disposition is inclined towards us, must be able to instruct the various barbarians to observe the law with care."[74] The incongruity practically converts the solemn genre of the *xi* into a comical and somewhat grotesque mockery of itself.

If Teng and Fairbank's translation reads like an unintentional echo of the 1858 ban on the super-sign *yi/barbarian*, one begins to wonder why the ban is so compelling that a modern translator must heed its call from across the space of a century. We find an interesting counterexample in the work of Arthur Waley, a translator and scholar of classical Chinese literature. Four years after the publication of Teng and Fairbank's retranslation of Lin's letter, Waley composed a slim volume titled *The Opium War through Chinese Eyes*, in which he, too, retranslated Lin's letter—not the official document included in Teng and Fairbank's book but Lin's very first draft—and converted Lin's *yi* back to "foreigner." Which of the two parties got the word wrong, Yuan Dehui and Waley or Teng and Fairbank? As we know, Waley was an experienced translator and seems to have known his Chinese classics better than Fairbank, since he authored many notable translations, including the *Book of Songs*, the *Analects of Confucius*, and the *Dao de jing (Tao te ching)*, as well as Tang poetry, vernacular novels, and other works. His acquaintance with the Confucian scholarship probably alerted him to the dangers of too facile an equation of the character *yi* with "barbarian," and he would have concurred with Samuel Wells Williams, the author of an enormously popular work, *The Middle Kingdom*, who noted in the late nineteenth century that "by translating *wai i* as 'outside barbarians,' foreigners have been misrepresented in the status they held among educated natives." Williams wrote further that "when used as a general term, without an opprobrious addition, *i* is as well adapted as any to denote all foreigners."[75] The "opprobrious addition" would have been *jian, ni,* or other such terms of moral condemnation.

One of Liu Fenglu's disciples, Wei Yuan, compiled his multivolume *Haiguo tuzhi* (An illustrated gazetteer of maritime countries) to help popularize knowledge of the geography and history of foreign nations. Little surprise that this important Gongyang scholar should promote the idea of *shi yi changji yi zhi yi* (emulating the strength of foreigners' technology in order to overcome them).[76] By that, Wei Yuan did not mean that the Chinese should master the technology of the barbarians. The verb *shi* in the phrase *shi yi changji* is the same character as the noun *shi* (teacher, master), suggesting the act of a student emulating his or her teacher, although in this instance the teacher was one's enemy at war with the Qing.[77] Prince Gong, who coordinated the work of W. A. P. Martin's translation of *Elements of International Law* (discussed in Chapter 4), employed the character *yi* in the same sense when he spoke of *shi yi zhi* (emulating the wisdom of the *yi*). The Confucian notion of *shi* denotes the respect one human being (student) should bestow on another (teacher), so it was not a contradiction of terms for Wei Yuan and Prince Gong to suggest a respect for one's enemy.

Thus far I have taken the reader along the diverse paths of "barbarian" and *yi* up to the point where they meet, intersect, and undergo a process of semiotic alchemy to become reified beyond their individual etymologies. The super-sign *yi/barbarian,* as an outcome of hostile encounters between the British and the Qing, encapsulates the story of nineteenth-century imperial rivalries, with its usual narrative intricacies and psychological twists and turns. The British and their allies strove to become the major powers of influence in the Great Game, whereas the Qing throne did its best to resist or comprise. Although the textbook history has endeavored to portray the super-sign *yi/barbarian* as a reflection of Chinese xenophobia, what it truly reflects is the important shift of geopolitical power that transformed international relations and modern society in the nineteenth century. This should not be taken to mean that the Chinese never adopted a hostile attitude toward the British. On the contrary, the hardships caused by the Opium Wars, treaty privileges, missionary work, and Western imperialism at large led to the increased anger and resentment that the gentry and ordinary people felt toward the presence of Westerners. The popular epithet *gui zi* or *fan gui*, commonly taken to mean "foreign devils," embodied that anger and steadfastly trailed the British troops and traders from south to north. More than any other Chinese words, *gui zi* or *fan gui* captured the popular sentiment of the time; that is, there was no love lost between the conqueror and the conquered.

Exorcising the Ghost of *Yi*

Two years after Lord Elgin and his ministers coerced the Qing government into signing the Treaty of Tianjin, the allied forces captured and sacked Beijing in a series of military campaigns.[78] The troops first pillaged and burned down the famous imperial Gardens of Perfect Brightness *(Yuanming yuan)* to the northwest of the city and then proceeded to set up legation quarters in the capital. Lord Elgin's Chinese secretary Thomas Wade, who had been a central figure at the negotiation of the Treaty of Tianjin, was promoted to counselor of the British legation. Wade was alert for slips of the tongue and regularly checked all official Chinese correspondence for signs of disrespect, whether it be the issue of elevating the Chinese characters for Great Britain to the same level as that for the Qing court or of using respectful language toward foreigners in published material. For example, Wade was furious when he discovered that the manuscript edition of the official newspaper *Jingbao* had failed to elevate the Chinese characters for "Great Britain" and went to great lengths to protest the infraction to Prince Gong, who headed the office of the Zongli yamen, the newly established foreign affairs ministry.[79]

The British authorities were constantly on the lookout for signs of disrespect, whether they originated from official communications or the popular press. Their anxieties were reflective of a general discourse of risk and mastery that helped build the character of the Victorian men who worked for the British Empire. Elaine Freedgood's research shows that "the quasi-hysterical separation of external expression from internal emotions—as implied in the idea of a stiff (or paralyzed) upper lip—indicates the severity of the need to immobilize and camouflage the anxieties that afflicted a nation struggling for mastery and authority in a period of unprecedented and heavily contested economic and territorial expansion."[80] Indeed, the development of the "laws" of classical political economy itself was driven by the conviction that, as the statistician William Farr put it, "knowledge will banish panic."[81]

Even with the law completely on their side, the panic with regard to the matter of respect would not go away. In 1879 the British residents of Shanghai organized a broad campaign, "The Charges of Discourtesy in Native Papers," for the express purpose of censoring all Chinese-language newspapers. Rudolf Wagner has revealed that even the *Shenbao*, a successful Chinese-language newspaper owned by the British entrepreneur John Major, could not escape the censorship. The paper came under attack from time to time for neglecting to leave honorary space for British dignitaries in the news articles it printed.[82] Censorship led to self-censorship until, at the turn of the twentieth century, the character *yi* and other "disrespectful" expressions made a permanent exit from most Chinese publications and government documents.

The spectacular success of the 1858 ban notwithstanding, the British continued to be haunted by the echoes of the super-sign, as the ghost of the (legally) dead word seemed to lurk behind the vernacular speech of ordinary people on the street and inside their homes and pop up in various other guises. Although the signs of disrespect in published or written media could be caught and brought to the attention of the appropriate authority charged with upholding the ban and punishing the transgressors, the use of the spoken word among the populace proved much more difficult to suppress. That, however, did not prevent the British from going after *fan gui* and its dialectal variant *gui zi* with the same sense of injury with which they had pursued the ban on the character *yi*. Eyewitness accounts by foreigners and Chinese alike attest to the manner in which the British censored the speech of ordinary Beijing residents during the 1860 occupation of the city. For example, a Chinese writer named Zhuiman Yesou (style name) described a scene of violent confrontation to caution his compatriots about the consequences of offending the armed troops:

There is a clause in the treaty that forbids us to call them *yi*. One cannot afford not to take notice of this. A few days ago, a retarded man caught sight of some *yi* people passing by the corner of the Three Turn Bridge outside the Chongwen Gate. Pointing at them, he laughed and called out, "The *gui zi* are here." A team of *yi* soldiers immediately set upon the poor idiot and beat him with such brutality that the man received mortal wounds and was close to dying. Having done that, the *yi* men stormed into the man's house and went on to beat his relatives, wounding them and smashing everything in sight. If the powerful could use their force this way, how can we not stay away from the words they have prohibited?[83]

It is almost as if *gui zi* had turned into the ghost of the character *yi* and assaulted the foreigners through the agency of the retarded man and in turn provoked frenzied reaction and physical violence. How does one account for this madness?

Contrary to the Frenchman's allegation to Zhang Deyi in 1871 mentioned earlier in this chapter, *gui zi* was not the exclusive appellation for Westerners in colloquial speech. Gützlaff reported that the local people had called him *xiyang zi* (Se-yang-tsze) or "child of the western ocean" on his first trip to the coast of Shangdong Province in 1831.[84] As we know, Gützlaff was one of the first Westerners to raise objections to the character *yi* and made lengthy comments about Chinese arrogance toward foreigners in his *Journal of Two Voyages along the Coast of China in 1831 and 1832.* From time to time, however, his journal would contradict those observations by noting, for example, that the natives on the southern coast of China were friendly and "seemed unused to see foreigners, and exceedingly delighted at our arrival. They ushered us into their houses, and gave us sweetmeats and tea."[85] On his 1832 voyage along the Chinese coast on board the *Lord Amherst*, the author discovered that "the Chinese character is exempt from misanthropy" and reports that "we had enjoyed the satisfaction of visiting the island [of Tsungming near Shanghai] undisturbed, and of seeing the Chinese character in its true light, that of friendliness and kindness toward foreigners."[86] If the people seemed friendly and kind on that occasion, what caused them to invent terms like *gui zi, bai gui* (white ghost), and *hei gui* (black ghost) to insult foreigners? Does the verbal violence tell us something about the history of interaction between locals and foreigners in China?

Negative portrayals of Westerners began in the early sixteenth century, when the first Portuguese traders appeared on the southern coast of China and committed random acts of pillage and homicide. Simão d'Andrade became especially notorious in the eyes of the local people for kidnapping Chinese women and children and selling them abroad into slavery. The threat the Portuguese posed to public safety alarmed the government censor He Ao and led him to memorialize the throne in 1520, proposing that all foreigners be expelled from China.[87] When the Jesuit missionary Matteo Ricci arrived decades later, he had to work very hard to overcome the unfavorable impressions that Simão d'Andrade had left behind. In the eighteenth century, as I have pointed out, the supercargoes of the British East India Company repeatedly got in trouble with the local government for homicides committed by Europeans against the Cantonese "natives." It was these acts of violence, rather than the exotic appearance of Westerners, that had contributed to the rise of the epithets *fan gui* and *gui zi* among the Cantonese and their spread to the rest of the country after the first Opium War. It has been observed that the overwhelming majority of the recorded usage of these epithets date from after the 1840s, and the Opium Wars appear to be the watershed events that disseminated the negative image of ghostly Westerners in the nineteenth century.[88] The fantastic figuring of the *gui zi* defined the enunciatory position of popular "outrage and pain over this period of subjugation by the West," similar to the semiotic throwing of stones and iron cash that I will discuss shortly.[89] The throwing of objects and verbal abuse had little to do with the people's actual knowledge or biased representation of the West; all it did was to gather illocutionary force to summon back the memories of violence from prior encounters and to mobilize the opposition against the British across the country.

The Opium Wars and "Foreign Devils"

The successful Sanyuanli campaign against the British in 1841 gave rise to an extraordinary output of verses, nursery rhymes, and other popular literary compositions that helped disseminate the expression *fan gui* to the rest of the country.[90] Within less than a year, the editor of the *Chinese Repository* took notice of this phenomenon and published an essay explicating the meaning of *fan gui:*

> The term *Fankwei* [*fan gui*].—This opprobrious epithet has become in this country a synonym for foreigner, and we may almost expect erelong to see it entered in our dictionaries, and defined a "term for a foreigner in China." We were asking a respectable native gentleman the other day what he supposed was the reason for the application of this term *Fan kwei* or "*Fan*

devils" to foreigners. He replied, "that he did not think *kwei* meant devil or demon in this connection, but something outlandish, uncouth, bizarre, something in short that was not celestial, i.e. Chinese. *Fan* was a term given to the petty, groveling island savages living in the southern ocean, as *man, i, ti,* &c., were the names of people dwelling on the northern and other frontiers of the empire. When foreigners first came to the shores of China, their close fitting dress, their squeaking shoes and cocked hats, their blue eyes and red hair, their swords, their unintelligible talk, their overbearing carriage, and the roaring guns of their ships, all astonished the people, who exclaimed *kwei! kwei!* Thus the term came into use, and gradually acquired circulation until it has become the general appellative of all far-traveled strangers." This explanation is probably somewhat near the truth, but must be considered rather *ex parte* evidence, and is, we think, really illustrative of Chinese contempt for other nations. The term is, however, the only one in common use among the people in this region to denote foreigners, and although it may be in many cases used without any intended disrespect, yet if the people entertained any particular respect for us, they would soon find a better term.[91]

The Sanyuanli resistance in the first Opium War, which was the immediate context of the dissemination of the epithet, is passed over in silence as the author concludes that *fan gui* illustrates the Chinese contempt for other nations. But the references to temporality such as "erelong" and "has become" drop hints of a world of action where words staged their own hit-and-run skirmishes on the discursive front and where ordinary people, old and young, tried to defend themselves against the roaring guns of the British ships. We have seen how the British were winning the battle with the Qing in its crusade against the super-sign *yi/barbarian*, but they seemed to be losing this one—the battle with the opprobrious epithet *fan gui*—largely because this time they were dealing with the anonymous and faceless masses rather than the plenipotentiaries and ministers of the Qing government.

The Chinese concept of *gui* (ghost, spirit) exhibits a much broader semantic reach than the English notion of "devil," ranging from the occult, fantastic, or repulsive to the spiritual, the exotic, and the playful. Because of its deep involvement in a grassroots social mobilization including women, children, even retarded people, *fan gui* registered stronger feelings of fear, revulsion, and hatred than "contempt." And it was doing so this precisely at the moment when the British and Qing officials were debating the meanings of the classical concept of *yi* at the negotiating table. A Westerner walking on the streets of Canton after the Opium War and accosted by children as a *fan gui* would be struck by the rudeness and hostility of the term. The author of the essay in the *Chinese Repository* includes several such anecdotes to help illustrate how the term was used by the locals in Guangzhou immediately after the war. For example, a friend of the author's was walking on the streets of Guangzhou when "one youngster among the crowd around him hooted after him so obstreperously, that turning suddenly he caught the urchin, and was about to teach him better manners, when the lad, turning up the white of his eyes, exclaimed, 'If I don't call you *fankwei,* what shall I call you?' And thus escaped."[92] In addition there is the tale of a mother who can "instantly quell the crying of her child by telling it that she would throw it to the *fankwei,* if it did not hush," and of a child whimpering and crying *fan gui* at the approach of the author himself.[93] But the author misses the point of his own anecdotes when he comments that "the use of this epithet however cannot be eradicated, until the people shall have had more familiar intercourse with those from other lands, and learned to regard them as fellowmen and friends, by receiving ocular demonstration of their claim to such titles."[94] The demonstration of the British claim to those titles, needless to say, was easily contradicted by the conspicuous movement of guns and battleships along the coast of China that could only have inspired fear, resentment, and resistance. One would suppose that the mother and the child had good reason to be afraid of the British and regard them as foe, not friends.

From the time that the Cantonese militia mobilized the villagers to combat the British, the dialectal term *fan gui* staged what seemed like a nation-wide guerrilla war against the intruders. When the British troops moved north along the coast of China, the epithets *fan gui* and *gui zi* followed them all the way to Beijing. Zhuiman Yesou's narrative about the foreign soldiers' censorship of street talk is partially corroborated by D. F. Rennie's eyewitness account from 1861. Rennie, who had been the staff surgeon on special service under the government of India, joined the British occupation forces in China in 1860. He kept a remarkably detailed journal about the daily routine of British military and diplomatic personnel in Beijing which later appeared in print as *Peking and the Pekingese: During the First Year of the British Embassy at Peking.*[95] There is an interesting episode in which Rennie describes how Thomas Wade confronted an old gentleman on the streets of Beijing and reprimanded him for using an offensive expression:

On April 6, 1861, Thomas Wade was riding through the streets of Peking on horseback when he overheard an old man with glasses on calling out to his friends inside to come out and see the foreign devils. Wade rode up to him, and corrected him for applying such a disrespectful term to him, informing him at the same time that they were not devils but ordinary men. The old gentleman denied having used the word, and the people assembled about him said that the expression was no doubt an objectionable one, and now that the old man is aware that it was one calculated to give offence, the probabilities are that he will not again use it. In passing some houses near the Foreign Office, we had several iron cash thrown at us. They are a small coin, about the size of a halfpenny, and not appreciated as currency. They were issued during a scarcity of copper, and the issue occasioned discontent. The coin consequently never got into general circulation.[96]

Wade's encounter with the old man may not be the same one recounted by Zhuiman Yesou. The two episodes, however, bear a striking resemblance to each other in their manner of narration, except that British brutality is conspicuously absent from Rennie's account. The situation brings to mind Robinson Crusoe's first encounter with Friday, which I analyzed in Chapter 1. Crusoe hails his gun as that "wonderful Fund of Death and Destruction" and succeeds in subduing Friday by semiotically displaying its killing power. Instead of the British finding Fridays who would worship them and their guns, a reverse deictic situation emerged in Beijing, where the residents greeted the British with thrown objects and hate epithets. The throwing of worthless iron cash is a significant detail, because we are dealing with two types of projectiles of which the throwing of cash is just as much an illocutionary act as the enunciation of words. The iron cash said the same thing as the verbal sign, and Rennie appears to have taken notice. Wade's desire to censor the speech of the locals shows that the illocutionary force of the iron cash and the verbal projectile was probably not lost on him as the weapons of the weak. His reaction to the epithet *gui zi* suggests, however, that he read an indexical and symbolic sign mimetically for its representational value. Imagining mimesis to be the horizon of verbal speech, he went after the old man to correct his mistaken notions about foreigners, a futile attempt, because the massive looting and desecration of palaces, temples, and people's homes during the initial months of British and French occupation had thrown into question the humanity of the British troops in Beijing and in the treaty ports newly opened up to the British.[97]

Article 11 of the Treaty of Tianjin added several more treaty ports besides those already granted to the British by the Treaty of Nanjing, namely, Zhuangzhou (Canton), Xiamen (Amoy), Fuzhou (Foochow), Ningbo (Ningpo), and Shanghai. The new treaty ports were Niuzhuang (Newchwang), Dengzhou (Tangchow), Taiwan, Chaozhou (Chawchow), and Hainan (Kiungchow).[98] The people in the latter areas organized resistance to the treaty agreement between the Qing and the foreign powers and openly denounced the British as *gui zi* in their speech and writing. During the time when the Qing capital was occupied by the Allied troops, the people of Chaozhou successfully barred the British from entering their town and were able to hold out for as long as six years. In anticipation of the arrival of the new British consul George Caine, the local gentry leadership issued a public document in 1860 announcing:

> It is said that the British are coming to the town of Chaozhou to survey the area with the intention of seizing and occupying the territory as they already did in Guangzhou and Shanghai. Their true mind is hard to tell but we must be prepared to defend ourselves. Some of our government officials are so terrified of the *fan gui* [foreign ghosts] that they grant them all their wishes. After some discussion, the gentry leadership has agreed that in the event that the *gui tou* ["ghost head," a dialectal variant of *guizi*] prefers to jump into the net by passing through our towns and villages, folk may proceed to kill them and receive an award of fifty *yuan* silver dollars per head or capture the *gui tou* alive and be awarded one hundred *yuan* silver dollars per head. If the *gui tou* obtains the assistance of a *han jian* [Chinese traitor], the award is fifty *yuan* silver dollars per head for killing the *han jian* and one hundred *yuan* silver dollars for capturing him alive. Each town and village must be prepared to use a banner and a gong to signal the coming of the *fan gui* so people will surround them from all sides. This matter is of grave importance for the local area. If the corrupt government officials dare to protect the *gui tou*, you, townsmen and villagers, are free to capture and execute those officials and need not hand them over to the government. You would be duly rewarded.[99]

Within months, the armed militia in the Chaozhou area sought out the residence of a representative of the Jardine and Matheson company for attack and destroyed the property of other foreign firms.[100] The local people regarded the Qing government as an accomplice to the enemy for ceding their port and livelihood to the foreigners. Numerous joint military expeditions and massacres of entire villages took place before the British and the Qing military could subdue the hostility and remove the opposition.[101] Even so, George Caine was pelted with stones and harsh epithets when he tried to pass through the town of Chaozhou under heavy escort by Qing troops many years later.[102] By comparison, the iron cash thrown at Wade and his entourage in Beijing seems a mere simulacrum of what the British were experiencing elsewhere in the country.

Samuel Wells Williams, who had not found the character *yi* offensive, observed that "this epithet of 'foreign devil' did much, in the course of years, to increase the contempt and ill will it expressed, not only there [Guangzhou] but throughout the Empire, for they [the British] were thereby maligned before they were known."[103] Williams believed, as did the author of the *Chinese Repository* essay quoted earlier, that *fan gui* was about Chinese contempt and ill will toward foreigners and not about the violence of the Opium Wars and the treaty arrangements. His reference to "the course of years," however, again reminds us of a sequence of historical events, from the first military skirmishes in Guangzhou to the Opium Wars, which cannot be separated out from the people's hostile reactions to the presence of the British. The curious etymology of the pidgin word "Wei-lo" which Rennie recorded in *Peking and the Pekingese* sheds further light on the sources of violence for verbal enunciations of this kind. Rennie writes:

> While Mr. Gibson, who is an excellent Chinese linguist, was riding in the city yesterday, a little boy called out "Wei-lo" to him, so he stopped the boy, and explained to him that "Wei-lo" was not an English word; and that, moreover, it was not one generally applied in a complimentary or respectful sense; consequently, that it would be better for him, even at the risk of being misunderstood, in future to confine himself to the Mandarin dialect, than to attempt to use foreign words, the meaning of which he did not understand. The crowd, that had formed round them while this conversation was going on, completely endorsed Mr. Gibson's views, and repeated his caution to the boy, in future to confine his observations to his own language. The word "Wei-lo" is an English corruption of the Chinese Hugh-lo, "to go," and originated amongst the soldiers during the first China war, since which time it has become identified in the minds of the Chinese with English, from being the word they most frequently hear foreigners make use of. The same word, Hugh-lo, in the north of China is pronounced Chu-lo. In the south, Li-lo means "to come"; hence, with Hugh-lo, the mixed

corruption "Wei-lo," now generic in pidgin (business) English for "to go." "He make-ee wei-lo," means that the person has gone.[104]

An interesting formulaic pattern emerges from Rennie's narratives of encounters with pedestrians in Beijing: A British man is riding through the city when an old man or a boy says something objectionable to him. The Englishman confronts the person as a crowd begins to form around them, and the crowd always endorses the views of the Englishman. In the scene just quoted, the missionary John G. Gibson's philological exercise appears more extravagant than Wade's treatment of similar instances, because his ears are alert for pidgin terms. Rennie and Gibson claim that "wei-lo" is not applied in a complimentary or respectful sense, but exactly how an English corruption of the word "Hugh-lo" suggests disrespect toward the British remains a mystery. If we can trust Gibson's ear or Rennie's transcription, "wei-lo" could be *waiguo lao*, meaning "foreign rogue" in the Beijing dialect, or some variant of *gui zi*, like *gui lao*, or simply a variant of "hello." Whether out of ignorance or unconscious evasion, Rennie and Gibson try to shield themselves from hearing what Wade has heard and determine that the word is a pidgin corruption for "to go."

To say "wei-lo" or not to say "wei-lo," that is not the question. The real cause of anxiety, as I suggested in the preceding chapter, was a certain perversion of familiar colonial discourse whereby the British attempted to contest their troubled self-image in the language of the other, be it *yi/barbarian, fan gui/foreign devil*, or any nonsense word that remotely suggested disrespect. Might we not glimpse in this obsession a rare moment of self-doubt within the imperial unconscious with regard to the mystified location of the "barbarian" and its relationship to the sovereign self? The sovereign subject is trying to root out the ghost of the "barbarian" from its own deep-seated uncertainty before it can become whole, positive, and real. The situation is not unlike the reflexive return of a conjuration that Jacques Derrida discusses in *Specters of Marx:* "Those who inspire fear frighten themselves, they conjure the very specter they represent. The conjuration is in mourning for *itself* and turns its own force against itself."[105] The trouble with Wade and Gibson was that, although the ban on the super-sign *yi/barbarian* was already in place by the time they arrived in Beijing, the spoken word had somehow escaped the legal sanction. To them, the ghost of the slain *yi* was roaming at large, carrying on endless guerrilla warfare with the imperial self.

John Thomson, the famous expedition photographer of the period, dubbed the camera the "forerunner of death" with a sense of self-irony. Thomson traveled to China in the wake of the second Opium War, where he produced some of the best-known photographic images of the Chinese landscape and its inhabitants. In the preface to the 1873 album *China and Its People*, Thomson observes:

> As the "Fan Qui" or "Foreign Devil" who assumed human shape, . . . I . . . frequently enjoyed the reputation of being a dangerous geomancer, and my camera was held to be a dark mysterious instrument, which, combined with my naturally, or supernaturally, intensified eyesight gave me power to see through rocks and mountains, to pierce the very souls of the natives, and to produce marvelous pictures by some black art, which at the same time bereft the individual depicted of so much of the principle of life as to render his death a certainty within a very short period of years.
>
> Accounted, for these reasons, the forerunner of death, I found portraits of children difficult to obtain, while, strange as it may seem in a land where filial piety is esteemed the highest of virtues, sons and daughters brought their aged parents to be placed before the foreigner's silent and mysterious instrument of destruction.[106]

Thomson was one of the few Englishmen in China who seems to have enjoyed being the "foreign devil" in a parodic mode. The deadly instrument, like the gun in the hands of Robinson Crusoe, turned the photographer into a powerful geomancer and gave him "naturally, or supernaturally, intensified eyesight." Thomson's narrative of colonial photography secures its scientific rationality by ironizing primitive ignorance. The sons and daughters in the land of filial piety who bring their aged parents to be placed before the foreigner's mysterious instrument of destruction transform the story of a devilish art into a moral parable about the ignorance and hypocrisy of the Chinese. A potential murder by the "foreign devil" undergoes a remarkable reversal to become a Chinese son's or daughter's potential patricide.[107]

"To haunt does not mean to be present," writes Derrida, "and it is necessary to introduce haunting into the very construction of a concept. Of every concept, beginning with the concepts of being and time. That is what we would be calling here a hauntology. Ontology opposes it only in a movement of exorcism. Ontology is a conjuration."[108] I find this observation remarkably lucid in light of the foregoing discussion and would extend Derrida's critique to the foreigner within the sovereign subject. The latter is haunted by the fear it projects onto the other but must secure the ontology of the self by exorcising that fear. Although Derrida's hauntology may not be the best alternative to ontology any more than I think that the human mind can conceptualize without conjuring, I believe that one can at least work with the idea of "haunting" to open up the monstrosity of super-signs like *yi/barbarian* or *fan gui/foreign devil* to show how particular meanings have been made or unmade and how, in general, it is possible to *mean* at all. In Chapter 4 I continue to ponder these issues as I move to the next phase of the foreign relations of the Qing. Known as the Tongzhi Restoration period, the new era saw the creation of the Tsungli yamen (Foreign Ministry) in 1861, the Tongwen guan (School of Languages) in 1862, and then the landmark translation and publication of *Wanguo gong fa*, or the Chinese edition of Henry Wheaton's *Elements of Law*, in 1863–64.

CHAPTER 4

Translating International Law

The conversion of Asian States, which before the nineteenth century had been members of the universal family of nations, into candidates for admission to this family or for recognition by the leading powers was brought about by doctrinal change, particularly by the abandonment of the natural law doctrine and adherence to positivism of the European brand.

—C. H. Alexandrowicz, Introduction to the History of the Law of Nations in the East Indies

Our understanding of modern international relations has tended to privilege the positivity of sovereign rights, often overlooking the immensely interesting processes of conjurations which I have tried to bring to light in the preceding chapters. We have seen how the sovereign subject conjured its wholeness, positivity, and reality by battling the ghost of the other within the self. In this chapter I explore the spectacular conjuring of the real in the translated articulations of international law in the nineteenth century and raise the question of how the text of international law negotiated the reality of its unfolding by insisting on a vision of the global that was yet to come. Henry Wheaton's *Elements of International Law* was a key text in that process. Published in 1836, the book circulated widely around the world and was reissued in numerous editions. In fact, it became one of the most popular texts of international law of the nineteenth century. During the author's lifetime, only one foreign-language edition was published, the 1846 French version, also known as the third edition, with Wheaton's final corrections and amplifications. After Wheaton's death, there appeared a succession of translations, including a Spanish translation published in Mexico in 1854, an Italian edition in 1860, and a classical Chinese translation under the title *Wanguo gongfa* in 1864 that appeared in print two years before Richard Henry Dana's authoritative English edition in 1866.

What do we make of this timely Chinese translation, an event that seems to have altered the course of history by participating in the power games between Japan and the West? Historians believe that the official adoption of Wheaton's text in China marked a turning point in the government's dealings with the outside world after the 1860 occupation, leading to the creation of the foreign affairs office (Zongli yamen) as well as the foreign legations in Beijing.[1] In fact, the classical Chinese translation introduced what seemed to be the first hypothetical equivalence between "sovereign right" and the neologism *zhuquan*. The existence of these and other hypothetical equivalents in the *Wanguo gongfa* assumes the double function of both securing the mutual intelligibility of philosophical and political discourses of two vastly different intellectual traditions and raising some fundamental issues concerning the logic of reciprocity in international law and its routes of circulation. Moreover, the colonial destinies of Taiwan and Korea were also prefigured in the intra-Asian circulation of this key text in Japan because the *Wanguo gongfa* traveled to Japan as early as 1865. The Japanese brought out a *kambun* transcription of the classical Chinese text within one year of the Chinese edition. This and a new Japanese edition of *Elements of International Law* in 1876 unleashed a wave of interpretations and discussions of *Bankoku kōhō* (international law) that had a directly impact on the rise of Japanese imperialism, Sino-Japanese relations, and Korean-Japanese relations in the years to come.[2]

Translatability: A Blind Spot in Colonial Historiography

The relationship between a translated text and its application in diplomatic practice is never a straightforward affair. Rather than assume a direct or indirect relationship between text and practice, it is important that we consider first how a translated text produces meaning—both intended and unintended—*between* the discursive contexts of the different languages involved, for neither international law nor its application can possibly exist independently of translingual interpretations in diplomatic negotiations. The situation is doubly interesting when we consider how meaning becomes possible between languages that had had limited contact before and must learn to speak in each other's political discourse for the first time. Such was the difficulty that the translators of *Elements of International Law* faced when they first embarked on the ambitious project and grappled with the minimal existence of equivalencies between English and classical Chinese in 1863.

The problem of translatability looms large in any such inquiry, but it would be futile to search for an ideal pairing of meanings when the matching of meanings is itself a historical phenomenon under investigation. The imagined *adequatio* of meanings as understood in traditional theories of translation is, therefore, a pseudo-problem as far as this study is concerned. Translatability means something entirely different here. It refers to the historical making of hypothetical equivalences between the semiotic horizons of different languages. These equivalences tend to be makeshift inventions in the beginning and become more or less fixed through repeated use or come to be supplanted by the preferred hypothetical equivalences of a later generation. As I have argued elsewhere, one does not translate between equivalents; rather, one creates tropes of equivalence in the middle zone of translation between the host and guest languages. This zone of hypothetical equivalence, which is occupied by neologistic imagination and the super-sign, becomes the very ground for change.[3]

Indeed, how are meanings initiated, legitimated, sabotaged, suspended, or put to practical use? I suppose that, even in cases where we need to consider how a text becomes involved in a larger diplomatic event, a question like this would suggest a more fruitful way of looking at the translation of international law in nineteenth-century China than a straightforward account of a text and its application in diplomatic practice. Both text and practice must be subjected to the same rigor of interrogation. What this means is that the Chinese translation of Euro-American international law in recent history is no longer a mere textual or diplomatic event. There is yet a third aspect which one might tentatively call an epistemological event. This intellectual event crosses paths with the textual and diplomatic to produce a triple event. It is in the sense of a triple event that the translation of international law assumes the importance that it does in the present discussion. I argue that the rise of so-called global (and later national) consciousness in East Asia falls precisely within the historical boundaries of this triple event.

Narratives of diplomatic history tell us repeatedly that the Manchus and Chinese were preoccupied with their ancient tributary protocols and consequently were unable to meet the challenge of modern European diplomatic usage. The resistance to British demands for trade and diplomatic representation is thus conveniently dismissed as a traditionalist's response to progress.[4] But the Chinese resistance to Western imperialism need not be "traditional" to be meaningful, any more than "unequal treaties" have been traditionally Chinese. Conceptually, such trivialization of resistance is oddly unhistorical because it means that the survival strategies that the Manchu court and the Qing official establishment had improvised and deployed on many occasions for the purpose of containing the encroachment of the Western powers in the Great Game were merely traditional responses to social change when they could have been understood as contemporary face-to-face and day-to-day struggles with global imperialist expansion, a novel phenomenon of the time indeed.[5]

The dismissal of the contemporary resistance as "traditional" lies at the heart of colonial historiography in the study of international relations and is by no means limited to Sino-Western relations. In my view, colonial historiography cannot be historical even by its own standards when it refuses to assign meaning to events or confront contemporary face-to-face and day-to-day struggles outside the predetermined conceptual models of tradition and modernity, backwardness and progress, particular and universal, and so on. That does not mean, however, that colonial historiography has not otherwise played a vital role. To British empire building and the imperial history of the West, colonial historiography has proved eminently useful and indispensable when it grants, for example, universal validity to Euro-American international law and to modern diplomatic practice while translating everything else into particular, hence less significant and culturally specific, moments. In this sense, the epistemological limits of the imperial history of the West are necessarily set and perpetuated by colonial historiography.

Marxist historiography, by contrast, always emphasizes the importance of organized resistance to colonialism and imperialism and has done much toward historicizing the violent moments of encounter between the colonizer and the colonized. Because of its primary attention to the mode of production in explaining historical change, however, Marxist theory has relied on a teleological view of history (the so-called progress from feudalism or the Asiatic mode of production to the capitalist mode of production) to characterize China's traumatic entrance into the modern international community.[6] This view of history has not been conducive to a fundamental questioning of colonial historiography in the matter of universal history and international relations or to asking questions such as how international law became universalized, and in turn it compels a universalist reading of world history and international law itself. In addition, when it comes to conceptualizing the historical real, Marxist historians have tended to fall back on a set of historiographic approaches and assumptions about the value of the data and ways of analyzing primary source materials which differ very little from those used in colonial historiography.

For example, the problem of *evidence* becomes intellectually meaningful only insofar as it enters into an argument about something else, be it an argument about imperialism or about national sovereignty. When the troublesome question of "translation" happens to surface and interfere with the historian's handling of evidence, it is either disregarded or promptly relegated to secondary importance. This extraordinary naïveté in the construction of evidence often results in collusive readings of primary documents by taking them at face value—regardless of what foreign-language sources they represent, whether Chinese, English, Japanese, French, or some other—and therefore in misguided conclusions about diplomatic events, as if these could take place in a transparent mode of exchange.[7]

Article 50 of the Treaty of Tianjin stipulates that the English originals were to be used to determine the final meaning of official communications; but within the circuit of diplomatic exchange, the originals that *actually* circulated between the two governments were often the Chinese-language documents. They were read in English only by the British government. Serious methodological problems would thus arise if one were to draw conclusions about what was going on based primarily on English-language sources. During the 1834 Napier crisis, the viceroy Lu Kun dispatched some officials and interpreters to visit Lord Napier, but the latter refused to speak through the Chinese interpreters, citing their incompetent language skills. The *Chinese Repository* translated Lu Kun's tenth proclamation as follows: "Still apprehending that their words might not be truly delivered, I commanded them [Qing officials] to take with them linguists, and proceed thither. When the flowery [*hua*] and barbarians [*yi*] have oral intercourse, linguists interpret what is said. Throughout the empire it is in all cases thus. Yet neither would the said barbarian *eye* employ the linguists to interpret for him, so that the deputed officers could not say everything."[8] The early phases of the Anglo-Chinese conflict were particularly susceptible to this politics of translation when the British side repeatedly rejected the Chinese interpreters hired by the Qing officials. One consequence of this struggle was that, in the words of J. Y. Wong,

> although the British government acted on these English translations and English originals, the Chinese government acted on neither. The Chinese government knew only the Chinese originals of their own dispatches, and recognized only the Chinese translations of those prepared and presented to them by the British. Therefore, Western historians who have so far used only the English translations and English originals may have to reconsider

their conclusions based on evidence of the despatches written in a language *that was not the medium of communication* between the British and Chinese diplomats."[9]

Indeed, if translation seems central to our study, it is because international relations have themselves been shaped by the processes of hetero-cultural and hetero-linguistic interpretation.

The Translator as Diplomat: W. A. P. Martin

The extraordinary afterlife of Wheaton's 1836 book (in its multiple cross-textual editions) is indebted to the symptomatic circularity exemplified by the exigencies of hetero-linguistic meaning making that govern most instances of diplomatic exchange. Perhaps the situation has more to tell us about the historical making of universalism than about the universal applicability of Wheaton's book or international law. What the circumstances surrounding the Chinese translations of international law suggest for our understanding of an earlier global and globalizing moment is that the coming into being of a global universal may be plotted as a series of *translated and contested* moments. The translator, who literally and figuratively plays the "diplomat," is a central agent in the colonial and cultural encounters. Many of the individuals I discuss in this book—Thomas Wade, Karl Gützlaff, W. A. P. Martin, Ku Hung-ming (Chapter 5), Ma Jianzhong (Chapter 6), and others—made history precisely in this sense.

The image of the translator as "diplomat" is useful also in the sense that a translated text relates to the original in more ways than one. Negotiations go in multiple directions and produce changes in the original text as well. The various later editions of the "original" European and American international law texts grew in volume and reference matter over an extended period of time as the authors and editors incorporated additional tribunal cases and international resolutions into the original texts. It is not atypical for an editor to cite the existence of foreign-language versions to prove the universal value (not merely applicability) of Wheaton's book. What this suggests is that later and *revised* editions can be just as illuminating as the original work in registering the process whereby international law has been globalized and universalized in the past two hundred years.

I would emphasize that the *revised* editions of international law texts in the original language inhabit the same space of global production and circulation as the foreign-language counterparts and should, therefore, be brought to the foreground of historical studies. For that reason, it is important to keep a double focus in this study. On the one hand, the complex circumstances of the nineteenth-century Chinese engagements with international law must be carefully laid out and analyzed; on the other hand, these engagements need to be brought into a meaningful circulatory relationship with the contemporary reissuing of the revised editions of the texts in the original settings in Europe and America. The double focus both explains and can be explained by the global circulatory networks of translated knowledge in modern international relations, thus imbuing the whole problematic of universal and particular with a new significance.

The *Wanguo gongfa* (Figure 6) was published under the official auspices of Prince Gong and his newly established foreign affairs office, the Zongli yamen.[10] The translation stood at the head of several major translation projects initiated and brought to fruition by an American missionary, W. A. P. Martin. Martin (also known as Ding Weiliang) was onetime president of the Imperial College, appointed by Prince Gong.[11] Assisted by his Chinese colleagues, he was also responsible for translating and publishing T. D. Woolsey's *Introduction to the Study of International Law*, J. C. Bluntschli's *Das Moderne Völkerrecht der Civilisierten Staten als Rechtsbuch dargestellt*, rendered from Charles Lardy's French version of the same text, *Le Droit international codifié*, and W. E. Hall's *Treatise on International Law* (1903). Moreover, Martin is credited with the Chinese edition of several diplomatic guidebooks such as *Le Manuel des lois de la guerre*, compiled by the Institut de Droit International, as well as Karl Freiherr von Marten's *Guide diplomatique*.

It was no accident that Martin took on the triple role of translator, diplomat, and missionary, which he played conscientiously. Like the other Christian missionaries of his time, Martin attached a "higher" purpose to his secular translations, although he would probably have given an evangelical name to the epistemological aspect of the triple role in which he was engaged. Most likely he would have called it the Christian moral truth. Martin was an American Presbyterian missionary from Indiana who was appointed to China by the Foreign Mission Board. He and his wife sailed from Philadelphia on November 23, 1849, and reached Hong Kong on April 10, 1850.[12] Martin spent the first decade of his mission work in Ningbo, during which time he occasionally offered his diplomatic services to the United States government as an interpreter. Long before undertaking the official task of translating international law for the Manchu government, he had been employed

Figure 6. The title page of the Chinese translation of Henry Wheaton's *Elements of International Law* (1864). Courtesy of the East Asian Library of the University of California at Berkeley.

by the U.S. minister William B. Reed as an official interpreter for the American legation during the Tianjin Treaty negotiations in 1858. After the next minister, John E. Ward, took office, Martin was hired again and interpreted for Ward during the Taku military confrontations between the Allies and the Manchu government. These and the other diplomatic posts at the American legation were conducive to Martin's interest in international law after 1860. A few years later he was to find a meaningful connection between his mission work and his secular translations.

Protestant missionaries who went to China following in Robert Morrison's footsteps after 1807 were aware of the proselytizing strategies that the Jesuits had found practical in the seventeenth century.[13] As the mandarins were uninterested in the theological explanations of Christian truths, the missionaries decided to camouflage religious doctrine with secular knowledge which they thought was either desired by or already inculcated into the Chinese elite. Martin read extensively about the work of the Society of Jesus in China under the Ming dynasty and greatly admired the Jesuit priest Matteo Ricci, whose example drove him to embark on the translation of international law.[14] He liked to think of himself as a Protestant Ricci. As one of the prominent missionaries of the nineteenth century, Martin straddles the evangelical traditions of both the past and his own time. His work raises some new questions about the role of the missionaries in the secularizing and globalizing processes of the modern world.

In what seems to be the first mention of his translation, Martin wrote to his friend Walter Lowrie, a fellow Presbyterian missionary in Ningbo, in a letter dated October 1, 1863. "I was led to undertake it, without the suggestion of anyone," he says, "but providentially I doubt not, as a work which might bring this atheistic government to the recognition of God and his Eternal justice; and perhaps impart to them something of the Spirit of Christianity."[15] That sounds genuine enough, but is not the whole story. Even at this initial stage, Martin did not make the decision entirely by himself, as his biographer Ralph Covell seems inclined to believe.[16] In a memoir titled *A Cycle of Cathay,* published many years later, Martin gives more details about the circumstances surrounding his translation and the reason why he chose the Wheaton book when he had first thought of translating Emmerich de Vattel (1714–1767). When he returned to China in 1862 after a furlough of two years back in America with his wife and children, Martin wanted to move north and open a mission in Beijing. But owing to the death of a colleague, William Culbertson, who had the editorial supervision of the mission press in Shanghai, he was temporarily detained in that city. "I employed a portion of my time in translating Wheaton's *Elements of International Law,* a work that was to exert some influence on two empires as well as on the course of my own life," Martin writes in his memoir. "The want of such a book had early forced itself on my attention, and I was proposing to take Vattel for my text, when Mr. Ward recommended Wheaton as being more modern and equally authoritative."[17]

The timely intervention by John Ward is significant. Martin had served as Ward's official interpreter during the Taku crisis and witnessed the military confrontations between China and the Allies. Ward's opinion mattered to his former interpreter because it represented the official view of the U.S. government. Wheaton's *Elements of International Law* was endorsed for being "more modern [than Vattel] and equally authoritative," but there is yet another reason that is not quite spelled out; that is, the author of the book was an American lawyer and diplomat who made no pretense of concealing his partiality toward the national interest of the United States. As early as 1855, the Department of State had sent a copy of Wheaton's book to the American commissioner in China, but it never arrived. So William B. Reed, the American minister who first employed Martin as official interpreter, purchased another copy at official expense in 1857.[18]

In his preface to the *Wanguo gongfa,* however, Martin does not and cannot spell out the interesting circumstances discussed here, which he occasionally mentions elsewhere but usually does not mention at all. For example, in the preface he offers an explanation that effectively erases the official policy implications of his choice of text:

> For the choice of my author, I offer no apology. My mind at first inclined to Vattel; but on reflection, it appeared to me that the work of that excellent and lucid writer might as a practical guide be somewhat out of date; and that to introduce it to the Chinese would not be unlike teaching them the Ptolemaic system of the heavens. Mr. Wheaton's book, besides the advantage of bringing the science down to a very recent day, is generally recognized as a full and impartial digest, and as such has found its way into all the cabinets of Europe. In England especially, it is employed as a text-book for the examination of candidates for the diplomatic service.[19]

This immediately follows Martin's praise for Robert Hart, who, according to the translator, overcame his national prejudices by endorsing "an American version of an American text-book." This might well have raised some eyebrows, since Wheaton's book was an American interpretation of international law and called for the author's defense of that choice. Fourteen years later, when Martin issued a translation of Theodore Dwight Woolsey's *Introduction to the Study of International Law*, once again an American text, he found it necessary to defend himself from charges of "patriotic partiality."[20] His subsequent inclusion of Bluntschli, Hall, and others represented a corrective attempt to balance the patriotic partialities among the Western writers on international law. For example, when the Chinese translation of Hall's *Treatise on International Law* was presented to the public, Martin confessed that he had introduced this British authority on the subject to "complete the list" of major international law texts.[21] Whether the list was complete or not, the national identity of the original authors casts a dubious shadow over the self-proclaimed impartiality of international law and shows that "authorship" in a broad sense does matter where the control over universal representation becomes a point of contention among the Western powers.

But back to Vattel, whom Martin briefly contemplated translating before changing his mind as a result of Ward's intervention. Vattel's *Le Droit des gens,* or *The Law of Nations,* was not unknown to the Chinese at this time. As early as 1839, Imperial Commissioner Lin Zexu had asked the American medical missionary Peter Parker (1804–1888) to translate three paragraphs of Vattel's book during the opium-suppression campaign in Guangzhou. Lin's visit was recorded by Parker in *The Tenth Report of the Ophthalmic Hospital* in 1839 as follows: "Case No. 6565. Hernia. Lin Tsihseu, the imperial commissioner . . . His first applications, during the month of July, were not for medical relief, but for translation of some quotations from Vattel's *Law of Nations,* with which he had been furnished: these were sent through the senior hong-merchant; they related to war, and its accompanying hostile measures, as blockades, embargoes, etc.; they were written out with a Chinese pencil."[22] Parker's translation was later included in *juan* 83 of Wei Yuan's multivolume *Haiguo tuzhi* (An illustrated gazetteer of maritime countries), the 1852 edition, with Vattel's name transliterated as Hua Da Er and the book title rendered as *Geguo lüli* (Laws and regulations of all nations).[23] Immanuel Hsü calls Parker's translation a travesty of Vattel's perspicuity because Parker did not try to reproduce the original but simply paraphrased Vattel and added his own comments in a labored and nonliterary style.[24]

As Commissioner Lin had difficulty understanding Parker's translation, which seemed to border on the unintelligible, he sought the help of Yuan

Dehui, "who, in view of the impending trouble with the British, first called Lin's attention to the authoritative work of Vattel."[25] Lin compared Parker's and Yuan's renderings of Vattel and decided to follow the course of action discussed in them. One of the passages Lin had Parker translate reads: "Every state has, consequently, a right to prohibit the entrance of foreign merchandises, and the nations that are affected by such prohibitions have no right to complain of it, as if they had been refused an office of humanity. Their complaints would be ridiculous, since they would only be caused by a want of that gain, refused by a nation that would not suffer it to be made at its own expense."[26] Despite Parker's obscure rendering of the original text, Lin gleaned some understanding of what Vattel was saying and followed international law to the letter by proclaiming opium contraband and demanding its destruction in 1839. Lin's use of international law in these transactions was entirely strategic, for the passages he had had Parker and Yuan translate for him were strictly confined to the issues of how nations go to war and impose embargoes, blockades, and other hostile measures.

In other words, Lin treated international law not as the universal truth but as a mode of persuasion that would enable him to argue against the harmful effects of the opium trade in a language he thought the British could understand. This strategic use of international law bears some superficial resemblance to the argument Martin would advance twenty years later when he wrote that his secular translation was intended to bring an atheistic government to the recognition of God and impart to them something of the "Spirit of Christianity." Whereas Martin took a holistic view of his secular and religious work and would not commit himself to translating anything less than the whole text of international law, even if it was just a paraphrase of the complete text, Lin was unconcerned with the integrity of the text and its holistic values. When he proclaimed opium "contraband" in 1839 and demanded its confiscation and destruction, he was responding to Britain's willful dismissal of the so-called traditional Chinese mode of persuasion during the government's campaign against the opium traffic.[27]

When neither the Chinese nor the Western mode of persuasion could produce the desired results, Lin resorted to force. As he issued the order to destroy the shipments of opium in Guangzhou, he was fully convinced of the moral righteousness and legal justification of his action even by the yardstick of Western international law. The Opium War, however, followed an entirely different course of development that would hold international law up to ridicule. Britain declared war against China and sought compensation for the damages caused by Lin's confiscation and destruction of its commodity. The rest is a familiar story: Hong Kong became a British colony, and five treaty ports were opened up along the Chinese coast. As the indemnities were being paid, Lin also had to pay for the consequence of his actions; he was forced into exile for having provoked the hostilities with the British. The historical irony is that China's entry into the family of nations had logical connections with Britain's violation of international law during the Opium War. These connections should help us locate Martin's translation of international law in a longer historical perspective.

Henry Wheaton's *Elements of International Law*

Twenty years after the first Opium War, when the British minister Frederick Bruce—Lord Elgin's brother—was informed of Martin's translation of *Elements of International Law*, he made a remark to Martin that once again spells out the interconnectedness of the West's violation of international law and China's simultaneous entry into the family of nations. "The work would do good," Bruce said, "by showing the Chinese that the nations of the West have *taoli* [principles] by which they are guided, and that force is not their only law."[28] Bruce was admitting that the Western nations went about conquering the rest of the world with weaponry in one hand and the law ("principles") in the other. Brute military force borrows the moral and legal authority of international law to justify seizing the world as an *œuvre civilitrice*. The act of justification in turn translates global killing and looting into a noble cause.

Bruce's endorsement of Martin's project suggests a need for belated justification for the British and other Western powers' violation of international law in the Opium War, the Arrow War, and other wars against China. The word "belated" is crucial here because it describes the circumstantial (that is, not exactly intended) meaning of Martin's work. After the various "unequal treaties" had been extorted from the Qing government and ratified at gunpoint, they were now in need of being monitored and implemented faithfully by the Zongli yamen and the imperial court according to the requirements of international law.[29] In that sense, the translation was both belated and timely.

In spring 1863, when the Manchu court was having diplomatic difficulties with France, Wen Xiang, a leading minister of the Zongli yamen, asked the U.S. minister in Beijing, Anson Burlingame, to recommend an authoritative work on international law which would be recognized by all Western nations. Like John Ward, Burlingame mentioned Wheaton's *Elements of International Law* and promised to have portions of the book translated. He wrote to Consul George Seward in Shanghai and was informed that by coincidence Martin was already doing the work.[30] Burlingame gave Martin encouragement and assured Martin of his aid in bringing the work before the mandarins. In June of the same year, Martin took passage for the North.[31] Further momentum was given to the arrangement when Chong Hou, Prince Gong's minister, who had been briefed on the translation by Martin at Tianjin in July 1863, offered to write to Wen Xiang to recommend this translation.[32]

On September 10, 1863, Burlingame formally introduced Martin to four members of the Zongli yamen with whom he had already become acquainted during the treaty negotiations in 1858.[33] Martin brought the unfinished translation to the meeting and showed it to the ministers. They were impressed. Wen Xiang mentioned a selection of important passages translated earlier for the Zongli yamen by Robert Hart when he was the chief assistant to Horatio N. Lay, the inspector-general of maritime customs. "Does it contain the 'twenty-four sections'?" Martin recalls Wen Xiang asking. "This will be our guide when we send envoys to foreign countries."[34] The "twenty-four sections" refers to Chapter 1 of Part 3 of *Elements of International Law,* in which the rights of legations are discussed.[35] In reply, Martin said that his translation was incomplete and asked the Zongli yamen to appoint a competent official to assist him in a final revision and to print it at public expense.[36] Subsequently, Prince Gong prepared a room for Martin near the Foreign Office and appointed a commission of four men—all of high literary competence, including one scholar working in the Hanlin Academy—to assist him in completing the translation.[37] In addition, Martin received five hundred taels to help cover the cost of printing and publication.[38] The work was done at the Yamen, and at the suggestion of Robert Hart, the newly appointed inspector-general, the book was printed for the use of the government.[39]

Martin dedicated the finished work to Burlingame, who, in Martin's words, "gloried in contributing something toward the introduction of international law into China."[40] Or as Anson Burlingame himself noted in his letter to the State Department on October 20, 1863, "This is the first time anything of the kind was ever done in China and I record the progress with patriotic pride."[41] The same may be said of Martin's own sense of achievement. But not everybody was as pleased. Several officials in the diplomatic establishment, Chinese as well as Europeans, questioned Martin's motivation. The French chargé d'affaires Count Michel Alexandr Klecskowski regarded Martin as a troublemaker and is said to have complained to Burlingame: "Who is this man who is going to give the Chinese an insight into our European international law? Kill him—choke him off; he'll make us endless trouble."[42] Likewise, Samuel Wells Williams expressed concern that the introduction of international law might stimulate China to reach the level of Western law and thus find legal grounds to abolish certain aspects of the "unequal treaties," such as extraterritoriality. In his letter to the State Department on November 23, 1865, Williams wrote:

> An attentive study of this work by the officials in both China and Japan will probably lead them to endeavor to apply its usages and principles to their intercourse with foreign countries. This will gradually lead them to see how greatly the principle of ex-territoriality contained in their treaties with those countries modifies the usages in force between western and European powers. How desirable it is that the latter should aim rather to elevate these eastern peoples to their own level than to urge this principle of ex-territoriality to the subversion of the native sway.[43]

It is interesting that Williams's concern was thwarted by those Chinese who suspected Martin of ulterior motives. They saw no disinterested benevolence in the work and surmised that Martin wanted to make a name for himself after the illustrious example of Matteo Ricci.[44] Only Prince Gong and Wen Xiang were enthusiastic supporters of Martin's work, as the Zongli yamen wanted to use the *Wanguo gongfa* as a practical manual for conducting diplomatic affairs with the Western powers. The book familiarized them with the protocols of the Western nations which had recently established legations in the capital after the crisis of 1860. The Zongli yamen desired to know what legal basis there was for the procedures that had been forced on China in the name of international law, such as unequal treaties, extraterritoriality, most-favored-nation treatment, tariff control, diplomatic representation, rights of war and peace, sovereignty, and so on.

A good number of Manchu and Chinese officials felt ambivalent or downright hostile toward Martin's translation. They were deeply suspicious and mistrusted the unspoken intention of his work "as Trojans did the gifts of the Greeks."[45] In response to such fears, Prince Gong memorialized the throne on August 30, 1864, arguing:

> He [Martin] says that this book should be read by all countries having treaty relations with others. In case of dispute it can be referred to. But since the

language is not fluent he asks us to help in his literary improvement, in order to have it printed. We, your ministers, guarding against such frequent
requests with books and possible attempts to make us follow them, have
told him that China has her own laws and institutions and that it would be
inconvenient to refer to foreign books. Martin, however, points out that although the Laws of the Qing Dynasty have been translated into foreign language, China never attempted to force western countries to practice them.
It cannot be that just because a foreign book has been translated into Chinese, China would be forced to practice it. Thus, he [Martin] pleaded repeatedly.

Prince Gong went on to emphasize the practical value of Western international law and added: "We your ministers, find that this book of foreign laws
does not entirely agree with our own laws, but there are in it occasional passages which are useful. For example, in connection with the case of Danish
ships captured by Prussia outside of Tientsin [Tianjin], we used some sentences from the book, without expressly saying so, as arguments. The Prussian minister acknowledged his mistake without saying a word. This seems a
good proof."[46] The incident involving Danish ships in Tianjin, which occurred as a result of Bismarck's war with Denmark, provided a useful occasion for the Zongli yamen to test the effectiveness of legal provisions as out-
lined in Wheaton's book. When the new Prussian minister to China, Guido
von Rehfues, arrived in China in a man-of-war in the spring of 1864, he
found three Danish merchant ships off the port of Taku. He immediately
seized them as war prizes. The Zongli yamen used the concept of maritime
territory and the treaty provisions between China and Prussia to protest the
extension of European quarrels to China. Prince Gong refused to grant an
interview to the new Prussian minister and condemned him for the way in
which he had begun his ministerial duties. The case was successfully re-
solved when von Rehfues relinquished the three Danish vessels, with a
compensation of $1,500.[47]

Prince Gong's memorial proved effective. Martin's manuscript received
imperial sanction and was allowed to be printed and distributed. But aside
from one or two isolated cases of effective uses of international law whereby
China was able to assert its sovereignty, how does the memorial articulate
the cultural implications of the ministers' endorsement of Martin's translation? It is interesting to note that Prince Gong appealed to a vague notion of
reciprocity at the suggestion of Martin himself. According to Martin, China

had never attempted to force Western countries to practice its laws any more than the West had intended to force its own laws on China. He does not, however, spell out the grounds of such imagined reciprocity. As we know, the earlier translation of the *Daqing lüli* (Collected statutes of the great Qing dynasty) by George Staunton following Macartney's mission had occurred under conditions in which there was absolutely no question of China's forcing the West to adopt its own laws. The Englishman had undertaken the task in order to provide his own government with useful information about China.

By the mid-nineteenth century, when Martin undertook to translate international law, however, the Western powers had already forced many of their demands and treaties on the Manchu government in the name of international law. So the alleged grounds of reciprocity did not exist between the *Daqing lüli* and the *Wanguo gongfa* to support Martin's argument of cultural relativism. Rather, as I argue in the next section, Martin's universalist agenda lies elsewhere. The fact that he pursued the translation at all may suggest a bona fide assumption of reciprocity and commensurability between English and Chinese. But reciprocity and commensurability are in every sense a *product* of deictic encounters between the two languages and not the other way around. This conception of reciprocity and commensurability opens up a hermeneutic space in which the significance of Martin's translation can be fruitfully grasped.

Insofar as Klecskowski's insistence on "our European international law" affirmed the brute instrumentality of that law, the French diplomat seems to have flatly denied universal status to the law. Likewise, Martin's cultural relativism, even if it was just a pretense, suggests a very much circumscribed sense of how far international law could go in making universal claims outside the West. If international law was thus circumscribed and contested by the Manchu, Chinese, and Westerners, none of whom knew for sure whose interest the book would best serve, how do we go about identifying and analyzing a historical process that seemed to gesture toward granting universal recognition to international law in the years to come? This is the question I try to answer in the next section.

Legislating the Universal

The opening pages of *Wanguo gongfa* greeted its targeted audience, the Manchu-Chinese officials, with a loud and clear message about the place of

China on the new "scientific" map of the world (Figure 7). This map represents the two hemispheres printed back to back with brief geographic narratives set in the margins and with names of the continents and oceans given in Chinese transliteration. The cartographic representation, which was not uncommon at the time, seeks to introduce a new order of universal knowledge and global consciousness to the Chinese elite so that this ancient civilization might be persuaded to join the family of nations.

But the spread of universal knowledge also meant overcoming the resistance of local languages at the textual level. Resistance was particularly strong in the mid-nineteenth century, when the hypothetical equivalence between English and Chinese had not yet been set in place and when there was a great deal of latitude as to what a word in one language might be taken to mean in the other. When Martin's manuscript was first presented to Prince Gong, the latter complained: "Examining this book, I found it generally deals with alliances, laws of war, and other things. Particularly it has laws on the outbreak of war and the check and balance between states. Its words and sentences are confused and disorderly; we cannot clearly understand it unless it is explained in person."[48] Prince Gong's reaction was at best ambivalent. He saw the usefulness of the book but thought it poorly written. Although his criticism was directed at the level of words and sentences, it should not be taken as merely a commentary on literary style; rather it was a reaction to the relative absence of evidence for the hypothetical equivalence between English and Chinese.

Martin's translations often employed neologisms at the expense of intelligibility. Some of the vocabulary seemed obscure at that time but has since grown self-evident. This is because the neologisms have been gradually assimilated into the language as modern Chinese itself underwent massive changes through increased exposure to translations of European texts over the past century. This process suggests that translatability and intelligibility emerged during the first encounter between the languages, but the significance of this tended to escape the immediate historical context only to achieve some level of clarity later in the language of future generations. It is one of those historical happenings that cannot be tied down to its immediate sociological origins or explained by naïve recourse to contemporary events and individual biographies.

One of the key concepts to emerge in the political discourse of modern China can be traced back to the neologisms invented by Martin and the Chinese translators of *Elements of International Law*. The concept I have in mind is *quanli*, or "right," which, like *zhuquan* (sovereignty) and many other nine-teenth-century coinages, no longer strikes us as strange or un-Chinese be-cause it has been naturalized in the history of Chinese (and Japanese) po-litical discourse and through repeated usage over nearly a century and a half. The situation was perceived differently, however, by those who lived in the mid-nineteenth century. This was duly documented by the translators themselves fourteen years after the fact, as they continued to feel a need to defend their "unwieldy" coinage. In a headnote to the 1878 translation of

EASTERN HEMISPHERE

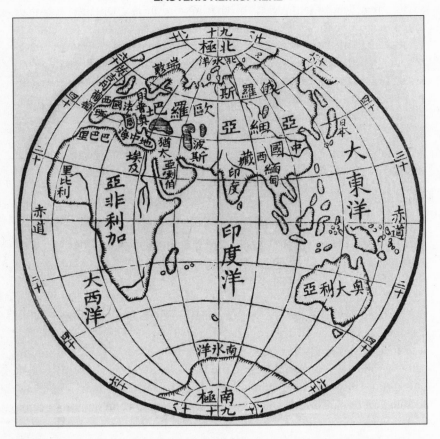

Figure 7. The world map printed in the first Chinese edition of *Elements of International Law* (1864). Courtesy of the East Asian Library of the University of California at Berkeley.

Woolsey's *Introduction to the Study of International Law,* known in Chinese as *Gongfa bianlan,* Martin and his Chinese collaborators describe how they had coined the neologism *quanli* to render the meaning of "right." Their tone was clearly apologetic:

International law is a separate field of knowledge and requires special terminology. There were times when we could not find a proper Chinese term to render the original expression, so our choice of words would seem less

WESTERN HEMISPHERE

than satisfactory. Take the character *quan,* for example. In this book the word means not merely the kind of power one has over others, but something every ordinary person is entitled to. Occasionally, we would add the word *li* [to form a compound], as, for example, in the expression *quanli,* meaning the born "rights" of the plebeian, etc. At first encounter, these words and expressions may seem odd and unwieldy, but after seeing them repeatedly, you will come to realize that the translators have really made the best of necessity.[49]

This approach is hardly surprising; in the beginning of the nineteenth century, when Robert Morrison first arrived in China, English and Chinese were still behaving like strangers to each other. Although translations of the Bible and religious tracts made some headway in the first half of the century, makeshift translations were the norm rather than the exception in political and philosophical discourse. It took a great deal of work for the first generation of translators, missionaries and their Chinese colleagues, to turn Chinese and English into each other's interlocutor for the sake of tolerable comprehensibility.

The Chinese noun *quan* thus underwent a drastic process of transvaluation through translation to be purged of some of its earlier connotations, often associated with *quanshi* (power, domination); likewise, the compound *quanli* took the word *li* (interest, profit) out of its usual commercial context to be rendered pliable enough to suggest something new in the context of international law. This positive meaning emerged entirely through the encounter with the English concept and introduced a very new concept into Chinese political discourse. Years later, the concept would take on a life of its own and garner increased respect, especially after the Sino-Japanese War, when liberal political thinkers of the West began to be translated and popularized through the writings of Yan Fu (1853–1921) and through Japanese translations.[50]

Still, it seems extraordinary that Martin should have been persuaded by his Chinese colleagues to pick two (negatively) loaded characters to coin an equivalent compound for the English word "right." We must keep in mind that the word *quanli* possessed more ambiguity in the 1860s than it does now precisely because the super-sign was unfamiliar and hovered somewhere between Chinese and English. The "excess" meanings are entirely capable of reflecting back on the original English word "right" and glossing its meaning according to a different mode of association.

This translingual process may be glimpsed with some hindsight from an interesting glossary of Chinese-English bilingual terminology of international law called "Terms and Phrases," prepared by Martin and his Chinese colleagues many years after the *Wanguo gongfa* had been issued. The text appeared as an appendix to their new translation of the *Gongfa xinbian* (W. E. Hall's *Treatise on International Law*) published in 1903. In this authoritative glossary, the word *quanli* is rendered back into English as "rights and privileges," which I take to be a significant reverse translation of the Chinese neologism. The convoluted translation has the effect of reinterpreting the English word "right" with a bit of a translingual echo of the original Chinese character *quan*, suggesting "power," "privilege," and "domination."[51] The original English word "right," once put into circulation, cannot but be reinterpreted in light of other possible meanings and other possible associations that always come with the translation. What is at issue is not a matter of right or wrong, good or bad translations. The situation, I believe, is much more interesting and subtle than a simple judgment of that kind, because it poses the question of whether a translation could actually jeopardize the transparency and self-evidence of the original concept.

Let us belabor this point a little further. We know that (human) rights discourse in Europe has figured prominently in the language of international relations and has been an inseparable part of international law since the Enlightenment. Kant, for example, called for a cosmopolitan order that would abolish war on the basis of moral practical reason, leading to the legal form of a federation of nations. In "Toward Perpetual Peace," Kant envisions a process by which all the peoples of the earth would enter into a universal community to the extent that "a violation of rights in one part of the world is felt everywhere; This means that the idea of cosmopolitan law is no longer a fantastical or overly exaggerated idea. It is a necessary complement to civil and international law, transforming it into public law of humanity."[52] Jürgen Habermas marvels at Kant's miraculous foresight in his interpretation of this eighteenth-century dream of a family of nations and makes a point of glossing the notion of "public law of humanity" to mean *Menschenrechte*, or human rights.[53] This meaning of "rights," as Habermas so acutely understands, places the discourse of "human rights" squarely in the historical unfolding of international law itself.

As I have argued throughout this chapter, the historical unfolding of international law cannot but include as well the multiple translations and circulations of international law in other languages. Habermas takes on a subject that has been glossed over and over again in Latin, English, French, Italian, Chinese, Japanese, and many other languages over the past two centuries. Unaware of this always already translated history, he is doing to Kant's notion of "perpetual peace" what the *Wanguo gongfa* did to Henry Wheaton's *Elements of International Law,* what Wheaton had done to August Wilhelm Heffter, the author of *Das Europäische Völkerrecht der Gegenwart,* in the nineteenth century, and so on ad infinitum. Namely, they all gloss the meaning of "law," "rights," and "human rights" with a specific historical and linguistic understanding of the stakes involved in each situated interpretation.[54]

Henry Wheaton, writing in English, refers the concept of "human rights" to the work of the famous German public law theorist Heffter, who introduced the idea to distinguish between two distinct branches of *Völkerrecht.* These are (1) human rights in general, and those private relations which sovereign states recognize in respect to individuals not subject to their authority; and (2) the direct relations existing among those states themselves. Wheaton cites Heffter to elaborate on these distinctions:

> In the modern world, this latter branch has exclusively received the denomination of law of nations, *Völkerrecht, Droit des Gens, Jus Gentium.* It may more properly be called external public law, to distinguish it from the internal public law of a particular state. The first part of the ancient *jus gentium* has become confounded with the municipal law of each particular nation, without at the same time losing its original and essential character. This part of the science concerns, exclusively, certain rights of men in general, and those private relations which are considered as being under the protection of nations. It has been usually treated of under the denomination of *private international law.*[55]

This provides a useful historical perspective for our understanding of human rights discourse in the past and the present. The concept of "human rights" is specifically glossed by Heffter as one branch of *Völkerrecht,* a commonly used German translation of the Latin *jus gentium* like the French equivalent *droit de gens* or the English "law of nations" of the time. "Human rights" has everything to do with an earlier understanding of private international law, and public law for that matter, and this is what I mean by the always already translated reading of *Menschenrecht* in Habermas's writing about Kant. In the Martin translation of this passage, "human rights" is rendered as *shiren ziran zhi quan,* or literally "human natural rights."[56] The clumsy phrase was the very first occurrence of the Chinese rendering of "human rights," which was later replaced by the neologism *ren quan*. Not surprisingly, this concept was first introduced as a term of international law and still plays a vital role in world politics today. As Jacques Derrida observes brilliantly in *Specters of Marx*, the discourse of human rights "will remain inadequate, sometimes hypocritical, and in any case formalistic and inconsistent with itself as long as the law of the market, the 'foreign debt,' the inequality of techno-scientific, military, and economic development maintain an effective inequality as monstrous as that which prevails today, to a greater extent than ever in the history of humanity."[57]

Indeed, as I have suggested, the noun *quan* commands a broad spectrum of meanings associated with "power," "privilege," and "domination" in the Chinese usage, much as the word *li* brings to mind "interest," "profit," and "calculation." Lurking behind the renderings of "rights" and "human rights," these banished meanings can always come back to haunt the supersign and unwittingly open up the word "right" or "human rights" to its suppressed "other" meanings such as "privilege" and "entitlement." The subtext of "excess" signification thus glosses the self-evident meaning of the English word "right" with something more than it ostensibly says. This is not to say that the translators were incapable of comprehending the true meaning of "right." On the contrary, the "excess" signification seems to heed the historical message of "rights" discourse in the *practice* of international law only too well, because it registers the fact that the idea had been brought into China by the nineteenth-century representatives of European international law who had asserted their "trade rights" and the "right" to invade, plunder, and attack the country. Their language of "rights" cannot but convey a loud message of threat, violence, and military aggression to the Qing government at the negotiation table and to the Chinese population at large.

Negotiating Commensurability

Martin and his Chinese colleagues undertook to create a preliminary level of *hypothetical equivalence* or makeshift translatability between the political discourses of two very different languages and intellectual traditions. They did so by negotiating a ground of commensurability between Chinese and Christian values, and that ground was where the intended readers were expected to get at the meaning of their translation. In the English preface to the *Wanguo gongfa,* Martin argues for cultural commensurability on the basis of natural law, explaining why the Chinese are capable of comprehending the principles of Western international law:

> To its fundamental principle, the Chinese mind is prepared to yield a ready assent. In their state ritual as well as their canonical books, they acknowledge a supreme arbiter of human destiny, to whom kings and princes are responsible for their exercise of delegated power; and in theory, no people are more ready to admit that His law is inscribed on the human heart. The relations of nations, considered as moral persons, and their reciprocal obligations as deduced from this maxim, they are thoroughly able to comprehend.[58]

Martin's understanding of commensurability between Chinese and Christian cultures carries strong connotations of natural law insofar as natural law is understood as the other side of the argument about positive law in Western theological and legal discourse. In the main text, Martin and his Chinese collaborators render "natural law" as *xingfa* and occasionally as *ziran zhi fa.* In contrast, "positive law" is rendered as *gongfa* (the same compound used to render "law of nations" and "public international law") and occasionally *lüfa.*

This is significant because they are essentially calling on the key Neo-Confucian notions *xing* (glossed as "nature" or "natural") and *gong* (glossed as "positive" or "public") to create a philosophical ground of commensurability between two very different intellectual traditions. The move is strongly reminiscent of the strategies that seventeenth-century Jesuit missionaries used to introduce grounds for reconciliation between Confucianism and Christianity. Nevertheless, Martin and his collaborators did not stretch the idea of natural law to make the moral principles of international law sound like the Confucian ethics of reciprocity. After all, they were trying to introduce new knowledge from the West. If one reads *xing* or *gong* with Neo-Confucian philosophy in the back of one's mind, as Martin's readers would have done, the Chinese word certainly changes the meaning of "natural law"; but it is also true that the meanings of the Chinese words are simultaneously transformed by a process of translation that engages them in a deictic manner with the English concept of "natural law" or "positive law" in *Elements of International Law.*

What happens is that neither Chinese nor English can lay exclusive claim to the meanings of the translated terms because those meanings reside somewhere in between, like the super-sign *yi/barbarian*, discussed in Chapter 2. Just as the neologistic use of *xingfa* and *gongfa* plucks the Neo-Confucian concepts *xing* and *gong* out of their familiar philosophical context, so do the same translations take the idea of "natural law" and "public law" out of Wheaton's local engagement with Western legal discourse to create a broader and more "universal" basis for the global claims of international law than either tradition could have accomplished on its own.

The seventeenth-century Dutch jurist Hugo Grotius (1583–1645) in his work *De jure belli ac pacis* (On the rights of war and peace) solidified the foundation for international law after Francisco de Vitoria made a crucial distinction between *jus naturale* and *jus gentium. Jus naturale* was based on the theological argument about the rules of human conduct prescribed by God to his rational creatures and revealed by the light of reason or the sacred scriptures. *Jus gentium* referred to the general or universal consent of nations to observe certain rules of conduct in their reciprocal relations. Those who endorsed natural law viewed nations and states as enlarged versions of moral beings (conveniently adapted by Martin to Confucian ethics) and thus treated international law as an extension of civil law.

In *Persian Letters*, for example, Montesquieu has one of his fictional characters, Usbek, express this view in a letter to another character named Rhedi: "You would almost think, Rhedi, that there were two entirely different types of justice: one, regulating the affairs of private individuals, rules civil law; the other, regulating the differences that arise between nations, tyrannizes over international law; as if international law itself were not a kind of civil law, not indeed the law of a particular country, but of the world."[59] If Montesquieu puts the words of contemporary theory in the mouth of his fictional characters in *Persian Letters*, he gives a straightforward treatment of international law on the basis of natural law in *The Spirit of the Laws*, joining the ranks of such prominent international law theorists as Leibniz (1646–1716) and Vattel.

"Natural law" and the "law of nations" represented two very different but related conceptualizations of the nature of human society and its ability to manage disputes and conflicts among nations. Grotius himself had defined the "law of nations" in terms of a binding consent among all nations to observe certain rules of conduct in their reciprocal relations, and this term was used interchangeably with "international law" by most European theorists. After Jeremy Bentham raised the objection that the "law of nations" sounded more like internal jurisprudence than laws governing states, "international law" gradually replaced "law of nations" as an umbrella term for the science. But the running theological debate over natural law and the law of nations continued unabated in the language of natural law and positive law (which partly explains why Martin and his collaborators considered the Chinese compound *gongfa* appropriate for rendering all three terms— "the law of nations," "positive law," and "public international law"—in the *Wanguo gongfa*). As the Western powers sought to increase their colonial possessions and conquer the world in the nineteenth century, the emphasis shifted more and more toward universal consent, treaties, balance of power, and international tribunals and away from commonly shared humanity or moral vision among the different nations. Thus, Henry W. Hallek, a well-known authority of international law of the nineteenth century, was able to give a supremely realistic picture. He simply called international law "the rules of conduct regulating the intercourse of states."[60]

Even so, the endorsement of a "natural law" position need not contradict such "realism" in the early nineteenth century. As early as 1838, Karl Gützlaff had argued that, when the British demanded the right to free intercourse among all nations, they were not merely seeking material benefits for Britain but were acting in accord with "international law." Chinese resistance to international trade amounted to defiance of God, who had decreed the brotherhood of all men. Those who denied their people access to truth, and to the manufactures of the West, were infringing on an inherent *human right*.[61]

The crude analogy Gützlaff draws between natural law and international trade puts a definitive historical spin on nineteenth-century discussions of natural law. Gützlaff's logic would sound familiar to his nineteenth-century European readers and not nearly as crude as it may seem now. He effectively exploited that logic, with all its moral and religious implications, to help justify the global expansion of the British Empire. As a missionary, diplomat, and translator, Gützlaff wrote and published these views at the height of Chinese resistance to the British opium traffic and only one year before Lin Zexu's famous visit to Parker's clinic to request a translation of Vattel. Lin, as I discussed earlier, had only those portions of Vattel translated which touched on the "positive" implications of Vattel's discussion of war: hostile measures, blockades, embargoes, and so on. The interesting contrast between Gützlaff's endorsement of "natural law" and Lin Zexu's pragmatic use of international law in the 1839 opium dispute is significant and reflective of the changing situation of universalism in the nineteenth century.

Henry Wheaton, an early-nineteenth-century theorist of international law, tried to tackle natural law in a critical review of earlier European international law theorists in *Elements of International Law* by adopting a more positive conceptualization of relations between modern states. Wheaton does not completely abandon natural law but attempts to imbue his notion of positive law with a vague notion of natural law. Thus, he defines international law among civilized nations (China is classified as semi-civilized) as "consisting of those rules of conduct which reason deduces, as consonant to justice, from the nature of the society existing among independent nations; with such definition and modifications as may be established by general consent."[62] Note that the emphasis here is not on the moral being or reciprocal obligation so much as on a positive understanding of "general consent."

Wheaton (with Friedrich Karl von Savigny) calls international law an imperfect positive law. It is imperfect "both on account of the indeterminateness of its precepts, and because it lacks that solid basis on which rests the positive law of every particular nation, the political power of the State and a judicial authority competent to enforce the law." He adds, however, that "the progress of civilization, founded on Christianity, has gradually conducted us to observe a law analogous to this in our intercourse with all the nations of the globe, whatever may be their religious faith, and without reciprocity on their part."[63] Wheaton's argument about progress and universalism is very different from the universalist argument about international law that takes cultural commensurability as its point of departure.

Where Wheaton simply equates Christianity with the universal and refuses to consider reciprocity, Martin, his translator, talks about reciprocal obligations and the communicability of universal laws across cultures and languages. Is Martin trying to manipulate Wheaton's complex arguments to suit his own evangelical purpose? It seems to me that the situation is more complex than the translator's intentional use or misuse of the original text. For no translator can afford to do away with a certain assumption of linguistic or cultural commensurability between the languages he or she works with. Doing so would be tantamount to contradicting the act of translation itself.

Instead, Martin and his collaborators made a choice that most translators would have made under the circumstance; namely, they turned the *desired commensurability* between English and Chinese into a *condition of universality*. Neo-Confucian overtones notwithstanding, *xingfa* and *gongfa* were taken to signify "natural law" and "positive law," and so on. These neologistic compounds borrowed the universalism of Neo-Confucian thinking to promote the translatability of international law. In that sense, the interjection of a notion of reciprocity and commensurability into Wheaton's argument by Martin and his collaborators did not help the cause of Confucianism so much as it did the universalist agenda of international law.

Both Wheaton and Martin lived at a time when the meaning of the universal in international affairs was undergoing fundamental changes. In his own way, Wheaton was very much in tune with the global events that were shaping the modern world with unprecedented speed and that in turn informed his own explication of the principles of both earlier and contemporary theories of international law. His reference to the "progress of civilization" as "founded on Christianity" is by no means a mere statement of the author's religious faith but rather a reworking of natural law principles in response to the unfolding of world events. Thus, we are told that

> the more recent intercourse between the Christian nations in Europe and America and the Mohammedan and Pagan nations of Asia and Africa indicates a disposition, on the part of the latter, to renounce their peculiar international usages and adopt those of Christendom. The rights of legation have been recognized by, and reciprocally extended to, Turkey, Persia, Egypt, and the States of Barbary. The independence and integrity of the Ottoman Empire have been long regarded as forming essential elements in the European balance of power, and, as such, have recently become the objects of conventional stipulations between the Christian States of Europe and that Empire, which may be considered as bringing it within the pale of the public law of the former.
>
> The same remark may be applied to the recent diplomatic transactions between the Chinese Empire and the Christian nations of Europe and America, in which the former has been compelled to abandon its inveterate anti-commercial and anti-social principles, and to acknowledge the independence and equality of other nations in the mutual intercourse of war and peace.[64]

Interestingly, the reference to China did not exist in the first edition of the *Elements of International Law* published in 1836, but found its way into the later revised and more definitive post-1846 edition that appeared after the Opium War (Martin used one of these editions in *Wanguo gongfa*). In this passage quoted from the revised edition, Wheaton is clearly referring to the Opium War and the subsequent treaties and settlements that opened China to foreign trade, marking the beginning of what some have called the period of semi-colonial history in China. This is intensely ironic in view of what had happened to Lin Zexu and his tragic use of Vattel. Whatever might have brought the Chinese government to the negotiation table following the Opium War, this fact is used by Wheaton as *evidence* of the triumph of the principles of Christian nations' "particular" international law.

The evidence that Wheaton enlists to prove the universal principles of European international law can be read as doing something else in the context of the later editions of his book. What I mean is that the so-called evidence has been the outcome of what it is supposed to prove. The post-1836 editions of Wheaton's book underwent constant revisions in order to accommodate the vast number of new treaties and tribunal cases that arose as the Western nations, armed with gunboats and international law, went out and conquered more territories and more societies. Like foreign-language translations, these cumulative editions of international law in the original language represent repeated *deictic engagements* (one speaking to the other) with other cultures and civilizations, though by no means on equal terms.

Of the various editions of Wheaton's book that appeared after the author's death, the 1866 edition by Richard Henry Dana was considered the authoritative and definitive text by diplomats and scholars of international law. Wheaton's main text and Dana's copious notes were frequently used to provide the legal grounds for many of the important decisions concerning international disputes in the nineteenth century. For our purpose, this edition contains an interesting reference to Martin's 1864 Chinese translation. In an appended note Dana calls our attention to the significance of Martin's work:

> The most remarkable proof of the advance of Western civilization in the East, is the adoption of this work of Mr. Wheaton, by the Chinese government, as a text-book for its officials, in International Law, and its translation into that language, in 1864, under imperial auspices. The translation was made by the Rev. W. A. P. Martin, D. D., an American missionary, assisted by a commission of Chinese scholars appointed by Prince Kung, Minister of Foreign Affairs, at the suggestion of Mr. Burlingame, the United States Minister, to whom the translation is dedicated. Already this work has been quoted and relied upon by the Chinese Government, in its diplomatic correspondence with ministers of Western Powers resident at Peking.[65]

Dana's footnote captures a uniquely circular situation. Namely, Wheaton's original text calls for translation because it possesses an inherent universal value, but it takes the existence of foreign translations to buttress its claim to universality. To aspire to the condition of the universal, the text demands universal recognition and demands to be translated.

When Wheaton's *Elements of International Law* was reissued in a centennial edition and published as part of the Classics of International Law series in 1936, the general editor, George Grafton Wilson, reiterated the point about the circulation of this American legal text abroad in the past century. Wilson mentions, for example, that *Elements of International Law* was translated into Chinese by W. A. P. Martin in 1864. "The edition published in China was quickly exhausted," writes Wilson, "The work had been received with much favour in Japan. An edition of this Chinese text reprinted and adapted for Japanese use was published in Kyoto, Japan, in 1865, and other editions were issued in the East."[66] The importance of the occasion is further noted in the official testimony of the U.S. minister Anson Burlingame, who wrote to the State Department in 1865: "The Chinese did not address me in writing, but called in person to mark their sense of the importance of the completion of the work, and when the Prince and suite kindly sat for their photographs, Fung Sun, who had superintended the translation, desired to be taken with a copy of Wheaton in his hand."[67] Wilson cites the existence of the foreign-language editions as the proof of the universal value of Wheaton's text, but, as I have argued throughout the chapter, it requires the circulation of that book to prove the self-same universality.

Decades after the completion of the *Wangguo gongfa*, Martin, reaching the age of seventy, was preparing a new Chinese translation of W. E. Hall's *Treatise on International Law* for publication. In 1901 he approached the Empress Dowager's most trusted minister and diplomat, Li Hongzhang, and asked him to write a foreword to the new book. Li had been a key player and a controversial figure in the negotiation of the unequal treaties and the handling of many of the crises that troubled the Qing reign during the Taiping Rebellion, the Sino-Japanese War, and the Yihe Tuan Uprising. In his foreword to Martin's new translation, Li summarizes China's experience of international law in the nineteenth century as follows:

Dr. W. A. P. Martin has been in China for fifty years. He has successively filled the Chair of President in the Tung Wên College and in the Imperial University. Last summer he was exposed to the dangers of the [Yihe Tuan] siege; but on escaping with his life, he at once resumed and completed the task of translating this book. In his preface, he states the causes of the siege but without a trace of resentment. In a note to the first chapter he speaks of the war with France; and adds that China's protection of French residents contrasted favorably with the way in which the French had treated the Germans. Proof that China had previously [to 1900] observed International Law in the spirit of peace. If this book could be hung up at our city gates and obeyed by nations beyond the seas there would be an end of strife, and all the world would be at peace; a state of things which I agree with Dr. Martin in hoping for.[68]

Li's tongue-in-cheek endorsement of Martin's labor articulates the negative condition of international law in theory and practice. Perhaps the desire for an alternative universal could only assert itself through the negativity of this situation: Can international law rise above its brute realism and submit to a higher ideal of peace, not a condition of war?

CHAPTER 5

The Secret of Her Greatness

> In discussing the right of woman, we are to consider, first, what belongs to her as an individual, in a world of her own, the arbiter of her own destiny, an imaginary Robinson Crusoe with her woman Friday on a solitary island. Her rights under such circumstances are to use all her faculties for her own safety and happiness.
>
> —Elizabeth Cady Stanton, "The Solitude of the Self"

The four long decades of the overlapping reigns of Queen Victoria (r. 1837–1901) and the Empress Dowager Cixi (effective reign behind the screen 1862–1908) saw a number of new social developments and historical events sweeping across the world. These raise some fundamental issues about gender and empire that no serious study of the nineteenth century can afford to downplay.[1] The political and symbolic rivalries between the Qing and British empires, each headed by a powerful female sovereign, suggest that the mode of sovereign thinking in the nineteenth century, religious and secular, could be further investigated with a view to exploring the role of gender—historically understood—in bringing about new ideas concerning political identity, loyalty, gift exchange, femininity, diplomacy, and international politics.

In England, Victorian middle-class culture was predominantly figured through the gender and self-representation of Queen Victoria as a devoted wife and mother; at the same time, Britain's imperial ambition led a large number of women—wives of missionaries and colonial officials as well as female missionaries themselves—to roam the world with unprecedented freedom. The traveling women took on different identities in colonial and foreign settings and were able to do things that had been off-limits to them at home, where the ideal of female passivity and domesticity prevailed. These colonial travels were almost evenly matched at this time by another striking

current of floating diasporic communities outside the metropole and between the metropole and the colonies, for the diasporic male elite of Chinese or hybrid descent and their families, for example, were also on the
move, shuttling back and forth between the Chinese communities abroad
and mainland China, as they triangulated love and politics among Britain,
Southeast Asia (under British colonial rule), Hawaii, California, and the
Qing. Although the familiar image of a *hua qiao* (overseas Chinese) in modern history is that of a man like Sun Yat-sen—the celebrated father of Chinese nationalism—who agitated for the revolution and practiced what Benedict Anderson has termed "long-distance nationalism," there were others,
Chinese as well as Western, who looked upon the Empress Dowager Cixi as
the mother of the nation and Queen Victoria's symbolic counterpart, if not
her rival.[2] In the eyes of some nineteenth-century *hua qiao*, the Empress
Dowager embodied an alternative political destiny and a sovereign ideal that
had come under the threat of the Western powers but had not otherwise
succumbed to colonial rule.

Keeping a dual focus in this chapter on the missionary women and the
Chinese diaspora, I explore how colonial travel produced new modes of sovereign thinking among the gendered subjects in the interstices between imperial powers and their colonies. In the first part of the chapter I analyze an
instance of gift exchange in 1894 involving the presentation of a Bible to
the Empress Dowager by a group of missionary women from Britain and
the United States. Although that exchange overtly took place between the
missionary women and the female sovereign of the Qing in China, it metonymically evokes the prior moments of colonial exchange between Queen
Victoria and the Africans of the British colonies. T. Jones Barker's painting of
Queen Victoria's presentation of the Bible to an unnamed African chief in
the early 1860s, for example, initiated a whole chain of metonymical exchanges reproducing the event at other times and in other places.[3]

Broadly connected to this global circuit of exchange, as we see in the second part of the chapter, is the story of Ku Hungming (1857–1928), a Malaysian of Chinese descent who received a European humanistic education in
Scotland and then turned around to shed his colonial identity as a subject of
the British Crown in order to adopt China as his mother country. Ku's life
story challenges the positivist theories of nationalism, citizenship, diaspora,
and decolonization that seem to dominate our thinking on these subjects,
for this man chose not to fight British colonialism in the country of his birth
but preferred to work it out elsewhere, chiefly by submitting himself to the

Empress Dowager Cixi. Ku's ambivalence toward Queen Victoria and his decision to adopt China as his "mother country" give us an opportunity to examine the problem of gender and empire from the angle of what I call the sovereignty complex of colonized men and their struggle to overcome the trauma of colonial abjection.

Imperial Gift Exchange: The Presentation New Testament

Shortly before the reign of the Empress Dowager Cixi, Christian missionaries had obtained extensive treaty privileges that enabled them to take aggressive steps to reach the inland population. Article 6 of the Chinese version of the French-Chinese Treaty of Tianjin stipulated that French missionaries be granted the freedom to rent and purchase land in the provinces of China and construct buildings there at will.[4] The same privileges were extended to the Protestant missionaries by the most-favored-nation clause. Paul Cohen has demonstrated that when the imperial government proceeded to implement the unequal treaties at the local level, it met with strong opposition from both the local gentry and ordinary people. Hundreds of mission incidents (jiao'an)—riots and massacres—erupted, culminating in widespread panic and rebellion.[5] For several decades, the Empress Dowager maintained a delicate, but not always successful, balance between her government's treaty obligations and her sympathies for the anti-Christian movements, until further crises forced her to change her position.

It was under those circumstances that the court's preparations for an elaborate celebration of the Empress Dowager's sixtieth birthday (November 7, 1894) got under way.[6] Protestant evangelists and women missionaries in China took the occasion seriously and spent many months raising money to create something special for Cixi. Their birthday present was an elegant classical Chinese edition of the Bible known as the Presentation New Testament. This legendary book was in royal quarto size (10" x 13" x 2"), printed on the finest paper available at the time and in the largest size of movable metallic type. The border around each page was set in gold, and the book was bound in solid silver boards engraved with the title "Complete New Testament" in large characters of solid gold. In the center of the cover was a gold plate bearing the inscription "Classic of Salvation for the World." The book was laid in a solid silver casket, similar in design to the covers of the book, and lined with plush, and the casket rested in a plush-covered box inside a teakwood case.[7] The Reverend John Hykes of the American Bible Society noted with special pride: "This is the first time, so far as we know, that a copy of the New Testament in the Chinese language has been received into the Imperial Palace. It is certainly the first time that such a gift has been made to one high in authority within the precincts of the Forbidden City. Followed as it is by the prayers of more than ten thousand Christian women, we have every reason to believe that it will be read, and to hope that it will make some 'wise unto salvation.'"[8]

The idea of presenting the Empress Dowager with a copy of the Bible had been proposed by the missionary women at the Shanghai Missionary Conference in February 1894. The board of the Missionary Association promptly endorsed their proposal and appointed a seven-member committee to put it into effect. The committee consisted of the Reverend William Muirhead of the London Mission; Archdeacon E. H. Thomson of the Protestant Episcopal Mission; Reverend Hykes, agent of the American Bible Society; Samuel Dyer, agent of the British and Foreign Bible Society, the Reverend John Stevenson, deputy director of the China Inland Mission; Mary M. Fitch of the American Presbyterian Mission; and Mary Richard of the Scotch United Presbyterian Mission.[9] The Missionary Association launched a fund-raising campaign to mobilize women converts across the nation and raised about $1,200 from these efforts. According to Hykes's correspondence with the American Bible Society, the Chinese women converts, representing a total of twenty-nine different missionary organizations, subscribed to the gift.[10] The work on the New Testament began in April at the Presbyterian Mission Press in Shanghai under the supervision of representatives of the American Bible Society and of the British and Foreign Bible Society.[11]

The committee decided to present only the New Testament, rather than the whole Bible, and selected the "Delegates" version (1847–1854) as the most scholarly of all the classical Chinese versions of the New Testament.[12] On March 26, Mary Fitch drafted the first of numerous circulars the committee would send out to all the Protestant mission stations around the country calling for nationwide donations. The full text of the announcement reads:

A proposition was lately made by the Ningpo missionaries that the Protestant Christian women in China, both native and foreign, should present the Empress-Dowager on her approaching 60th birthday with a copy of the Sacred Scriptures in a suitable casket. They referred the whole matter to a Committee in Shanghai. This Committee unanimously approved of this proposition and have decided to present Her Majesty with a handsomely-bound copy of the New Testament.

Would you kindly make arrangements at your station and out-stations for receiving contributions from the native Christian women, who can also be empowered to collect from their friends? Please forward these sums at your earlier convenience, along with any contributions from their foreign sisters—missionary or non-missionary—to Mrs. Timothy Richard, No. 1 Quinsan Road, Shanghai.

As the time is limited and the style of casket depends on the amount of funds to hand, we beg that this matter may receive your immediate attention. Also kindly mention that number of Christian women, native and foreign, who have contributed the funds which you send.

In order that the gift may be as widely representative as possible we sincerely hope that *all* the native Christian women will be afforded an opportunity of contributing funds, however small, and thus show their loyalty, and also their admiration of the Empress-Dowager's able and beneficent Regency.[13]

Headed by the missionary women, the campaign targeted women converts and received generous contributions from them. The Bible was intended as a gift from the Christian women of China as a token of their loyalty to their female sovereign, although the book itself had to be presented through the usual diplomatic protocols of male institutions. On October 29, 1894, the Presentation New Testament was transported by a group of male missionaries from Shanghai to Tianjin, where it was picked up by the Reverend H. H. Lowry and brought to Beijing. The presentation itself did not take place until the morning of the twelfth, when the British minister Sir Nicholas Roderick O'Conor and the U.S. minister Charles Denby took the book to the ministers of the Zongli yamen, and from there it was forwarded on to the Empress Dowager.

The Christian missionaries had long regarded Buddhism, Confucianism, and indigenous religious practices as obstacles to progress and evangelicalism. William Muirhead, who authored the general introduction to the Presentation New Testament, does not hesitate to dismiss the Confucian classics and Buddhist scriptures: "In these twenty-seven portions of the sacred classic," he writes, "the doctrine of Christ is definitely announced for the benefit of his disciples that they may truly believe in it, diligently observe it, and faithfully follow its teachings. Outside of this book, is there any other that can be compared with it? None. There are many treatises on morality and such like, which are the mere product of the human mind, but this book is the production of God's Holy Spirit, inspiring the minds of wise and holy men who spoke accordingly."[14] Since the time of Robert Morrison, the first Protestant missionary to enter China in 1807, the missionaries had worked hard to destroy the pagan idols and to replace the indigenous classics with the holy Scriptures, but they ran into the formidable task of having to produce first-rate translations of the Bible in classical Chinese comparable to the elegance and sophistication of the Buddhist scriptures or the authoritative status of the Confucian classics. The Presentation New Testament was a proud statement of what the missionaries had accomplished to date.[15]

Accompanying the Presentation New Testament was a congratulatory memorial drafted by Mary Richard, the missionary Timothy Richard's wife, in the name of the women converts of the Protestant Christian Church in China. The memorial begins: "Your Imperial Majesty, having, by Divine appointment, undertaken the government of China in times of unparalleled internal and external trouble, and having by your great energy and wisdom restored profound peace throughout the whole empire, and established friendly relations with all nations, has called forth the admiration not only of your own subjects but those of other nations far and wide as well." Richard goes on to emphasize that the Christian subjects owed their protection to the laws established by the Empress Dowager and wanted to express their gratitude to her on this happy occasion. She continues: "Therefore, we, a few thousand Protestant Christian women throughout the various provinces of your Empire, though mostly poor, cannot let the auspicious occasion of your Imperial Majesty's 60th birthday pass without testifying our loyalty and admiration. We do so by presenting your Majesty with the New Testament, which is the principal Classic of our Holy Religion, namely the religion of Jesus Christ, which is the only religion that practically aims at the salvation of the whole world from sin and suffering." She concludes by explaining why the New Testament has been chosen as a particularly suitable birthday present for the sovereign head of a nation: "We hear it is a custom in the West to present Empresses, Queens, and Princesses with a copy of this book on happy occasions in their lives." The memorial is signed collectively "Your Majesty's most faithful subjects, the women of the Protestant Christian Church in China."[16] There is no existing testimony or any independent source to substantiate how the Chinese converts themselves regarded Cixi, if they thought about her at all, apart from what is represented here by Richard. We know, however, that the actual gift exchange took place not between the Chinese converts and the Empress Dowager but between the

Protestant missionary representatives of the women converts and the Qing sovereign or, more accurately, between the United States and Britain on the one hand and the Qing empire on the other. This raises the interesting issue of what kinds of gift exchange the presentation of the Bible set in motion among the ministers, missionary organizations, and the Empress Dowager herself. Did the Bible figure religion, sovereignty, feminine bonding, a reminder of the Treaty of Tianjin, or something else?

Queen Victoria and the Empress Dowager

The gift of the Bible in the nineteenth century was not as innocuous as Mary Richard suggested in her memorial. Although the initiation of gift exchange between the Chinese Christian converts and the Empress Dowager is said to mimic a Western custom, Richard does not specify which Western custom authorizes the giving of the New Testament to the ruler of a non-Western society by Christians from the West. The Protestant monarch Queen Victoria had given Bibles in situations that suggested vastly different meanings from that of the intra-European custom of presenting "Empresses, Queens, and Princesses with a copy of this book on happy occasions in their lives." In fact, one well-known portrait depicting this subject was completed by T. Jones Barker in the early 1860s (1863?). Called *The Secret of England's Greatness*, it is known also as *Queen Victoria Presenting a Bible to an African Chief* (Figure 8). The iconicity of empire lies in the contrasting composition of the dignified pose of the richly attired queen, who is seen holding out the Bible, and a kneeling African whose bent back and outstretched arms and the eager look in his eye all mark him as the racial and cultural inferior. Behind them, under a canopy, stand British officials and the prince consort (who had just died), lending an atmosphere of royal augustness to the occasion. Adrienne Munich has shown that Barker's painting went on tour after its completion through the provinces to the far reaches of the British Isles, including an 1864 exhibit in Belfast. The tour effectively demonstrated to those Britons who had never seen an African or an Indian where the empire stood in relation to the heathens and how "the barbarian undergoes domestication under biblical and monarchical authority."[17]

It was during one of these tours that W. T. Stead, the author of the Golden Jubilee memoir of Queen Victoria, *Her Majesty the Queen: Studies of the Sovereign and the Reign* (1887), first viewed the painting and was deeply impressed by its powerful enunciation of British sovereignty. Stead describes what the

Figure 8. Thomas Jones Barker, *The Secret of England's Greatness,* oil on canvas (ca. 1863). Courtesy of the National Portrait Gallery, London.

painting had meant to him as a strictly reared Protestant of a Methodist cast when he beheld it as a young boy in a gallery in Newcastle upon Tyne and how common people such as rude coal heavers "used to tell over and over again how the Queen had given the Book of Books, the Book of our Salvation, to the heathen from afar who sought to know what it was that made England Great."[18] Recalling his experience, Stead writes: "The swarthy African, highly idealised, I fear, flashing with gems and picturesque in his native garb, bows low before a youthful queen—resplendent in white satin, if I remember right—who advancing to meet with the inquiring savage, presents him with a copy of the Bible as the answer to his question. 'What is the secret of England's Greatness?'"[19] The African prince's alleged question, which gives the painting its famous title, is answered by the queen's act of presenting the Bible to the "savage." This catechism of imperial ideology frames the rhetoric of the visual spectacle in a powerful pedagogical address and allows the narrativity of the painting to enunciate the allegorical nature of the Bible to the viewer. As one of the first-generation viewers of Barker's painting and a witness to others' reactions to it, Stead offers some remarkable insights into the way the painting touched a chord in the British viewing public during the 1860s, generating metonymical reverberations throughout England, Ireland, and the provinces and colonies that the painting and its future replicas passed through. Particularly revealing is Stead's confession that "I began to gain a glimmering of the uses of the Sovereign as Grand Certificator for the truth and excellence of that which is best worth holding by in church and state."[20]

Although the actual event depicted in Barker's painting has not been documented, Munich suggests that it probably did occur in some form. She mentions an unidentified print at the National Portrait Gallery that shows a youthful Victoria "handing a Bible to a dark-skinned man wearing a feather headdress and earrings while uniformed white-skinned dignitaries attend the ceremony."[21] A documented scene that bears a striking resemblance to Barker's painting occurred much later in Windsor Castle. In *Life with Queen Victoria*, Marie Mallet recalled that on November 20, 1896:

> The Queen received the [African] Chiefs in the White Drawing Room seated on a Throne like a chair, and the Chiefs advanced through a long line of Life Guards with drawn swords . . . The Queen welcomed them and they presented their gifts, three Karosses or rugs of leopard skins of doubtful smell but intrinsic worth. Then the Queen spoke saying she was glad to have them under her rule and protection and felt very strongly the necessity of preventing strong drink from entering their lands. This was duly interpreted and they replied each in turn. Then the Queen gave them a New Testament in their tongue with her own hands and huge framed photos, and an Indian Shawl was handed to each of them by Lord Clarendon, and with grateful grunts they retired backwards leaving us much impressed by their quiet dignity and wonderful self possession. I could see they were immensely impressed but they tried not to show their feelings and succeeded admirably.[22]

The "quiet dignity" of the African chiefs can be appreciated only after they have submitted themselves to the queen's rule and protection. This scene reiterates the colonial iconicity of Barker's painting in all its essential detail, except that the African chiefs also gave the queen three leopard skin rugs, which signified primitive Africa. The three magical objects the queen conferred on the Africans in return are the symbols of religious authority, technology (photography), and colonial possession.[23] With regard to this last item, Queen Victoria had been in the habit of giving Indian shawls to foreign visitors since she was declared empress of India in 1876. Commenting on the Queen's new habit, Munich makes an apt observation: "If she had not personally visited the jewel in her crown, she imported India to England, not simply through such relatively light things as shawls but through animals and people as well. India captured Victoria's imagination, but one can only infer what Victoria's India might have meant to her or what she imagined it was like. For her, as for many subjects, India gave Britain a symbol of empire."[24] The fact that the queen presented the New Testament to the Africans in conjunction with these other symbols of empire calls for a reading of the Bible itself as a symbol of empire.

In light of this, the presentation of the New Testament to the Empress Dowager by the missionary women in 1894 was hardly an isolated event. Mary Richard and her husband had been sent to the China field by the Scotch United Presbyterian Mission. Had she viewed the popular Barker painting in her youth when it was touring Scotland? Was she self-consciously emulating Queen Victoria when she proposed the idea of presenting the New Testament in Shanghai? If it were possible to document these aspects of Richard's life, we would be in a better position to detect the actual points of connection among these acts of imperial gift exchange. Short of establishing the biographical linkage, can the circumstances of the events themselves reflect on one another to help illuminate the colonial condition of nineteenth-century gift exchange between the empires? For instance, what can the Barker painting tell us about the missionary women's presentation of the Bible to the Empress Dowager? Conversely, what does the 1894 presentation of the Bible in Beijing tell us about Queen Victoria's gifts to the Africans in 1896? If an event is capable of replicating some prior event (or iconic event), regardless of authorial intentions, and joining a chain of endless replicas and metonymical exchanges, then what is the semiotic process that drives the itinerancy and simulacra of colonial iconicity in the act of imperial gift exchange?

As I suggested at the outset, the Empress Dowager had remained disastrously ambivalent between her government's obligations to honor the treaties and her personal sympathy for the anti-Christian movements. This was a time when the missionaries and the colporteurs hired by the Bible societies to distribute the Scriptures inland were prone to getting into trouble. When a plague was raging in the South in the fall of 1894, two of the colporteurs from the American Bible Society found themselves being accused of carrying poisonous drugs in their "scent bags" and causing the epidemic. By the account of Reverend Hykes, these men were attacked by an infuriated crowd and severely beaten. The literal interpretation of the figure of the Scriptures as poisonous drugs inadvertently corroborates the potency of the Book as implied by the Barker painting, except that this time the magical symbol turns deadly and causes widespread paranoia.

Under the very nose of the Empress Dowager, colporteurs and preachers were increasingly subjected to random harassment by angry locals. As the agent of the American Bible Society, Reverend Hykes wrote on September 20, 1894:

> Some of my men have had trouble in the city [Peking]. A few days ago they were preaching and selling books at the corner of the street in which is one of the Presbyterian Mission Stations when a crowd of men headed by a well dressed Manchu kicked over the piles of books which were on show and asked them why they had not left the city "along with the devils whom they followed." They reviled them and their ancestors and declared their intention to stop the sale of the "devil's books." I think the people are getting stirred up on account of the war, and, of course do not distinguish between Japanese and other foreigners.[25]

With indirect reference to the frequent and widespread outbreaks of anti-Christian violence, Mary Richard took care to include the following language in her congratulatory memorial, stating that "among the many just laws which your Majesty has established not the least is that which commands the same protection to your Christian subjects as to those of all other religions."[26] The New Testament was intended to be a timely reminder to the sovereign of the Qing that treaty privileges had been conceded to the missionaries and native Christians and that it was her responsibility to stop the violence and bloodshed in the provinces.

The Presentation New Testament could not have served as a symbol of sovereign exchange without the patriarchal institutions of diplomacy despite the missionaries' emphasis on the strictly gendered economy of women converts paying homage to their female sovereign. In fact, the Presentation Committee in Shanghai was dominated by men; so was the work of translating and publishing the Delegates version of the Bible. Patrick Hanan has shown that the Delegates' version of the New Testament had been the work of Walter Henry Medhurst and three Chinese assistants, including the eminent scholar Wang Tao (1828–1897).[27] On this particular occasion, Wang Tao was once again invited to translate the general introduction to the Presentation New Testament drafted by William Muirhead of the London Mission. These men were then joined by the British and American ministers and their counterpart at the Zongli yamen, who took charge of forwarding the present to the Empress Dowager.

Was Mary Richard's representation of the women converts in her memorial a rhetorical conjuration? In what sense does gender matter to sovereign thinking and to the missionary women's attempt to cast Cixi as one of their own? Was the idea of universal womanhood real and substantial enough to bind the Empress Dowager to the missionaries on the one hand and the lower-class female converts on the other? How did the Empress Dowager respond to the missionaries' appeal to her womanhood? A fascinating detail from Princess Der Ling's account of Cixi's daily life suggests that Cixi did not always think of herself as a woman and insisted that the Guangxu emperor address her as "father," not as "mother." Der Ling wrote: "Her Majesty always wanted to be a man and compelled everyone to address her as if she were actually one. This was only one of her many peculiarities."[28] Cixi's own favorite colloquial soubriquet, Lao Fo Ye (literally, "Old Buddha"), was clearly gendered in this manner, the character *ye* being an honorific suffix for males.[29] This seems to suggest that Cixi comprehended sovereign power in gendered terms and thought of herself as the patriarchal sovereign vested with the power to emasculate the emperor chosen by herself.[30] The events that followed the delivery of the birthday present appear to support this reading. On the occasion of the presentation, Cixi hijacked the missionary women's game of gender and played it on her own terms.

The Empress Dowager received the Bible with a display of graciousness and requested to know the names of the subscribers to the gift. The names of Mrs. Richard (Mrs. Li) and Mrs. Fitch (Mrs. Fei), as well as a list of twenty women from several missions, were submitted. The list, however, apparently did not include the names of the native converts who had contributed. Shortly after the names had been submitted, the American minister, Colonel Denby, received a memo indicating that the Zongli yamen had received from the Empress Dowager imperial gifts to confer on the women whose names were on the subscriber list. In an official letter from the princes and ministers of the Zongli yamen to the British minister, dated December 15, 1894, the presents are described as follows:

On the 27th of November, the yamen received from Mr. Cheshire, Chinese Secretary to the United States Legation, a letter enclosing a list of names of

nü jiaoshi [female missionaries] who had offered their congratulations on
the occasion, and on submitting it for Imperial inspection, they were hon-
ored with the receipt of a Degree from H. M. the Express Dowager, con-
ferring a roll of Nanking silk, a roll of large satin, a box of needle work,
and two cases of handkerchiefs each upon Mesdames Li [Richard] and Fei
[Fitch] who had taken the leading part in the movement, and a case of
handkerchiefs and a roll of Huchow crape, each, upon Madame Ma and 19
other ladies who had assisted in the undertaking. The foregoing articles
were sent to the American Legation on the 8th instant with a request that
they might be distributed amongst the female converts whose names were
given on the list. On the 10th December the Yamen received a note in reply
from the American Legation intimating that the articles had been duly
handed over, as requested, and it becomes the duty of the Princes and Ministers to write this note for the information of H. E. the British Minister.[31]

Interestingly, the copy of the original letter that was kept on file together
with the English translation at the American Bible Society refers to the
women on the subscriber list as *nü jiaoshi* (women missionaries), whereas
the English version reads "female converts" (the standard Mandarin equivalent of which would be *nü jiaomin*). The discrepancy is not without its illocutionary suggestiveness, because the sleight of hand in the English translation
represents the meaning of the gift exchange to the home board in the United
States differently from how the original letter was interpreted by the diplomatic communities in China. To the home board, the missionaries implicitly
claimed that the Christian "women converts" were communicating directly
with the Empress Dowager. The "practical and unmistakable evidence of her
appreciation of the gift" demonstrated that the work of the missionaries in
China had finally gained sovereign recognition and therefore was worthy
of continued support from the home board.[32] From the viewpoint of the
princes and ministers of the Zongli yamen, however, the actual gift exchange took place not between the women converts and the Empress Dowager but between the Protestant *nü jiaoshi* and the Qing sovereign and, by
extension, between the United States and Britain on the one hand and the
Qing empire on the other.

   We have seen that Cixi's appreciation of the Presentation Bible came in
the form of Nanking silk, a roll of "large satin," a box of needlework, two
cases of handkerchiefs, and so on, objects that the *North China Herald* described at the time as "a set of embroidery requisites."[33] These "feminine

trifles" seem to suggest that the Empress Dowager was corroborating a code of female exchange practiced universally among queens, princesses, and wives of foreign ministers in a diplomatic world still very much dominated by aristocratic social etiquette. But the ground of femininity as imagined by the missionary women when they initiated the exchange cannot be sought in the universal aristocratic code of feminine gift giving. There is something novel about the missionaries' carefully crafted communication with the female sovereign of their non-Western converts. The novelty can perhaps be best explained by the unprecedented hetero-cultural circulation of gender in the nineteenth century.

The Foreign Mission Exemplar

Protestant missionaries and their wives began to travel to Asia and other distant parts of the world to preach the Gospels in the early nineteenth century. Women's own organized mission did not take off until the second half of the century. In her research on the American women missionaries, Jane Hunter shows that fewer than a dozen single women had managed to affiliate themselves with relatives or with married couples to venture out in the mission field before the 1860s, including women such as Eliza Agnew and Fidelia Fiske, who had pioneered work in education and evangelism in Ceylon and Persia in the 1840s. Because gender taboos barred men from preaching to the female half of the population in some non-Western societies, the general mission boards believed that the role of missionary wives would be crucial to the success of their cause. Designated as assistant missionaries, the wives were expected to see to their special task, but it was not until the arrival of single women missionaries after the Civil War that a sustained program for women began to emerge and flourish. American women's experience with organized work during the Civil War had given them confidence that they could create their own boards to do collectively what individual women had struggled to do alone. The Woman's Board of Missions (1869), which was affiliated with the Congregational Church, was the first denominational board for women, followed in the same year by the Methodist Woman's Foreign Missionary Society and others. By 1900, forty-one American women's boards of varying size had come into existence, and women in the mission field had begun to outnumber the men.[34]

Inspired by the Second Great Awakening, the women missionaries made it their goal in China to save the native female population from idol worship and traditional forms of submission and patriarchal oppression. Scorning foot-binding, female illiteracy, and polygamy, the missionaries saw themselves as liberated individuals who represented the best values of Western civilization. Their own understanding of womanhood was limited, however, to the role of the enlightened mother and caring wife, for the evangelical upbringing of these women had led many of them to believe that women's God-ordained place was in the home. The extent to which they could imagine themselves as liberated individuals and gain their own freedom from patriarchal bondage depended on their physical removal from the network of patriarchal institutions at home. Colonial travel introduces a distancing factor, insofar as the Victorian ideals of womanhood and femininity are concerned.

The growing importance of the women's boards notwithstanding, white women remained shut out from philological work, and, in particular, from the exegesis and translation of the Bible, which had been the sole prerogative of learned men. In 1895, within a year of the presentation of the New Testament in Beijing, the leading American suffragist Elizabeth Cady Stanton published her controversial work *The Woman's Bible* in New York to protest the exclusion of women from theology and the interpretation of Scripture by the church establishment. One of the factors that prompted the writing of *The Woman's Bible* was that in 1870 the Church of England had established a Revising Committee to re-edit the 1611 King James version of the Bible. No woman was allowed to sit on the committee. Stanton protested that male theologians kept reproducing versions of the Scriptures that favored men and promoted the image of God as male.[35] This patriarchal theological tradition, in Stanton's view, was directly responsible for the oppression of women, robbed them of their dignity, and limited them to the supposedly divinely ordained sphere of domesticity.

Stanton argued that the Bible, which had given Western civilization its values and worldview, had contributed to the suppression of women by shaping their low self-image. Freedom for women, therefore, meant more than obtaining the vote, for women first had to be freed from the psychological oppression that had kept them enslaved for so long. To that end, she conceived *The Woman's Bible* in 1886 and tried to enlist the help of friends and associates, but it was not until the 1890s that the project obtained the support of other women and took off.

In her commentary in *The Woman's Bible* on Matthew 25:1–12, Stanton writes:

In their ignorance, women sacrifice themselves to educate the men of their households, and to make of themselves ladders by which their husbands, brothers and sons climb up into the kingdom of knowledge, while they themselves are shut out from all intellectual companionship, even with those they love best; such are indeed like the foolish virgins. They have not kept their own lamps trimmed and burning; they have no oil in their vessels, no resources in themselves; they bring no light to their households nor to the circle in which they move; and when the bridegroom cometh, when the philosopher, the scientist, the saint, the scholar, the great and the learned, all come together to celebrate the marriage feast of science and religion, the foolish virgins, though present, are practically shut out; for what know they of the grand themes which inspire each tongue and kindle every thought? Even the brothers and the sons whom they have educated, now rise to heights which they cannot reach, span distances which they cannot comprehend.[36]

Stanton turns the parable of the wise and foolish virgins into a lesson in the cultivation of courage and self-reliance for women. Her feminist reinterpretation of this and other passages from the Old and New Testaments was shocking and unacceptable to most of her contemporaries. In fact, the publication of the first volume of *The Woman's Bible* provoked a storm of controversy within the National American Woman Suffrage Association in 1896 that resulted "in a vote that amounted to censure."[37] The threat Stanton's work posed to the ecclesiastical establishment and the "respectable" women's suffrage movement may well reveal the limits of women's liberation at the turn of the century. But the one thing that bound together Stanton's "kingdom of knowledge" and the National Woman Suffrage Association's demands was precisely their insistence on sovereign rights as the basis of modern subjectivity.

In some of her earliest discussions of woman's inalienable rights, Stanton was already interpreting such rights as sovereign rights. For example, in 1869 she cast husband and wife in the figure of sovereign nations that come together to form a kind of interstate alliance through the institution of marriage:

Two nations each acknowledging the unlimited sovereignty of the other acting therefore perfectly in the capacity of equals may enter into entangling alliances which will destroy the independence and freedom of each as may bind each other by impolitic and oppressive treaties and even by conditions impossible of execution without ruin to each other, so may two individuals thoroughly ensnare each other with the [?] founded in particularly in [sic] their mutual differences and needs. I know parties, man and wife, who have worked hard and honestly almost for a lifetime and together in behalf of what has been known as women's rights . . . working in the equality of the sexes, neither of whom dares say their souls were their own, making each other mutually and equally the abject slaves, simply because each has classified and established the right of ownership over the other and because each had in ignorant good faith—conceded the right, had in a word abdicated their own individual sovereignty—sinking it in the cortex of marriage.[38]

Stanton does not spell out at what point the analogy should end so that the terms of national sovereignty might articulate the condition of marriage partners in a more grounded sense. Her use of the concept of national sovereignty seems to point away from itself and remains largely at the level of metaphoric substitution.

In her later works, Stanton did develop a notion of "self-sovereignty" that aimed to clarify the connections between individual rights and sovereign rights. In "The Solitude of the Self," a lecture originally delivered at a convention of the suffragist movement on January 18, 1892, Stanton proceeded to model her concept of woman's birthright to "self-sovereignty" on the male narrative of subjectivity and colonial encounter. She argues that "in discussing the right of woman, we are to consider, first, what belongs to her as an individual, in a world of her own, the arbiter of her own destiny, an imaginary Robinson Crusoe with her woman Friday on a solitary island. Her rights under such circumstances are to use all her faculties for her own safety and happiness."[39] The unabashed allusion to Defoe's fiction of desire suggests that the early feminist imagining of subjectivity and autonomy was very much indebted to the colonial notion of subjectivity. Who was Stanton's female Robinson Crusoe? And who might her woman Friday be? Were race and colonialism integral to the early feminist thinking on woman's right?[40] Is it mere coincidence that Stanton's casting of the female citizen in the figure of a female Robinson Crusoe who must claim her share of the savage Friday took place at a time when the number of women missionaries working at the outposts of civilization was about to outstrip the total number of males in the field?

Margaret Homans's analysis of John Ruskin's famous lecture "Of Queens'

Gardens" shows how extensively the British critic drew on Queen Victoria's monarchy to help construct the image of Victorian woman in the public sphere. Ruskin credited middle-class British women, in particular, with the "power to heal, to redeem, and to guard. Power of the scepter and shield; the power of the royal hand that heals in touching,—that binds the fiend, and looses the captive; the throne that is founded on the rock of Justice, and descended from only by steps of mercy. Will you not covet such power as this, and seek such throne as this, and be no more housewives, but queens?"[41] Ruskin's empowerment of women through the trope of monarchy sheds interesting light on Stanton's rhetoric of woman's rights, for the public realm represented more than a departure from domesticity. It also suggested the entry into and participation in empire which is borne out by Stanton's enthusiastic endorsement of global evangelism.[42] Stanton saw a fitting analogy between the state's legislation for the best interests of the nation and the Christian conversion of the world. In "Address to the New York State Legislature," she went so far as to say that if the state cannot wait for the criminal to ask for his prison term or for the insane, the idiot, the deaf and dumb to request their asylum, does "the Christian, in his love to all mankind, wait for the majority of the benighted heathen to ask him for the gospel? No; unasked and unwelcomed, he crosses the trackless ocean, rolls off the mountain of superstition that oppresses the human mind, proclaims the immortality of the soul, the dignity of manhood, the right of all to be free and happy."[43] The upshot of her argument is that if the majority of women remained ignorant of matters of government and had not demanded the right to vote, this constituted no legitimate ground for denying women their inalienable rights. The analogy with criminals, the insane, and the benighted heathen may have dangerous implications that subvert the author's own argument, but it is not a spurious analogy, especially with regard to the last group. In Stanton's view, the success of women missionaries abroad held out a glimmer of hope for the suffragists because their work prefigured what might yet be accomplished on the home front.[44] "Might we not find here new fields of effort?" asked Stanton. "The Christian work of devout women has been specially [?] in India and the missionary islands, might it not be equally effective in Harvard, Yale, and Columbia?"[45] In an effort to emulate the missionaries who had gone out to conquer the uncivilized, heathen world, Stanton and her co-editors conceived the ambitious multivolume *History of Woman's Suffrage* (1881–1922) as a project that would in turn "bear the glad gospel of woman's emancipation to all civilized nations."[46]

Murray Rubinstein's study of American Protestant missions in China reveals that the evangelical missionaries considered themselves at war from the very day of their arrival and applied military metaphors and a predominantly militant mindset to their mission work. On the Chinese front, the evangelicals saw their enemies as fourfold: first, the heathen multitude who practiced "exotic and barbaric rites"; second, the Chinese government which, before 1858 and the Treaties of Tianjin, prohibited the missionaries from propagating their religion freely; third, the Catholic Church and the various Catholic missionary societies, especially the Jesuits and Dominicans, which had converted thousands to their faith; and finally, a community of Western merchants in Canton who were openly contemptuous of the missionaries and their cause.[47] The Protestant evangelical thinkers advocated the forceful opening of China and were eager to see the Opium Wars come about. The theological justification for the use of force was that human action could play a part in the process of bringing closer the day of Christ's triumphant return. "Disinterested benevolence," as Rubinstein points out, "was the term used for the process of human action: the active cooperation of man in the working out of God's own plan for humankind. The Millennium was the goal. When the two concepts were placed together they formed the core of a theology of mission. Thus was born not only a revitalized Millennial sensibility but a rationale for missionary enterprise as well."[48] As I discussed in Chapter 2, the missionary Karl Gützlaff had appealed to his English readership in these terms in a work published seven years before the outbreak of the first Opium War: "In the merciful providence of our God and Saviour, it may be confidently hoped, that the doors to China will be thrown open. By whom this will be done, or in what ways, is of very little importance."[49] The example of colonial evangelism that animated Stanton's vision of self-sovereignty indicates that the genealogies of sovereign rights and women's rights were deeply involved in the cross-currents of imperial conquest and colonial travel in recent history.

When a male compatriot observed to Stanton that she ought to be thankful, for there was no country in the world where women enjoyed a higher status than American women, Stanton rebutted by asking: "Is my political position as high as that of Victoria, Queen of the mightiest nation on the globe? Are not nearly two millions of native-born American women, at this very hour, doomed to the foulest slavery that angels ever wept to witness?"[50] It may sound strange that Stanton puts herself on a par with Queen Victoria, but the analogy is not so incongruous as it first appears. This is be-

cause Queen Victoria's monarchy was itself embroiled at this time in the debate and agitation over electoral reform, which eventually culminated in the
passage of the Reform Bill of 1867. As Margaret Homans has shown, the
queen attempted to fashion her own image on a model of middle-class
womanhood (devoted wife and grieving widow) and played a potent but
ambivalent role in women's suffrage at the time.[51] Homans draws our attention to the equivocal meanings of the queen's "representation" of the people—between symbolic representation (favoring a strong monarchy and ar-
istocracy) and direct democratic representation—that were played out in the
context of electoral reform. The equivocal nature of Victoria's monarchy
thus gave rise to a tautology of political representation of the people
whereby the queen "rules because she represents them, and she represents
them because she is like them, although she is like them because they follow
her example, after the fashion of Hobbes's mutually creating subjects and
monarchs."[52] The implications of her gendered identity for the politics of
electoral reform were evident when the defenders of female suffrage argued
in Parliament that Britain was governed "by our Sovereign Lady the Queen"
to justify a political change to which the queen herself had objected.[53]
Charles Kingsley, a contemporary reviewer of the queen's book *Leaves from
the Journal of Our Life in the Highlands* (1865), wrote, "By telling her own
story, simply, earnestly, confidently, Her Majesty has appealed to women's
suffrage, of a most subtle and potent kind."[54]

Stanton's close contact with the British women suffragists led her to construct woman's self-sovereignty in specifically Victorian terms. She did not
literally put herself on a par with Queen Victoria, but she responded to the
terms of the British debate on electoral reform and woman suffrage in the
1860s in which the queen, though ostensibly withdrawn from public view
in mourning for the death of Prince Albert, had a significant role to play. If
the queen claimed to represent the people, and succeeded in doing so, the
women suffragists took the tautology of political representation seriously
and gave it a literal reading by insisting on the gendered identity of Queen
Victoria and by projecting their desires onto her sovereign body.

The desire for the female sovereign cannot but mirror back the queen's
own mirroring of the desired image of the people she represents. The circularity of this politics of representation constitutes the conceptual ground of
Stanton's reflections on North American women's self-sovereignty. But as
we have seen, Queen Victoria was not the only object of desire thus constructed. A similar sort of fascination for the Empress Dowager Cixi pre-

vailed among the women missionaries of Stanton's generation, to the extent that one could point to a symbiosis of sovereign thinking circulating from the suffragists' interest in Queen Victoria to the Protestant missionaries' interest in the Empress Dowager. In what ways can we argue, then, that the queen's giving the New Testament in their own tongue to the Africans and the missionary women's presentation of the Chinese New Testament to the Empress Dowager constituted a continuum of sovereign exchange in the nineteenth century?

Feminine Trifles in Sovereign Transactions

The answer to the question must be sought in colonial evangelism. Would Mary Richard have thought of the idea, much less been able to coordinate the effort, of presenting the Bible or other gifts to Queen Victoria on the occasion of her birthday? The likelihood seems remote. Foreign mission work provided one of the few opportunities for (white) women to travel and engage in certain activities abroad that they could not participate in at home, either because of their social standing or because of their gender. The flocking of women into the field in the 1880s and 1890s caused some male officials on general mission boards to remind women of their place. Jane Hunter writes that "although many general boards were successful in limiting the scope of women's missionary activity to ministration to women, the numerical imbalance threatened to define the nature and reputation of the mission force. By 1888, the opposition to women's work had changed from concern about its impropriety to a beleaguered effort by men of the general boards to retain minority control over a majority of female workers."[55] The Congregationalist board granted women neither the right to vote nor the right to speak at the station meetings, so women missionaries had no choice but to bring their crocheting and sit in as silent observers. By 1894, the American Board of Commissioners for Foreign Missions (ABCFM) decided that women in the field should have a voice, but only "in consideration of questions touching their own work," a policy that remained in effect until the 1920s.[56] That may explain why the women's proposal for a Presentation New Testament at the Shanghai Missionary Conference in 1894 not only gained the support of male missionaries but also led to the appointment of Mary Richard and Mary Fitch to the Presentation Committee. The exchange between the women and the Empress Dowager was considered legitimate because it belonged within the gendered realm of "their own work."

But no woman was ever appointed to committees that made decisions about Bible translations. What often happened at the mission stations was that women were expected to sacrifice themselves for their husbands and households, and were excluded from the "kingdom of knowledge" and "intellectual companionship," a situation not that different from Stanton's assessment of the domestic situation in *The Woman's Bible*. Among mission couples, for example, the superior skill of the wife in the acquisition of the foreign language, a precondition for professional success, often caused both husband and wife dismay. Martha Crawford, one of the missionary women discussed by Hunter in her book *The Gospel of Gentility*, agonized over her competitive edge over her husband, T. P. Crawford, who felt ashamed at his inadequacy in speaking Chinese. Martha Crawford writes in her diary: "The contrast would be observed always unfavorably to him. It would be bitter that he [be] in any respect inferior to his wife. It would be a continual trial. This was unexpected to me. I had prayed long and earnestly that God would make me willing to see my husband daily outstripping me . . . but I was not prepared for this."[57] Likewise, Pearl Buck wrote of her father, Andrew Sydenstricker, who found his wife's skill "a little trying . . . reared as he had been in the doctrine of male superiority." Sydenstricker, however, exerted himself in the mastery of written Chinese characters, rarely considered necessary for women to acquire, which turned him into a "real scholar" and reestablished his linguistic preeminence in this marriage.[58] The late-nineteenth-century mission boards instituted language examinations which young missionaries had to pass as a condition of their continuing service, but wives were sometimes exempt or required to meet substantially lower standards than their husbands. The lack of encouragement, in addition to their family responsibilities, led the women to relinquish any hope of mastering the written characters.[59] Stanton's analogy of sovereign nations competing with each other and making compromises within the marriage institution is literally borne out by the lives of these mission couples, who survived primarily on the basis of international treaties and concessions.

The conception of the Presentation New Testament in 1894 was a brilliant move by women such as Mary Richard and Mary Fitch, as it allowed them to imagine themselves against all odds as positive sovereign subjects. Relying on a discursive conjuration of universal womanhood in symbolic rapport with the sovereign body, they were able to rally a good number of women converts as well as men to their cause. As if mocking these efforts, the reciprocal presents from the Empress Dowager consisted mostly of "feminine trifles," carrying a differently coded message about what gender or sovereign exchange might mean under the circumstances. Cixi appeared to be playing her own game of femininity as she reciprocated the Book of Books with articles that were "not of much intrinsic worth" in themselves, as Reverend Hykes noted at the time.[60] The latter's observation on "value" brings to mind Marie Mallet's words when she characterized the three leopard skin rugs the African chiefs had presented to Queen Victoria as "of doubtful smell but intrinsic worth." In return, Victoria bestowed on the Africans a copy of the New Testament, huge framed photos, and an Indian shawl, as I suggested earlier, three important symbols of the British Empire—representing the Protestant spirit, the technology of mechanical reproduction, and the pride of colonial rule—and the key to the secret of Britain's greatness.

In contrast, the "feminine trifles" with which the Empress Dowager reciprocated the missionaries' birthday present were ordinary trade items that had long linked the economies of China and Europe until the rise of the opium economy. Queen Victoria's Indian shawl and the Empress Dowager's "feminine trifles" do, nevertheless, speak to each other in meaningful ways, for they participate in the same colonial circuit of desire and exchange. If the Indian shawl signifies Britain's imperial supremacy in the world, the "feminine trifles" respond to the threat of the same imperial presence in the Qing territories by shielding the giver from the incriminating need to demonstrate one way or the other where she stood on the question of the New Testament and Christianity. In other words, the "feminine trifles" gave the Empress Dowager the luxury of being noncommittal. As she continued to harbor sympathies for the rising anti-Christian sentiment across the country, these insignificant objects helped stage a diplomatic masquerade with a strategy of deferral that aimed to forestall accusations of treaty violation and further demands from the Western powers for indemnity payments.[61]

The court photographs taken after 1900 offer rare glimpses into Cixi's thoughts on gender and religion at the time. These highly theatrical images depict the Empress Dowager rising from a bed of lotus flowers dressed in the costume of Avalokiteśvara (Guanyin), with her first eunuch Li Lianying and her second eunuch Xue Yugui standing on either side, costumed as attendants of the bodhisattva (Figure 9). Der Ling, who was present when the photographs were taken, recalls that this picturesque idea came from the Empress Dowager herself. "Whenever I have been angry, or worried over anything,'" she quotes the Empress Dowager as saying, "by dressing up as the Goddess of Mercy it helps me to calm myself, and so play the part I represent. I can assure you that it does help me a great deal, as it makes me remember that I am looked upon as being all-merciful. By having a photograph taken of myself dressed in this costume, I shall be able to see myself

Figure 9. The Empress Dowager Cixi posing as Avalokiteśvara (Guanyin). Photograph by the court photographer Yu Ling (ca. 1903), reproduced from Liu Beisi and Xu Qixian, eds., *Gugong zhencang renwu zhaopian huicui* (Exquisite figure-pictures from the Palace Museum) (Beijing: Forbidden City Publishing House of the Palace Museum, 1994).

as I ought to be at all times."[62] Der Ling interprets Guanyin as the "Goddess of Mercy" for the English audience, inadvertently fixing the gender of Avalokiteśvara as female. Like all bodhisattvas in Mahāyāna Buddhism, however, Avalokiteśvara cannot be said to possess any gender characteristics in a doctrinal sense, although the early icon of the deity in India, Southeast Asia, Tibet, and China up to the Tang dynasty depicted a handsome and princely young man. After the Five Dynasties, Guanyin began to undergo a process of feminization in the course of the indigenization of Buddhist iconography and became identified as a female deity by the Ming.[63] Was Cixi attracted to the implied androgyny of the hetero-cultural Avalokiteśvara as Guanyin when she acted out the role in those photographs?[64]

It is well known that, as we have seen, the Empress Dowager compelled those around her to call her Lao Fo Ye (Old Buddha), and, as Der Ling puts it, she liked being treated as a (powerful) man. What do we make of her act of bestowing "feminine trifles" on the missionary women besides noting the effect of a diplomatic masquerade? Was she responding positively to the idea of universal womanhood that had united in spirit the missionary women and their converts in the first place? There is no evidence for that other than Reverend Hykes's claim that the return gifts showed the "practical and unmistakable evidence of her appreciation of the gift."[65] Another way to look at the situation is to view the gendering of the silks, the satin, the handkerchiefs and boxes of needlework as an outcome of patriarchal circuits of symbolic exchange rather than an expression of female bonding or feminine diplomacy. Old Buddha bestowed the "feminine trifles" upon the missionaries from the position of a patriarchal sovereign, an act that would put the recipients back in their place—a gendered domestic sphere—and remind them of their womanly duties. As we can see, this is an ironic reversal of what the missionary women had hoped to achieve, for the sovereign transaction was supposed to help them transcend the patriarchal determinations of gender and domesticity both at home and abroad.

According to Reverend Hykes, the story of the Presentation New Testament had a happier ending than seems to be suggested by the "feminine trifles." On November 21, 1894, the very day when the Bible was received at the palace, Hykes recorded the following anecdote:

A finely dressed eunuch, named Li, who said he was one of the "inner palace" men, went to our bookstore to buy some books. He carried a slip of paper on which was written, "one Old Testament, one New Testament." Wang Yu Chou, my helper at the store, who was an educated fellow, was struck by the uncommon look of the characters, and was led to ask who had written them. The Eunuch replied: "Wansuiye" (The Emperor). "Indeed," said Wang, "Today the women of the Christian Church in China have presented the Empress Dowager with a copy of the New Testament." "Yes," answered the Eunuch, "The Emperor has seen it, and now wishes to see copies of the books of the Jesus religion."[66]

This story of the Guangxu emperor's (1875–1908) new interest in Christianity after seeing the Presentation New Testament cannot be verified by independent sources. But the enunciatory act of repeating the anecdote carries its own truth value and speaks to the moment in powerful ways. Like the silks, the satin, the handkerchiefs, and boxes of needlework, Hykes's story of triumph participated in a procession of simulacra of sovereign exchange that metonymically evoked the other narrative accounts I have examined in the course of this chapter, from Stead's narrative about his youthful viewing of the Barker painting of Queen Victoria giving the Bible to the African chiefs to Mallet's journal entry about the queen's exchange of the New Testament with the Africans' gift of leopard skin rugs. Interestingly, the Qing emperor himself emerges in this account as the potential protagonist in a future fiction of conversion yet to be written.

Fully anticipating narrative closure, the prolepsis of conversion was to be authored on the eve of the collapse of the imperial Qing dynasty when some Chinese Christians and overseas converts, men as well as women, decided to replicate the 1894 episode by reproducing four facsimile copies of the Presentation New Testament and giving them to the imperial family.[67] Preparations for the presentation of the Scriptures to the imperial family began in 1909. This time the idea appeared to originate with some Chinese converts. With the help of a missionary, the native Christians submitted a call for contributions in the *Chinese Recorder* and all the leading papers for native Christians, proposing that each Christian donate at least two copper cash. The money would be used for a presentation copy of the Scriptures from the Chinese to their emperor. The native pastors in Shanghai formed a General Executive Committee with a Pastor Yü as their secretary and treasurer.[68] By March 1911, the Presentation Committee had raised $1,412.35 (Mexican dollars), although the actual expenses were Mexican $1,549.49.[69]

The four copies of the Presentation New Testament were each set in large type and bound in silver covers that illustrated scenes from the life of Jesus Christ; the preface was printed in pure gold on red paper (Figures 10 and 11). The Ningpo carvers made an elaborate casket for each book, each with a

Figure 10. The front cover of the 1911 edition of the Presentation New Testament in Chinese. Courtesy of the American Bible Society.

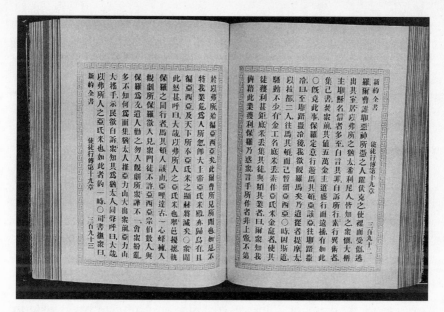

Figure 11. The text of the 1911 edition of the Presentation New Testament. Courtesy of the American Bible Society.

carving portraying a New Testament scene. The books were first put on display in the Chinese YMCA in Shanghai and then exhibited at four well-known local business houses. According to the records of the British and Foreign Bible Society: "At a general meeting of the Chinese Christians held in the Martyrs' Memorial Hall, Shanghai, Pastor Yü Kueh-chen and Mr. Czar Lien-fu were delegated to take the books to Peking. Considerable difficulty and delay, not to say obstruction, were experienced in arranging for the actual presentation, which in the end was satisfactorily completed."[70] But the *China Mission Year Book* gives us a somewhat different version of the story. It shows that the Chinese converts encountered many bureaucratic hurdles when they reached Beijing, and "strange to say, the delegation was compelled to send in the volumes through the Board of Foreign Affairs. It is to be hoped that the volumes reached those for whom they were intended, though one can never be sure."[71]

Three distinguishing characteristics set this event apart from the previous missionary presentation. First, it was decided early on that the Presentation New Testament should be the work of Chinese Christians, with no foreign help whatsoever. Nationalist pressures were clearly on the rise and would soon impact the overall direction and identity of Christian organizations in China. Second, men as well as women were encouraged to subscribe to the gift, and no argument of gender was made this time. Third, and most important, the contributions came from Chinese Christians in China and all over the world. Facilitated by the print media, the fund-raising campaign was a global endeavor, involving the diasporic communities in America, Hawaii, the Straits Settlements, and Africa.[72]

The involvement of the worldwide Chinese community raises some interesting issues concerning the ways in which the diasporic Chinese, Christian and non-Christian, related to the sovereign image of the Qing in the last years of the dynasty. Did their intimate experience of colonialism outside China breed a particular love for the land of their ancestors? Might that love mask a potent form of the sovereignty complex, a condition more germane to colonial abjection than perhaps a positive manifestation of patriotism or nationalism? I noted at the outset of this chapter that the missionaries were not the only ones who traded place for identity in the course of colonial expansion, for the diasporic Chinese were just as busy traveling back and forth between the metropole and the colonies. Some of them looked on the Qing as an embodiment of alternative political destiny, a way out of colonial abjection. The Malaysian-born and European-educated Ku Hung-ming was one such man.[73]

Ku's legendary loyalty to the Empress Dowager, inexplicable to some and reactionary to others, opens a window onto the unique conditions of migrant nationalism and sovereign thinking at the close of the Qing and Victorian eras. Ku entered the diplomatic service of the Qing government in the mid-1890s and rose to be the top aide and translator for the powerful imperial viceroy Zhang Zhidong, appointed by the Empress Dowager. Ku published numerous articles during the 1900 uprising of the *Yihe Tuan* in defense of the Empress Dowager. (The Allies' defeat of this popular nationalist movement led to the second round of massive looting by the Western powers and their possession of the throne chair, an incident I discuss in the concluding chapter.) It should be pointed out that Ku's devotion to the Empress Dowager was not just another case of patriotism, because his respect for Queen Victoria also led him at times to shield the British Crown from the atrocities that the British troops were committing in China. In fact, his unresolved ambivalence toward Queen Victoria, his former sovereign, is no less fascinating than his loyalty to Cixi, whom he called *guomu* or "the mother of the nation." Love and politics were ceaselessly triangulated in the life of this

Malaysian man between Southeast Asia and Europe, between Europe and China, and between China and Southeast Asia.

Triangulating Love and Politics

In examining the work of the early Chinese interpreters who had served Commissioner Lin in his 1839 campaign against the opium trade, I discussed briefly the academic background of Yuan Dehui, who traveled to Malaysia and studied English at John Milne's Anglo-Chinese College. The other known interpreters on Lin's translation team either were born in South or Southeast Asia or had spent considerable time in a foreign country. Ya Meng, the son of a Chinese father and a Bangladeshi mother, was raised a Christian in Serampore. He assisted the Baptist missionary Joshua Marshman—the translator who had competed with Robert Morrison to publish the first Chinese Bible—in the latter's evangelical work among the diasporic Chinese communities in India.[74] Ya Lin (Liaou Ahsee, also called William Botelho), another member of Lin's translation team, had attended a mission school in Cornwall, Connecticut, in 1822 and went on to study in Philadelphia in 1824—probably the first Chinese student to be educated in the United States.[75] The youngest member of Lin's team, Liang Jinde, was the son of Liang Afa, the first Protestant convert of Robert Morrison and the first indigenous Protestant priest. As Jonathan Spence shows in his book *God's Chinese Son*, Liang Afa's Chinese tracts, *Quan shi liang yan* (Good words exhorting the world), served as a significant source of inspiration for Hong Xiuquan's Taiping Rebellion.[76] His son, Liang Jinde, lived for eight years with the missionary Elijah Bridgman, the founder of the journal the *Chinese Repository*, and also pursued his studies in colonial Singapore.[77] Ku Hungming's appointment as the top aide and interpreter of Viceroy Zhang Zhidong in the late 1880s may well have replicated a pattern originally established by Commissioner Lin. His role, however, greatly exceeded that of his predecessors, and his reputation as a writer and philosopher traveled far and wide.

The British novelist Somerset Maugham paid a personal visit to Ku Hungming in 1921 and described his impressions in an essay, "The Philosopher." Maugham wrote that he had undertaken the trip to Beijing because "here lived a philosopher of repute the desire to see whom had been to me one of the incentives of a somewhat arduous journey. He was the greatest authority in China on the Confucian learning. He was said to speak English and

German with facility. He had been for many years secretary to one of the Empress Dowager's greatest viceroys, but he lived now in retirement."[78] Maugham's rendezvous with the philosopher turned out to be a disaster. He recalled: "I hastened to express my sense of the honour he did me in allowing me to visit him. He waved me to a chair and poured out the tea. 'I am flattered that you wished to see me,' he returned, 'Your countrymen deal only with coolies and with compradores; they think every Chinese must be one or the other.' I ventured to protest. But I had not caught his point. He leaned back in his chair and looked at me with an expression of mockery."[79] Ku emerges from the pages of Maugham's essay as a ranting old man who seemed bitter, lost, and deeply insecure on behalf of his adopted country. It is almost as if the Englishman's physical presence in his room was too much for him and he had to fight it off in self-defense. In one poignant moment, Maugham quotes Ku as pontificating:

> Do you know that we tried an experiment which is unique in the history of the world? We sought to rule this great country not by force, but by wisdom. And for centuries we succeeded. Then why does the white man despise the yellow? Shall I tell you? Because he has invented the machine gun. That is your superiority. We are a defenceless horde and you can blow us into eternity. You have shattered the dream of our philosophers that the world could be governed by the power of law and order. And now you are teaching our young men your secret. You have thrust your hideous inventions upon us. Do you not know that we have a genius for mechanics? Do you not know that there are in this country four hundred millions of the most practical and industrious people in the world? Do you think it will take us long to learn? And what will become of your superiority when the yellow man can make as good guns as the white and fire them as straight? You have appealed to the machine gun and by the machine gun shall you be judged.[80]

Maugham did not enjoy being scapegoated by Ku's impassioned oratory. In his commentary he speaks sarcastically of Ku's mannerisms and style of speech, writing: "I could not help thinking him a somewhat pathetic figure. He felt in himself the capacity to administer the state, but there was no king to entrust him with office; he had vast stores of learning which he was eager to impart to the great band of students that his soul hankered after, and there came to listen but a few, wretched, half-starved, and obtuse provincials."[81]

Maugham's disappointment is genuine and reasonable, but he does not seem to comprehend the pathos of Ku's neurotic behavior or appreciate the literal meaning of his tropes of sovereign rule, such as "administering the state" and "no king to entrust him with office," which could have led to a better understanding of Ku's situation.[82] Did Ku's sovereign complex turn to paranoia? Was his ranting that of a schizophrenic or an uncanny prophet? (If we substitute nuclear warheads for the machine gun, Ku's words would probably ring true as the new millennium witnesses yet another round of military buildups and the nuclear arms race in the Asian Pacific region.) Was Ku speaking to the ghosts of his own memory, the ghost of a former self that had lingered behind in Penang, Singapore, Berlin, Edinburgh, and a host of other places where he had lived and studied?

Ku Hung-ming was born into a family of *nanyang* ethnic Chinese (*nanyang* meaning "the South Sea," an old Chinese term for Southeast Asia). He received early schooling at the Prince of Wales' Island Central School, then, when he reached the age of thirteen, he was brought to Edinburgh by his Scottish godfather, Forbes Brown, and stayed with the Brown family while furthering his education in Europe. For the next decade or so, Ku immersed himself in the European humanistic curriculum and mastered an impressive array of languages, including Greek, Latin, French, and German. As one of the handful of Eurasians or ethnic Chinese studying the humanities in nineteenth-century Europe, Ku became conversant with the classics as well as the modern literature and philosophy of the West.[83] After finishing an M.A. degree at the University of Edinburgh, he went on to study civil engineering in Germany for a period of time. In 1880 he returned to Southeast Asia and began a career in the colonial administration of Singapore.[84]

A chance encounter with the Chinese scholar and senior diplomat Ma Jianzhong (1844–1900)—who will be discussed in the next chapter—as Ma was passing through Singapore and Penang in 1881 is said to have brought about a miraculous transformation in Ku's outlook on life and the world.[85] Almost immediately after the two became acquainted, Ku made what would become for him a life-changing decision: he quit his job with the colonial secretary in Singapore and renounced his identity as "an imitation Western man." Ku relates: "I was too impatient to wait for the boss's reply to my note of resignation. I simply jumped on board a departing steamer and returned to my old home Penang. The moment I arrived, I announced to the head of our clan who was my cousin that I was going to grow a queue and adopt the Chinese long gown."[86] Undaunted by the fact that he had to acquire Mandarin and classical Chinese in his mid-twenties in order to become Chinese, Ku plunged into an intensive course of study; within three years he had learned to read and write classical Chinese and had a tolerable command of the Confucian classics. In 1885 Ku sailed for China and soon afterward was appointed top secretary-interpreter in the office of Viceroy Zhang Zhidong. He rose to become a senior diplomat in Zhang's office of foreign affairs aim played an important role in the management of the 1900 crisis.

Ku's conversion was both thorough and tragically at odds with the currents of his own time. Not only did he declare himself an orthodox Confucian just as classical Chinese learning was in the process of disintegrating and giving way to the models of Western education in which he himself had been brought up, but also he began to insist on the importance of the queue as a sign of his identity and loyalty to the Qing dynasty at the point when the dynasty was on the verge of catastrophic collapse. Indeed, with the demise of the Qing in 1911, the much-hated queue, long regarded as an oppressive foreign code imposed on Chinese males by the Manchu regime, was the first thing to go—often by violent means.[87] Ku's steadfast refusal to cut his queue many years after the overthrow of the Qing turned him into a national laughingstock in the young Republic and caused him no small measure of pain and isolation at Beijing University, where he taught English literature in the Department of Foreign Languages until his retirement. During Maugham's visit, Ku pointed to his queue: "'You see that I wear a queue,' he said, taking it in his hands. 'It is a symbol. I am the last representative of the old China.'"[88] After his English works were translated into French, German, and Japanese, Ku became better known as a Confucian philosopher in the West than in China. His idiosyncratic translations of the Confucian classics were eagerly read and discussed by liberal intellectuals in Europe, including Maugham, Tolstoy, and Georg Brandes.[89]

Ku's lifelong devotion to the sovereignty of the Qing has struck many as oddly conservative. After renouncing his colonial Malaysian identity, why would he declare allegiance to a Manchu sovereign whose alien authority had been contested by the Chinese for over two hundred years? Is it not a contradiction to let the queue stand or fall as a symbol of the old China? If the queue signifies the old China, what might the old China signify for Ku? Does it signify the overcoming of his colonial abjection? Ku's decision to serve the Qing when the Chinese nationalists were in the midst of plotting against the regime highlights the conceptual limits of the sovereign state as the realm of freedom. Inasmuch as national independence movements aim at a satisfactory resolution of sovereign rights by taking the telos of the state as the guarantor of freedom, they share the same conceptual limits as individuals like Ku who opt out of colonial abjection by traveling elsewhere.[90] I regard these limits as the threshold of any inquiry into the condition of possibility of sovereign right and its ability to evolve into the ultimate test of independence, freedom, dignity, and the logic of reciprocity in the modern world—all that we have since become so intimately aware of.

In that sense, Ku's emotional attachment to the Qing is best seen as colonial negativity masquerading as nationalism. By that I mean that Ku's sovereign complex always recognizes the Empress Dowager as the equivalent of Queen Victoria. In other words, the Empress Dowager is *guomu* for him to the same extent that Queen Victoria is the Mother of the Nation in the eyes of the British. Psychoanalysts may find this level of attachment to a mother figure enormously interesting and perhaps can search through Ku's childhood experience for clues as to why this should be the case. But Ku was notoriously reticent about his parents and never once spoke of his mother, whose ethnic identity—Chinese, Malay, or a hybrid of Asian and white—remains to this day shrouded in mystery.

There are important aspects of Ku's attachment to a female sovereign that cannot, however, be accounted for by the psychoanalytic model of family romance and sexuality. Further clues must be sought in the dynamic interplay of nation and empire at a time when Queen Victoria stood as the world's most powerful symbol of national sovereignty and imperial rule. Earlier in this chapter I showed how the queen's giving the New Testament to Africans led to a series of replicas in artistic representation and in the actual circumstances of colonial exchange. In North America, Queen Victoria had a powerful hold on Elizabeth Cady Stanton's imagination as the latter was developing her feminist notion of "self-sovereignty." It could be argued that Mary Richard, W. T. Stead, T. Jones Barker, and Stanton all had their share of the sovereignty complex, as did the most of the other figures I mention in this book. Since Ku was a former subject of Queen Victoria from colonial Malaysia and lived in Scotland and Europe for many years, the question arises: Was his sovereignty complex, and his adopted loyalty to the Empress Dowager, linked in fundamental ways to what Queen Victoria and Britain meant to him?

Ku, an outspoken critic of British imperialism, wrote nearly all of his polemics in English. His chief statement in defense of the Qing sovereign was published in response to the Allies' retaliation against the popular *Yihe Tuan* uprising in 1900. This and his other articles appeared in an English-language newspaper, the *Japan Mail*, published in Yokohama, and in the *North China Daily News*, the largest-circulation English newspaper in China. In one of his polemics, Ku wrote: "Whenever modern scientific men of Europe meet with any extraordinary manifestation of human soul which they cannot explain, they call it fanaticism. But what is fanaticism? It is this. The only impulse which can drive men to extraordinary acts of courage and heroism, and make them sacrifice themselves, is the impulse inspired by a desire to defend something which they in their hearts admire, love and reverence."[91] The "something" Ku endorsed turned out to be the sovereign ideal embodied in the person of the Empress Dowager. Indeed, the stakes of sovereignty were now extremely high because the Allies were demanding the heads of the princes and "Boxer" rebels, and the Empress Dowager was forced into exile for the second time.

The *Guomu:* Defending the Mother of the Nation

The *Yihe Tuan*, or *Yihe Quan*, were dubbed "the Boxers" by the missionaries and Western journalists in China; hence the "Boxer Rebellion." Ku objected to the Western media representation of the *Yihe Tuan* as "the Boxers," saying, "The name of the original legitimate first so-called 1900 society 'Yi-ho-t'uan' may be translated as 'friendly society of good men and true' or 'society of honest men for mutual defence.'"[92] The fact that Ku's position in the office of Viceroy Zhang Zhidong was unique and prominent drew public attention to his criticisms. The British commander Lord Salisbury took notice and found Ku's attack on "bastard" British imperialism particularly offensive. Salisbury lodged a formal complaint to Viceroy Zhang with the purpose of silencing Ku and preventing him from publishing more polemics in the English-language media. Ku, however, went on to expose Salisbury's blackmail attempt by printing a short notice preceding his article "For the Cause of Good Government in China" in the *Japan Mail:* "I understand the British authorities have taken umbrage at my writing, and have formally complained to H. E. the Viceroy. I, of course, hold myself amenable to His Excellency's displeasure. I do not know whether the action of the British authorities is sanctioned by the British Government. But in view of it, I think it useful here to bring publicly to the notice of Lord Salisbury, a cipher telegram which I sent to his Lordship last summer."[93]

Ku wrote his defense of the Manchu sovereign on July 27, 1900, when the Allied Forces were advancing to Beijing to relieve the legations and seek revenge against the Manchu princes and the Empress Dowager. Viceroy Zhang had entrusted him with the task of translating a joint official telegram on behalf of the southern viceroys urging the British authorities and the Allies to respect the personal safety of the Empress Dowager.[94] In the course of translating the telegram, Ku took the initiative of elaborating on the official statements and turning the text into a lengthy article, which he subsequently published in the *Japan Mail* under the title "Moriamur pro Rege, Regina! A Statement of the True Feelings of the Chinese People Towards the Person and Authority of H. I. M. the Empress Dowager." In a letter to the editor of the newspaper, Ku explained the circumstances under which he had written the article:

> I had at first obtained authority from H. E. the Viceroy to prepare a translation of the substance of his telegram for publication. But afterwards on learning that I had made a long article of his telegram, His Excellency, under advice and other extraneous influence, which I could not control, withdrew his authorization. I did not submit to His Excellency my whole article beforehand, because, for one reason, in order to make him see the force of it, it would have taken me a long time to put the article into proper Chinese literary form, and, in the agony of the situation, every minute was precious. For *I had intended with this article to save Peking as well as the Legations there*. I believed then,—and I almost believe it now,—that if I could have succeeded in arresting and allaying somewhat the storm of indignation, natural at the moment, on the part of foreigners against H. I. M. the Empress Dowager and her Government, the panic and mutual agony on both sides would calm down a little to enable those responsible persons in authority to take a clearer view of the situation and to solve it without any unnecessary bloodshed.[95]

In a doomed attempt to stop the war and influence the policy of Britain and the Allies, Ku took the step of forwarding his article to the attention of Lord Salisbury. Although the Allies spared the life of the Empress Dowager in the aftermath of the suppression, they punished the princes and rounded up victim after victim for execution.[96] Ku recalled: "The cool, callous, persistent demand for heads was, I must say, an act of moral helplessness and cynicism on the part of responsible statesmen more disgraceful to the state of civilization at the present day than even the savagery of the foreign troops in North

China. I really pity the men who were responsible for the suicide of the Chinese Princes and State Ministers."[97]

The essay "Moriamur pro Rege, Regina!" was motivated by the need to defend the Empress Dowager as the supreme sovereign of the Chinese people. To make his own opinion heard, Ku overstepped the bounds of his official position as translator and presented his argument in a way that ran counter to Viceroy Zhang's political objective, namely, to exonerate the Empress Dowager from the actions of the insurgents. Ku defended the insurgents, as well as the Empress Dowager, on the grounds that these men were trying to protect the *guomu* (the mother of the nation) and were doing so by throwing their young lives at the muzzles of European guns. His main argument states:

> It is plain therefore that the real "causa belli," the real passionate impulse which has led the people of China to assume a warlike attitude actually in the North and virtually in the South, is the conviction that insult was offered or intended to be offered to the person and liberty of H. I. M. the Empress Dowager. It is, I may say, a war of the people, not of the Government; in fact, it is rather in spite of the Government. That is the unfortunate reason why what are called the strict rules of civilized warfare have not been scrupulously observed.
>
> Now, I do not know whether the more or less democratic people of Europe and America, who are at the present day very enthusiastic about "patriotism," are able or willing to remember from their past history that there is still a more genuine word than modern patriotism, a word the meaning of which I have tried to convey by using the Latin phrase at the head of this article, namely "Loyalty," the loyalty of the servant to his master, the loyal devotion of a child to his parents, of a wife to her husband, and lastly, summing up all these, the loyalty of a people to their sovereign! If the people of Europe and America will remember the meaning of that word, they will understand why the Chinese people—and not the Government—are now in a state of war, at bay against the whole world. For the cry from one end of China to the other is "Moriamur pro Rege, Regina!"[98]

Ku's comment on the loyalty shown by ordinary people to the sovereign is worth pondering. Whether or not the author correctly diagnoses the origins of the 1900 uprising is beside the point. We are not reading a historical essay for the author's objective assessment of the situation any more than we would trust the objective archival value of the contemporary eyewitness accounts by missionaries such as Arthur Smith and Arthur Brown.[99] It is the mode of argumentation in the form of what Benedict Anderson calls the "quotidian universals" of newspaper writing that mattered at the moment and shaped the moment.[100]

Ku's manner of securing the universals of the "people" and their "sovereign" along a set of exchangeable registers—history, loyalty, patriotism—appears very much like a free translation between Chinese and English. The argument of the *guomu* makes sense only insofar as the Empress Dowager is understood as an equivalent of the British sovereign (the mother of the nation and the empire) and China as an equivalent of other sovereign nations. The exchangeability and reciprocity of sovereign rights articulate the legal ground on which Queen Victoria and the Empress Dowager should act and be seen to act. In a sentimental move, Ku believes that the only solution to the Anglo-Chinese conflict is to let the female heads of state speak directly to each other. At the conclusion of "Moriamur Pro Rege, Regina!" he proposes "that H. B. M. the Queen, as the Doyenne of the Lady Sovereigns of the world, be graciously pleased to send, as soon as possible, a direct open telegram to H. I. M. the Empress Dowager—not in official language, but in simple language of the heart,—expressing sympathy for the trials and hardships which H. I. M. the Empress Dowager, her son and her suffering people have gone through in the present trouble."[101] The appeal to Queen Victoria as "the Doyenne of the Lady Sovereigns of the world" is made with particular attention to how the "simple language of the heart"—an imaginary feminine language—would differ from the official language of men. Ku admits that his proposal sounds sentimental in the context of the war but attempts to justify it by the hard, practical, commonsense reason of *politique du cœur*.

From what we know of how the Empress Dowager and Queen Victoria treated each other, Ku's proposal for *politique du cœur* does seem like an extravagant fantasy. When the first organized military looting took place in Beijing in 1860, Lord Elgin ordered the destruction of the imperial Gardens of Perfect Brightness *(Yuanming yuan)*. Out of the looting, Queen Victoria received a Pekingese dog, the first to be seen in the West, to which she gave the apt name of "Looty."[102] In *Queen Victoria's Secrets*, Adrienne Munich has shown how Queen Victoria's intimacy with her dogs contributed to the Victorian cult of domesticity.[103] The addition of Looty certainly gave an imperial twist to that feminine cult, and the Empress Dowager, who had the reputation of showing more affection for her dogs than for the people surrounding her, would not have been happy about this symbolic event.[104] After the suppression of the uprising of the *Yihe Tuan*, which was followed by the death of Queen Victoria in 1901, the Empress Dowager was quoted as saying: "I have often thought that I am the most clever woman that ever lived and others cannot compare with me. Although I have heard much about Queen Victoria and read a part of her life which someone has translated into Chinese, still I don't think her life was half so interesting and eventful as mine. My life is not finished yet and no one knows what is going to happen in the future."[105] Der Ling, who lived for two years in the imperial palace as the first lady in waiting, recorded many of the Empress Dowager's conversations in her memoir *Two Years in the Forbidden City*. If her account can be trusted, the following remarks have also been attributed to Cixi:

> England is one of great powers of the world, but this has not been brought about by Queen Victoria's absolute rule. She had the able men of parliament back of her at all times and of course they discussed everything until the best result was obtained, then she would sign the necessary documents and really had nothing to say about the policy of the country. Now look at me. I have 400,000,000 people, all dependent on my judgment. Although I have the Grand Council to consult with, they only look after the different appointments, but anything of an important nature I must decide myself.[106]

There is no doubt that the circumstances of imperial rivalry would have precluded the talk of the heart that Ku wanted to se/e come about between the two female sovereigns. Even if it had been possible, the conversation would have had to take place within the larger framework of international law and figure the sovereign exchange in a relation of reciprocity understood to govern the family of nations at that time. Ku was certainly familiar with the contemporary discourse of international relations and had his own thoughts about it, which are conveyed in a treatise titled "For the Cause of Good Government in China." He wrote:

> The broad and vital issue of the Chinese Problem is this. The foreign Powers must distinctly and absolutely decide either to take over the responsibility of Government in China or to leave that responsibility to the Imperial Government. If the Powers decide to take over the responsibility: well and good. But if the Powers, on the other hand, decide to demand responsibility of good government from the Imperial Government, then the Powers' plain duty is to absolutely recognize and respect all the rights of the Imperial Gov-

ernment as an independent State—with the exception, at present, of juris-diction over foreign subjects.[107]

When recognition is employed as a discretionary instrument for making or breaking sovereign entities, this suggests that we are in the realm of a logic of reciprocity in positive law that came to prevail in the course of imperial conquest.[108] Ku's appeal to the sovereign rights of his imperial government could no more escape this logic than the Qing government could shirk its responsibility to sign the unequal treaties without abdicating its sovereign rights. In my earlier discussion of Henry Wheaton's *Elements of International Law* and its translation and circulation in East Asia, I analyzed the process whereby the Chinese neologism *quanli* was constructed in reciprocity with the English "rights." The same process of reciprocity can be observed in the birth of the super-sign *zhuquan/sovereign right,* in which the neologism *zhuquan* conjures the projected universalism of "sovereign right" for the *Wanguo gongfa* and Wheaton's *Elements of International Law.*

Wheaton was among the first legal theorists to propagate a constitutive notion of recognition for international law. In it, Wheaton argues that while the independence of a state is sufficient to establish its internal sovereignty, its external sovereignty "may require recognition of other States in order to render it perfect and complete." Emphasizing this crucial distinction with respect to the rights of a new state, he writes that as long as a state confines its actions to its own citizens and to the limits of its own territory, it may well dispense with recognition by others.

> But if it desires to enter into that great society of nations, all the members of which recognize rights to which they are mutually entitled, and duties which they may be called upon reciprocally to fulfill, such recognition becomes essentially necessary to the complete participation of the new State in all the advantages of this society. Every other State is at liberty to grant, or refuse, this recognition, subject to the consequences of its own conduct in this respect; and until such recognition becomes universal on the part of other States, the new State becomes entitled to the exercise of its external sovereignty as to those States only by whom that sovereignty has been recognized.[109]

By the late nineteenth century, the English jurist W. E. Hall flatly mandated that "states outside European civilization must formally enter into the circle of law-governed countries. They must do something with the acquiescence of the latter, or of some of them, which amounts to an acceptance of law in its entirety beyond all possible misconstruction."[110]

The threat of nonrecognition not only affects the entitlement of states and communities outside Europe to positive existence but also touches on the inner lives of individuals who must endure the trauma of colonial abjection. To rise above the fate of colonial abjection, Ku Hung-ming journeyed to China in search of the sovereign embodiment of dignity and devoted his best years to defending the *guomu* and his adopted mother country. In a poignant way, his battle was lost not so much to the British as to the nationalist revolutionaries who overthrew the Qing dynasty in 1911 to establish a new Republican state.

CHAPTER 6

The Sovereign Subject of Grammar

> To make him talk pidgin is to fasten him to the effigy of him, to snare him, to imprison him, the eternal victim of an essence, of an *appearance* for which he is not responsible.
>
> —Frantz Fanon, *Black Skin and White Masks*

In March 1864 the American linguist William Dwight Whitney (1827–1894) delivered a lecture, "On the Principles of Linguistic Science," to an audience of the Smithsonian Institute. The text was subsequently expanded into a series of twelve lectures, which appeared in print under the title *Language and the Study of Language* in 1867. In his first lecture Whitney expounded a theory of the linguistic sign by bringing the notions of recognition, conventionality, and consent to bear upon the study of language. He stated:

> We recognized no tie between any word and the idea represented by it excepting a mental association which we had ourselves formed, under the guidance, and in obedience to the example, of those about us. We do indeed, when a little older, perhaps, begin to amuse ourselves with inquiring into the reasons why this word means that thing, and not otherwise: but it is only for the satisfaction of our curiosity; if we fail to find a reason, or if the reason be found trivial and insufficient, we do not on that account reject the word. Thus every vocable was to us an arbitrary and conventional sign: *arbitrary*, because any one of a thousand other vocables could have been just as easily learned by us and associated with the same idea; *conventional*, because the one we acquired had its sole ground and sanction in the consenting usage of the community of which we formed a part.[1]

The quoted passage instantly brings to mind Saussure's famed formulation of the linguistic sign. How substantial were the intellectual ties between

Whitney and Saussure? The opening chapter of *Course in General Linguistics* contains an explicit remark by Saussure stating that his first inspiration had come from Whitney, the author of *The Life and Growth of Language*.[2] This acknowledgment somehow baffled the historian Hans Aarsleff, who wrote a book documenting the evolution of linguistic ideas from Locke to Saussure. Aarsleff believed that Taine and Bréal had probably contributed more to the development of Saussure's theory of the sign than Whitney, and so "it remains a puzzle why Saussure made so much of him [Whitney], especially of points that few contested such as the social and conventional nature of language."[3]

   John E. Joseph, who analyzed the Whitney family papers, has shown that Whitney and Saussure first met in Berlin in 1879 and corresponded briefly afterwards.[4] The earliest record of Saussure's reflections on general linguistics exists in the forty pages of notes he had prepared on the occasion of the Whitney Memorial Meeting, where he was invited to present a paper at the invitation of the American Philological Association in Philadelphia on December 28, 1894. Interestingly, the Whitney connection also caught the attention of Roman Jakobson when he tried to explain the fundamentals of Saussure's general linguistics:

> The essence of this striking innovation rests upon Whitney's thesis that language is a human institution: "that changed the axis of linguistics" [Saussure's words]. The substantial particularity of this institution consists in the fact that "language and writing are *not founded on a natural connection of things*. There is no connection at any time between a certain sibilant sound and the form of the letter S, and likewise it is no more difficult for the word *cow* than the word *vacca* to designate a *vache* ['cow']." It is this which Whitney never tired of repeating, in order better to make understood the fact that language is a pure institution.[5]

By questioning the "natural connection of things," Whitney sought to depart from the centuries-long European search for the perfect language, as reflected, for example, in the works of Leibniz and Christian theologians who tried to identify a natural order and logic of meaning underlying all known languages.[6] The idea of "conventionality" directs our attention to the consenting usage of a community and suggests strong connections with the contemporary theories of positive law and its concept of recognition, which I discussed in the preceding chapters. Can we identify and establish those connections in Saussure's writings to help work out the puzzle as to why he singled out Whitney and acknowledged the latter's impact on his notion of the sign when Saussure was also clearly indebted to the insights of the other contemporary linguists suggested by Aarsleff? Does the novelty of Whitney's work lie in the idea of "the social and conventional nature of language" or somewhere else? The answers to these questions will throw further light on what I have termed the semiotic turn of international politics in the long nineteenth century as we investigate the role that comparative grammar and philological studies played in the globalizing process.

The Indo-European Hypothesis

Since the publication of Edward Said's landmark study *Orientalism*, postcolonial scholarship has flourished, greatly enriching our understanding of how modern European philology arose and evolved as a colonial regime of knowledge which helped fashion not only identities and racial subjects but also the very notions of the Occident and the Orient, and of self and other. Thomas Trautmann's study of Sanskrit scholarship in British India shows further how Arya *(ārya)*, a name originally taken from Sanskrit that had referred to the first speakers of Sanskrit, Latin, Greek, Gothic, Celtic, and Old Persian, was turned into an Aryan story of Indo-European brotherhood, authorizing a new theory of language families in the nineteenth century.[7] The Indo-European hypothesis gave rise to classifications and rankings of all known languages on an evolutionary scale. The German *indogermanisch* scholars, in particular, took pains to demonstrate that the evolution of linguistic forms must pass through three stages of development and refinement, from monosyllabism to agglutination and further to inflection.[8] On the basis of a hypothesized common origin of the Indo-European language family, they speculated that all primitive languages were monosyllabic, and that only some had evolved into sophisticated forms owing to the introduction of formal principles of inflection and declension. The scale of human evolution and progress inverted the notion of "the primitive language," previously understood in the sense of origin, legitimacy, and authority, and relegated it to backwardness indexed by racial inferiority. Thus, Max Müller proposed "a correlation between phonological complexity and mental progress and believed that 'a very imperfect alphabet will suffice for the lower states of thought and speech.'"[9] Wilhelm von Humboldt saw nations such as the Germans and the British as more qualified than others to construct higher forms of language and attributed the lower, "petrified" languages to the inability of the national mind to advance. He made this comparative point explicit by asserting that, in the grand scheme of world languages, Chinese was the polar opposite against which all grammars are to be contrasted. Chinese, which had been exalted as the crown of all languages by Leibniz and others in the seventeenth century, was now degraded and held to be barbaric and backward.[10] The value of this backward language for linguistic science, however, was not lost on comparative philologists like Friedrich von Schlegel, who stated that Chinese "presents a remarkable instance of a language almost without inflection, every necessary modification being expressed by separate monosyllabic words, each having an independent signification. The extraordinary monosyllabic form, and perfect simplicity of its construction, make the consideration of it important as facilitating the comprehension of other languages."[11]

Trained in continental Europe, Whitney joined the ranks of German comparative grammarians such as Bopp, Humboldt, and Schleicher as one of the foremost North American linguists. He had inherited the concept of symbiosis of language and race from the Europeans but did more than many of them to popularize white supremacist views. Whitney wrote:

> The importance of the Indo-European races in history is, then, legitimately to be included among the titles of Indo-European philology to the first attention of the linguistic scholar. Moreover, since the relation between the capacity of a race and the character of the tongue originated and elaborated by that race is a direct and necessary one, it could not but be the case that the speech of the most eminently and harmoniously endowed part of mankind should itself be of the highest character and most harmonious development, and so the most worthy object of study, in its structure and its relations to mind and thought. And this advantage also, as we shall see more plainly hereafter, is in fact found to belong to Indo-European language: in the classification of all human speech it takes, unchallenged, the foremost rank.[12]

I should emphasize that it is Whitney's view of language *as grammar*, rather than his blatant pronouncements about race and character, that deserves special notice here, because grammar was regarded as that unmarked territory of linguistic science where racism could muster the support of neutral, scientific evidence, especially as comparative grammarians claimed to have developed a set of objective criteria for understanding human speech. Classifying all known tongues into grammatical forms entailed making decisions about the relative standing of each language within a coherent hierarchy governed by the sovereign subject of linguistic science. Here, the politics of recognition and nonrecognition noted in Chapters 4 and 5 could be played out at the technical levels of verb conjugation and parts of speech.

The comparative philologists agreed that the primitive monosyllabism of the Chinese language was valuable, and even indispensable, by virtue of its negativity and exceptionality, to the task of identifying and establishing the proper norms of Indo-European grammar for the common good of linguistic science. Their method of comparison was driven by a circularity of reasoning that required the object of analysis to stand simultaneously as the point of departure and the point of arrival, as, for example, when Chinese was called on to witness the truth of the Indo-European hypothesis negatively but required the same hypothesis a priori to verify its own truth as a tongue that "has never advanced out of its primitive monosyllabic stage; its words remain even to the present day simple radical syllables, closely resembling Indo-European roots, formless, not in themselves parts of speech, but made such only by their combination into sentences."[13] In making this observation, Whitney gave as evidence the example of a classical Chinese text, which he translated from one of August Schleicher's earlier German translations:

> How different is the state of monosyllabism which precedes inflection from that which follows it in consequence of the wearing off of inflective elements, may be in some measure seen by comparing a Chinese sentence with its English equivalent. The Chinese runs, as nearly as we can represent it, thus: "King speak: Sage! not far thousand mile and come; also will have use gain me realm, hey?" which means, "the king spoke: O sage! Since thou dost not count a thousand miles far to come (that is, hast taken the pains to come hither from a great distance), wilt thou not, too, have brought some thing for the weal of my realm?"[14]

The original episode referred to in the quoted passage is taken from a Confucian classic, the first book of the *Mencius*, in which the sage Mencius pays a visit to King Hui of the state of the Liang. According to James Legge's English rendering of the original (see the Glossary for characters), King Hui says to Mencius: "Venerable sir, since you have not counted it far to come here, a distance of a thousand *li*, may I presume that you are provided with counsels to profit my kingdom?" Mencius replies, "Why must your Majesty use that word 'profit'? What I am provided with, are counsels to benevolence and righteousness, and these are my only topics."[15] The quotation cited by Whitney had appeared in Schleicher's book *Die Sprachen Europas in Systematischer Übersicht* (European languages in systematic overview), but, as Haun Saussy has pointed out, Schleicher's own quotation was a German retranslation of Stanislas Julien's French translation of the Chinese text.[16] What Whitney's English version did was to participate in a chain of quotations and retranslations of the same lines from the *Mencius,* further removing them from the text it claimed to represent literally.

Whitney's example masquerades as a literal figuring of the Chinese words—understood as non-translation—when the fact is that his mimicking of Chinese characters in broken English syntax is no less a translation than the otherwise grammatical representation of the same words in parentheses. Why break up English syntax, rather than simply using foreign-sounding nonsense syllables, for the effect of creating radical difference? Saussy has given us some good insights into the rhetorical mechanism of such literal translations in his essay "Always Multiple Translation, or How the Chinese Language Lost Its Grammar." He points out that the rendering of the *Mencius* passage into pidgin English was for Whitney "an imaginative tunnel through which we journey back to a primitive state, the state at which all words are roots and nothing but roots. Formal parataxis is the representation in present speech of a history that should have taken place but never did, leaving the Chinese in 'the primitive stage' preceding the fusions and inflections of actual linguistic history."[17] In short, pidgin English has a representational value as a signifier of primitive otherness; just as Friday never learns to speak grammatical English during many years of living with and serving Robinson Crusoe, so must Whitney hear the sound of pidgin English coming from a classical Chinese text.

Where does the English language proper stand in all of this? Having left primitive languages at the other end of his imaginary tunnel, Whitney must now confront an anomaly within the Indo-European family—namely, his own native tongue—because English has dropped much of its inflection and declension and exhibits what Ernest Renan called a reverse evolutionary trend with implications for a contrary hypothesis that perhaps primitive languages began with polysyllabic forms and evolved toward monosyllabic conditions. Whitney responds to that critique by introducing a necessary distinction between primitive monosyllabism and other kinds of monosyllabism:

The English, it is true, has been long tending, through the excessive preva-
lence of the wearing-out process, toward a state of flectionless monosyllabism; but such a monosyllabism, where the grammatical categories are
fully distinguished, where relational words and connectives abound, where
every vocable inherits the character which the former possession of inflection has given it, where groups of related terms are applied to related uses,
is a very different thing from a primitive monosyllabism like that to which
the linguistic analyst is conducted by his researches among the earliest representatives of Indo-European language.[18]

The denial of commensurability between English and Chinese brings into
sharp relief Whitney's decision to adopt pidgin English—which acts like a
system of super-signs extending in the direction of both languages but becomes neither—in translating the *Mencius*. That translation, as noted earlier,
derived not from the Chinese original but from Schleicher's German version. A quick comparison of the two translations reveals that Whitney in-
tentionally altered Schleicher's text to suit his need for a pidginized image
of the Chinese language. For instance, Schleicher had provided a tentative
rendering of person as "(ich) mein Reich" for *wu guo* to allow for both difference and commensurability. Whitney eschewed the obvious "(I) my country" to match the German pronouns for *wu guo*, writing instead "me country." Whereas Schleicher represented the last character, *hu*, in the *Mencius*
quote with a simple question mark, adding "Fragepartikel" (question particle) in parentheses, that character became "hey?" in Whitney's English version, a translation that disavowed the minimal functionality of the interrogative particle Schleicher had granted to the Chinese character.[19] The travesty
we are trying to bring to light here has little to do with the accuracy or inac-
curacy of renderings of a particular text (since no one, including Schleicher,
can be immune from infelicities of this kind) or the fact that there are a limited number of choices with which a translator must work to get the best
possible result. Rather, Whitney's careful rewording of Schleicher's German
translation while footnoting the latter as the source of his own version advanced a silent theoretical argument about cultural incommensurability
that troubles the raison d'être of comparative work itself.

To be sure, Whitney was neither the first nor the last to treat an existing
European-language translation of a Chinese text in this manner.[20] In a move
reminiscent of Whitney's pidgin rendering of Schleicher's German transla-

tion of a French rendering of classical Chinese, the twentieth-century historian Jean-Claude Martzloff cited a 1607 classical Chinese translation of Euclid's *Elements* by Xu Guangqi (1562–1633) and Matteo Ricci (1552–1610) to establish a case for linguistic incommensurability between Latin and classical Chinese by pointing to the "absence of the copula" in the latter. Roger Hart takes a close look at Martzloff's truncated transcription of classical Chinese syntax and argues that Martzloff's French translation makes the mistake of assuming that Clavius' Latin version of the *Elements* represented "an uncorrupted original by remaining untranslated and dehistoricized: effaced are the problems of translation from Greek to Latin to French and English, the complex history of the translation and editions of this text."[21] Against this conglomerate of originals are then contrasted the radical difference and incommensurability of classical Chinese and the need for a literal rendering of the sounds of the Chinese characters. If we were to follow Whitney's and Martzloff's method of literality to its logical end, there would be nothing to prevent us from doing the same with a literal translation from Latin into English, producing the same pidgin travesty of the original. By mirroring the syntactical order of the original, we would discover that the Latin text, too, had been missing the copula, prepositions, the definite article, and so on. The radical incommensurability Martzloff tries to establish with his literal translations turns out to be an artifact of the choices he made in the process of retranslation.

This brings us back to the question of reciprocity I discussed in the context of international law. I have shown how the positivist understanding of reciprocity in the nineteenth century typically operated around the issues of exclusivity, recognition, and nonrecognition whereby that which constitutes the *inside* of the family of nations depended very much on that which defines its *outside*. The positivist law of reciprocity imagines difference as a problem of equivalence (either equal or not equal to the Indo-European family) but cannot do so without tautology. The tautology of difference as value within a structure of unequal exchange, as I have argued elsewhere, can victimize that difference by translating it as non-universal value.[22] The argument of incommensurability has to enter the space of a larger argument and worldview to be able to sustain any sort of hypothesis about cultures, races, and civilizations. What is the worldview that underscores Whitney's claim of incommensurability and the conviction that linguistic science is the foundation of "the science of ethnology, the science which investigates the genealogy of nations"?[23]

In the preceding chapters we have seen how positive law demanded that states outside European civilization formally enter into the world of sovereign nations and be admitted into the international community by the West. Like Wheaton, Dana, and the other contemporary jurists of his time, Whitney regarded the European nations as the vanguard of world history and the sole enlightened and privileged race. He pointed to the fact that the European nations had circled the globe and dispatched their ships to every corner of the world for the purpose of trade or conquest. "The weaker races are perishing off the face of the land from inherent inability to stand before the superior race," he observed.[24] So the scepter of universal dominion now passed into the hands of the European nations, which ruled over a vast world and were worthy rulers because their sway brought "physical well-being, knowledge, morality, and religion to those over whom it is extended."[25] By extension, the Indo-European language family had the proper historical pedigree to rule the linguistic territory of the world.

Perhaps it is time for us to reconsider Whitney's notion of arbitrariness, universally attributed to Saussure, in light of the worldview he elaborated concerning race, nations, imperial sovereignty, and international conflicts. We find that, rather than rehashing one of those received ideas about the social and conventional nature of language, Whitney developed a sustained argument about the nature of the linguistic sign, the significance of which has since been obscured by the work of Saussure and other structural linguists. In 1874 Whitney published a seminal essay titled "Phusei or Thesei— Natural or Conventional?" in *Transactions of the American Philological Association*, in which he argued that the connection between a sign and its sense is one of mental association just as artificial as the connection between the sign 5 and the number it stands for or the sign π and 3.14159+. "Not a single item of the traditional English speech received by us from our forefathers has a vestige of right to claim to exist $\Phi\acute{v}\sigma\epsilon\iota$ in any one of the innumerable individuals that employ it, to have been produced by him under government of an internal, instinctive impulse, that made it what it is and no other."[26] In place of the naturalist fallacy, he proposes a notion of the sign in what amounts to a legal definition:

He who answers $\Phi\acute{v}\sigma\epsilon\iota$, therefore, to the question we have been discussing, lays himself open to the charge of total misapprehension of the most fundamental facts of language-history; he who answers $\theta\acute{\epsilon}\sigma\epsilon\iota$ needs only to show by due explanation that he does not mean to imply that any individual can

successfully fasten any name he pleases upon any idea he may choose to select; since every change must win the assent of a community before it is
language, and the community will ratify no arbitrary and unmotivated
changes or fabrications.[27]

The opposition of Φύσει and θέσει translates the nineteenth-century debate between natural law and positive law into linguistic terms. Whitney's
notion of "community," which found its way into Saussure's work, refers
specifically to a republic of speakers whose sovereignty is conferred by general suffrage and in which the members are permitted to make changes to
the common speech insofar as the community "ratifies" the changes. In an
interesting move that anticipated J. L. Austin's theory of the speech act,
Whitney wrote:

> When the first schooner ever built, on the coast of Massachusetts, slid from
> her stocks and floated gracefully upon the water, the chance exclamation of
> an admiring by-stander, "Oh, how she *scoons!*" drew from her contriver and
> builder the answer, "A *scooner* let her be, then," and made a new English
> word. The community ratified his act, and accepted the word he proposed,
> because the new thing wanted a new name, and there was no one else so
> well entitled as he to name it; if, on the other hand, he had christened a
> man-of-war a *scooner,* no one but his nearest neighbours would ever have
> heard of the attempt.[28]

Austin would be erecting a set of theoretical premises on similar kinds of
parables decades later. On closer examination, however, Whitney's anecdote
seems less concerned with speech acts than with recognition and ratification. The builder of the vessel reserves the right to authorize and confirm the
name "scooner," but it is up to the community to ratify or refuse to ratify the
neologism. What is the conceptual ground on which a community makes
such decisions, that is to say, if the decisions are not made for them by an authority or sovereign figure? It is interesting that the language of ratification
used in each of the quoted passages speaks of the individual and the community *as if* they were organized states or political bodies hashing out treaty
agreements under the aegis of positive law. Rather than a model of democratic society, Whitney's choice of words evokes the image of an international community in which signs and super-signs could be agreed on and
ratified among states, and he was writing at a time when the proliferation of

international treaties was exerting a major impact on the political life of language and language studies.

The linkage Daniele Gambarara identified between Saussure's notion of conventionality on the one hand and the novelty of international assemblies and treaty meetings on the other could fruitfully be extended back to Whitney.[29] If Saussure witnessed the birth of a brave new world of signs where international conventions were turning into primary venues for the standardization and adoption of various artificial sign systems, Whitney was no stranger to the ways in which sovereign states and imperial powers were in the process of regulating maritime signals, signs, codes, and other semiotic systems through the second half of the nineteenth century. The exclusion of states from the international community on the grounds of withdrawal of recognition by other sovereign states was to positive law what the rejection of natural connections between things was to a theory of language that sought to impose its imperial desire and vision on the linguistic territory of the world. The invention of the super-sign *yi/barbarian*, which I analyzed in Chapter 2, confirms and is confirmed by this novel view of the linguistic sign and of the international community. Of course, the ratification of treaties within the setting of the Opium Wars was almost always shadowed by a British "man-of-war" nearby. The novelty of Whitney's notion of the linguistic sign, if one has to speak in such terms, might be said to be its manifesting a positivist strain of sovereign thinking that was elsewhere transforming the colonial discourse of war, sovereign rights, women's rights, and international legal matters pertaining to imperial warfare.

Ma Jianzhong and His Grammar Book

What would happen when imperial warfare took comparative grammar to a foreign country where the culture or race had been othered by the Indo-European hypothesis? Would the translation of such knowledge lead to a form of the sovereignty complex, or could it cause a fundamental shift in the conceptual thinking of comparative studies itself? I ponder these questions by turning to the work of Ma Jianzhong, the author of a classical Chinese grammar book published in 1898 titled *Mashi wentong* (Ma's universal principles of classical Chinese). Ma's name came up briefly in Chapter 5, where I described his meeting and conversation with Ku Hung-ming in Southeast Asia and Ku's subsequent decision to leave colonial Singapore for China.

The mission that took Ma to Singapore in the summer of 1881 was part of the Qing government's ongoing effort to reduce and eventually stop the opium trade through diplomatic means. Ma had studied and earned a degree in France. Upon his return to China in 1880, he joined the diplomatic corps of the imperial government and was appointed head of a government delegation dispatched to British India. His delegation made a stop at the Straits Settlement, where they met with the colonial officials Cecil Clementi Smith and Sir Frederick Aloysius Weld, and investigated the opium situation there. The Straits Settlement, situated just above the equator at the end of the Malay Peninsula, consisted of Singapore, Penang, and Malacca, all colonies of the British Crown at the time. Singapore was one of the centers of opium manufacture, sale, and distribution in the British colonial economy.[30]

Ma's diplomatic career ran parallel to those of the other translator-diplomats I have been discussing in the course of this book, such as Thomas Wade, W. A. P. Martin, and Ku Hung-ming. The central role he played during the Korean crisis and the Sino-French war is largely overshadowed by his reputation as the pioneering scholar of Chinese grammatical studies. His monumental grammar book was completed during the intervals between catastrophic wars at the end of the nineteenth and beginning of the twentieth centuries. Within two years of the publication of *Ma's Universal Principles of Classical Chinese*, the author died in the midst of the British and Allied military campaign against the *Yihe Tuan* movement, which I discussed in connection with Ku Hung-ming. Ma, who had long since retired from government service, was recalled by Viceroy Li Hongzhang to help translate the volumes of diplomatic exchanges that poured in during the crisis. His brother Ma Xiangbo, a Catholic priest, described the circumstances of Ma Jianzhong's death as follows:

> After the Empress Dowager blindly endorsed the anti-foreign and pro-Qing sentiments of the rebels, the Governors-General of the southern provinces decided on a policy of autonomous rule rather than follow the decree of the Qing court. This turn of events brought Viceroy Li Hongzhang to Shanghai to take control of the situation there. Li then summoned my brother Jianzhong to his temporary residence to work with him [negotiating with the Western powers]. In mid-August, Li received a 7,000-word telegram from the court of Russia declaring that Russian troops would blockade the Wusong area should China refuse to meet their demands. Jianzhong spent a whole night translating the telegram and, when the work was finished, he was exhausted. He fell ill with a high fever and died on the morning of August 14 [1900]."[31]

Li Hongzhang and Zhang Zhidong were the two most powerful viceroys in the service of the Empress Dowager at this time, and Zhang had taken Ku Hung-ming under his wing. Whereas Ku survived the harsh realities of the war, Ma Jianzhong became a casualty. As a matter of fact, both Ma and Robert Morrison died in the midst of translation work they were performing for their respective governments during military confrontations.

The standard textbook assessment of *Ma's Universal Principles of Classical Chinese* is that the author single-handedly initiated modern grammatical studies in China and brought progress to the antiquated philological tradition of a backward nation. Without diminishing the novelty and importance of his work, we should perhaps raise a few questions and ask, for example, why it was deemed desirable and necessary in Ma's time to model classical Chinese *wen* (text/textuality, writing) on Latin or Indo-European grammar. Certainly, grammar books of the Chinese language modeled on Latin did not begin with *Ma's Universal Principles of Classical Chinese* but can be traced back to the sixteenth century, when European Catholic missionaries first arrived in China. By W. South Coblin's and Joseph A. Levi's account, the earliest known grammar of Mandarin, called *Arte de la lengua China,* was written by a Dominican, Juan Cobo (d. 1592/3). Cobo is said to be the author of two other similar works, the *Arte de las letras Chinas* and *Lingua Sinica ad certam revocata methodam.* A second Mandarin grammar, attributed to another Dominican, Francisco Díaz (1606–1646), was printed in the Philippines in 1640 or 1641, although its title is not recorded. The third is by the well-known Dominican missionary Juan Bautista de Morales (1597–1664). But the first published work in this series of "Dominican grammars" was completed by Francisco Varo in 1682. Titled *Arte de la Lengua Mandarina,* it had circulated in manuscript during the author's lifetime and was published in Guangzhou by a Franciscan friar, Pedro de la Pinuela, in 1703. Coblin and Levi point out that "this book is apparently the earliest published grammar of any form of Chinese and is therefore of considerable interest and importance, both because of its position in the history of Chinese linguistics and because of the concrete data it furnishes on the phonology, syntax, and lexicon of 17th-century Mandarin."[32] Indeed, the grammars produced in this period focused on Mandarin or other spoken forms, as they were intended for use primarily in the teaching of Mandarin to the Europeans who traveled to China or to neighboring countries. The text of *Arte de la Lengua Mandarina* provides numerous examples to demonstrate that Varo's understanding of Mandarin grammar was driven not only by the Latin model but also by the religious agenda of the Roman Catholic Church.

Ma's Universal Principles of Classical Chinese arrived on the comparative grammatical studies scene under rather different circumstances. I have argued that a single textual event, such as the translation and publication of the Chinese edition of *Elements of International Law* in 1864, can be read simultaneously as a threefold event, with textual, diplomatic, and epistemological implications. *Ma's Universal Principles of Classical Chinese* is precisely such a multiple event. Besides being the first comprehensive grammar book on classical Chinese written in the Chinese language, this work is unique and important in that it speaks powerfully to the conditions of colonial abjection and complicity between military conquest and linguistic science in the nineteenth century and to the desire to transcend that abjection. We have seen how comparative grammar joined forces with positive international law and participated in the imperial game of conjuring a sovereign subject for the Indo-European language family. That process of conjuration, however, did not end there any more than imperial desire could cease to project itself elsewhere. If imperial desire gains self-knowledge by conjuring the other, the other may resist the conjuration by recasting himself or herself in the desirable image of the sovereign subject. This process leaves traces of the sovereignty complex in those who are othered by the hegemony of the Indo-European hypothesis and who find themselves negotiating a subject position by appropriating a comparative paradigm that is itself grounded in Indo-European grammar. If the act of appropriation cannot free them from the continuum of conjurations honoring the legitimacy of imperial desire, does it further subjugate them? This is one of the questions posed by the birth of *Ma's Universal Principles of Classical Chinese*.

The reader will recall that Whitney represented the quotation from *Mencius* in pidgin English as "King speak: Sage! not far thousand mile and come; also will have use gain me realm, hey?" Granted that Whitney's travesty is absurd, what would be a plausible explication of the *Mencius* phrase? Would an indigenous scholar such as Ma Jianzhong be able to make sense of its grammatical components? Can the classical Chinese sentence be considered *grammatical*, that is, from the point of view of Latin and Indo-European languages? These questions are not entirely fortuitous, for the same *Mencius* quotation finds its way into *Ma's Universal Principles of Classical Chinese* and is there for the sole purpose of illustrating the grammaticality of classical Chinese. In the ninth chapter, the author identifies six types of functional suffixes for interrogative sentences in classical Chinese that pertain to the character *hu* in the *Mencius* quotation—represented as "hey" by Whitney—

and classifies them under *chuanyi zhu zi* (aid characters for interrogative structures). The aid character belongs in turn to a category called *xu zi* (empty character), which can be positioned at the beginning or at the end of a sentence to help complete the meaning. In addition to the character *hu*, Ma lists five other aid characters commonly found in interrogative sentences—*zai, ye, yu, fu,* and *zhu*—which satisfy the diverse rhetorical needs of classical Chinese, such as straight questions, rhetorical questions, exclamation, and so on.[33] Ma sees the category of empty characters as a classical Chinese equivalent of verb conjugation and makes a comparative observation:

> Western languages are phonetic tongues. The meaning of a word must follow the sound, which is why the verb ending changes to suit the needs of different expressions. Some verbs in Greek and Latin can have up to sixty or seventy different endings duly reflected in the different ways of pronouncing them. The vernacular languages [in Europe] have since evolved and varied greatly, with English being the simplest of all. Because verbs in these languages are inflected, they do not need the category of aid characters. The aid characters are unique to the Chinese language and make up for whatever lack there is due to the non-changing endings of its verbs.[34]

Ma's insistence on the grammaticality of classical Chinese is the outcome of a comparative method that models the study of the Chinese language on Latin, Greek, and other European tongues. Whitney relied on the comparative approach to develop an evolutionary hierarchy of inflectional and non-inflectional languages and a theory of incommensurability.[35] Ma's comparativism tends toward an opposite argument, namely, if the empty character achieves the same end as the verb conjugation, the grammatical function of the one must be commensurate with that of the other. In that regard, the phonetic rendering of *hu* as "hey" in Whitney's idiosyncratic representation of a sound misses the function of the empty character, whereas Schleicher's use of a question mark is confirmed by Ma's category.

Hu is not the only reason why the same *Mencius* quotation is repeatedly brought up in Ma's *Universal Principles*. In the eighth chapter, the first part of the quotation appears under the heading "Connectives" to help illustrate the use of the empty character *er*.[36] The remaining characters from the *Mencius* passage are addressed, respectively, in sections on the verb and predicate as well as on personal pronouns. The *you yi* phrase, rendered as "have use" by Whitney, is explained by Ma as having a verb *(you)*–preposition *(yi)* structure that typically omits the object of the transitive verb.[37] In James Legge's translation, the omitted object "counsels" is then restored to the verb-preposition phrase to read "be provided with counsels." Ma's classification and analysis of the parts of speech appear to support the decision made by Legge in consultation with Chinese scholars such as Wang Tao, whose role in the translation of the Bible I discussed in Chapter 4. In the matter of personal pronouns, Ma's theory is that first-person pronouns in classical Chinese are marked by grammatical case, and the character *wu* is commonly seen in the subjective or possessive case. Whitney, as I noted earlier, has rendered *wu guo* in the objective case as "me kingdom" by altering Schleicher's German "(ich) mein Reich," thus marking *wu* as a perverse reflection of pidgin English. Ma shows that in the structure of the *Mencius* quotation the character *wu* can be used in the possessive case only, and, unlike another character *wo*, *wu* never appears in the objective case except when the preceding verb is accompanied by a negative such as *bu*.[38]

Ma's implicit argument with the European and North American philologists runs throughout the vast collection of illustrative examples the author laboriously culled from the Chinese classics. His work is relentlessly comparative in the sense that all the evidence he collected goes to support the idea that the grammatical principles abstracted from classical usage are comparable or identical to their counterparts in Latin or modern European languages. Scholars have labored to identify the European grammar book(s) that served as a model for Ma's *Universal Principle*, because there seems strong internal evidence that Ma had been exposed to a number of well-known texts on Indo-European grammar or Chinese grammar books written by Jesuit missionaries and other Western scholars. We know that the author and his priest brother had come from a prominent gentry family in the Dantu prefecture of Jiangsu Province which is said to have been converted to Christianity since the time of the Jesuit priest Matteo Ricci. Ma Jianzhong was baptized Mathias. His mother was a devout Roman Catholic who taught her sons to read Matteo Ricci's *Tianzhu shi yi* (True meaning of the Lord of heaven) along with the four books of Confucius and the five classics.[39] When the brothers grew up, they were sent to the newly founded Jesuit College of St. Ignatius (Xuhui gongxue) in Shanghai, where they studied Latin, Greek, English, French, the sciences, and the Chinese classics.[40]

Alain Peyraube has suggested that a compelling model for Ma's *Universal Principles of Classical Chinese* is a work called *La Grammaire générale et raisonnée* by Antoine Arnauld and Claude Lancelot (1660), better known as *La Grammaire de Port-Royal*. This book had exerted the greatest impact on the study of language in Europe up until the birth of comparative grammar. Between 1803 and 1846, *La Grammaire de Port-Royal* was reissued six times in Paris and was simply known as *La Grammaire* at the time. Ma would have come into contact with the work when he went to study in France in 1875 (or 1876) if not earlier at the College of St. Ignatius in Shanghai. Peyraube's comparative analysis of the analytical categories used in *Ma's Universal Principles* and those found in *La Grammaire de Port-Royal* reveals some extraordinary parallels between the two works.[41] Of course, there are other significant sources to consider, such as Joseph de Prémare's *Notitiae Linguae Sinicae* (written in 1728 but not published until 1831 in Malacca) and Jean-Pierre Abel-Rémusat's *Elémens de la Grammaire chinoise* (Paris, 1822), but *La Grammaire de Port-Royal,* argues Peyraube, appears to provide the basic philosophical framework for the conceptualization of *Ma's Universal Principles*.[42] The Port-Royal grammarians assumed the existence of a universal grammar in all languages and exigencies of human thought, but unlike the comparative grammarians who came later, they were not trying to show that all languages must have case systems or use inflectional devices. On the contrary, as Noam Chomsky argues, "they repeatedly stress that a case system is only one device for expressing those relations . . . It is important to realize that the use of the names of classical cases for languages with no inflections implies only a belief in the uniformity of grammatical relations involved, a belief that deep structures are fundamentally the same across languages, although the means for their expression may be quite diverse."[43]

If Ma follows the philosophical thrust of the Port-Royal model in his belief in the universality of grammatical relations such as the case, can he prove the existence of universal grammar without first translating the grammatical categories from *La Grammaire de Port-Royal* and forcing classical Chinese into the borrowed mold? The tension appears to lie in the idea of universal grammar itself. Otto Jespersen makes a good point when he observes that the Port-Royal grammarians "tried to eliminate from a language everything that was not strictly conformable to the rules of logic, and to measure everything by the canon of their so-called general or philosophical grammar. Unfortunately they were too often under the delusion that Latin grammar was the perfect model of logical consistency, and they therefore laboured to find in every language the distinctions recognized in Latin."[44] Does Ma's work suffer from the same delusion?

Ma's Universal Principles makes a painstaking effort to demonstrate that classical Chinese has its full share of parts of speech, grammatical structure, and formal elements comparable to inflection and declension and is not marked by lacks and absences. The comparative impulse that led to Ma's explanation of classical Chinese in terms of Latin grammar ends up grafting the one onto the other. In that sense, Ma's experiment does seem run into the conceptual limits of his own comparative paradigm. Nevertheless, the book is as much about the claims of commensurability and sovereign thinking as it is about grammar. Ma's agenda was very much driven by the desire to (re)establish the sovereign status of the Chinese language and put it on a par with Indo-European grammars.

Grammaticality and Beyond

The publication of *Ma's Universal Principles of Classical Chinese* was greeted by the Chinese scholarly community as something of a novelty. This was not due to any lack of an indigenous philological tradition; on the contrary, there had been a deep-rooted, continuous scholarly tradition that evolved into highly specialized systems of knowledge by the nineteenth century. With a view to making grammatical studies accountable to the existing scholarship, Ma wrote in the preface to the *Universal Principles:*

> The ancient sages accomplished the work of civilization by creating the written characters to replace the knotted strings; hence the rise of the *wen zi.* Of the *wen zi,* the pictographs were called *wen* and the phonetico-ideographs were called *zi,* but with the passage of time, the *wen* and the *zi* both altered and transformed until they lost their original sense. To restore the vanishing traces of the ancient thoughts, there arose in the Han dynasty a generation of scholars such as Zheng Xuan [127–200] and Xu Shen [58–147] who inherited the seeds of fire from the Qin dynasty and whose works led to the invention of the *xiao xue* [Small Learning] which, since the Han, has branched into special fields. Ouyang Yongshu said: "*Er ya,* a work of the Han dynasty, was devoted to the rectification and clarification of names and things, leading to the rise of the *xun gu* [paleography/etymology]. Xu Shen wrote *Shuo wen jie zi* [Explicating texts and analyzing characters] with which he inaugurated the study of the *pian pang* [radical forms]. The need to interpret the changing forms of inscriptions and ancient scripts led to the knowledge of the *zi shu* [epigraphy]. Sun Yan, who identified the five tones and sound patterns as well as the interdependence of vowels and consonants, was the first to study the pronunciation of words and launched the

yin yun [sound/rhythm analysis]." On that basis, Wu Jingfu proposed three major fields of learning: epigraphy, paleography, and sound/rhythm analysis. Hu Yuanrui believed that Small Learning covered a dozen fields of learning including the *wen*, semantics, sound, epigraphy, evidential scholarship, commentaries and annotations, and so on but they all boiled down to these three: paleography, sound/rhythm studies, and epigraphy.[45]

The lacuna Ma perceived in the threefold tradition was a lack of interest in grammar. Traditional pedagogy, he argued, had emphasized textual exegesis and focused on the written character and did not encourage students to master their language through grammar. But laws of grammar did exist in classical Chinese, and one need only delve into the language to bring them to light. Ma regarded Chinese writing and Latin alike as the guardians of the great civilizations of the past, East and West, because each had the advantage of transcending the local dialects and vernacular languages of individual countries and regions. He pointed out, "One cannot claim to master classical Chinese until one is well versed in the Small Learning, and, by the same token, one must know Latin and Greek in order to understand the living European tongues that descend from the archaic languages. Scholars in England and France follow the routine of analyzing archaic terms from Latin and translating them into their own tongues."[46] Interestingly, Ma's brother had begun composing a book called *Lading wentong* (Universal principles of Latin) shortly before Ma Jianzhong embarked on the project on Chinese grammar.[47]

Ma saw an urgency for grammatical studies and linked it to the survival of Chinese culture and its ability to compete with the West in the contest of civilizations. "Over the past four millennia," Ma wrote, "our accumulated wisdom and talents have been expended asking the question why the Dao must carry and why reason must shine forth but we have been ignorant of that which carries the Dao and that which enables reason to shine forth. In comparison with the Westerners who have mastered the Dao and grasped reason, it goes without saying who will emerge as the superior and wiser one in this contest."[48] The project of discovering the laws of grammar in classical Chinese was inherently comparative because it was not enough to delve into the language itself. One must draw on preexisting concepts and analytical categories translated from Indo-European grammar books, as Ma acknowledges in the preface to the *Universal Principles:* "This book would be named *gelangma* [transliteration of "grammar"] in the West. The etymology of *gelangma* goes back to ancient Greek, meaning 'syntax' or rules for learning a language. All nation have grammars and the grammars are more or less identical; the differences show mainly at the level of the phonetics and the writing systems."[49] Ma attributed the existence of universal grammar to the human desire for meaning (*yi*) and argued that the desire for meaning allowed the races to transcend the limited horizons of their individual languages. "From ancient times to the present in this vast world, the different races, yellow, white, red, or black, are human beings and as human beings they are naturally endowed with the heavenly reason to understand and communicate meaning."[50] This is a very different sort of argument about race and language from what we have been hearing from the European and American comparative grammarians, and it brings him closer to the philosophical project of the Port-Royal grammarians.

Liang Qichao, the foremost Qing reformer, had long admired Ma Jianzhong by reputation. He became acquainted with the Ma brothers in the fall of 1896, when he arrived in Shanghai to start his newspaper *Shiwu bao* (Current affairs). In the course of that year, Liang and the brothers became close friends and conversed on a regular basis. Ma Jiangzhong gave Liang Latin lessons two hours a day, and it was at this time that Ma first showed Liang his unpublished grammar book as well as a volume of essays titled *Shikezhai jiyan* (Essays from the Shike studio, 1896), for which Liang wrote a foreword.[51] Ma Xiangbo and Liang had witnessed together the making of *Ma's Universal Principles of Classical Chinese* in Shanghai. Liang later recalled the time he had spent with the Ma brothers:

> Meishu [Ma Jiangzhong's style name] was well versed in the European languages and conceived of his grammar book on the model of well-organized grammatical categories of European grammar. Before that, he had already benefited from a deep knowledge of Wang Yinzhi's *Jing zhuan shi ci* (Explications and exegesis of the classics) and Yu Yinfu's *Gu shu yiyi juli* (Instances of contested interpretations in the classics). In 1896 Ma resided on Shouchang Road in Shanghai and was writing his grammar book when I moved there and became his next-door neighbor. Whenever Ma finished a section, I would be the first one to read it; modest as he was, Ma would consult my opinion from time to time. To this day, whenever I think of Ma, I feel inspired by his spirit and dedication to scholarship.[52]

Ma had retired from a diplomatic career in order to devote his time and energy to the writing and completion of his *Universal Principles;* he died less than two years after the book came out in print. We can gather from the paratexts surrounding the *Universal Principles,* such as the author's preface, the note on the text, and the epilogue, that his avowed intent was pedagogical. Commenting on how ineffective traditional schooling in China was in his time, Ma intended the book to be an effective aid in expediting the learning process so students could be freed from cumbersome rote learning and move quickly to the study of the sciences.[53] Liang Qichao concurred with the pedagogical story when he published the news of Ma's work in *Shiwu bao* in 1896:

> Schoolchildren in the West learn to read the alphabet first and are exposed to the study of grammar next by reading books that are designed to teach them how to turn words into sentences and how to compose essays by stringing the sentences together. I have watched Ma Meishu working on a book of Chinese grammar that is yet to be finished. In my pedagogical experience, I have taught schoolchildren the art of writing in classical Chinese. What I did was to give them a vernacular phrase for them to rephrase and correct them when they got it wrong. Going from simple subjects through preliminary reasoning, I would begin with a single sentence and then move on to three, four, and ten sentences until by the end of the second month they have mastered over thirty sentences. After acquiring this number of sentences, they will have nearly arrived at the point of knowing how to write classical Chinese. This is much less painful for the students and the teacher than if they were to adopt the common practice of composing the eight-legged essay and were asked to follow the rules for "cracking a topic," "introducing the subject," "making an argument," and "completing the exposition" and pore over the intricacies of sections and paragraphs. There is a world of difference between these two methods. We expect Ma's book, once completed, to provide us with a detailed analysis of how the order [of classical Chinese] works.[54]

After Ma's *Universal Principles of Classical Chinese* appeared in print, Liang celebrated the author's pathbreaking contribution to the development of modern Chinese scholarship but did not emphasize the pedagogical value of this work. He clearly saw that the novelty of Ma's book lay in its inauguration of a new discipline for China and called the book "an extraordinary accomplishment unprecedented in our history," one that "marked the beginning of grammatical studies in China."[55]

The nationalist leader Sun Yat-sen was among the first to see the value of grammatical studies for nation building, but his opinion of *Ma's Universal Principles of Classical Chinese* appeared lukewarm in contrast with Liang Qichao's enthusiastic endorsement. Sun expressed his views in the seminal text *Jianguo fanglue* (Blueprint for nation building):

> What is a grammar? It is what the Westerners call *gelangma*, a branch of learning that teaches people how to classify parts of speech and how to combine words to make a sentence. All Western nations boast of grammatical studies and publish books each in its own language for the edification of language learners . . . As we did not develop our own grammatical studies, we could not take the shortcut to reach the goal quickly. It was as if we were trying to cross a river but had no bridge or boat to do it with and must make a detour of a hundred times as far. Chinese men of letters had to endure this inconvenience to await the arrival of *Ma's Universal Principles of Classical Chinese*. That was when they discovered the existence of a discipline called grammatical studies. Ma claimed that he had spent more than ten long years in the researching and writing of this book, but from a practical viewpoint, the book has done little else than prove that grammar existed in ancient Chinese writing. As an indispensable tool, grammar books ought to be in the hands of Chinese scholars to help expedite their learning and progress. Ma's work might be useful to people who have already mastered classical Chinese for further reference but can hardly be used as a "bridge" by first-time learners.[56]

Sun's criticism brings Ma's and Liang's earlier pedagogical argument into question. The erudition and theoretical sophistication of Ma's book are clearly beyond the comprehension of well-educated individuals outside the small circle of language specialists and seem to defeat the author's stated pedagogical purpose. If Sun is right to observe that Ma's monumental work merely proves the existence of the laws of grammar in ancient Chinese writing, does the economy of sovereign thinking warrant a work of such magnitude and labor?

No doubt Sun had his own pedagogical goals in mind. By mapping out a nationalist agenda for humanistic studies, he envisioned a new generation of grammarians who could produce grammar books for schoolchildren that truly lived up to the pedagogical promise of helping students master their native tongue. But Sun's idea of modernity is just as invested in the economy of sovereign thinking as Liang's assessment of the value of Ma's work, except that the gains and losses of the grammarian's labor are weighed differently. Neither man took issue with the conditions of comparative grammar in general or Ma's modeling of classical Chinese on Indo-European language in particular, as these conditions have been assumed for the development of the modern Chinese academic study of Chinese language and writing. Opening up these conditions to further inquiry will enable us to understand better the grammatical figuring of the linguistic sign in comparative philology and how Ma negotiated the terms of commensurability between the concept of *zi* (character) and that of "word" within that framework.

The *Zi* versus the "Word"

Ma's *Universal Principles* sets out to identify and classify the parts of speech of classical Chinese *zi* in two broad conceptual categories. The first category, called *shi zi* (full character), encompasses substantives, demonstratives, adjectives, verbs, and adverbs, while in the latter category, *xu zi* (empty character), belong the prepositions, connectives, auxiliaries, and exclamations.[57] The notions of *shi zi* and *xu zi* were not new to indigenous Chinese textual exegeses; as we have seen, Ma's familiarity with the works of the classical scholars Wang Yinzhi and Yu Yinfu was remarked on by Liang Qichao. But the *shi zi* and *xu zi* do not automatically correlate with "parts of speech" as understood in the grammars of inflectional languages. That correlation was introduced into the study of Chinese by the Western missionary grammarians, primarily Joseph de Prémare, who needed a Chinese equivalent for the idea of parts of speech in Latin grammar. Alain Peyraube notes the connection when he states that, "like Prémare, Ma regards the *zi* as the basic grammatical unit of language, and he adopts the traditional division between 'empty words' and 'full words' to divide them subsequently according to the discursive categories of the West."[58] Ma's familiarity with Prémare's *Notitiae Linguae Sinicae* and with the indigenous classical scholarship probably led to his endorsement of Prémare's appropriation of "empty character" and "full character" in a translingual mode of theory making. What is more important, he could not treat the *zi* as the basic unit for grammatical analysis or identify the *zi lei* (parts of speech) without having already endorsed the hypothetical equivalence between the *zi* and the "verbum" (word) and, therefore, endorsed the truth of the super-sign *zi/verbum/word/mot* (hereafter *zi/word*)

The consolidation of the super-sign *zi/word* in *Ma's Universal Principles of*

Classical Chinese has caused the logocentric concept of "word" to destabilize the Chinese notion of *zi* on a massive scale and has led to heated debates among Chinese grammarians over the past century, often with confusing but fascinating results. What is a *zi?* Is it a written character, a "word," or a combination of the two? If, on the one hand, the *zi* is a word, what are the formal markers of the *zi lei* (parts of speech) of that word? If, on the other hand, the *zi* is a written character with phonetic-ideographic semantemes capable of combining with other characters to form "words," is it still meaningful to talk about the part of speech of a particular *zi* at this level?

Indeed, to think of the *zi* in terms of its super-sign *zi/word* is to overlook the fact that each Chinese written character comes with a minimal semanteme whose signification is independent of phonetic determination. This is not because the written characters are abstract pictures or pictographs, for the majority of them are not, but because the characters satisfy a wide range of semiotic conditions by adopting, among others, the functions of the *zhi shi* (indexical), the *xiangxing* (mimetic), and the *hui yi* (suggestive), according to Xu Shen's original classification of the *liu shu*, the Six Types (of written characters). Joseph de Prémare himself wrote a dissertation in 1721 in Chinese under the Chinese pseudonym Wen Gu Zi to offer a theological interpretation of the ancient theory of the *liu shu*.[59] It would be interesting to know whether C. S. Peirce was aware of Prémare's or Leibniz's work when he was developing the semiotic idea of indexicality for his trichotomy of signs—icon, index, and symbol—which I discussed in Chapter 1. He would have been inspired by their representation of the written Chinese character as a signifying entity rather than a mere verbal unit. Peirce used the example of a weathercock and a road sign to explain the function of the indexical sign. The former indicates the direction of the wind without imitating anything, while the latter points down the road in a manner that evokes the signifying process of Chinese ideographs, such as *shang* 上 (up) and *xia* 下 (down), independently of how the characters are pronounced in Mandarin, Japanese, Korean, Vietnamese, or the various dialects. Peirce's concept of the symbolic or general sign is particularly germane to the ways in which the radicals form Chinese ideographic characters, because the symbolic sign derives its meaning by being associated with other signs through usage. That is to say, signs nestle inside other signs and generate more signs that may or may not be "words."

In one of the passages quoted earlier, Ma mentions the threefold tradition in the indigenous studies of the *zi* but does not ponder its implications for future grammatical work. Broadly defined, the *xun gu* tradition includes the paleographic and etymological studies of the *zi* and *zi*-related phenomena; the *yin yun*, or sound analysis, focuses on the systems of attributable phonetic value associated with the *zi;* and the *zi shu*, or epigraphy, is devoted to the analysis of ancient inscriptions and the evolution of the written character. The *zi* bears the semantic value represented by the material sign of the written character, and, at the same time, all characters carry material sound values secondary to the written sign and indeterminate insofar as the written character can be pronounced in many different ways across a vast array of languages and dialects. Individuals within a radius of a hundred miles may not be able to understand one another's speech, but an educated Chinese would have little trouble communicating with an educated Japanese or Korean with the help of the writing brush (brush talk or pen talk has even survived language reform in each of these countries).[60] The portability of the material sign of the *zi* enables the semantic value of the Chinese character to travel more freely than its local pronunciation, since the *zi* need not be pronounced in any particular manner or pronounced at all to be meaningful, any more than it makes sense to talk about the meaning of Arabic numerals in terms of monosyllabism and polysyllabism.

The study of the ideographic character of the *zi* parallels and overlaps with the indigenous studies of the systems of attributed phonetic value, such as tonal patterns, in poetics and music. I have coined the term *attributed phonetic value* (hereafter APV) to emphasize the fluidity of the abstract phonetic value assigned to the written character as opposed to its actual pronunciation in speech, whether Mandarin, Cantonese, Japanese, or otherwise. The APV is what brings the written character and speech together, joining them in an unstable union, as the actual pronunciation of the character varies greatly from language to language, dialect to dialect. The APV corresponds to a cluster of phonemes rather than a specific phonemic value. The Chinese *yin yun* scholarship has relied on the *qie* method (cross-spelling), using the APVs of two written characters to transcribe the APV of a third character. The way the *qie* system works is that it borrows the *sheng* (consonant) of the first character and the *yun* (vowel and tone) of the second to define the pronunciation of the third. It is a native spelling system devised out of the existing characters and has the advantage of transcribing the APVs within the writing system as well as across the languages and dialects that employ the Chinese writing system. What the *qie* transcribes is not the actual pronunciation of a given character, which may vary from language to language and dialect to dialect, but the exchangeability or substitutability of attributed phonetic values among the written characters that are pronounced according to the phonetic systems of the languages or dialects in which they appear.

When a written character is used to designate the attributed phonetic value of another character, the "phonetic" character is not to be equated with the actual syllable of ordinary speech in a given linguistic environment. The failure to distinguish between the "phonetic" character and the syllable of linguistic enunciation is what caused Whitney's and other linguists' misconception of "the Chinese language" as a monosyllabic tongue characterized by an excessive number of homophones. According to that view, the excess of homophones in Chinese is due to a limited number of syllables, which explains why the tones are needed to stand in as additional phonemes. It is as if they mapped the Chinese language onto the written characters first and then determined on the monosyllabic basis of the individual written characters that the Chinese language itself is monosyllabic. But if two or more characters are found to share the same syllable with identical tones, the reverse is true as well, because each written character can be shown to represent as many different sound values as there are dialects and languages that share the Chinese writing system. In short, the illusion of the monosyllabic character of the Chinese language results from a blind projection of the APV of the written character onto speech so that the excess of homophones is attributed to the linguistic system itself rather than to the semiotic function and evolution of the written characters.

Xu Shen's principles of the *liu shu* have guided the Chinese understanding of the written character for the past two millennia. The basic assumption underlying the *liu shu* idea is that the pool of written radicals (along with their attributed phonetic values) available for forming new characters is limited, but the combinations can be infinite. (I should mention in passing that most Chinese word-processing software incorporates the *liu shu* principles to devise the *zao zi,* or character creation function.) Therefore, tension exists, primarily not between the insufficient number of syllables (or tones) and the needs for expression within the total horizon of the spoken language, but between the written character and the spoken language. The birth of the super-sign *zi/word* further aggravates that tension and, moreover, raises the thorny issue of how the Chinese *zi* could be grasped in terms of "word." Does the super-sign *zi/word* in this new, translated sense cross paths with the *liu shu* concept of the *zi?* Is the written character included in the super-sign?

The slippage between the *zi* and the "word" caused by the invasion of the super-sign has created an enormous conceptual burden that all Chinese grammarians since Ma must grapple with one way or the other before they can build their own systems by following or rejecting Ma's original conception. When Zhang Shizhao wrote his *Intermediary Mandarin Grammar* on the model of *Ma's Universal Principles of Classical Chinese* in 1907, he tried to resolve the issue by substituting the character *ci* for Ma's *zi* to classify the parts of speech in Mandarin. Likewise, Liu Bannong (Liu Fu) contested Ma's classificatory system and offered an alternative schema in his *Comprehensive Grammar of the Chinese Language* (1920), as did Jin Zhaozi in his *Studies in Chinese Grammar* (1922).[61] The concept of *ci* popularized by the works of the May Fourth scholars quickly became the standard equivalent of the English "word" to produce a new super-sign, *ci/word*. The concept of *ci* did appear within the system of Ma's grammar but was reserved for naming syntactical components such as the *qi ci* (subject) or the *zhi ci* (object) of a sentence. The substitution of *ci* for *zi* in the works of these grammarians caused Ma's neologistic designation of *ci* to undergo a new round of semiotic revisions. There is no reason why the character *ci* should be considered more accurate than the *zi* as a representation of the English "word." It was simply introduced to help the later scholars bypass the inimical slippage between the written character and the "word" in a super-sign that troubled Chinese grammatical studies from the outset.

Bypassing that slippage, however, has not solved the problem, because it leaves us to deal with a new super-sign, *ci/word*, that could no more banish the written character from grammatical analysis than one could compose a Chinese grammar without employing written characters. At the heart of grammatical analysis still lie traces of the *zi*, without a proper name, that nonetheless haunt the grammarian's attempt to name and fix things for the Chinese language and the writing system. Ma's slippage at least had the advantage of revealing, not hiding, the secret of what was really at stake, namely, the remaking of the written character, *zi*, in terms of its foreign other.

The contemporary Chinese artist Xu Bing has intuitively grasped the central problem here and tried to work with the slippage in his art installations. What he has done is to invent thousands of "fake" written Chinese characters and carve them one by one onto printer's woodblocks, printing the sheets and binding some of them in the manner of woodblock publications. The work has become known as the *Tian Shu* (A book from the sky), a title that comments directly on the undecipherability of the writing thus produced (Figure 12). Now, how do we comprehend the undecipherability of his fake characters and woodblock prints? Xu Bing's characters are made up of radicals from the Chinese writing system, and these radicals, along with their attributed phonetic value, as I have pointed out, are limited in number, but out of them the total number of possible combinations seems unlimited. Not surprisingly, the artist has also experimented with the English alphabet in a later work to achieve the same effect.

But the *Tian Shu* has accomplished much more than the arbitrary combination of known radicals. Xu Bing's simulacra of characters also explore the time-honored tension between the printed character and the spoken language and, more recently, the tension within the super-signs *zi/word* and *ci/word* which I have demonstrated. The artist pushes the tension to such an extreme that the printed character retains its Chinese-looking radicals, but they are not identifiable as words. The conception is brilliantly hyperfactual, because each of the *zi* looks like a word and is drawn from the fund of recog-

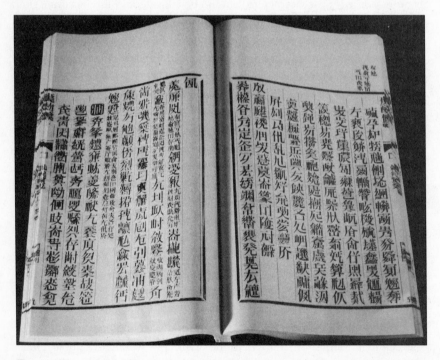

Figure 12.   Woodblock print with fake Chinese characters, from the art installation *The Book from the Sky* (1988). Courtesy of the artist, Xu Bing.

nizable radicals from the Chinese writing system but is meant to be a *non-word*. The printed character is there to tease and challenge, but not to be read or pronounced. The *Tian Shu* effectively parodies the printed character to subvert its association with the super-signs *zi/word* and *ci/word* and, ultimately, the very concept of "word" itself. This extraordinary understanding of the written character would have made little sense had the collision of the *zi* and the "word" not entered the space of translingual imagination in the first place through the works of Prémare, comparative philologists, and *Ma's Universal Principles of Classical Chinese*. In its quiet way, the *Tian Shu* brings the chapter on the sovereign subject of grammar to a close.

The Emperor's Empty Throne

This possibility of being in relation with desire is not simply the fact of the poetic, fictional, or imaginary practice of discourse: the discourses on wealth, on language *(langage)*, on nature, on madness, on life and death, and many others, perhaps, that are much more abstract, may occupy very specific positions in relation to desire.

—Michel Foucault, *The Archaeology of Knowledge*

I began this book by reflecting on my visit to London in the summer of 1997, when I explored the archives on Anglo-Chinese relations in the British Library and the Public Record Office. It was the eve of Hong Kong's scheduled return to China. My research coincided with the timing of the historical happening in that eventful summer and has been transformed by it. In the intervening years the world has experienced new wars, new acts of violence, the shock of September 11, 2001, the bombing of Afghanistan, U.S. imperialist expansion, global antiwar movements, the rift within NATO, the crisis of the UN, the war on Iraq launched by the Bush administration in the name of the American people, and so on. The list goes on.

Fear, death, border control, refugees, the nuclear arms race, questions of humanity, livelihood, rights, security, and dignity. Our world seems haunted by the ghost of terrorism that knows how to mimic the violence it attacks and become its shadow. Where does the ghost come from and who will be its next victim? Has sovereign thinking entered a new phase of enemy making and self-invention in our time? The answer depends on who is looking and which side of the *them and us* global divide one lives or has lived on. Half a century ago, Frantz Fanon wrote that he was shaken and overcome by grief when he saw "an Arab with his hunted look, suspicious, on the run, wrapped in those long ragged robes that seem to have been created especially for him." The grief leads Fanon to repeat, "Every citizen of a nation is

210

responsible for the actions committed in the name of that nation."[1] Apparently, things have not improved much since then, and have even grown worse. Now the whole world watches the spectacles of suffering on the television screen: Arabs, Africans, Asians, women and children on the run, desperate and dying, with that poignant empty look in their eyes after their homes have been bombed and destroyed by an enemy they did not make. Can we still grieve for them as Fanon did, or mourn the loss of our own imagination and sense of history?

The writing of this book has provided me with the opportunity to explore what I have called the nineteenth-century legacy of sovereign thinking, which has survived through our own times and continues to show robust signs of life. It is very clear that today's imperial warfare has not given up on evoking the rhetoric of barbarity and civilization, the logic of us versus them, Christian evangelism, appeals to friendship, human rights, honor, injury, dignity, and sovereignty. And yet, as I have argued and endeavored to show throughout this book, such discourses should not be taken as one-dimensional, for these ideas always get translated into other languages that contribute to the making of a larger story about world history. And it is that larger, hetero-cultural and translingual story that this book is after and that I have tried to put together for the reader.

The super-sign is the theoretical direction my investigation has pursued because it promises a level of conceptual uniqueness and precision that I have not been able to find in the work of other theorists. The idea has been immensely helpful in illuminating the strange ban that the British imposed on the Chinese character *yi* in Article 51 of the Anglo-Chinese Treaty of Tianjin, in showing how the character acquired the meaning it has in recent memory, and in analyzing the circumstances surrounding the translation of Henry Wheaton's *Elements of International Law* as well as those surrounding the birth of Ma Jianzhong's pioneering Chinese grammar book. The theory of the super-sign is also intended to help overcome the implicit monolingual assumptions of our inherited language theories and semiotic work in recognition of the fact that the majority of the world's populations today are increasingly bilingual or trilingual. Such awareness ought to have a significant bearing on our study of empire and the history of empire because the phenomenon of multilingualism is the outcome of the colonial and imperial warfare of the past. The contentiousness between the British and Qing empires, which I have analyzed in detail, placed the issue of language at the heart of nineteenth-century arguments about entitlement, injury, and sovereign rights, often with deadly consequences. Furthermore, the circulation of the Bible through the channels of imperial gift exchange in Britain and the Qing dynasty brought gender and religion into the purview of inter-imperial studies and refocused the early feminist notion of self-sovereignty in the light of missionary travel and imperial expansion.[2] I conclude by reflecting on the role of colonial memory and image making in the reiteration of imperial desires and the reinvention of sovereign subjectivity in the twentieth century. I focus on the spectrality of sovereign thinking in the physical removal and the fetishizing of the Qing emperor's throne chairs and the simultaneous circulation of their photographic images in the contemporary world.

Colonial Visuality

Terry Castle has called photography "the ultimate ghost-producing technology of the nineteenth century."[3] Photography is known for its uncanny ability to conjure memory by fixing the shadow of an image.[4] When the daguerreotype first came into existence in the 1840s, it was dubbed "the mirror with a memory," but the new technology quickly expanded its mimetic/mnemonic ambitions to take on a ghostly life of its own.[5] In both the popular imagination and the fantastic literature of nineteenth-century Europe, the camera obscura came to be associated with witchcraft and was made to act like a witch-machine at times. In "The Time Machine," for example, H. G. Wells explored the metaphysical implications of the new technology by letting his narrator speak the photographic language of "double exposure" in describing "a ghostly, indistinct figure sitting in a whirling mass of black and brass for a moment—a figure so transparent that the bench behind, with its sheets of drawings, was absolutely distinct; but this phantasm vanished as I rubbed my eyes."[6]

That the spectrality of the camera obscura has something to do with the colonial exploitation of primitivism has been suggested by recent scholarship in literary criticism, art history, and visual culture. Michael Taussig's reading of early documentary films comes to mind as a postcolonial intervention in the contemporary study of early visual anthropology. The magic of the camera lens, or of a talking machine such as the gramophone, is said to conjure the phantasmagoria of the self in the act of documenting and staging the primitive's fetishizing of modern technology.[7] With enthusiasm, the colonial traveler pursues the magical effect of being fascinated by someone else's fascination with his or her own technology. Above and beyond the imputed mimetic power of the camera lens, the encounters with the unfamiliar seem to hold out the attractive prospect of exorcising the ghostly other from within the self so that the West's own obsession with dark magic, all in the name of science and technology, may be simultaneously played out and disavowed.[8] Paul Gauguin's use of photography in some of his Tahiti paintings, as suggested by Nancy Perloff, thematizes the European artist's confrontation with the other as well as with the ghostly other within the self; hence, the need to exercise control over the processes of enchantment and exorcism.[9]

The legacy of colonial anthropology notwithstanding, one need not take too literal a stand on the issue of primitivism by assuming that colonial narratives are single-mindedly preoccupied with the primitivizing of the other. To do so would be to occlude the perverse, ignoring in the interpretive process the troublesome zone where the colonial traveler might have permitted himself or herself to trade places inadvertently with the fictitious "native" and, therefore, felt a particular urgency to narrativize, combat, or otherwise cope with the specter of primitivism that haunts the self. The literal approach is narrow-minded in that one tends to forget that the colonial legacy is all about sovereign thinking and sovereign claims. The primitivizing of the other is meaningful only insofar as it articulates meaningfully to the story of how the modern sovereign subject wills itself into being.

For in the matter of subject formation, the perverse—or, if you will, the "return of the repressed"—is in every sense integral to the process of self-making and can shed important light on what has heretofore been occluded by the positive studies of nationalism, modern history, and colonial photography. That which has been occluded, I argue, is the spectrality of sovereign thinking in the formation of modern subjectivities and collectivities. But how do we go about proving this? In what follows, I examine the ways in which the museum and the camera frame the ghostly shadow of the imperial throne chair in order to see how modern technology spawns spectral beings even as it claims to have brought the superstitions and specters of the human imagination under control.

The Victoria and Albert Museum

Craig Clunas, the British art historian who has investigated the looting of the imperial thrones from China, has given us a poignant account of his adolescent experience inside the Victoria and Albert Museum the very first time he saw the imperial throne. The experience made such an impression that many years later, long after he had become a curator in that museum, he remembered the incident:

> When I was fourteen I came to London with my father. We were on the way to Cambridge, where I was to investigate the possibility of studying Chinese. I visited the Victoria and Albert Museum for the first time, and there in a large room titled "Far Eastern Art" I was enthralled to see a great carved lacquer seat, labeled "Throne of the Emperor Ch'ien-lung." While the uniformed warder looked or pretended to look away, I knelt down and put my forehead to the black linoleum in homage.[10]

In the narrative account of his "embarrassing personal engagements and secret fetishisms, which threaten to reopen the space between the viewer and the artifact," Clunas directs our attention to the spectacle of sovereign enchantment in the display of dead emperors' throne chairs and other regalia in a British museum (Figure 13).[11] The Qing emperor's throne chair, in the

Figure 13. The alleged throne of the Qianlong emperor. Courtesy of Victoria and Albert Museum, London.

prized collections of the Victoria and Albert, transports the viewer to a different time and place in Clunas's telling of the story. It is almost as if the ghost of the Qianlong emperor had perched on the throne chair and turned the inert object into a spectral being. In the potent moment of enchantment, the emperor's throne chair appears to be unoccupied but, in another sense, crowded with old dreams, new fantasies, and much, much more.

Fetish objects under colonialism are itinerant signs that generate new meanings as they move from place to place. The central sign-events I have examined in this book—the invention of the super-sign *yi/barbarian*, the presentation of the New Testament, the translation of international law, and the writing of grammar books—all demonstrate the extent to which sovereign thinking depends on the movement of itinerant signs and objects across space and time. The emperor's throne chair is the ultimate fetish and object of desire. It seems that the disenchantment of the modern world has not been so thorough as to cause the fetish to lose its meaning and power of enchantment in our own time. The specific appeal of a dead emperor's throne not only extends to rulers who have gone out and conquered territories but also relates in some strange, fundamental way to the inner experience of ordinary individuals who visit museums, view photographs, watch films, read history books and novels, and so on. I have shown that this ultimate sign of sovereign thinking has continued to speak to the psyche of the modern individual in ways that have largely escaped the notice of the theorist of modern subjectivity.

In a study of British looting in India, Richard Davis provides an illuminating perspective from which we may reinterpret the meaning of looting and of loot for the nineteenth century:

> When we trace the histories of these objects, often we find that they have been dislodged from their initial settings during moments of official pillage, where the practice of looting has been public, more or less orderly, lawful (within the moral parameters of the looting party), and motivated as much by symbolic and representational as by economic intentions. This kind of looting most often forms part of imperial projects, by which conquering polities have sought to establish and represent asymmetrical political relations and cultural hegemonies.[12]

The looting episode Davis studies here is the pillage of Delhi by the British after they had suppressed the Indian uprising in 1857. Three years later some of the same troops would be deployed to Beijing and begin another looting incident as they entered the royal palaces of the Qing emperors. Military looting, however, should not be taken for granted as a natural expression of human greed any more than the throne of the Chinese emperor was a mere war trophy claimed by the victorious British army during the military campaigns. As Davis's and James Hevia's studies have shown, there were specific legal and moral codes governing the orderly transactions involving looted objects and their destination in the art market or other international venues.

The throne chair in the Victoria and Albert Museum did not formerly belong to the Forbidden City. Clunas's research shows that it had been looted from an imperial hunting park, Nan haizi, to the south of Beijing when the Allied Forces of the Eight Powers occupied the city at the time of the so-called Boxer Uprising.[13] This late-eighteenth-century imperial chair embarked on a somewhat obscure trip abroad after leaving its original home and did not turn up on the London art market until twenty years later. The owner of the chair at the time was Michael Girs, a White Russian émigré and former tsarist ambassador, who sold the piece for £2,250. At the time of its acquisition by the Victoria and Albert in 1922, the director Cecil Harcourt Smith wrote to the benefactor J. P. Swift, who had raised the money and donated the throne to the museum: "I have had an opportunity of bringing the gift to the personal notice of the Queen who had already seen the Throne and expressed a hope that, by some means, it might find a place in our collections; and I am commended to inform you that Her Majesty desired me to convey to you her warm appreciation of your generosity and spirit."[14] From the time of its acquisition to the removal of the collection on the eve of World War II, the throne was the main attraction in a gallery (room 42) devoted to Chinese and Japanese lacquer and woodwork. It was singled out as the most significant item in the room by the authors of *The Victoria and Albert Museum: Brief Guide* (1924) and *The Victoria and Albert Museum: A Short Illustrated Guide* (1937).

Cecil Harcourt Smith's acquisition of the alleged "Throne of the Emperor Qianlong" for the Victoria and Albert Museum had, he notes, won the appreciation of the queen. With hindsight, her endorsement may well be read as a direct assertion of the sovereign right of the British Crown vis-à-vis that of the Chinese state. This understanding of sovereignty seems to suggest a mode of reciprocity familiar to us all. Clunas argues, for example, that by acquiring the throne in 1922, "the British state was obtaining more than a splendid piece of craftsmanship, it was staking a claim which supported at a symbolic level the political and commercial rights that it had extorted from the government of the Chinese empire, and would uphold against the claims of the Chinese Republic."[15] While I agree with much of what Clunas says in his fine study, the notion of the "symbolic" does not seem to capture the performativity of sovereign rights as a *retroactive act of redress*. For when the British took possession of the throne chair, they specifically insisted without proving it that the throne belonged to the Qianlong emperor, which cannot but bring to mind the memory of Lord Macartney's mission at the court of the Qianlong emperor in 1793.

The Macartney audience had long preoccupied the imagination of British imperial subjects who fought to defend Britain's interests in the Opium War, the Arrow War, and the subsequent suppression of the 1900 uprising. The overwhelming rhetoric for waging war against China invariably evoked the perceived need to redeem the honor and cultural superiority of the British, which had been compromised in the earlier encounter between Lord Macartney and the Qianlong emperor. As I have shown, the official dispatches and unofficial exchanges between the British and Chinese governments attest to a startling level of neurotic fixation that had driven the British ruling class to engage in one military campaign after another in China.[16] One must be vigilant about reading such emotional behavior as a mere ideological sham to cover up the commercial interests of the British in the nineteenth century. Without downplaying the economic motivation, I suggest that the will to retaliate against the Chinese for the humiliation of the British on the symbolic front was very real, no less so than the trade interest. Such psychic investment often exceeded the calculated political and economic objectives of the British and led to costly and fanatical destruction of human lives and property in military campaigns. Taking possession of the throne chair of the Qianlong emperor and putting it on display in the Victoria and Albert Museum amounted to settling an old score with a dead Qing emperor.

From the Qianlong emperor's death in 1799 to Britain's taking possession of the throne chair in 1922, the retroactive act of redress took more than a century to accomplish. That time lag was identical with none other than the long nineteenth century, in the course of which the notion of universal sovereignty was being significantly eclipsed by the positive construct of sovereign rights as an object of recognition. The British Crown was not only staking out a symbolic claim to the political and commercial rights it had extorted from the Qing regime but also asserting a view of sovereignty and reciprocity that went back to the looting of the Qianlong emperor's European-style palaces during the destruction of the Gardens of Perfect Brightness in October 1860. On that occasion, as Hevia has shown, British troops found a cannon of European manufacture and identified the object as a gift from King George III. The Macartney embassy had brought the gift to the Qianlong emperor on behalf of the king of England, but it was being "repatriated" to the Royal Arsenal at Woolwich, "the site where it had been manufactured and where armaments were produced for empire."[17] This manner of repossession and repatriation canceled out the earlier mode of reciprocity and substituted a politics of nonrecognition for the economy of gift exchange.[18] The British annulment of the eighteenth-century communication between King George III and the Qianlong emperor suggests a changing condition of sovereign exchange in recent history that gives the possession and permanent display of the Chinese emperor's throne at the Victoria and Albert Museum its historical meaning and unique expression of sovereign will.

Nevertheless, the story of the Chinese emperor's throne chair should not and need not end in London or Edinburgh, for we find similar displays of the emperor's empty throne chairs within the audience halls of the Forbidden City, now the Palace Museum in Beijing. Some of those throne chairs are similarly caught up in a discontinuous history of displacement and reappropriation although they may not have been physically removed beyond the thick walls of the Forbidden City. The museum display of the Qing emperor's throne chairs in the original setting of the imperial audience halls raises the issue of what purposes these objects might be serving for a modern state. Are the fetishes regarded as cultural relics of the past and thus valuable to the tourist industry of the nation? Or have they been incorporated into the national imaginary of the People's Republic? If so, in what ways do they conjure the sovereignty of a modern republic that opposes its raison d'être to the dynastic rule of the past? Is the historicity of the imperial artifacts in the Palace Museum linked in some fundamental ways to that of looted objects on display in London and elsewhere?

Lost and Found: The Imperial Throne in the Forbidden City

Fifteen years after the looting of the throne chair from the imperial hunting park by the Allied troops, the magnificent throne chair in the Hall of Supreme Harmony in the Forbidden City was also removed from its original setting and soon vanished without a trace. This particular throne, having seen the successive reigns of the Qing rulers, was the most august of all throne chairs adorning the emperor's audience halls, because the Hall of Supreme Harmony was exclusively reserved for the coronation of Qing emperors and other grand occasions of state. General Yuan Shikai removed the original throne chair in 1915 when he proclaimed himself the new emperor of China. Yuan decided to modernize the old throne chair in the Hall of Supreme Harmony and had a new imperial throne of hybrid Chinese and European design built for him (Figure 14). The old one was banished to some obscure corner and was not to reemerge until half a century later. Yuan's

Figure 14. General Yuan Shikai furnished the Hall of Supreme Harmony with a new throne chair in 1915. Photograph reproduced from Zhu Chuanrong, ed., *Dijing jiuying* (As dusk fell on the imperial city) (Beijing: Forbidden City Publishing House of the Palace Museum, 1994).

emperorship was short-lived. After his death in 1916, the new throne chair continued to occupy the Hall of Supreme Harmony for decades.[19]

In 1947 the Palace Museum of the Nationalist government took charge of the relics of the imperial household. The curator of the museum attempted to remove Yuan's throne and restore the original Qing furniture to the Hall of Supreme Harmony. The search for the original chair proved more daunting than the museum staff had imagined. After combing through the warehouses of the Forbidden City, they were unable to find anything to match the original screen and dais in the Hall of Supreme Harmony. The search was resumed in 1959 after the founding of the People's Republic, and Zhu Jiajin, the curator of the Palace Museum, was put in charge of the task. Interestingly, using a 1901 photograph of the Hall of Supreme Harmony to identify the old throne, Zhu found it in a pile of dilapidated furniture and broken timber in an obscure corner of the Forbidden City (Figure 15). The original

Figure 15. The 1901 Japanese photograph of the Qing emperor's throne chair in the Hall of Supreme Harmony of the Forbidden City, reproduced from *Photographs of Palace Buildings of Peking*. Courtesy of the Library of Congress, Washington, D.C. Curator Zhu Jiajin and his team relied on this photograph to restore the broken throne chair to its present state.

throne chair was damaged beyond recognition; its left arm was completely missing and the rest was otherwise in disrepair. With the support of the central government, a restoration team led by Zhu spent several years reconstructing the throne, carefully reproducing the original details as shown in the 1901 photograph.

The itinerancy of the old throne preoccupied me when I visited Zhu Jiajin himself in a small office near the Shenwu Gate of the Forbidden City in the spring of 2000.[20] In the course of our conversation, Zhu showed me a reproduction of the photograph he had used to restore the old throne chair. It had been taken by a Japanese photographer named Kazumasa Ogawa, who was one of four Japanese academics dispatched to Beijing by the Imperial University of Tokyo after Japan had joined the Western powers in the suppression of the *Yihe Tuan* uprising. The other three members of the team were Chiuta Itō of the College of Engineering; Jiun-ichi Tsuchiya, a member of the University Hall; and Tsunegorō Okuyama, also a professor at the College of Engineering.[21] The photographing of the imperial throne in the Hall of Supreme Harmony by the Japanese team took place in the same time period as the looting of the throne chair from the imperial hunting park, which has been studied by Clunas.

During the Allies' occupation of Beijing in 1900–1901, Japanese and Western photographers were admitted into the Forbidden City to photograph the imperial palace and the emperor's audience halls for propaganda literature, while at the same time the Western troops were looting the Western Palace of the Empress Dowager (the Yiluan Palace); they torched the building afterwards. One of the most celebrated images of the Allies' victory was taken inside the Qianqing audience hall, showing a European officer sitting on the imperial throne chair (Figure 16). When the Empress Dowager returned from exile, she saw some of the photographs and expressed resentment at the fact that "several foreigners sat on my throne and had their photos taken."[22]

Zhu Jiajin's family had owned a large house on Legation Street where the foreign diplomatic community lived. Before the foreign troops entered the city, the Zhu family had left the residence to the care of their servants and taken refuge in the countryside. On returning the next year, they found the building in ruins. Zhu's father retrieved from the rubble only a bronze mortar for grinding herbal medicine and an iron hammer. "I was not born yet," Zhu writes, "but I could imagine how my parents' generation had felt when the loss of the nation also meant the loss of one's own home. As I look at the

Figure 16. An officer of the Allied Forces sits on the throne chair of the Qianqing audience hall during the 1900–1901 occupation of Beijing. Photograph from Liu Beisi and Xu Qixian, eds., *Gugong zhencang renwu zhaopian huicui* (Exquisite figure-pictures from the Palace Museum) (Beijing: Forbidden City Publishing House of the Palace Museum, 1994).

photographs of those years, they always remind me of the Allied Forces' crimes against China, and no Chinese should forget them. More important, they remind me of the catastrophic losses suffered by my own family. That trauma has been deeply imprinted on my memory."[23] In some ways, Zhu's personal anecdote mirrors the anecdote Clunas told about his own adolescent experience, quoted at the outset of this chapter. At the time of his writing about the throne chair, Clunas was the curator of Far Eastern art at the Victoria and Albert Museum, while Zhu Jiajin was in charge of the relics of the imperial household at the Palace Museum in Beijing. Their respective engagement with the emperor's throne chairs in one or the other museum suggests that the personal trauma in Zhu's story and the secret fetishism of which Clunas spoke are both embedded in the absent figure of the sovereign. That powerful void from the violent past of colonial encounter is what enables the empty throne chair to speak to the present and to the new desires and forms of sovereign thinking in our own time.

Zhu's mention of old photographs is significant. Beginning in the second half of the nineteenth century, war journalists had become a common sight, traveling with the imperialist troops to document their colonial exploits. The army and the Imperial Civil Service of the British Empire numbered among their ranks thousands of amateur photographers who pioneered in photojournalism. A military photographer, Linnaeus Tripe, published as many as ten books in 1857 and 1858.[24] Military technology provided the material context in which the work of the pioneering photographers in China such as Ernst Ohlmer, John Thomson, and Osvald Siren should be viewed. Ohlmer was a German photographer who took some of the earliest photographs of the Gardens of Perfect Brightness before they were looted and completely destroyed by the British-French Allied troops. In the words of Thomson, the photographer was the "forerunner of death," who witnessed the beheading of rebels as well as the destruction of palaces, temples, and mansions. The modern writer Lu Xun began his literary career after experiencing the trauma of watching a propaganda slide made by Japanese military photographers showing the execution of a fellow Chinese man during the Russo-Japanese War (1904–5).[25]

The Palimpsest of Desire: Bertolucci's *The Last Emperor*

When I first watched Bernardo Bertolucci's film *The Last Emperor* in 1987, I was baffled by the oppressive pull of nostalgia the film sought to produce and force into the subjectivity of the viewer. The strange narrative of obsession was blatantly seductive, if not immobilizing, as the film attempted to impress on the audience a hypnotic rhetoric of past imperial splendor.

Bertolucci's camera seizes on the royal throne of the emperor of China, in particular, with a fetishistic intensity and reverence that call for the repeated assertion of that object throughout the film. The throne is there to haunt the viewer. I, for one, tend to lose track of the total number of shots devoted to that singular object, but the last shot of the imperial site is truly unforgettable. The scene includes several sentimental close-ups of the aged Pu Yi (played by John Lone), who is making what appears to be his last visit to the Forbidden City. There he encounters, or fantasizes about encountering, a young boy who appears out of nowhere and addresses him as he approaches the vacant throne. The boy's age is roughly the same as that of Pu Yi when he had first been crowned in the Hall of Supreme Harmony the boy emperor of China (Figure 17). No doubt the film is trying to stage an allegorical encounter between Pu Yi and his ghostly former self across the monumental divide of the Republican revolution, World War II, and the Communist revolution. For a long period of time I struggled, albeit unsuccessfully, to figure out why this particular brand of nostalgia had been able to cast such a spell on its audience and why the experience of watching Bertolucci's film both repelled and fascinated me.[26]

Looking back, I must have been repelled and fascinated by Bertolucci's own fascination with the Chinese throne, but I was unable to put my finger on either source of fascination until I visited Britain in the mid-1990s. In the Asian Art Museum in Edinburgh I stumbled on what looked like a Chinese throne chair. Glancing at the caption next to it, I learned that this handsome object had been donated to the museum by a Scottish brigadier and his wife.

Figure 17. The coronation of the child Pu Yi as the last emperor of the Qing dynasty in Bertolucci's film *The Last Emperor.*

The caption did not, however, disclose by what means the couple had come to own this object. On my visit to the Victoria and Albert Museum in London, I was brought face to face with the alleged throne chair of the Qianlong emperor in the permanent collection there, which made me wonder if there was not something peculiar about these reified images of the imperial throne in the modern West. The thing that had astonished me the most was the discovery that I had somehow neglected to pay attention to the display of the imperial thrones in their original settings, namely, the emperors' audience halls in the Forbidden City. After all, I had made a good number of visits to the Palace Museum in the Forbidden City before journeying out to the West in 1984. Had I not been made to see through someone else's eyes—through Bertolucci's camera and the museum exhibitions—I would not have cast more than a passing glance at these relics of the past, which, I thought, could have little material impact on the contemporary world. But now it was as if I were looking at the objects for the first time. It was not that I had rediscovered the colonial and postcolonial life story of the imperial objects through someone else's eyes but rather that I was fascinated by *someone else's fascination* with spectral beings.

What seemed to have begun as a viewer's spontaneous reaction to the film *The Last Emperor* and to the museum displays led me to ask questions about the spectral relationship between subjectivity and sovereign thinking that I have been trying to address in this book. The curious multiple encounters I have had with the imperial thrones over the years have worked to change my mind about time, memory, selfhood, desire, and sovereignty so that I can no longer take the materiality of things for granted. If the genealogical history of the museum as an imperial institution seems to carry less weight in my analysis of the display of the throne chairs in London and Beijing, it is because it cannot answer the question of how the economy of sovereign thinking produces targets of neurotic fixation among those who participate in imperial acts and fantasies, past and present.[27]

To judge from the director's cut of *The Last Emperor,* Bertolucci primarily used the Hall of Supreme Harmony as the setting for his film.[28] The Hall of Supreme Harmony is where the boy emperor's coronation and the final scene of Pu Yi's ghostly encounter with his childhood self take place. As I have described it, the latter scene includes several sentimental close-up shots of Pu Yi during his last visit to the Forbidden City. As he walks into the Hall of Supreme Harmony, a young boy appears and begins asking him questions. In this fabricated episode, Pu Yi gives the boy the cricket box he had hidden underneath the throne many years before. Miraculously, a live cricket begins to emerge from the box as if Pu Yi's own cricket had never left since the emperor's coronation. The boy is enthralled by the little creature, as is the audience, but as the camera's eye turns to behold the old man Pu Yi once again, he vanishes from the frame without a trace. (The subtitle informs us that Pu Yi died in 1967.)

The manipulation of cuts and reverse shots helps stage a miraculous encounter and the equally miraculous disappearance of the emperor. Bertolucci's camera, however, is not the first ghost-producing machine that contemplates the emperor's throne in this uncanny manner. As we have seen, the film followed in the wake of successive projections of imperial desire onto the emperor's throne from the time of the Allies' occupation of Beijing in 1900. The seeming transparency of the cinematic shots in *The Last Emperor* constitutes one of the palimpsest layers of previous snapshots motivated by earlier conquests and earlier moments of sovereign thinking. In short, the magical image of the throne is always already fetishized. We can also think of this transparency in terms of a metonymic "double exposure," as I observed in connection with H. G. Wells's "ghostly, indistinct figure" in "The Time Machine." This figure is so transparent that the bench behind it (or the throne in this case), covered with sheets of drawings, is absolutely distinct; but this phantasm vanishes as the narrator rubs his eyes.

As I noted earlier, the Japanese photographer Kazumasa Ogawa secured one of the first film exposures of the emperor's throne in the Hall of Supreme Harmony in 1901. Fifteen years later the original throne disappeared from the hall during the rule of Yuan Shikai. But it remained a ghostly figure in the Japanese photograph until Zhu Jiajin rediscovered the remains of the throne chair, which he identified based on that ghostly figure. The restoration team copied the image of the figure to make an exact replica of the original emperor's throne for the Palace Museum. This is what Bertolucci saw when he brought his film crew to the Forbidden City to document the original royal regalia in the Hall of Supreme Harmony. Instead of the original throne, his camera merely copied what was itself a refurbished copy of the ghostly figure captured by the camera of an earlier generation of foreign photographers. As if haunted by the ghost of the Japanese military photographer, *The Last Emperor* includes a scene depicting a Japanese film crew working in Manchuria on the eve of World War II. One fascinating frame shows a Japanese photographer directing his camera at the Qing emperor, this time during the re-coronation of the puppet emperor Pu Yi for the purpose of imperialist propaganda (Figure 18).[29] With a powerful sense of imperial nostalgia, these moments of *mise en abîme* replay a history of desire and sovereign thinking that has been central to the making of the modern world.

Figure 18. A Japanese military photographer documenting Pu Yi's recoronation in Manchuria as puppet emperor, from Bertolucci's *The Last Emperor*.

Appendix: Lin Zexu's Communication to Queen Victoria

Translation published in *Chinese Repository* 8, no. 10 (February 1840)	The original document titled "Ni yu yingjili guowang xi" (A draft declaration to the sovereign of England) jointly submitted by Lin Zexu, Deng Tingzhen, and Yi Liang	Translation published in Ssu-yü Teng and John K. Fairbank, *China's Response to the West* (1954), pp. 24–27
Letter to the queen of England from the high imperial commissioner Lin, and his colleagues. From the Canton Press	林則徐、鄧廷楨、怡良會奏《擬諭英吉利國王檄》	Lin Tse-hsü's Moral Advice to Queen Victoria, 1839
Lin, high imperial commissioner, a president of the Board of War, viceroy of the two Keäng provinces, &c., Tang, a president of the Board of War, viceroy of the two Kwang provinces, &c., and E., a vice-president of the Board of War, lieut.-governor of Kwangtung, &c., hereby conjointly address this public dispatch to the queen of England for the purpose of giving her clear and distinct information (on the state of affairs) &c.	欽差大臣湖廣總督部堂林 兵部尚書兩廣總督部堂鄧 廣東巡撫怡良	[Official titles omitted]

Translation in *Chinese Repository* (1840)	The original document, "Ni yu yingjili guowang xi"	Translation in *China's Response to the West* (1954)

It is only our high and mighty emperor, who alike supports and cherishes those of the Inner Land, and those from beyond the seas-who looks upon all mankind with equal benevolence—who, if a source of profit exists anywhere, diffuses it over the whole world—who, if the tree of evil takes root anywhere, plucks it up for the benefit of all nations;—who, in a word, hath implanted in his breast that heart (by which beneficent nature herself) governs the heavens and the earth! You, the queen of your honorable nation, sit upon a throne occupied through successive generations by predecessors, all of whom have been styled respectful and obedient. Looking over the public documents accompanying the tribute sent (by your predecessors) on various occasions, we find the following: "All the people of my country, arriving at the Central Land for purposes of trade, have to feel grateful to the great emperor for the most perfect justice, for the kindest treatment," and other words to that effect. Delighted did we feel that the kings of your honorable nation so clearly understood the great principles of propriety, and were so deeply grateful for the heavenly goodness (of our emperor):—therefore, it was that we of the heavenly dynasty nourished and cherished your people from afar, and bestowed upon them redoubled proofs of our urbanity and kindness. It is

為照會事：洪惟我大皇帝，撫綏中外，一視同仁，利則於天下公之，害則為天下去之，蓋以天地之心為心也。貴國王累世相傳，皆稱恭順。觀歷次進貢表文云："凡本國人到中國貿易，均蒙大皇帝一體公平恩待"等語。竊喜貴國王深明大義，感激天恩，是以天朝柔遠綏懷，倍加優禮，貿易之利，垂二百年。該國所由以富庶稱者，來由此也。

A communication: magnificently our great Emperor soothes and pacifies China and the foreign countries, regarding all with the same kindness. If there is profit, then he shares it with the peoples of the world; if there is harm, then he removes it on behalf of the world. This is because he takes the mind of heaven and earth as his mind.

The kings of your honorable country by a tradition handed down from generation to generation have always been noted for their politeness and submissiveness. We have read your successive tributary memorials saying, "In general our countrymen who go to trade in China have always received His Majesty the Emperor's gracious treatment and equal justice." and so on. Privately we are delighted with the way in which the honorable rulers of your country deeply understand the grand principles and are grateful for the Celestial grace. For this reason the Celestial Court in soothing those from afar has redoubled its polite and kind treatment. The profit from trade has been enjoyed by them continuously for two hundred years. This is the source from which your country has become known for its wealth.

Translation in *Chinese Repository* (1840)	The original document, "Ni yu yingjili guowang xi"	Translation in *China's Response to the West* (1954)

merely from these circumstances, that your country—deriving immense advantage from its commercial intercourse with us, which has endured now two hundred years—has become the rich and flourishing kingdom that it is said to be!

But, during the commercial intercourse which has existed so long, among the numerous foreign merchants resorting hither, are wheat and tares, good and bad; and of these latter are some, who, by means of introducing opium by stealth, have seduced our Chinese people, and caused every province of the land to overflow with that poison. These then know merely to advantage themselves, they care not about injuring others! This is a principle which heaven's Providence repugnates; and which mankind conjointly look upon with abhorrence! Moreover, the great emperor hearing of it, actually quivered with indignation, and especially dispatched me, the commissioner, to Canton, that in conjunction with the viceroy and lieut.-governor of the province, means might be taken for its suppression!

惟是通商已久，眾夷良莠不齊，遂有夾帶鴉片，誘惑華民，以致流毒各省者。似此但知利己，不顧害人，乃天理所不容，人情所共憤。大皇帝聞而震怒，特遣本大臣來至廣州與本總督部堂巡撫部院會同查辦。

But after a long period of commercial intercourse, there appear among the crowd of barbarians both good persons and bad, unevenly. Consequently there are those who smuggle opium to seduce the Chinese people and so cause the spread of the poison to all provinces. Such persons who only care to profit themselves, and disregard their harm to others, are not tolerated by the laws of heaven and are unanimously hated by human beings. His Majesty the Emperor, upon hearing of this, is in a towering rage. He has especially sent me, his commissioner, to come to Kwangtung, and together with the governor-general and governor jointly to investigate and settle this matter.

Translation in *Chinese Repository* (1840)	The original document, "Ni yu yingjili guowang xi"	Translation in *China's Response to the West* (1954)

Every native of the Inner Land who sells opium, as also all who smoke it, are alike adjudged to death. Were we then to go back and take up the crimes of the foreigners, who, by selling it for many years have induced dreadful calamity and robbed us of enormous wealth, and punish them with equal severity, our laws could not but award to them absolute annihilation! But, considering that these said foreigners did yet repent of their crime, and with a sincere heart beg for mercy; that they took 20,283 chests of opium piled up in their store-ships, and through Elliot, the superintendent of the trade of your said country, petitioned that they might be delivered up to us, when the same were all utterly destroyed, of which we, the imperial commissioner and colleagues, made a duly prepared memorial to his majesty;—considering these circumstances, we have happily received a fresh proof of the extraordinary goodness of the great emperor, inasmuch as he who voluntarily comes forward, may yet be deemed a fit subject for mercy, and his crimes be graciously remitted him. But as for him who again knowingly violates the laws, difficult indeed will it be thus to go on repeatedly pardoning! He or they shall alike be doomed to the penalties of the new statute. We presume that you, the sovereign of your honorable nation, on pouring out your heart before the altar of eternal justice, cannot but command all foreigners with the deepest

凡內地民人販鴉片食鴉片者，皆應處死。若追究夷人歷年販賣之罪，則貽害深而攫利重，本為法所當誅。為念眾夷尚知悔罪乞誠，將躉船鴉片二萬二百八十三箱，由領事官義律稟請繳收，全行毀化，叠經本大臣等據實具奏。幸蒙大皇帝格外施恩，以自首者情尚可原，姑寬免罪，再犯者法難屢貸，立定新章。量貴國王嚮化傾心，定能諭令眾夷，兢兢克法，但必曉以利害，乃至天朝法度，斷不可以不懍尊也。

All those people in China who sell opium or smoke opium should receive the death penalty. If we trace the crime of those barbarians who through the years have been selling opium, then the deep harm they have wrought and the great profit they have usurped should fundamentally justify their execution according to law. We take into consideration, however, the fact that the various barbarians have still known how to repent their crimes and return to their allegiance to us by taking the 20,283 chests of opium from their storeships and petitioning us, through their consular officer [superintendent of trade], Elliot, to receive it. It has been entirely destroyed and this has been faithfully reported to the Throne in several memorials by this commissioner and his colleagues.

Fortunately we have received a specially extended favor from His Majesty the Emperor, who considers that for those who voluntarily surrender there are still some circumstances to palliate their crime, and so for the time being he has magnanimously excused them from punishment. But as for those who again violate the opium prohibition, it is difficult for the law to pardon them repeatedly. Having established new regulations, we presume that the ruler of your honorable country, who takes delight in our culture and whose disposition is inclined towards us, must be able to instruct the

Translation in *Chinese Repository* (1840)	The original document, "Ni yu yingjili guowang xi"	Translation in *China's Response to the West* (1954)

respect to reverence our laws! If we only lay clearly before your eyes, what is profitable and what is destructive, you will then know that the statutes of the heavenly dynasty cannot but be obeyed with fear and trembling!

We find that your country is distant from us about sixty or seventy thousand miles, that your foreign ships come hither striving the one with the other for our trade, and for the simple reason of their strong desire to reap a profit. Now, out of the wealth of our Inner Land, if we take a part to bestow upon foreigners from afar, it follows, that the immense wealth which the said foreigners amass, ought properly speaking to be portion of our own native Chinese people. By what principle of reason then, should these foreigners send in return a poisonous drug, which involves in destruction those very natives of China? Without meaning to say that the foreigners harbor such destructive intentions in their hearts, we yet positively assert that from their inordinate thirst after gain, they are perfectly careless about the injuries they inflict upon us! And such being the case, we should like to ask what has become of that conscience which heaven has implanted in the breasts of all men?

查該國距內地六、七萬里，而夷船爭來貿易者，為獲利之厚故耳。以中國之利利外夷，是夷所獲之厚利，皆從華民分去，豈有反以毒物害華民之理！即夷人未必有心為害，而貪利之極，不顧害人，試問天良何在？

various barbarians to observe the law with care. It is only necessary to explain to them the advantages and disadvantages and then they will know that the legal code of the Celestial Court must be absolutely obeyed with awe.

We find your country is sixty or seventy thousand *li* [three *li* make one mile, ordinarily] from China. Yet there are barbarian ships that strive to come here for trade for the purpose of making a great profit. The wealth of China is used to profit the barbarians. That is to say, the great profit made by barbarians is all taken from the rightful share of China. By what right do they then in return use the poisonous drug to injure the Chinese people? Even though the barbarians may not necessarily intend to do us harm, yet in coveting profit to an extreme, they have no regard for injuring others. Let us ask, where is your conscience?

Translation in *Chinese Repository* (1840)	The original document, "Ni yu yingjili guowang xi"	Translation in *China's Response to the West* (1954)

We have heard that in your own country opium is prohibited with the utmost strictness and severity:—this is a strong proof that you know full well how hurtful it is to mankind. Since then you do not permit it to injure your own country, you ought not to have the injurious drug transferred to another country, and above all others, how much less to the Inner Land! Of the products which China exports to your foreign countries, there is not one which is not beneficial to mankind in some shape or other. There are those which serve for food, those which are useful, and those which are calculated for re-sale; but all are beneficial. Has China (we should like to ask) ever yet sent forth a noxious article from its soil? Not to speak of our tea and rhubarb, things which your foreign countries could not exist a single day without, if we of the Central Land were to grudge you what is beneficial, and not to compassionate your wants, then wherewithal could you foreigners manage to exist? And further, as regards your woolens, camlets, and longells, were it not that you get supplied with our native raw silk, you could not get these manufactured! If China were to grudge you those things which yield a profit, how could you foreigners scheme after any profit at all? Our other articles of food, such as sugar, ginger, cinnamon, &c., and our other articles for use, such as silk piece-goods, chinaware, &c., are all so many necessaries of

聞該國禁食鴉片甚嚴，是固明知鴉片之為害也。既不使爲害於該國，則他國尚不可移害，況中國乎！中國所行與外國者，無一非利人之物，利於食，利於用，並利於轉賣，皆利也。中國曾有一物爲害外國否！況如茶葉、大黃，外國所不可一日無也。中國若靳其利而不恤其害，則夷人何以爲生！有外國之呢羽嗶嘰，非得中國絲斤，不能成織。若中國亦靳其利，夷人何利可圖。其餘食物自糖料、姜桂而外，用物自綢緞、瓷器而外，曷可勝數。而外來之物，皆不過以供玩好，可有可無，既非中國要需，何難閉關絕市！乃天朝與茶、絲諸貨，悉任其販運流通，絕不靳惜，無他，利於天下公之也。

I have heard that the smoking of opium is very strictly forbidden by your country; that is because the harm caused by opium is clearly understood. Since it is not permitted to do harm to your own country, then even less should you let it be passed on to the harm of other countries—how much less to China! Of all that China exports to foreign countries, there is not a single thing which is not beneficial to people: they are of benefit when eaten, or of benefit when used, or of benefit when resold: all are beneficial. Is there a single article from China which has done any harm to foreign countries? Take tea and rhubarb, for example; the foreign countries cannot get along for a single day without them. If China cuts off these benefits with no sympathy for those who are to suffer, then what can the barbarians rely upon to keep themselves alive? Moreover the woolens, camlets, and longells [i.e., textiles] of foreign countries cannot be woven unless they obtain Chinese silk. If China, again, cuts off this beneficial export, what profit can the barbarians expect to make? As for other foodstuffs, beginning with candy, ginger, cinnamon, and so forth, and articles for use, beginning with silk, satin, chinaware, and so on, all the things that must be had by foreign countries are innumerable. On the other hand, articles coming from the outside to China can only be used as toys. We can take them

Translation in *Chinese Repository* (1840)	The original document, "Ni yu yingjili guowang xi"	Translation in *China's Response to the West* (1954)

life to you; how can we reckon up their number! On the other hand, the things that come from your foreign countries are only calculated to make presents of, or serve for mere amusement. It is quite the same to us if we have them, or if we have them not. If then these are of no material consequence to us of the Inner Land, what difficulty would there be in prohibiting and shutting our market against them? It is only that our heavenly dynasty most freely permits you to take off her tea, silk, and other commodities, and convey them for consumption everywhere, without the slightest stint or grudge, for no other reason, but that where a profit exists, we wish that it be diffused abroad for the benefit of all the earth!

Your honorable nation takes away the products of our central land, and not only do you thereby obtain food and support for yourselves, but moreover, by re-selling these products to other countries you reap a threefold profit. Now if you would only not sell opium, this threefold profit would be secured to you: how can you possibly consent to forgo it for a drug that is hurtful to men, and an unbridled craving after gain that seems to know no bounds! Let us suppose that foreigners came from another country, and brought opium into England, and seduced the people of your country to smoke it, would not you, the sovereign of the said country, look upon such a procedure with anger, and in your just

該國帶去內地貨物，不特自資食用，且得以分售各國，獲利三倍，即不賣鴉片，而其三倍之利自在。何忍更以害人之物，自無厭之求乎！設使別國有人販鴉片至英國誘人買食，當亦貴國王所深惡而痛絕之也。向聞貴國王存心仁厚，自不肯以己所不欲者施之與人。並聞來粵之船，皆經頒給條約，有不許攜帶禁物之語，是貴國王之政令，本屬嚴明。只因商船眾多，前此或未加查，今行文照會，明知天朝禁令之嚴，定必使之不敢再犯。

or get along without them. Since they are not needed by China, what difficulty would there be if we closed the frontier and stopped the trade? Nevertheless, our Celestial Court lets tea, silk, and other goods be shipped without limit and circulated everywhere without begrudging it in the slightest. This is for no other reason but to share the benefit with the people of the whole world.

The goods from China carried away by your country not only supply your own consumption and use, but also can be divided up and sold to other countries, producing a triple profit. Even if you do not sell opium, you still have this threefold profit. How can you bear to go further, selling products injurious to others in order to fulfill your insatiable desire?

Suppose there were people from another country who carried opium for sale to England and seduced your people into buying and smoking it; certainly your honorable ruler would deeply hate it and be bitterly aroused. We have heard heretofore that your honorable ruler is kind and benevolent. Naturally you would not wish to give unto

Translation in *Chinese Repository* (1840)	The original document, "Ni yu yingjili guowang xi"	Translation in *China's Response to the West* (1954)

indignation endeavor to get rid of it? Now we have always heard that your highness possesses a most kind and benevolent heart, surely then you are incapable of doing or causing to be done unto another, that which you should not wish another to do unto you! We have at the same time heard that your ships which come to Canton do each and every of them carry a document granted by your highness' self, on which are written these words "you shall not be permitted to carry contraband goods"; this shows that the laws of your highness are in their origin both distinct and severe, and we can only suppose that because the ships coming here have been very numerous, due attention has not been given to search and examine; and for this reason it is that we now address you this public document, that you may clearly know how stern and severe are the laws of the central dynasty, and most certainly you will cause that they be not again rashly violated!

Moreover, we have heard that in London the metropolis where you dwell, as also in Scotland, Ireland, and other such places, no opium whatever is produced. It is only in sundry parts of your colonial kingdom of Hindostan, such as Bengal, Madras, Bombay, Patna, Malwa, Benares, Malacca, and other places where the very hills are covered with the opium plant, where tanks are made for the preparing of the drug; month by month, and

竊聞貴國所都之蘭頓及斯葛蘭、愛倫等處，本皆不產鴉片。惟所轄印度地方，如孟阿拉、曼達拉、薩孟買八、達拿默拿、麻爾洼數處，連山栽種，開池製造，累月經年，以厚其毒，臭穢上達，天怒神恫。貴國王誠能與此等處，拔盡根株，盡鋤其地，改種五穀。有敢再圖種造鴉片者，重治其罪。此真興利除害之大仁政，天所佑而神所福，延年壽、長子孫，必再此舉矣！

others what you yourself do not want. We have also heard that the ships coming to Canton have all had regulations promulgated and given to them in which it is stated that it is not permitted to carry contraband goods. This indicates that the administrative orders of your honorable rule have been originally strict and clear. Only because the trading ships are numerous, heretofore perhaps they have not been examined with care. Now after this communication has been dispatched and you have clearly understood the strictness of the prohibitory laws of the Celestial Court, certainly you will not let your subjects dare again to violate the law.

We have further learned that in London, the capital of your honorable rule, and in Scotland *(Su-ko-lan)*, Ireland *(Ai-lun)*, and other places, originally no opium has been produced. Only in several places of India under your control such as Bengal, Madras, Bombay, Patna, Benares, and Malwa has opium been planted from hill to hill, and ponds have been opened for its manufacture. For months and years work is continued in order to accumulate the poison.

Translation in *Chinese Repository* (1840)	The original document, "Ni yu yingjili guowang xi"	Translation in *China's Response to the West* (1954)
year by year, the volume of the poison increases, its unclean stench ascends upwards, until heaven itself grows angry, and the very gods thereat get indignant! You, the queen of the said honorable nation, ought immediately to have the plant in those parts plucked up by the very root! Cause the land there to be hoed up afresh, sow in its stead the five grains, and if any man dare again to plant in these grounds a single poppy, visit his crime with the most severe punishment. By a truly benevolent system of government such as this, will you indeed reap advantage, and do away with a source of evil. Heaven must support you, and the gods will crown you with felicity! This will get for yourself the blessing of long life, and from this will proceed the security and stability of your descendants!		The obnoxious odor ascends, irritating heaven and frightening the spirits. Indeed you, O King, can eradicate the opium plant in these places, hoe over the fields entirely, and sow in its stead the five grains [millet, barley, wheat, etc.]. Anyone who dares again attempt to plant and manufacture opium should be severely punished. This will really be a great, benevolent government policy that will increase the common weal and get rid of evil. For this, Heaven must support you and the spirits must bring you good fortune, prolonging your old age and extending your descendants. All will depend on this act.
In reference to the foreign merchants who come to this our central land, the food that they eat, and the dwellings that they abide in, proceed entirely from the goodness of our heavenly dynasty: the profits which they reap, and the fortunes which they amass, have their origin only in that portion of benefit which our heavenly dynasty kindly allots them: and as these pass but little of their time in your country, and the greater part of their time in ours, it is a generally received maxim of old and of modern times, that we should conjointly admonish, and clearly make known the punishment that awaits them.	至夷商來至内地，飲食居住，無非天朝之恩膏；積聚豐盈，無非天朝之樂利。其在該國之日猶少，而在粤東之日轉多。弱教明刑，古今通義。譬如别國人到英國貿易，尚需遵英國法度，況天朝乎！今定華民之例，買鴉片者死，食者亦死。試思夷人若無鴉片帶來，則華民何由轉賣，何由吸食，是姦夷實陷華民於死，豈能獨予以生！彼害人一命者，尚須以命抵之。況鴉片之害人，豈止一命已乎！故新例於帶鴉片來内地之夷人，定以斬絞之罪，所謂為天下去害者此也。	As for the barbarian merchants who come to China, their food and drink and habitation are all received by the gracious favor of our Celestial Court. Their accumulated wealth is all benefit given with pleasure by our Celestial Court. They spend rather few days in their own country but more time in Canton. To digest clearly the legal penalties as an aid to instruction has been a valid principle in all ages. Suppose a man of another country comes to England to trade, he still has to obey the English laws; how much more should he obey in China the laws of the Celestial Dynasty?

Translation in *Chinese Repository* (1840)	The original document, "Ni yu yingjili guowang xi"	Translation in *China's Response to the West* (1954)

Suppose the subject of another country were to come to England to trade, he would certainly be required to comply with the laws of England, then how much more does this apply to us of the celestial empire! Now it is a fixed statute of this empire, that any native Chinese who sells opium is punishable with death, and even he who merely smokes it, must not less die. Pause and reflect for a moment: if you foreigners did not bring the opium hither, where should our Chinese people get it to re-sell? It is you foreigners who involve our simple natives in the pit of death, and are they alone to be permitted to escape alive? If so much as one of those deprive one of our people of his life, he must forfeit his life in requital for that which he has taken: how much more does this apply to him who by means of opium destroys his fellow-men? Does the havoc which he commits stop with a single life? Therefore it is that those foreigners who now import opium into the Central Land are condemned to be beheaded and strangled by the new statute, and this explains what we said at the beginning about plucking up the tree of evil, wherever it takes root, for the benefit of all nations.

Now we have set up regulations governing the Chinese people. He who sells opium shall receive the death penalty and he who smokes it also the death penalty. Now consider this: if the barbarians do not bring opium, then how can the Chinese people resell it, and how can they smoke it? The fact is that the wicked barbarians beguile the Chinese people into a death trap. How then can we grant life only to these barbarians? He who takes the life of even one person still has to atone for it with his own life; yet is the harm done by opium limited to the taking of one life only? Therefore in the new regulations, in regard to those barbarians who bring opium to China, the penalty is fixed at decapitation or strangulation. This is what is called getting rid of a harmful thing on behalf of mankind.

Translation in *Chinese Repository* (1840)	The original document, "Ni yu yingjili guowang xi"	Translation in *China's Response to the West* (1954)

We further find that during the second month of this present year, the superintendent of your honorable country, Elliot, viewing the law in relation to the prohibiting of opium as excessively severe, duly petitioned us, begging for "an extension of the term already limited, say five months for Hindostan and the different parts of India, and ten for England, after which they would obey and act in conformity with the new statute," and other words to the same effect. Now we, the high commissioner and colleagues, upon making a duly prepared memorial to the great emperor, have to feel grateful for his extraordinary goodness, for his redoubled compassion. Any one who within the next year and a half may by mistake bring opium to this country, if he will but voluntarily come forward, and deliver up the entire quantity, he shall be absolved from all punishment for his crime. If, however, the appointed term shall have expired, and there are still persons who continue to bring it, then such shall be accounted as knowingly violating the laws, and shall most assuredly be put to death! On no account shall we show mercy or clemency! This then may be called truly the extreme of benevolence, and the very perfection of justice!

復查本年二月間，據該國領事義律，以鴉片禁令森嚴，稟求寬限。凡印度港腳 [country merchant] 屬地，請限五月，英國本地，請限十月，然後即以新例遵行等語。今本大臣等奏蒙大皇帝格外天恩，倍加體恤。凡在一年六個月之內，誤帶鴉片，但能自首全繳者，免其治罪。若過此限期，仍有帶來，則是明知故犯，即行正法，斷不寬貸，可謂仁之至義之盡矣！

Moreover we have found that in the middle of the second month of this year [April 9] Consul [Superintendent] Elliot of your nation, because the opium prohibition law was very stern and severe, petitioned for an extension of the time limit. He requested an extension of five months for India and its adjacent harbors and related territories, and ten months for England proper, after which they would act in conformity with the new regulations. Now we, the commissioner and others, have memorialized and have received the extraordinary Celestial grace of His Majesty the Emperor, who has redoubled his consideration and compassion. All those who from the period of the coming one year (from England) or six months (from India) bring opium to China by mistake, but who voluntarily confess and completely surrender their opium, shall be exempt from their punishment. After this limit of time, if there are still those who bring opium to China then they will plainly have committed a willful violation and shall at once be executed according to law, with absolutely no clemency or pardon. This may be called the height of kindness and the perfection of justice.

Translation in *Chinese Repository* (1840)	The original document, "Ni yu yingjili guowang xi"	Translation in *China's Response to the West* (1954)

Our celestial empire rules over ten thousand kingdoms! Most surely do we possess a measure of godlike majesty which ye cannot fathom! Still we cannot bear to slay or exterminate without previous warning, and it is for this reason that we now clearly make known to you the fixed laws of our land. If the foreign merchants of your said honorable nation desire to continue their commercial intercourse, they then must tremblingly obey our recorded statutes, they must cut off for ever the source from which the opium flows, and on no account make an experiment of our laws in their own persons! Let then your highness punish those of your subjects who may be criminal, do not endeavor to screen or conceal them, and thus you will secure peace and quietness to your possessions, thus will you more than ever display a proper sense of respect and obedience, and thus may we unitedly enjoy the common blessings of peace and happiness. What greater joy! What more complete felicity than this!

我天朝君臨萬國，盡有不測神威，然不忍不教而誅，故特明宣定例，該國夷商欲圖長久貿易，必當懍遵憲典，將鴉片永斷來源，切勿以身試法。王其詰姦除慝，以保乂爾有邦，益昭恭順之忱，共享太平之福。幸甚！幸甚！

Our Celestial Dynasty rules over and supervises the myriad states, and surely possesses unfathomable spiritual dignity. Yet the Emperor cannot bear to execute people without having first tried to reform them by instruction. Therefore he especially promulgates these fixed regulations. The barbarian merchants of your country, if they wish to do business for a prolonged period, are required to obey our statues respectfully and to cut off permanently the source of opium. They must by no means try to test the effectiveness of the law with their lives. May you, O King, check your wicked and sift your wicked people before they come to China, in order to guarantee the peace of your nation, to show further the sincerity of your politeness and submissiveness, and to let the two countries enjoy together the blessings of peace. How fortunate, how fortunate indeed!

Let your highness immediately, upon the receipt of this communication, inform us promptly of the state of matters, and of the measure you are pursuing utterly to put a stop to the opium evil. Please let your reply be speedy. Do not on any account make excuses or procrastinate. A most important communication.

P.S. We annex an abstract of the new law, now about to be put

接到此文之後，即將杜絕鴉片緣由，速行移覆，切勿諉延，須至照會者

After receiving this dispatch will you immediately give us a prompt reply regarding the details and circumstances of your cutting off the opium traffic. Be sure not to put this off. The above is what has to be communicated. [Vermilion endorsement:] This is appropriately worded and quite comprehensive (Te-t'i chou-tao).

Translation in *Chinese Repository* (1840)	The original document, "Ni yu yingjili guowang xi"	Translation in *China's Response to the West* (1954)

in force. "Any foreigner or foreigners bringing opium to the Central Land, with design to sell the same, the principals shall most assuredly be decapitated, and the accessories strangled; and all property (found on board the same ship) shall be confiscated. The space of a year and a half is granted, within the which, if any one bringing opium by mistake, shall voluntarily step forward and deliver it up, he shall be absolved from all consequences of his crime."

This said imperial edict was received on the 9th day of the 6th month of the 19th year of Taoukwang, at which the period of grace begins, and runs on to the 9th day of the 12th month of the 20th year of Taoukwang, when it is completed.

Notes

1. The Semiotic Turn of International Politics

1. Frantz Fanon, *Black Skin, White Masks*, trans. Charles Lam Markmann (New York: Grove Press, 1967), p. 12.
2. For a critical interpretation of the psychohistory of colonial repression in Fanon's writing, see Emily Apter, *Continental Drift: From National Characters to Virtual Bodies* (Chicago: University of Chicago Press, 1999), pp. 77–95.
3. Jean-Luc Nancy, *Being Singular Plural*, trans. Robert D. Richardson and Anne E. O'Byrne (Stanford: Stanford University Press, 2000), p. 108.
4. Benedict Anderson, *Imagined Communities: Reflections on the Origin and Spread of Nationalism*, 2nd ed. (London: Verso, 1991), p. 6.
5. Edward Said, *Orientalism* (New York: Vintage Books, 1979), p. 18.
6. Samuel Morse's electromagnetic system, superseding Claude Chappe's optical device in 1836, was conceived during a time when writing systems and cryptology were drawing intense interest. In 1822 Jean-François Champollion successfully deciphered ancient Egyptian hieroglyphs, in 1829 Louis Braille invented the system of writing for the blind, and in 1834 F. X. Gabelsberger devised the first modern system of stenography. Moreover, elaborate attempts were made to establish an international artificial language, from Volapük (Johann Martin Schleyer, 1879) to Esperanto (Lejzer L. Zamenhof, 1887), and the Délégation pour l'adoption d'une langue auxiliaire internationale was formed in 1901.
7. For an overview of cryptography and its rapid development in modern warfare, see Simon Singh, *The Code Book: The Science of Secrecy from Ancient Egypt to Quantum Cryptography* (New York: Anchor Books, 2000).
8. See David Lyndon Wood, "The Evolution of Visual Signals on Land and Sea" (Ph.D. diss., Ohio State University, 1976), p. 359. The first *British Manual of Instruction of Army Signaling* was issued in 1880 to all armies of the British Empire. The manual divided military communication into three phases: (1) electric telegraph; (2) visual signaling; (3) mounted orderlies. Ibid., pp. 98–99.
9. Ibid., p. 86.

10. The following excerpt from General Randolph B. Marcey's book *Thirty Years of Life on the Border* makes that connection very clear: "Their [the Indians'] language is verbal and pantomimic. The former consists of a very limited number of words, some of which are common to all prairie tribes. The latter is used and understood with great facility and accuracy by all the tribes from the Gila to the Columbia, the motions and signs to express ideas common to all. This pantomimic vocabulary, which is exceedingly graceful and significant, when oral communication is impracticable, constitutes the court language of the Plains; and what was a fact of much astonishment to me, I discovered that it was nearly the same as that practiced by the mutes in one of our deaf and dumb institutions that I visited." Albert J. Myer, *A Manual of Signals*, quoted in Wood, "The Evolution of Visual Signals," p. 86.

11. These systems fall under what Derrida calls "phonetic writing" in his critique of Saussure's proposition that "language and writing are two distinct systems of signs; the second exists for the sole purpose of representing the first." See Jacques Derrida, *Of Grammatology*, trans. Gayatri Chakravorty Spivak (Baltimore: Johns Hopkins University Press, 1974), p. 30.

12. See Ferdinand de Saussure, *Course in General Linguistics*, trans. Wade Baskin (New York: McGraw-Hill Book Company, 1966), p. 16. Also Daniele Gambarara, "The Convention of Geneva: History of Linguistic Ideas and History of Communicative Practices," in *Historical Roots of Linguistic Theories*, ed. Lia Formigari and Daniele Gambarara (Amsterdam: John Benjamins Publishing Company, 1995), p. 288.

13. Derrida, *Of Grammatology*, p. 47.

14. Gambarara, "Convention of Geneva," p. 286.

15. See ibid.; also Armand Mattelart, *Mapping World Communication: War, Progress, and Culture* (London: Routledge, 1997).

16. For a critique of the Saussurian sign, see my essay "The question of Meaning-Value in the Political Economy of the Sign," in *Tokens of Exchange in Global Circulations*, ed. Lydia Liu (Durham: Duke University Press, 1999).

17. Peirce's definition of the sign is as follows: "A sign, or *representamen*, is something which stands for something in some respect or capacity. It addresses somebody, that is, creates in the mind of that person an equivalent sign, or perhaps a more developed sign. The sign which it creates I call the *interpretant* of the first sign. The sign stands for something, its *object*. It stands for that object, not in all respects, but in reference to a sort of idea, which I have sometimes called the *ground* of *representamen*." *Collected Papers of Charles Sanders Peirce*, vols. 1–6, ed. by Charles Hartshorne and Paul Weiss (Cambridge, Mass.: Harvard University Press, 1931–1935), 2:228.

18. Peirce's signs are divided into the "qualisign" (a mere idea or a quality of feeling), the "sinsign" (an existent token, thing, or event), and the "legisign" (general, regular, repeatable, and lawlike, such as the linguistic sign). The object of the sign is likewise divided into immediate object and dynamic object, just as the interpretant, an important concept that is missing from Saussure's binary

system, can be divided into the immediate interpretant, the dynamic interpretant, and the final interpretant, with each of them being subdivided further. There is an infinite chain of semiosis whereby interpretants, which are themselves signs, lead to other interpretants and so on. For a succinct summary, see Dinda L. Gorlée, *Semiotics and the Problem of Translation: With Special Reference to the Semiotics of Charles S. Peirce* (Amsterdam: Rodopi, 1994), pp. 64–65.

19. Peirce, *Collected Papers*, 2:297.

20. Derrida, *Of Grammatology*, p. 47.

21. A good example is the anachronistic etymology of the word *yi* given by twenti-eth-century Chinese language dictionaries, such as *Cihai*, which nods toward the English equivalent "barbarian" without naming or identifying it.

22. The gendered pronominals in modern Chinese exemplify the making of modern super-signs through translation. See my discussion of the invention of the Chinese characters for the third-person feminine *ta/she* and third-person masculine *ta/he* on the model of European pronouns in *Translingual Practice: Litera-ture, National Culture, and Translated Modernity—China, 1900–1937* (Stanford: Stanford University Press, 1995), pp. 36–39. The Chinese compound *minzhu*, now rendered as "democracy," is but the latest manifestation of the making of the super-sign *minzhu/republic* that first emerged from the 1864 Chinese trans-lation of Henry Wheaton's *Elements of International Law.* For my discussion of this text, see Chapter 4.

23. Charles Sanders Peirce, *The Essential Peirce: Selected Philosophical Writings,* ed. the Peirce Edition Project (Bloomington: Indiana University Press, 1998), 2:6. This work corresponds to MS 404. Portions of it were published in *Collected Papers of Charles Sanders Peirce,* 2:281, 285, and 297–302. The passage I cite here was not included in the *Collected Papers* but is available in the unabridged version under the title "What Is a Sign?" in *The Essential Peirce.*

24. Ibid., 2:6–7.

25. Daniel Defoe, *Robinson Crusoe,* ed. Michael Shinagel, 2nd Norton Critical Edi-tion (New York: W. W. Norton and Company, 1994), p. 153.

26. For a new critique of Althusser's notion of subjectivity, see Judith Butler, *The Psychic Life of Power: Theories in Subjection* (Stanford: Stanford University Press, 1997), pp. 106–131.

27. Emile Benveniste, *Problems in General Linguistics,* trans. Mary Elizabeth Meek (Coral Gables: University of Miami Press, 1971), pp. 219–220. From a feminist point of view, it is remarkable that the French linguist should take the un-marked use of the masculine pronoun for granted even as he theorizes the na-ture of the pronoun.

28. Elizabeth Cady Stanton, "Collected Papers," in Beth M. Waggenspack, *The Search for Self-Sovereignty: The Oratory of Elizabeth Cady Stanton* (New York: Greenwood Press, 1989), p. 159.

29. For postcolonial studies of empire and women's suffrage, see the essays in-cluded in Ian Christopher Fletcher, Laura E. Nym Mayball, and Philippa Le-

vine, eds., *Women's Suffrage in the British Empire: Citizenship, Nation, and Race* (London: Routledge, 2000).

30. See Michel Foucault, "Faire vivre et laisser mourir: la naissance du racisme," *Temps modernes* 46, no. 535 (February 1991): 39.

31. Michel Foucault, *The History of Sexuality: An Introduction*, trans. Robert Hurley, vol. 1 (New York: Vintage Books, 1990), p. 136.

32. Ibid., p. 137.

33. Ann Laura Stoler, *Race and the Education of Desire* (Durham: Duke University Press, 1995), p. 15.

34. Ibid., pp. 192–193.

35. Michel Foucault, *Discipline and Punish: The Birth of the Prison*, trans. Alan Sheridan (New York: Random House, 1979), p. 30.

36. Stoler notes that the last of Foucault's Collège de France lectures in spring 1979 suggests a departure from his earlier position on this issue. Here Foucault was willing to entertain the idea that the sovereign right to kill might have undergone a transformation in modernity rather than being replaced, for racism is what establishes the "positive relation between the right to kill and the assurance of life" through the permanency of warlike relations inside the social body. Stoler, *Race and the Education of Desire*, p. 86. Foucault's lecture raises the stakes of race and racism in the study of the modern biopolitical state, as Stoler has rightly observed, but does not push on to the point of analyzing modern subjectivity as a reinvention of sovereignty.

37. See George Steinmetz, "Precoloniality and Colonial Subjectivity: Ethnographic Discourse and Native Policy in German Overseas Imperialism, 1780s–1914," *Political Power and Social Theory* 15 (2002): 135–228.

38. Daniel Philpott argues: "Sovereignty need not lie in a single individual, as Bodin thought, or in a body above the law, as both Bodin and Hobbes thought. It could also reside in a triumvirate, a committee of public safety, the people united in a General Will (as Rousseau thought), the people ruling through a constitution, or the law of the European Union. Popular constitutional rule governs the majority of modern states, although even here, in some matters, international law or European Union Law may be sovereign." See Daniel Philpott, *Revolutions in Sovereignty: How Ideas Shaped Modern International Relations* (Princeton: Princeton University Press, 2001), p. 17.

39. Butler, *Psychic Life of Power*, p. 102. Wendy Brown's analysis of "wounded attachments" throws important light on how the strategies of inclusion used by feminists and other politically marginalized groups to protest exclusion from the universal category of citizen are themselves characteristic of the Western liberal tradition. See Wendy Brown, *States of Injury: Power and Freedom in Late Modernity* (Princeton: Princeton University Press, 1995), p. 75.

40. Butler, *Psychic Life of Power*, p. 104.

41. Georges Bataille, *The Accursed Share: An Essay on General Economy*, trans. Robert Hurley, vols. 2–3 (New York: Zone Books, 1993), pp. 240–241.

42. G. W. F. Hegel, *The Phenomenology of Spirit*, trans. A. V. Miller (Oxford: Oxford University Press, 1977), pp. 109–110.

43. Fanon, *Black Skin, White Masks,* pp. 220–221.

44. Ibid., p. 216.

45. Fanon talks only about the subjectivity of black men, not women. Gender enters his work primarily in terms of a race situation that structures the socio-erotic relationship between white men and (dominated) black women or that between black men (wanting revenge) and white women. In his chapter of *Black Skin, White Masks* on Mayotte Capécia, the female author of *Je suis Martiniquaise,* Fanon attempts to unravel the situation but reveals at the same time his own misogyny.

46. Ironically, Michael Hardt and Antonio Negri believe that "for a thinker like Fanon, the reference to Hegel suggests that the Master can only achieve a hollow form of recognition; it is the Slave, through life-and-death struggle, who has the potential to move forward toward full consciousness." Their reading curiously distorts Fanon's critical dialogue with Hegel and makes the former sound just like Hegel. See Michael Hardt and Antonio Negri, *Empire* (Cambridge, Mass.: Harvard University Press, 2000), p. 129.

47. Fanon, *Black Skin, White Masks,* p. 218.

48. Sartre quoted ibid., p. 29.

49. Fanon's engagement with Sartre and, through him and other French thinkers, with the Hegelian legacy merits special attention here because Fanon was writing at a time when the revival of the Hegelian philosophy of subjectivity in France coincided with the country's experience of the violence of decolonization abroad. In *Black Orpheus,* Sartre writes: "The black man who asserts his negritude by means of a revolutionary movement immediately places himself in the position of having to meditate, either because he wishes to recognize in himself certain objectively established traits of the African civilizations, or because he hopes to discover the essence of blackness in the well of his heart. Thus subjectivity reappears: the relation of the self with self; the source of all poetry, the very poetry from which the worker had to disengage himself. The black man who asks his colored brothers to 'find themselves' is going to try to present to them an exemplary image of their negritude and will look into his own soul to grasp it. He wants to be both a beacon and a mirror; the first revolutionary will be the harbinger of the black soul, the herald—half prophet and half follower—who will tear Blackness out of himself in order to offer it to the world; in brief, he will be a poet in the literal sense of *vates.*" Jean-Paul Sartre, *Black Orpheus,* trans. S. W. Allen (Paris: Présence africaine, 1976), pp. 297–298. Fanon, for his part, refuses to consider the "black problem" as such. As long as he is among his own people, writes Fanon, the black man has no occasion except in minor internal conflicts to experience his being through the other. There is always an impurity, a flaw that prevents an ontological explanation of the *Weltanschauung* of the colonized people. This is because not only must the black man be black; he must also be black in relation to the white man. The "black problem," therefore, is born of the colonial legacy and must be tackled on that front. For Fanon, the *struggle for recognition* operates differently in colonial relations because it is a revolutionary struggle to overcome colonial rule

and establish sovereign independence simultaneously. For an analysis of the place of Hegel studies in twentieth-century France, see Judith Butler, *Subjects of Desire: Hegelian Reflections in Twentieth-Century France* (New York: Columbia University Press, 1987).

50. Giorgio Agamben, *Homo Sacer: Sovereign Power and Bare Life*, trans. Daniel Heller-Roazen (Stanford: Stanford University Press, 1998), p. 28.

51. Ibid., p. 84.

52. Ibid., p. 83.

53. Hardt and Negri, *Empire*, p. 87.

54. Ibid., p. 137.

55. Unfortunately, Hardt and Negri lump the postmodern and postcolonial critics together and portray them as making the outrageous statement that "if the modern is the field of power of the white, the male, and the European, then in perfectly symmetrical fashion the postmodern will be the field of liberation of the non-white, the non-male, and the non-European" (ibid., p. 141). It seems to me that no self-respecting postcolonial critic has said as much or would put the matter in this manner. The caricature of postcolonial scholarship by the authors of *Empire* misses the opportunity to engage seriously with the challenge that postcolonial scholars, especially in the field of empire studies, have presented to their own work and to intellectual discourse in general.

56. See James Brown Scott, *The Spanish Origin of International Law: Francisco de Vitoria and his Law of Nations* (Oxford: Clarendon Press, 1934).

57. Anthony Pagden, *The Fall of Natural Man: The American Indian and the Origins of Comparative Ethnology* (Cambridge: Cambridge University Press, 1982), p. 65.

58. Anthony Pagden, "Dispossessing the Barbarian: The Language of Spanish Thomism and the Debate over the Property Rights of the American Indians," in *The Language of Political Theory in Early Modern Europe*, ed. Anthony Pagden, (Cambridge: Cambridge University Press, 1987), p. 79.

59. David Kennedy, "Primitive Legal Scholarship," *Harvard International Law Journal* 27, no. 1 (Winter 1986): 23.

60. Pagden, "Dispossessing the Barbarian," pp. 86–87.

61. Ibid., p. 87. Pagden's discussion of the Salamanca school of Spanish scholastics includes a range of different positions represented by Vitoria and others such as Melchor Cano and Juan de la Peña. Without meaning to downplay the complexity of the theological debates in Vitoria's own time, I am here mainly concerned with the potentiality of the key theoretical concepts that Vitoria developed for the law of nations and with his impact on the subsequent development of international law.

62. For my discussion of "barbarian" and its relation to antiquity, see Chapter 2.

63. See Gerrit W. Gong, *The Standard of "Civilization" in International Society* (Oxford: Clarendon Press, 1984), p. 37.

64. For further discussion, see Anthony Anghie, "Finding the Peripheries: Sovereignty and Colonialism in Nineteenth-Century International Law," *Harvard International Law Journal* 40 (Winter 1999): 1–80.

65. For a discussion of primitive legal concepts, see David Kennedy, "Primitive Legal Scholarship."
66. C. H. Alexandrowicz, *An Introduction to the History of the Law of Nations in the East Indies: Sixteenth, Seventeenth, and Eighteenth Centuries* (Oxford: Clarendon Press, 1967).
67. See Philpott, *Evolutions in Sovereignty*, p. 34.
68. Alexandrowicz, *Introduction*, p. 11.
69. Ibid., p. 65.
70. Quoted ibid., p. 45.
71. Ibid.
72. C. H. Alexandrowicz, *The European-African Confrontation: A Study in Treaty Making* (Leiden: A. W. Sijthoff, 1973), p. 6.

2. The Birth of a Super-Sign

1. Edith Hall points out that it was the Persian wars that first produced a sense of collective Panhellenic identity and the idea of the barbarian as the universal other. She dates the simultaneous invention of Greek identity and the barbarians as the universal anti-Greek to the fifth century B.C.E. The Greek term *barbaros* was oriental in origin, formed by reduplicative onomatopoeia. See Edith Hall, *Inventing the Barbarian: Greek Self-Definition through Tragedy* (Oxford: Oxford University Press, 1989), pp. 1–19.
2. Lord Elgin, who was assisted by his Chinese secretaries Thomas Wade and Horatio Lay, represented the British government at the negotiating table. Guiliang (Kweiliang) and Hua shana (Hwashana) represented the Qing imperial government. Lord Elgin, or James Bruce (1811–63), was the eighth earl of Elgin and twelfth earl of Kincardine, the son of the famous Elgin, Thomas Bruce (1766–1841), who had removed the Greek marbles, allegedly with the permission of the Turkish authorities, and shipped them to England in the early part of the nineteenth century. James Bruce himself had served as the colonial governor-general of Jamaica (1842–1846) and of Canada (1846–1854) before arriving in East Asia to become the Queen's High Commissioner and Plenipotentiary of China and Japan in 1856. For the colonial exploits of the Elgin family, see Sydney Checkland, *The Elgins, 1766–1917: A Tale of Aristocrats, Proconsuls, and Their Wives,* (Aberdeen: Aberdeen University Press, 1988).
3. *Treaties, Conventions, etc., between China and Foreign States,* 2nd ed., 2 vols. (Shanghai: Statistical Department of the Inspectorate General of Customs, 1917), 1:419.
4. Ibid., 1:418. Article 3 of the French-Chinese Treaty of Tianjin makes a similar provision but adds a number of conditions that include some degree of reciprocity between the Chinese and French. The article reads: "Les communications officielles des Agents diplomatiques et consulaires Français avec les autorités Chinoises seront écrites en français, mais seront accompagnées, pour faciliter le service, d'une traduction Chinoise aussi exacte que possible,

jusqu'au moment où le Gouvernement Impérial de Péking, ayant des interprètes pour parler et écrire corretement le Français, la correspondance diplomatique aura lieu dans cette langue pour les Agents Français, et en chinois pour les fonctionnaires de l'Empire. Il est convenu que jusque-là, et en cas de dissidence dans l'interprétation à donner au texte Français et au texte Chinois, au sujet des clauses arrêtées d'avance dans les Conventions faites de commun accord, ce sera le texte français qui devra prévaloir. Cette disposition est applicable au present Traité. Dans les communications entre les autorités des deux Pays, ce sera toujours le texte original et non la traduction qui fera fois." Ibid., p. 816. Interestingly, the Chinese version of Article 50 is closer to the French text than to the English original.

5. The interpreter Thomas Wade and his assistant Horatio Lay played a major role throughout the negotiating process because the plenipotentiaries met only at the initiation and the signing of the treaties. See Masataka Banno, *China and the West, 1858–1861: The Origins of the Tsungli Yamen* (Cambridge, Mass.: Harvard University Press, 1964), pp. 18–25.

6. James Hevia, *Cherishing Men from Afar: Qing Guest Ritual and the Macartney Embassy of 1793* (Durham: Duke University Press, 1995), p. 25.

7. See my discussion of the Manchu-Chinese translation in light of the Qing promotion of the imperial ideology of the Center and the Outer as a single family in Chapter 3.

8. In the emperor's edicts and the Qing officials' memorials of the period, one finds *yi* and *xiyang* appearing in the same sentence or paragraph without any significant change of rhetoric. Consult *Zhupi yuzhi: Yongzheng* (Vermilion edicts: the Yongzheng emperor) (Shanghai: Dianshizhai, 1887).

9. For published documentary evidence of this usage, see the Chinese official memos, memorials, and proclamations from the years 1834–1839 included in Sasaki Masaya, *Ahen senso zen Chu-Ei kosho bunsho* (Documents from Anglo-Chinese official exchanges before the Opium War) (Tokyo: Gannando Shoten, 1967). See also Feng Erkang, *Yong Zheng zhuan* (Biography of Yongzheng) (Beijing: Renmin chubanshe, 1985), p. 407.

10. This functional distinction between *yi* and *yang* in the pre–Opium War years has been largely neglected in the studies of the war and of Chinese foreign relations. Chen Xulu, whose essay on the words *yi* and *yang* is widely cited by scholars, makes no mention of the Hong merchants as *yang shang*. See Chen Xulu, "Bian 'yi,' 'yang'" (Analyzing "yi" and "yang"), in *Chen Xulu xueshui wencun* (Collected works of Chen Xulu) (Shanghai: Shanghai renmin chubanshe, 1990).

11. Naoki Sakai, *Translation and Subjectivity: On "Japan" and Cultural Nationalism* (Minnesota: University of Minneapolis, 1997), p. 15.

12. See Ferdinand de Saussure, *Course in General Linguistics,* trans. Wade Baskin (New York: McGraw-Hill Book Company, 1966), pp. 74–75.

13. Jacques Derrida's reading of Saussure's concept of the sign in *Of Grammatology* misses an important aspect of Saussure's semiological work, which is precisely

to bring out the limits of etymological thinking in the study of language to which Derrida himself succumbs in his frequent play with the Greek and Latin roots of words. See my critique of semiology for a theory of translation in "The Question of Meaning-Value in the Political Economy of the Sign," in *Tokens of Exchange: The Problem of Translation*, ed. Lydia Liu (Durham: Duke University Press, 1999), pp. 24–27.

14. In his own context, Pufendorf is critical of the "Holy Roman Empire of the German Nation" and its incoherence as a collection of independent state powers. See J. G. A. Pocock, "States, Republics, and Empires: The American Founding in Early Modern Perspective," in *Conceptual Change and the Constitution*, ed. Terence Ball and J. G. A. Pocock (Lawrence: University Press of Kansas, 1988), p. 67.

15. Part two of the second volume of *The Cambridge History of China* covers the late Qing period from 1800 to 1911. The chapters on China's foreign relations represent a typical Fairbankian approach in the sense that the authors evoke the English word "barbarian" ubiquitously in the spirit of Article 51 to impute sinocentrism without having interrogated the documentary evidence for that usage or reflected on the incongruity of their multilingual sources. The story in this authoritative textbook cannot be taken as a reliable account of the foreign relations of the Qing, as it perpetuates a certain representation of facts that would not contradict Article 51 in the past or jeopardize its mode of survival in the future. See Denis Twitchett and John K. Fairbank, eds., *The Cambridge History of China*, vol. 2, pt. 2 (Cambridge: Cambridge University Press, 1980).

16. Hevia, *Cherishing Men from Afar*, p. 27.

17. My debt to that scholarship is indicated by the citations, references, and discussions throughout this book.

18. Hosea Ballou Morse, *The Chronicles of the East India Company Trading to China, 1635–1834*, 4 vols. (Oxford: Clarendon Press, 1926), 4:332; vol. 5 (1742–1774) (Oxford: Clarendon Press, 1929).

19. See ibid., 4: 333. The dates Gützlaff gives in his journal show a slight variation: departing on February 25 and returning on September 5. See Charles (Karl) Gützlaff, *The Journal of Two Voyages along the Coast of China in 1831 and 1832* (New York: John P. Haven, 1833), pp. 126 and 297.

20. This is confirmed by Chinese-language sources relating to that trip, which indicate that the petition was submitted on the twenty-second day of the fifth month of the twelfth year of the Daoguang reign. See Xu Dishan, ed. *Dazhong ji* (Arriving at the inner truth) (Shanghai: Shangwu yinshuguan, 1928), pp. 47–49.

21. Gützlaff, *Journal of Two Voyages*, pp. 227–230. This book appeared in print in 1833, although some of its chapters had been published in the *Chinese Repository* in 1832. In 1834 Gützlaff published the journal of his third voyage, along with a reprint of the first two journals, in *Journal of Three Voyages along the Coast of China in 1831, 1832, 1833 with Notices of Siam, Corea, and the Loo-choo Islands*.

22. Gützlaff, *Journal of Two Voyages*, p. 233.

23. The entries for both *yi ren* and *fan ren* are listed under the ninth radical, *jin* or *ren* (human). The written character *yi* also comes under the heading of the thirty-seventh radical, known as *da* (great), whose English definition shows multiple usages but makes no mention of "barbarian." See Rev. Robert Morrison, *The Dictionary of the Chinese Language*, 3 vols. (Macao: East India Company Press, 1815), 1:61 and 586–587.

24. The factory records of the East India Company tell a very different story about the word *yi* and its English equivalents. As one often encounters in the translation of government proclamations to the foreign business community and Chinese merchants in Canton, the word *yi* was equated with "foreign" or "foreigner." The proclamation issued by Kong Yuxun, the viceroy of Guangdong and Guangxi, which I transcribed from the archives of the East India Company is a case in point. Kong's various memorials to the Yongzheng emperor in the 1720s had been instrumental in the emperor's decision to reopen and reorganize foreign trade in Canton. For Kong's role in the Yongzheng emperor's trade policy in the early eighteenth century, see Feng Erkang, *Yongzheng zhuan* (Biography of Yongzheng) (Beijing: Renmin chubanshe, 1985), pp. 402–415; and Wang Zhichun, *Qingchao rouyuan ji* (Records of Qing foreign relations) (1891; reprint, Beijing: Zhonghua shuju, 1989), pp. 58–60). Dated August 20, 1728, the English version of Kong's proclamations was supplied to the company by a Roman Catholic priest in Canton who had rendered it from an earlier French version of the Chinese original. An excerpt from this English text (with the original eighteenth-century spelling) reads:

"I, Tsunto, Viceroy and Mandareen of the Customs, the head and eyes lifted up, I regard with respect and with all possible attention how great is the goodness of the Emperor to treat forreigners so favourably and that by benefits without bounds, which obliges me to redouble my attention to assist forreigners. Therefore you forreigners who come here to trade, you can help by applying yourselves to, and trusting the chiefs of Hongs; take care they are men of worth who are faithfully just and of good correspondence, that your merchandize may be soon ready, and that you may be soon ready to return home from hence, for there are a sort of merchants, imposters and deceitfull, who by fraudulent means endeavours to engage forreigners and afterwards defer dayly to fulfill their contracts, not having their merchandize ready, and by their villainy forreigners hazard their being caught and loosing the monsoon; it's certain heretofore forreigners have been reduced to this condition by the tricks of fraudulent merchants.

"For this cause I publish now this placart to prohibit you from acting in that manner, and by this I signify to you forreigners and to you chiefs of Hongs who deall with Europeans, to you Linguists [interpreters] and all others, that each of you may be instructed in and do his duty. I ordain then that forreign ships coming into our ports, that the merchants have liberty to choose the chiefs of Hongs who are men of worth and whom they can trust, that poor merchants may no more deceive forreigners & ruin their commerce. I prohibit to Linguists and others to introduce their friends or adventurers to forreigners to deceive them, and if you should violate this order I shall punish you rigorously. As to the houses built at Wampo, it is permitted them in the daytime to sell all eatables. I prohibit selling wine to the sailors for to shun disorders, and if you have the boldness to resist this my command you shall be taken and chastised on the place. In short, you forreigners, attend to the choice you make of merchants, don't give ear indifferently to all sorts of people for fear of falling into the hands of villains, that afterwards you have cause to repent in suffering by them. This is the principall aim of this placart, given the 23rd of the 7th Moon in the 6th Year of the reign of Emperor Yong Tching, the 28th August NS 1728." "Diary and Consultation of the Council for China," in "East India Company Factory Records (1595–1840)," British Library, G/12/27, Canton, August 20, 1728, pp. 49–51.

Since Kong's Chinese text has been lost to time, a direct comparison with the original is impossible. But one striking feature of this translation is its repeated use of "foreigner" and the total absence of "barbarian." What could be the Chinese term of which the word "foreigner" is a translation? Kong's memorials to the emperor which have survived employ *xiyang ren* (men of the western ocean) and *yi* interchangeably. As the quoted proclamation is addressed simultaneously to the Hong merchants and the foreign business community, we are left with the word *yi* as the only possible candidate, because the distinction between the foreign merchant and the Hong merchant was maintained through the contrastive use of *yi* and *yang* in the official language of the Qing. This is confirmed by the work of Robert Morrison, the first Protestant missionary to enter China, who followed the past practice of the East India Company in glossing the word *yi* as "foreign" and "foreigner" in his 1815 *Dictionary of the Chinese Language.*

25. Morse, *Chronicles of the East India Company,* 4:284.
26. Gützlaff was not the first translator to render *yi* as "barbarian." Jesuit missionaries such as Matteo Ricci himself had given similar translations in Latin, using "barbari." What Gützlaff did that the Jesuit missionaries would not have done was to exclude alternative eighteenth-century English translations in favor of "barbarian" and then turn *yi* into a legal problem and a super-sign on the basis of that translation.
27. In a study of the missionaries of the period, Patrick Hanan has discovered that Gützlaff even pioneered a genre of missionary novels written in vernacular Chinese, in addition to the many other activities he engaged in. Hanan aptly summarizes the career of this extraordinary nineteenth-century missionary, who has been called "opportunistic, ebullient, flamboyant, hyperactive, and indestructible. His ambitions are said to have been fueled by egotism. He has been described as an inveterate optimist, a man of fanatical zeal, a visionary, a missionary adventurer, an astute publicist, and, in the most sweeping generalization of all, that by Arthur Waley, as 'a cross between a parson and a pirate, charlatan and genius, philanthropist and crook.' Even his physical qualities im-

pressed people. A fellow missionary describes him as 'personally short, stout, gross in his tastes and manners, active in his movements, rapid in speech, and cheerful and engrossing in conversation,' while another acquaintance refers to his 'great' face and 'sinister eye.'" Patrick Hanan, "Missionary Novels in Nineteeth-Century China," *Harvard Journal of Asiatic Studies* 60, no. 2 (December 2000): 420.

28. Gützlaff, *Journal of Two Voyages,* pp. 123–124.

29. See my discussion below of the signing of the treaty later in this chapter.

30. This material comes from the archives of the East India Company and is now housed at the Bodleian Library of Oxford University as Ms. Chin. C. 23. It is not utilized in Morse's multivolume *Chronicles of the East India Company.* Morse's and Gützlaff's accounts of the voyage should be checked against this body of Chinese-language sources. The published version of Ms. Chin. C. 23 was the work of Xu Dishan, who transcribed, edited, and published the material under the title *Dazhong ji* (Arriving at the inner truth) in 1928.

31. Xu Dishan, *Dazhong ji,* pp. 49–50.

32. Ibid., pp. 51–52. For a detailed analysis of eastern *yi* on the basis of classical textual studies and modern archaeological findings, see Pang Zhenggao, "Dongyi jiqi shiqian wenhua shilun" (A study of the prehistory of eastern *yi* culture), *Lishi yanjiu* 3 (1987): 54–65. The Chinese etymology should not be confused with, or be glossed in terms of, the translation problem I am addressing here. The former also has an interesting story to tell and is related to the story of the super-sign *yi/barbarian* in some unexpected ways. I discuss in the next chapter the changing situation of *yi* and its importance to the imperial classical scholarship of the Qing through an analysis of the Yongzheng emperor's *Tayi juemi lu* (Awakening to Supreme Justice), in which the emperor defended his sovereign rule over China by citing the same Mencius quotation that Admiral Wu cited to Lindsay.

33. The reference to the British colonies is interesting. In his written memos and petitions, Lindsay consistently translated the word "colony" or "colonies" as *shu difang.* In Gu Changsheng's description of this exchange in *Cong Ma lixun dao Situ leideng* (From Morrison to John Leighton Stuart), however, the characters *shu difang* are inexplicably left out of the quotation from Lindsay's petition to Wu Qitai: "As we permit the ships from Shanghai to sail into our own [English] harbors, I believe we reserve the right to visit your place." Gu Changsheng, *Cong Ma lixun dao Situ leideng,* (Shanghai: Shanghai renmin chubanshe, 1985), p. 54. This is clearly a misquotation of the original petition, for there were no Chinese ships being sent from Shanghai to England. The words Lindsay adopted were actually the British *shu difang* (colonies), not England itself. By that Lindsay meant, of course, India and Southeast Asia, where Chinese merchants had been conducting business for centuries. In the original petition, Lindsay wrote: "Junks from your honorable country and merchant ships from Shanghai county visit the ports of the colonies of Great Britain every year and are well treated there. The trade has been exceedingly profitable.

The merchants of our country believe that it makes good sense to conduct the trade in mutually beneficial terms and hope to be able to trade along the north coast of China." Xu Dishan, *Dazhong ji,* pp. 47–48. It should be noted that the argument of reciprocity pertains to the relationship between China and the British colonies, not that between China and England.

34. Xu Dishan, *Dazhong ji,* pp. 53–54.

35. The Chinese document is dated the ninth day of the sixth moon of the twelfth year of the Daoguang reign. Ibid., p. 59.

36. As quoted in John Francis Davis, *The Chinese: A General Description of the Empire of China and Its Inhabitants,* 2 vol. (1836; reprint, London: C. Cox, 1851), 1:49. For a critial evaluation of the philological endeavor of Joseph de Prémare, see David Porter, *Ideographia* (Stanford: Stanford University Press, 2001), pp. 66–72.

37. Davis, *The Chinese,* p. 49. The same English quotation is repeated in Samuel Wells Williams's popular book *The Middle Kingdom: A Survey of the Geography, Government, Literature, Social Life, Arts, and History of the Chinese Empire and Its Inhabitants,* 2 vols. (New York: Charles Scribner's Sons, 1883), 2:450.

38. For Su's original essay, see "Wangzhe buzhi yi di lun" (Sovereigns apply non-rule to the *yi di*), in *Sushi quanji,* 3 vols. (Shanghai: Shanghai gu ji chubanshe, 2000), 2:671–672. Su's concept of *bu zhi,* or non-rule, can be traced back to the thinking of He Xiu, one of the most important commentators on Confucius's *Spring and Autumn Annals,* about which He wrote: "The sovereign applies non-rule to the *yidi.*" Su's views about ethnic minorities should be evaluated with reference to the repeated efforts to conquer China by militant foreigners coming from the north in the Song dynasty. For an informed study of Han literati and ethnic relations in the Song, see Peter K. Bol, "Seeking Common Ground: Han Literati under Jurchen Rule," *Harvard Journal of Asiatic Studies* 47, no. 2 (December 1987): 461–538.

39. The agency of the faceless Chinese scholar who helped draft the exchanges in classical Chinese cannot be ascertained from the existing sources. The official interpreter on board the *Lord Amherst* was Gützlaff, who made or approved decisions about the meanings of the Chinese prose written out by the Chinese scholar.

40. See Viscount Palmerston to Lord Napier, January 25, 1834, *British Parliamentary Papers,* China 30, Correspondence Orders in Council, and Reports Relative to the Opium War in China, 1840, p. 242.

41. For published Chinese-language communications among Lu Kun, the imperial court, and the Hong merchants regarding the Napier expedition, see Sasaki Masaya, *Ahen senso zen Chu-Ei kosho bunsho* (Documents from Anglo-Chinese official exchanges before the Opium War) (Tokyo: Gannando Shoten, 1967).

42. Fairbank suggested that the Chinese characters for Napier's name, Lü Laobei, meant "laboriously vile." See John King Fairbank, *Trade and Diplomacy on the China Coast: The Opening of the Treaty Ports, 1842–1854* (Cambridge, Mass.: Harvard University Press, 1953), p. 79.

43. Robert Morrison was appointed Chinese secretary and interpreter by Lord
    Napier on July 16, 1834, with an annual salary of £1,300 and was instructed to
    wear a vice consul's uniform, with the king's buttons, instead of a preacher's
    gown. See Eliza A. Morrison and Samuel Kidd, *Memoirs of the Life and Labours of
    Robert Morrison*, 2 vols. (London: Longman, Orme, Brown, and Longmans,
    1839), 2:524. Apparently, Morrison's decision to accept Napier's offer was
    prompted by his family's financial needs. In his letter to the treasurer of the
    London Missionary Society on November 9, 1832, Morrison had complained:
    "Twenty-five years—the one-half of my life—I have been labouring abroad for
    the Missionary Society, and other benevolent Institutions—the Bible, Tract,
    School, and Prayer-Book Societies. I feel old age creeping upon me. The East
    India Company has declined to assign me a pension, such as they give to sur-
    geons and chaplains; probably thinking that other societies afford me pecuni-
    ary aid for my personal concerns. It would not be unreasonable, that those I
    have served so long, should unite, and provide me a retiring pension." Morri-
    son and Kidd, *Memoirs*, 2:468. Before his appointment as the Chinese secretary
    of the British government, Morrison had expressed some grave concerns about
    the rhetoric of free trade in a letter to Sir George T. Staunton, dated January
    31, 1834, to this effect: "I pretend not to foretell the consequences. They ap-
    pear to me to be great, and I pray that they may be beneficial—not only to
    England, but to China; for I am not that patriot who would wish to aggrandize
    my own country by the injury or ruin of another. I do not think that Christian-
    ity admits of such patriotism. But how few consider the welfare of China in all
    their speculations about free trade, &c." (ibid., 2:505).
44. *Chinese Repository* 3, no. 4 (August 1834): 187. This number contains a total of
    five translated edicts by the governor-general (pp. 187–192).
45. Ibid., p. 188. The *Chinese Repository,* edited by E. C. Bridgman, shows signs of
    confusion and uncertainty during this period as to how to translate the word
    yi, as "barbarian" or "foreigner." Checking the translated texts against the orig-
    inal edicts, I noticed that the same word *yi* would be rendered as "barbarian,"
    as in "the barbarian *eye*," but would appear as "foreign" in the very next sen-
    tence or paragraph. Compare, for example, the second paragraph of edict no. 2
    (p. 187) with the Chinese original in Sasaki Masaya, *Ahen senso zen Chu-Ei kosho
    bunsho*, p. 4. For a recent study of this influential journal, see Murray A.
    Rubinstein, "The Wars They Wanted: American Missionaries' Use of the *Chi-
    nese Repository* before the Opium War," *American Neptune* 48, no. 4 (Fall 1988):
    271–282.
46. Fairbank, *Trade and Diplomacy,* p. 79.
47. The echoes of "the barbarian eye" continue to reverberate in our own times.
    For example, they recently reappeared in the title of a book, *Barbarian Eye,* by
    Priscilla Napier, who is married to one of Lord Napier's descendants. The au-
    thor suggests that William John Napier was called a "barbarian eye" because
    the Chinese government suspected him of being a dangerous spy. A 1998 book
    on photography, titled *Barbarian Lens,* also plays self-consciously on the Napier

note. See Priscilla Napier, *Barbarian Eye: Lord Napier in China, 1834, the Prelude to Hong Kong* (London: Brassey's, 1995).

48. *Chinese Repository* 3, no. 6 (October 1834): 286. "Reverently obedient" is a translation of *gog shun,* an official stock expression connoting "politeness" *(gong)* and "deference" *(shun).*

49. For the number of casualties caused on each ship, see *Chinese Repository* 3 (November 1834): 332.

50. Morrison died on August 1, 1834, in the midst of the Napier affair. For the circumstances of his death, see John Robert Morrison's letter to Mrs. Morrison in Morrison and Kidd, *Memoirs,* 2:531–538.

51. P. C. Kuo, *A Critical Study of the First Anglo-Chinese War with Documents* (Shanghai: Commercial Press, 1935), p. 26.

52. See Jack Beeching, *The Chinese Opium Wars* (1975; reprint, New York: Harcourt Brace Jovanovich, 1977), pp. 61–62 and 141–142.

53. "The Petition of British Subjects in Canton, to the King's Most Excellent Majesty in Council," *Chinese Repository* 3, no. 8 (December 1834): 357. See also W. C. Costin, *Great Britain and China, 1833–1860* (Oxford: Oxford University Press, 1937), p. 27.

54. For detailed discussion, see Dilip Basu, "Chinese Xenology and the Opium War," paper presented at the University of California at Berkeley, 1997. I should add a relevant detail here. Karl Gützlaff had translated a similar word in his account of the first voyage along the coast of China. The word *toumu* (Towmuh) was rendered by him as "head man," not literally as "head eye." See Gützlaff, *Journal of Two Voyages,* p. 46.

55. See Basu, "Chinese Xenology," p. 9.

56. The first duke of Wellington, Arthur Wellesley (1769–1852), served as foreign secretary from November 1834 until April 1835, when Lord Palmerston took over again on April 18.

57. Wellington to Napier, *British Parliamentary Papers,* China 30. February 2, 1835. See also Costin, *Great Britain and China,* pp. 26–27. Costin mentions the words of a Roman Catholic missionary who witnessed the incident and criticized Napier for making "un long numéraire de ses titres sans oublier celui de sa noblesse, moins encore sa qualité de Representant de Sa Majesté très puissante le Roi de la Grande Bretagne" (a long string of titles never forgetting his title of nobility, much less his eminent quality as the Representative of His Majesty the King of Great Britain) (p. 27n2).

58. Costin, *Great Britain and China,* p. 28. The laws of the Qing were clear and perhaps erred on the side of overspecification. See note 110.

59. The Chinese equivalent of the title "the Chinese secretary" was *Zheng fanyi guan* and after 1856 *Hanwen zhengshi.* See F.O. 682/1987/21 and F.O. 682/1992/25b, British Foreign Office Records.

60. Neither the British government nor the Qing government trained professional interpreters in this early period. Both relied on the service of missionaries, whose income and allegiance turned on the well-being of the British Empire

even if they themselves were not British by national origin, such as the independent Prussian missionary Gützlaff.

61. Wakeman wrote that "the British Chinese Secretary's office had a thriving intelligence network in Canton's yamens: subclerks who smuggled copies of memorials and decrees out for a fee." See Frederic Wakeman Jr., *Strangers at the Gate: Social Disorder in South China, 1839–1861* (Berkeley: University of California Press, 1966), p. 103.

62. For the roles played by Chinese Secretary Thomas Wade and Assistant Chinese Secretary Horatio Lay during the negotiation of the Treaty of Tianjin, see Banno, *China and the West*, pp. 18–25.

63. Fairbank, *Trade and Diplomacy*, p. 119.

64. A successful diplomat and sinologist, Wade was invited to fill the first endowed chair of Chinese at Cambridge University after retirement from foreign service. He is chiefly remembered as a scholar who helped design and promote the Wade-Giles romanization system that has now largely been replaced by the Pinyin system. In the nineteenth century, however, he was a key player in the drafting of a series of unequal treaties at the negotiating table, including the Anglo-Chinese Treaty of Tianjin and all the way through the Anglo-Chinese Treaty of Yantai, signed with Li Hongzhang in 1876. See James Hevia, "An Imperial Nomad and the Great Game: Thomas Francis Wade in China," *Late Imperial China* 16, no. 2 (Summer 1995): 1–22.

65. Lord Palmerston (Henry John Temple, 1784–1865) served as Britain's foreign secretary from November 1830 to November 1834 under Earl Grey, again from April 1835 to September 1841 under Lord Melbourne, and finally from July 1846 to December 1851 under Earl Russell.

66. Palmerston to Elliot, July 22, 1836, *British Parliamentary Papers*, China 30, Correspondence Orders in Council, and Reports Relative to the Opium War in China, 1840, no. 65. For the Chinese version of Elliot's communication, see Sasaki Masaya, *Ahen senso zen Chu-Ei kosho bunsho*, p. 87.

67. Elliot to Palmerston, January 12, 1837, *British Parliamentary Papers*, China 30, no. 87.

68. In his original instructions to Napier, Palmerston had prevented Napier from using the *bing* genre by insisting that "Your Lordship will announce your arrival at Canton by letter to the Viceroy." Palmerston to Napier, January 25, 1834, ibid.

69. Palmerston to Elliot, June 12, 1837, ibid.

70. *Treaties, Conventions, etc., between China and Foreign States*, 1:355.

71. James Hevia, "Making China 'Perfectly Equal,'" *Journal of Historical Sociology* 3, no. 4 (December 1990): 394. Hevia's article provides some fascinating insights into the British obsession with Manchu court rituals such as the sedan chair, palace ways, and audience halls in the aftermath of the so-called Boxer Uprising.

72. See Guo Weidong, "'Zhaohui' yu zhongguo waijiao wenshu jindai fanshi de

chugou" ("Communication" and the invention of modern genres of diplomatic communication in China), *Lishi yanjiu* 3 (2002): 99. Guo's study gives the most thorough analysis of the issue of equality in Anglo-Chinese diplomatic communication published to date.

73. For Yu Qian's memorial, see Liang Tingnan, *Yifen jiwen* (Recollections of the *yi* menace) (1874; reprint, Shanghai: Commercial Press, 1937), p. 40. The governor-general's memorial was not signed, but contemporaries and historians attribute it to Yu Qian. See Guo Weidong, "'Zhaohui' yu zhongguo waijiao wenshu jindai fanshi de chugou," p. 100n6. The governor-general committed suicide in October 1841 after the British bombarded and took the city of Ningbo during the Opium War. See Kuo, *Critical Study,* p. 157.

74. *Qing daoguang chao liuzhong mizou* (Confidential memorials in the court of the Daoguang emperor in the Qing dynasty), vol. 3, pp. 514 and 516; quoted in Guo Weidong "'Zhaohui' yu zhongguo waijiao wenshu jindai fanshi de chugou," p. 100.

75. Ibid.

76. Herman Merivale, *Lectures on Colonization and Colonies* (Oxford: Oxford University Press, 1928), p. 675.

77. See Kenneth Bell's note, ibid., p. A1.

78. F. Sidney Ensor, ed., *The Queen's Speeches in Parliament from Her Accession to the Present Time* (London: W. H. Allen & Co., 1882), p. 22.

79. For Elliot's and Qishan's respective falls from grace, see Fairbank, *Trade and Diplomacy,* pp. 81–82.

80. See Zhang Xi, "Fuyi riji" (Journal of the pacification of the *yi*), in *Yapian zhanzheng* (The Opium Wars), 6 vols. ed. Qi Sihe et al. (Shanghai: Shenzhou guoguang she, 1954), 5:389.

81. T. Mullet Ellis, *The Fairies' Favourite: or The Story of Queen Victoria Told for Children* (London: Ash Partners, 1897), p. 31; quoted in Adrienne Munich, *Queen Victoria's Secret* (New York: Columbia University Press, 1996), p. 73.

82. See Zhang Xi, "Fuyi riji," 5:390. The maximum was more likely twenty-one. For example, when the signing of the Treaty of Nanjing took place on August 29, 1842, the British fired a twenty-one-gun salute to celebrate the birthday of Queen Victoria on the same day.

83. Ibid., pp. 382–383 and 385.

84. Fairbank, *Trade and Diplomacy,* p. 196.

85. *Daqing gaozong chun huangdi shilu* (The veritable records of the supreme Qing emperor) (Taipei: Huawen shuju, 1964), p. 21327.

86. Ibid. For a new interpretation of this episode, see Zhao Gang, "Shi shenmo zhebi le shijia de yanjing: Shiba shiji shiye zhong de majiaerni shituan lai hua shijian" (What is it that has blindfolded the historian? Revisiting the Macartney embassy to China in the eighteenth century), *Shijie* 9 (February 2003): 3–28.

87. See Hevia, *Cherishing Men from Afar,* p. 72.

88. See C. H. Alexandrowicz, *An Introduction to the History of the Law of Nations in the East Indies: The Sixteenth, Seventeenth, and Eighteenth Centuries* (Oxford: Clarendon Press, 1967), p. 17.

89. Thomas R. Trautmann, *Aryans and British India* (Berkeley: University of California Press, 1997), p. 17.

90. Roy Harris, "Comparative Philology: A 'Science' in Search of Foundations," intro. to Franz Bobb, *Über das Gonjugationssystem der Sanskritsprache* (London: Routledge, 1999), p. 17.

91. Frantz Fanon, *Black Skin, White Masks,* trans. Charles Lam Markmann (New York: Grove Press, 1967), p. 99.

92. George Bonham had formerly been the governor of Singapore. He arrived to replace Sir John Davis as plenipotentiary and governor of Hong Kong on March 16, 1848. See Wakeman, *Strangers at the Gate,* pp. 90–91.

93. Xu Guangjin and Bo-gui to Bonham, July 27, 1852, F.O. 23/75, British Foreign Office Records.

94. The earlier translation of *yi* as "foreign" or "foreigner" had the potential of becoming a super-sign but had not fulfilled its destiny (by absorbing the Manchu signified within its semantic reach) when it came to be replaced by *yi/barbarian.* See my discussion of the Manchu discourse of *yi di* and *tulergi aiman* in the respective reigns of the Yongzheng and Qianlong emperors in the next chapter.

95. For my discussion of the concept of deixis in Emile Benveniste's work, see Chapter 1.

96. James Boswell, *Life of Johnson.* 6 vols., ed. G. B. Hill and L. F. Powell (Oxford, 1934), 3:339; quoted in Porter, *Ideographia,* p. 76.

97. Morse, *International Relations of the Chinese Empire,* 2:38.

98. Ibid., p. 39. The origin of the Anglo-Chinese fleet goes back to the imperial government's suppression of the Taiping Rebellion, in the course of which the government had made occasional use of chartered foreign vessels under foreign officers in order to impose some check on the supply of arms to the rebels. It was suggested in 1862 to the Qing authorities that a properly organized navy should be created, manned by Europeans, for the purpose of hemming in the Taiping forces. Robert Hart, who would himself become the next Inspectorate General in 1863, took advantage of the situation and proposed to Prince Gong that the imperial government should instruct Lay, who was in England at the time, to purchase and equip a steam fleet there and bring it out to China. This Lay did. The fleet was commanded by Captain Osborne. See ibid., 2:34–35.

99. See George Steinmetz, "Precoloniality and Colonial Subjectivity: Ethnographic Discourse and Native Policy in German Overseas Imperialism, 1780s–1914," *Political Power and Social Theory* 15 (2002): 185–186.

100. Quoted ibid., p. 188. Steinmetz shows that, although the annexation of Qingdao came later, the German colonial imaginings of China began as early as the first and second Opium Wars. In fact, one of the most notorious champions of an explicitly colonial approach to China, leading up to the colonizing of Qingdao, was Baron Ferdinand von Richthofen. Richthofen accompanied the

first Prussian embassy to the Qing court in 1860 and returned to China in 1868 to travel for four years, scouting out sites for future mines and ports in thirteen of the eighteen Chinese provinces (ibid., p. 187). For my discussion of Prince Gong's handling of the capture of Danish ships off the coast of Tianjin in 1864 by the Prussian minister to the Qing, see Chapter 4.

101. I thank Tamara Chin for drawing my attention to the Elgin cartoon.

102. Anthony Pagden, "Dispossessing the Barbarian: The Language of Spanish Thomism and the Debate over the Property Rights of the American Indians," in *The Language of Political Theory in Early Modern Europe,* ed. Anthony Pagden (Cambridge: Cambridge University Press, 1987), p. 79.

103. Ibid., p. 87.

104. Jonathan M. Hall, *Ethnic Identity in Greek Antiquity* (Cambridge: Cambridge University Press, 1997), p. 47.

105. Ibid.

106. See Anthony Pagden, *The Fall of Natural Man: The American Indian and the Origins of Comparative Ethnology* (Cambridge: Cambridge University Press, 1982), p. 20.

107. See Michel de Certeau, *Heterologies: Discourse on the Other,* trans. Brian Massumi (Minneapolis: University of Minnesota Press, 1986), p. 71.

108. Ibid.

109. The incident resonates uncannily with the scene, discussed in Chapter 1, from *Robinson Crusoe,* published only three years before this incident.

110. The statutory punishments in the *Da qing lüli,* or the Penal Code of the Qing, were translated into English by Sir George Thomas Staunton and published as early as 1810. The articles that would apply to the Europeans who committed homicide in Guangzhou are contained in book two, section 282, under the heading "Preconcerted Homicide; Murder," which stipulates that "in every case of persons preconcerting the crime of homicide, whether with or without a design, against the life of a particular individual, the original contriver shall suffer death, by being beheaded after the usual period of confinement." Section 290, "Killing with an Intent to Kill, and Killing in an Affray," states that "all persons guilty of killing in an affray; that is to say, striking in a quarrel or affray so as to kill, though without any express or implied design to kill, whether the below was struck with the hand or the foot, with a metal weapon, or with any instrument of any kind, shall suffer death, by being strangled, after the usual period of confinement. All persons guilty of killing with an intent to kill, shall suffer death by being beheaded, after being confined until the usual period. When several persons contrive an affray, in the course of which an individual is killed, the person who inflicts the severest blow or wound, shall be strangled, after the usual period of confinement. The original contriver of the affray, whether he engages in it or not, shall be punished at the least, with 100 blows, and perpetual banishment to the distance of 3000 *lee.* The rest of the party concerned shall be punished with 100 blows each." George Thomas Staunton, *Ta Tsing Leu Lee* (London: Cadell & Davies, 1810), pp. 303 and 311–

312. It is important to keep these statutory punishments in mind, because the British first brought up the desirability of extraterritoriality, contrary to the European international law of the time and to the Penal Code of the Qing in the eighteenth century.

111. Morse, *Chronicles of the East India Company,* 1:174–175.

112. Ibid., 1: 175.

113. Ibid., 1:168.

114. Ibid., 1:169.

115. This would fall under book two, section 290, of the *Daqing lüli,* which specifies the kinds of punishment for "killing with an intent to kill, and killing in an affray." For the detailed language of this section, see note 110.

3. Figuring Sovereignty

1. Chen Xulu, "Bian 'yi,' 'yang'" (Analyzing "yi" and "yang"), in *Chen Xulu xueshui wencun* (Collected works of Chen Xulu) (Shanghai: Shanghai renmin chubanshe, 1990), p. 303.

2. Compare the 1844 draft of Xu's *Yinghuan kaolüe* with the 1849 edition of *Yinghuan zhilüe.* The character *yi* was weeded out completely from the section on England in the latter edition. That this happened before the formal institution of the ban shows how much pressure the British had been putting on Chinese publishers even then.

3. *Chouban yiwu shimo* (A complete account of the management of foreign affairs) (Beijing: Gugong bowuguan, 1930), 3:812–813; quoted in Chen Xulu, "Bian 'yi,' 'yang,'" p. 304.

4. "The Central States" is a literal rendering of the Chinese self-appellation Zhongguo. See my critical assessment later in this chapter of both "China" (used by foreigners) and *Zhongguo* (used by the Chinese) as legacies of contested naming and self-naming.

5. Frank Dikötter, *The Discourse of Race in Modern China* (Stanford: Stanford University Press, 1992), p. 3. I owe this insight to Tamara Chin, who pointed out Dikötter's misquotation in an unpublished essay. Chin also notes that where Dikötter introduces a misquotation of Legge's translation, the Chinese scholar Yang Bojun adopts a modern neologism, *zhongzu* (from the Japanese *kanji* phrase *shuzoku,* used to translate Western terms of "race"), to introduce a similar slippage of translated terms between *zulei* (Legge's "kin") and *zhongzu* (Dikötter's "race") in the commentaries to a twentieth-century edition of the same *Zuo Commentaries* text. Compare Legge's rendering of *zulei* in *The Chinese Classics,* trans. James Legge (Hong Kong: Hong Kong University Press, 1960), 5:335.

6. Nicola di Cosmo, *Ancient China and Its Enemies: The Rise of Nomadic Power in East Asian History* (Cambridge: Cambridge University Press, 2002), p. 97. Di Cosmo's reading of the early texts and their historical contexts questions the notion that "a consciousness had been achieved among the Chou [Zhou] states of a clearly

demarcated 'us' and 'them' and that such a demarcation indicates a mature notion of cultural unity within China expressed in the classic opposition between a unified Hua-Hsia [Hua-Xia] community and non-Chou 'barbarians.'" He shows that the binome *yi-di* began to appear in the *Guliang* and *Gongyang Commentaries* but was not found in the earlier *Zuo Commentaries*. In the *Guliang* tradition, the *yi-di* were those who inhabited the reverse side of virtue and morality, and one could punish them without paying overmuch attention to the rules of propriety otherwise supposed to govern interstate relations; hence the famous pronouncement, "As for Yi and Ti [Di], one cannot speak of right or wrong." But who were the *yi-di?* If the nomenclature drew a clear boundary between "us" and the foreigners so named, it was fluid enough to "be applied to states normally regarded as part of the Chou political and cultural system. The states of Chin [Qin], Ch'u [Chu], and Wu were all branded at one time or another as Yi-Ti [*yi-di*] because of their violation of accepted norms" (p. 100).

7. Anthony Pagden, *The Fall of Natural Man: The American Indian and the Origins of Comparative Ethnology* (Cambridge: Cambridge University Press, 1982), p. 7.

8. As quoted in Fang Hao, *Zhongxi jiaotong shi* (A history of Sino-Western relations) (Taipei: Zhonghua wenhua chuban shiye weiyuanhui, 1954), p. 165. The original date given was the twenty-sixth day of the tenth month of the fifty-fifth year of the Kangxi reign.

9. When I was revising this chapter, the British Library opened an exhibit in London in the spring of 2002, called "Trading Places," to showcase the history of the East India Company. The exhibit drew fire from the Chinese community in London as critics pointed out that the organizers played down the aggression of the British in China by omitting to cover the Opium Wars that led directly or indirectly to the death of 17 million Chinese (yet to be confirmed) in the nineteenth century. A Web site dedicated to the protest notes that the exhibit "continues to keep silent on the horror of British military action to force the will of the East India Company on what the British Library in 2002 calls the company's 'trading partners'." See *www.thetruthabouttradingplaces.org.uk*.

10. For anti-Manchu movements in the early Qing, see Mi-chu Wiens, "Anti-Manchu Thought during the Qing," *Papers on China* 22A (1969): 1–24; Yu Xinhua, "Qing chu kang Qing hanren de huayi guan yanjiu: yi Wang Fuzhi, Gu Yanwu, Fu Shan wei zhongxin" (A study of the notions of *hua* and *yi* in the works of the anti-Manchu Han in the early Qing: with a focus on Wang Fuzhi, Gu Yanwu, and Fu Shan) (Ph.D. diss., Beijing University, 1999).

11. See Federic Wakeman Jr., *The Great Enterprise: The Manchu Reconstruction of Imperial Order in Seventeenth-Century China*, 2 vols. (Berkeley: University of California Press, 1985), 1:649.

12. For Gu Yanwu and Wang Fuzhi, see Ian McMorran, *The Passionate Realist: An Introduction to the Life and Political Thought of Wang Fuzhi* (Hong Kong: Sunshine, 1992); Alison Harley Black, *Man and Nature in the Thought of Wang Fu-chi* (Seattle: University of Washington Press, 1989); Thomas Bartlett, "Ku Yen-wu's Response to 'The Decline of Human Society'" (Ph.D. diss., Princeton University,

1985); Willard. J. Peterson, "The Life of Ku Yen-wu (1613–1682)," *Harvard Journal of Asiatic Studies* 28 (1968): 114–156; 29 (1969): 201–247; see also Kaiwing Chow, *The Rise of Confucian Ritualism: Ethics, Classics, and Lineage Discourse* (Stanford: Stanford University Press, 1994), pp. 80–84.

13. Pamela Crossley, *A Translucent Mirror: History and Identity in Qing Imperial Ideology* (Berkeley: University of California Press, 1999), p. 341.

14. In *Qing Colonial Enterprise: Ethnography and Cartography in Early Modern China* (Chicago: University of Chicago Press, 2001), Laura Hostetler argues that "although the term *Zhongguo* is found in ancient Chinese texts, it came to be used consistently to refer to a unified China only relatively recently. For early periods the term is more appropriately translated as the 'central states.' The Ming (1368–1643) and Qing dynasties often referred to the territory they controlled as the Great Ming *(da Ming)* and Great Qing *(da Qing)*, respectively, as well as by a number of more literary terms—Zhonghua (Central [Cultural] florescence), Shenzhou (the Spiritual Region), Jiuzhou (the Nine Regions), and Zhongtu (the Central Land)—but not commonly as 'China' *(Zhongguo)*. The present use of the term *Zhongguo* to refer to all of China is concurrent with the country's status as a modern nation-state" (p. 27). Hostetler's point is well taken, although she could have gone on to interrogate "China," which she seems to treat as the unproblematic signified of *Zhongguo*, to highlight the "colonial" or "international" making of *Zhongguo*.

15. Huang Zunxian, *Riben guo zhi* (An Account of the state of Japan), in *Xuxiu Siku Quanshu* (Sequel to the Four Treasures) (Shanghai: Guji chubanshe, 1995), vol. 745, p. 49.

16. Liang Qichao, "Zhongguo shi xulun" (Introduction to Chinese history), in, *Yinbing shi heji* (Collected essays from the ice-drinker's studio), (Shanghai: Zhonghua Shuju, 1936), 6: 3.

17. Zhang Taiyan, "Zhonghua minguo jie" (Interpreting the Republic of Zhonghua), *Minbao* 15 (July 1907): 2413.

18. An alternative story about the origins of the Sanskrit term *cīna* has been proposed by the Chinese scholar Su Zhongxiang. Su argues that the state of the *Jing*, also known as the *Chu* (an ancient culture existing along the Yangzi River and in the extensive areas south of the Yangzi and of the Central States) was a better candidate than the *Qin* as a possible source for *cīna*. Su speculates that the Sanskrit word might be a transcription of the name of the kingdom of Jing via the ancient trade routes in the southwest, with connections to Sihuan and India, which had existed before the Silk Road of the Han dynasty. His rejection of *Qin* as the Chinese equivalent for *cīna* is based on the dating of the primary Sanskrit texts, the *Rāmāyana* and the *Mahābhārata*, which he claimed went back to the fifth century B.C.E. and predated the rise of the unified Qin dynasty. He also cited the Hebrew term *Ciyniym* from the Old Testament Book of Isaiah as another instance of the earlier sources. The King James Version of the Bible translates the relevant lines as "Behold, these shall come from far: and lo, these from the north and from the west, and these from the land of Sinim."

The New Revised Standard Version (1989), however, represents the Hebrew term as "Syene," a name used for Aswan. If the Sanskrit and the Old Testament sources can each be determined to postdate the founding of the Qin dynasty, they could have been transcriptions of the latter. Su's speculation that the Sanskrit terms *cīna* and "outer *cīna*" correspond to *Jing* and *wai Jing* from the Chinese-language sources provides us with no hard evidence, however. The Sanskrit scholarship he used to date the earliest fragments of the *Rāmāyana* and the *Mahābhārata*, as we will see, is not very reliable. See Su Zhongxiang, "Lun 'Zhina' yi ci de qiyuan yu Jing de lishi he wenhua" (A study of the origins of the term *Zhina* and the history and culture of the Jing), *Lishi yanjiu* 4 (April 1979): 34–48. Su mentions a medieval usage of the term *Zhina* in the Chinese Buddhist canon that had been translated from the Sanskrit. This is probably the earliest Chinese transcription of the Sanskrit term before the appearance of the Japanese *Shina,* which derived from European sources. See Joshua Fogel, *Cultural Dimension of Sino-Japanese Relations: Essays on the Nineteenth and Twentieth Centuries* (Armonk, N.Y.: M. E. Sharpe, 1995), p. 68.

19. Alf Hiltebeitel, *Rethinking the Mahābhārata: A Reader's Guide to the Education of the Bharma King* (Chicago: University of Chicago Press, 2001), p. 31.

20. Patrick Olivelle, "The Laws of Manu," unpublished ms. I am grateful to Madhav Deshpande, who drew my attention to Olivelle's forthcoming new edition of the Laws of Manu, and I thank the author for permitting me to quote from his manuscript.

21. At the beginning of the twentieth century, Kang Youwei speculated on the historical transformation of the phonetic patterns of *zhuxia* and *cīna* and argued on the basis of morphological analysis that *cīna* must have been related to an earlier name, *zhuxia,* from the age of the Three Dynasties, but this view still remains speculation. See Kang Youwei, "Zhuxia yin zhuanwei zhuhua yin zhuan wei zhina kao" (A study of the morphological transformation of *zhuxia* to *zhuhua* and *cīna*), in *Wanmu Caotang yigao waibian* (A collection of miscellaneous essays from the Grass-Roof House among Ten-thousand Trees), ed. Jiang Geilin (Taipei: Chengwen chuban she, 1978).

22. For a historical and philological argument about the meaning of *Da Qin,* see Shen Fuwei, *Zhongguo yu feizhou: zhongfei guanxi er qian nian* (China and Africa: two thousand years of Sino-African relations) (Beijing: Zhonghua shuju, 1990). Relying on archaeological and textual sources, Shen clarifies an important point, namely, that *Da Qin* does not refer to southern India as is suggested by scholars such as Feng Binjun in *Zhongguo nanyang jiaotongshi* (History of Chinese South Sea trade). The term actually refers to the Roman Empire, especially Alexandria. The mistaken reference to India may be attributed to the confusion between the term *Da Qin* in volume 88 of the *History of the Latter Han* and a much later term "*daqin* Brahman," which appeared in the ninth-century *Man shu* (Barbarian book). According to Shen, "*daqin* Brahman" was itself an erroneous transcription of "*da* Brahman" (p. 68).

23. *History of the Latter Han,* (Beijing: Zhonghua Shuju, 1965), *juan* 88, p. 2919.

24. Joshua Fogel contends that *Shina* has no derogatory connotations in modern Japanese usage, any more than the word "Negro," the latter being "the respectful term in use" before the mid-1960s with "no intended offense." Fogel's judgment illustrates the severe limitation of keyword studies and conventional etymologies that construe the meanings of words in their purported statement value rather than their situated enunciations. The illocutionary force of a verbal enunciation *which also generates meaning* is completely elided in Fogel's representation of how the issue was debated between China and Japan in the twentieth century. Interestingly, that elision has not prevented Fogel himself from taking sides in the Japanese debate about *Shina* and *Shina jin* or endorsing the similar views of Takeuchi Yoshimi or the June 1930 editorial in the *Tokyo Daily News* while impulsively dismissing the arguments of Guo Moruo and Liu Shengguang. See Fogel, *Cultural Dimension of Sino-Japanese Relations*, p. 75.

25. On the imitation of Western imperialism in Meiji Japan, Robert Eskildsen offers a convincing analysis in "Of Civilization and Savages: The Mimetic Imperialism of Japan's 1874 Expedition to Taiwan," *American Historical Review* 107, no. 2 (April 2002): 388–418.

26. Conventional loanword analysis is useful but cannot substitute for the study of the super-sign that I pursue in this book. To prevent possible confusion, I should reiterate that a super-sign is not a word but a signifying chain that crosses the semantic fields of different languages simultaneously and makes a material impact on the meaning of established verbal units, whether it be indigenous words, loanwords, or other discrete verbal phenomena that linguists can identify. See Chapter 1 for a detailed discussion of this phenomenon.

27. For the grounds of Lu Xun's objection to *Shina jin*, see my *Translingual Practice: Literature, National Culture, and Translated Modernity—China, 1900–1937* (Stanford: Stanford University Press, 1995), p. 67.

28. Takeuchi Yoshimi noticed this contradiction when he responded to the insistence of the Chinese on using the English translation of their state's name as "the National Republic of China" yet asking the Japanese not to use *Shina*. Wanting to be consistent, the Japanese called the new republic "the National Republic of Shina" in the face of repeated protests by the Chinese government. See Fogel's summary of the Japanese position in the 1930s debate in *Cultural Dimension of Sino-Japanese Relations*.

29. The earlier usage of the English term "China" in the seventeenth and early eighteenth centuries was understood in the sense of "chinaware" as well as the place where porcelain and other desirable oriental goods were manufactured. See my article "Robinson Crusoe's Earthenware Pot," *Critical Inquiry* 25, no. 4 (Summer 1999): 728–757.

30. *Han ren* (men or women of the Han nationality) is used when the distinction from ethnic minorities is called for. *Han ren* is often confused with *Zhongguo ren* in English because "the Chinese" always lumps them together. For a clarification of the specific historical meanings of the ethnic classification of *Han ren* and its implications in the Manchu imperial policy, see Crossley, *Translucent Mirror*, p. 46.

31. Zhang Deyi, *Sui shi faguo ji* (Travels with the embassy to France) (Changsha: Hunan renmin chubanshe, 1982), pp. 181–182.

32. Qian Mu's research shows that leading Chinese scholars, such as Song Lian, thought little of their identity as the *hua* and felt rather ambivalent, if not contemptuous, toward the Ming. See *Zhongguo xueshu sixiang shi luncong* (Essays in the history of Chinese thought and scholarship), 8 vols. (Taipei: Dongda tushu youxian gongsi, 1978), 6:77–200.

33. *Mengzi (Mencius)*, 4.33. James Legge rendered *dongyi* as "a man near the wild tribes on the east" and *xiyi* as "a man near the wild tribes on the west." I have slightly modified his translation to stay as close to the original as possible; thus *dongyi* becomes "eastern *yi*" and *xiyi* "western *yi*." Legge's translation of *zhongguo* was "the Middle Kingdom," which was a popular nineteenth-century English term for China. I believe "the Central States" is more accurate for referring to the ancient states.

34. Peter K. Bol, "Seeking Common Ground: Han Literati under Jurchen Rule," *Harvard Journal of Asiatic Studies* 47, no. 2 (December 1987): 535.

35. Mark C. Elliott, *The Manchu Way: The Eight Banners and Ethnic Identity in Late Imperial China* (Stanford: Stanford University Press, 2001), p. 34.

36. Feng Erkang, *Yongzheng zhuan* (Biography of Yongzheng) (Beijing: Renmin chubanshe, 1985), pp. 222–242.

37. Ibid., p. 225.

38. See Crossley, *Translucent Mirror*, pp. 251–252. On the reading of "a secret counsel" in the commentarial tradition of the *Spring and Autumn Annals*, see Wiens, "Anti-Manchu Thought during the Qing."

39. The work was "Zhixin lu" (Records of the knowledge of the new). The manuscript was destroyed during the inquisition. What remains of it survives in the emperor's own rebuttal. See Feng Erkang, *Yongzheng zhuan*, pp. 224–225.

40. Feng Erkang, *Yongzheng zhuan*, p. 228.

41. Yongzheng emperor, *Dayi juemi lu* (Great righteousness resolving confusion) (Beijing: Zhongguo chengshi chubanshe, 1999), p. 2.

42. For a summary of Yongzheng's views in English, see Crossley, *Translucent Mirror*, pp. 255–258.

43. Yongzheng emperor, *Dayi juemi lu*, p. 42.

44. See *Qing shilu* (Veritable records of the Qing), 4433 *juan* (Beijing: Zhonghua shuju, 1985), *juan* 130, pp. 21–23.

45. An Shuangcheng, *Man han da cidian* (A Comprehensive Manchu-Chinese dictionary) (Shenyang: Liaoning minzu chubanshe, 1993), p. 633. The collapsing of two Chinese terms into one in the Manchu translation suggests that foreigners were primarily foreign merchants. This is how Lin Zexu used the term *yiren* in his communication with Queen Victoria. See my English translation of Lin's text in the Appendix.

46. Crossley, *Translucent Mirror*, pp. 258–265.

47. In Qianlong's reign, there was a tendency to collapse the characters *yi* and *yi²* (see the Glossary) into one, although the interchangeability of *yi* and *yi²* can be dated back to the *Zuo Commentaries* on the *Spring and Autumn Annals*. The Em-

peror's Authorized Bibliography of the Four Treasures of the Imperial Library, edited and approved by Qianlong himself, defines yi^2 in these terms: "The Central Territory occupies the center of the land mass, surrounded by the high seas on all sides. Residents who live near the seas are called yi^2. Yi^2 means borderland." In his annotations of the Four Treasures project, however, Qianlong shows his displeasure at the popular scholarly practice of suppressing the characters *yi* and *di* and replacing them with homophonous characters. See *Qinding siku quanshu zongmu* (Beijing: Zhonghua shuju, 1997), 1:7.

48. Benjamin Elman, *Classicism, Politics, and Kinship: The Ch'ang-chou School of New Text Confucianism in Late Imperial China* (Berkeley: University of California Press, 1990), p. 217.

49. See Zhuang Jifa, "Qing Gaozong chi yi *Si shu* de tantao" (A study of the imperial commissioned translations of the four Confucian classics in the Qing emperor Qianlong's reign), in *Qingshi lunji* (Collected essays on the history of the Qing) (Taipei: Wen shi zhe chubanshe, 2000), p. 66. I thank Zhao Gang for drawing my attention to this essay.

50. See *Qingding siku quanshu zongmu*, 1:368–369. For the work of Hu Anguo, see Elman, *Classicism, Politics, and Kinship*, pp. 152–153.

51. See *Qinding siku quanshu zongmu*, 1:345 and 368–369.

52. Crossley, *Translucent Mirror*, p. 221.

53. See Zhuang Jifa, *Xie Sui Zhi gong tu manwen tushuo jiaozhu* (Annotated edition of Xie Sui's illustrated Manchu version of the Imperial Tributaries Scrolls), (Taipei: Guoli gugong bowu yuan, 1989), p. 81.

54. I thank Yang Lihua for suggesting the Gongyang sources in the Qing elaboration of the *hua/yi* distinction.

55. See Elman, *Classicism, Politics, and Kinship*, pp. 231–234. For a study in Chinese, see Chen Qitai, *Qingdai Gongyang xue* (The Gongyang studies of the Qing) (Beijing: Dongfang chubanshe, 1997).

56. See Elman, *Classicism, Politics, and Kinship*, pp. 216–217. For Liu's explication of these terms, see Huang Aiping, "Liu Fenglu yu qingdai jinwen jing xue" (Liu Fenglu and the New Text scholarship in the Qing), *Qingshi yanjiu* 1(1995): 102–110. The phrase "outer *fan*" is semantically equated with the Manchu *tulergi aiman* (outer native), which has also been used to translate *yi di*. See An Shuangcheng, *Man Han da cidian*, p. 633. The archaic etymology of the character *fan* had been associated with "fences," or "borders," and the concept took on new meanings in the Qing imperial geography. Peter Bol's translation of *fan* as "border" is an accurate rendering of the etymology. See Bol, "Seeking Common Ground," p. 536. Also Bao Wenhan, "Qingdai 'fan bu' yi ci kaoshi" (An etymological study of "fan bu" in the Qing dynasty), *Qingshi yanjiu* 4 (November 2000): 98–105.

57. Elman, *Classicism, Politics, and Kinship*, p. 217.

58. Alexander Barton Woodside, *Vietnam and the Chinese Model: A Comparative Study of Vietnamese and Chinese Government in the First Half of the Nineteenth Century*, Harvard East Asian Monograph Series, no. 52 (1971; reprint, Cambridge, Mass.: Harvard University Press, 1988), p. 118.

59. See Alexander Woodside, "Territorial Order and Collective-Identity Tensions in Confucian Asia: China, Vietnam, Korea," *Daedalus* (Summer 1998): 198. Woodside draws an interesting analogy between the common literacy in classical Chinese and Confucian learning shared by the Qing, Vietnamese, and Korean courts, on the one hand, and the family resemblance between Italian Renaissance humanists and more northerly European ones such as Erasmus, on the other. He writes: "Encouraged by the existence of civil-service examinations generally similar to China's, Korean and Vietnamese writers could even hold direct but silent writing-brush dialogues with each other during their interacting visits to China as diplomats, as in the 1597 'summit' colloquy in Beijing between the Vietnamese scholar-envoy Phung Khac Khoan and the Korean historian Yi Su-gwang" (p. 195).

60. Another analogy drawn by Woodside might be helpful in thinking about the situation. "Just as the Christian Bible might resonate differently in the minds of Scottish Calvinists, German Lutherans, or Polish Catholics, so too could such texts as the Confucian Analects be read differently by Chinese or Korean academicians or Vietnamese village teachers." Ibid., p. 194.

61. For a study of Confucian thinking in Korea, see Ren Guichun, "Shi lun shiba shiji qing wenhua dui chaoxian de yingxiang: yi lichao chushi Qing chao de shijie wenti wei zhongxin" (A preliminary analysis of the impact of eighteenth-century Qing culture on Korea, with a focus on the envoy of the Li mission to the Qing court), *Qingshi yanjiu* 4 (1995): 28–39. For the Japanese situation, see Hao Bingjian, "Shiba shiji zhong ri zhengzhi sixiang de fan cha" (Differences in the political thoughts of China and Japan in the eighteenth century), *Qingshi yanjiu* 1 (1995): 1–12; David L. Howell, "Territoriality and Collective Identity," *Daedalus* (Summer 1998): 105–132; and Yan Qinghua, "Zhong ri jindai hua zhi chu de liangzhong dui wai kaifang guan: 'zhongti xiyong' yu 'hehun yangcai' sixiang bijiao" (Two views on how to open up to the outside world in the early stages of Chinese and Japanese modernity: a comparison of "Chinese essence versus western utility" and "Japanese soul versus foreign talents"), *Jingji pinglun* 2 (1995): 66–71.

62. See Chapter 4 for my discussion of Commissioner Lin's use of international law and *le droit des gens.*

63. Lin Zexu et al., "Ni yu yingjili guowang xi" (A draft declaration to the sovereign of England), in *Lin Zexu nianpu xinbian* (Revised chronicles of Lin Zexu's life), ed. Lai Xinxia (Tianjin: Nankai daxue chubanshe, 1997), p. 342. The Chinese original for "foreign" in this passage is *wai guo* (outer country). Lin uses *wai* for foreign country and reserves *yi* for foreign people in his writing.

64. Lin did not trust the English mail carriers and made multiple copies of the letter for the captains of other European ships to take to England. For dating and related circumstances surrounding the letter, see Lai Xinxia, *Lin Zexu nianpu xinbian*, pp. 311–313.

65. Lin's writings carefully maintained the distinction between *liang yi* and *jian yi*. See *Lin Zexu ji gongdu* (Collected official communications of Lin Zexu) (Beijing: Zhonghua shuju, 1965), pp. 58–60.

66. Examples are ubiquitous in the *Chouban yiwu shimo*, 27: 25b–26, as well as the earlier Qing documents.

67. See Wang Zhichun, *Qingchao rouyuan ji* (Records of foreign relations in the Qing dynasty) (1891; reprint, Beijing: Zhonghua shuju, 1989), p. 128. The Qianlong emperor's policy was similar to that of the Yongzheng emperor with regard to the foreign community in Canton. Compare, for example, his edict with the proclamation of Kong Yuxun in Chapter 2, note 24.

68. The translator put a religious spin on Lin's rhetoric by employing expressions such as "the tree of evil," "Providence," and "pouring out your heart before the altar of eternal justice." I thank Stephen Owen for noting the connection with the anti-opium campaigns among the religious communities inside and outside China.

69. What seems to be the very first English translation of an official document by one of Lin's own translators appeared in print in the *Chinese Repository*. No punctuation was used in this text, and the English was not idiomatic. The editor of the journal noted: "So far as we know, this is the first document which ever came from the Chinese language. This is evidently the work of the commissioner's senior interpreter [Yuan Dehui], who has for many years been in the employment of the government, at Peking. Its idioms are perfectly Chinese; and, like all the documents in their own language, it is without punctuation. If our readers should be able to understand what it means, they will here see the 'great imperial commissionary's' compassion manifested, and his earnest desire shown that the English ships should enter the Bogue as usual, promising that he 'will never treat you foreigners by two manners of ways.' It is a document worthy of being put on record." (*Chinese Repository* 8, no. 3 (July 1839): 168. For a study of Commissioner Lin's translators, see Lin Yongyu, "Lun Lin Zexu zuzhi de yiyi gongzuo" (A study of Lin Zexu's organizing of the work of translation), in *Lin Zexu yu ya pian zhan zheng yanjiu lunwen ji* (Collected essays in the study of Lin Zexu and the Opium War), History Institute of the Fujian Academy of Social Sciences (Fuzhou: Fujian renmin chubanshe, 1985), pp. 118–137.

70. *Chinese Repository* 8, no. 2 (June 1839): 77. For detailed information about the background of Lin's interpreters, see Chapter 5.

71. See Lai Xinxia, *Lin Zexu nianpu xinbian* p. 295.

72. William C. Hunter, *Bits of Old China* (London: Kegan Paul, Trench, & Co., 1885), pp. 260–263. Hunter called Yuan his schoolmate because they had known each other when Hunter was taking Chinese lessons at the Anglo-Chinese College in Malacca.

73. See Lin Yongyu, "Lun Lin Zexu zuzhi de yiyi gongzuo" pp. 122–123. See also Qi Sihe, *Yapian zhanzheng,* (The Opium Wars) (Shanghai: Shenzhou Guoguang she. 1954), 6:440.

74. Ssu-yü Teng and John K. Fairbank, *China's Response to the West: A Documentary Survey, 1839–1923* (Cambridge, Mass.: Harvard University Press, 1954), p. 25. For the full texts of both translations, see the Appendix.

75. Samuel Wells Williams, *The Middle Kingdom: A Survey of the Geography, Govern-ment, Literature, Social Life, Arts, and History of the Chinese Empire and Its Inhabit-ants,* 2 vols. (New York: Charles Scribner's Sons, 1883), 2: 461–462. But Wil-liams showed his own limited understanding of the situation when he objected to the British translation. For example, he stated that the word "*yi* has been raised into notice by its condemnation in the British Treaty as an epithet for British subjects or countries. This word, there rendered '*barbarian*,' conveys to a native but little more than the idea that the people thus called do not under-stand the Chinese language and usages, and are consequently less civilized. This epithet *barbarian* meant to the Greeks those who could not speak Greek, as it did to Shakespeare those who were not English; likewise among the Chi-nese, under *i* were included great masses of their own subjects" (p. 461). As we have seen, the actual situation was much more complex than Williams's analo-gies suggest.

76. Wei Yuan, *Haiguo tuzhi* (An illustrated gazetteer of maritime countries), 100 *juan,* (N.p., 1852), *juan* 1, p. 1.

77. Among those who shared Wei Yuan's views were Gong Zizhen, Lin Zexu, and others, down to Liang Qichao's generation, all of whom were steeped in the Gongyang learning. Gong Zizhen, who was Lin's close friend, became one of the most important Gongyang scholars of the period. He had studied under Liu Fenglu in 1819 and espoused the latter's rejection of the *hua/yi* distinction as well as distinctions between "what is close and what is distant and between what is great and what is humble." To confront the crisis brought on by the opium trade, Gong reinterpreted the three epochs to call for a radical reform of the Qing and wrote to Lin Zexu to give his friend the moral support he needed to launch the campaign against the opium trade. For an important interpreta-tion of Gong's role in the Gongyang studies and contribution to the imperial geographical scholarship, see Wang Hui, "Liyi zhongguo de guannian yu diguo de hefaxing wenti: jinwen jingxue de 'nei wai' guan yu qingchao de diguo shiye jiqi yanbian" (The concept of a ritual China and the legitimacy of empire: the notion of "inner/outer" in the changing imperial vision of the Qing dy-nasty), *Zhongguo shehui kexue pinglun* 1, no. 1 (2002): 181–185.

78. Historians call it the second Opium War. For a well-documented and reliable study of this war, see John Y. H. Wong, *Deadly Dreams: Opium, Imperialism, and the Arrow War (1856–1860) in China* (Cambridge: Cambridge University Press, 1998).

79. See Rudolf G. Wagner, "The *Shenbao* in Crisis: The International Environment and the Conflict between Guo Songtao and the *Shenbao*," *Late Imperial China* 20, no. 1 (June 1999): 122. Wagner refers to the correspondences between Wade and Prince Gong between March 21 and 26, 1872, F.O. 230/89, Public Record Office, London.

80. Elaine Freedgood, *Victorian Writing about Risk: Imagining a Safe England in a Dan-gerous World* (Cambridge: Cambridge University Press, 2000), p. 92.

81. Ibid., p. 13.

82. See Wagner, " *Shenbao* in Crisis," p. 127.

83. *Di er ci yapian zhanzheng* (The Second Opium War), ed. Qi Sihe et al. (Shanghai: Renmin chubanshe, 1979), 2:20.

84. See Charles (Karl) Gützlaff, *Journal of Two Voyages along the Coast of China in 1831 and 1832* (New York: John P. Haven, 1833), p. 84.

85. Ibid., pp. 126–127.

86. Ibid., p. 243.

87. For the early interactions between Europeans and Chinese, see Zhou Jinglian, *Zhong pu waijiao shi* (A history of the foreign relations between China and Portugal) (Beijing: Shangwu yinshu guan, 1991); Fang Hao, *Zhongxi jiaotong shi* (A history of Sino-Western relations) (Taipei: Zhonghua wenhua chuban shiye weiyuanhui, 1954); and Andrew Ljungstedt, *Historical Sketch of the Portuguese Settlements in China* (Boston, 1836).

88. See Meng Hua, "The Chinese Genesis of the Term 'Foreign Devil,'" in *Images of Westerners in Chinese and Japanese Literature,* ed. Meng Hua and Sukehiro Hirakawa (Amsterdam: Rodopi, 2000), p. 34.

89. Ibid., p. 36.

90. For a historian's account of this episode in English, see Frederic Wakeman Jr., *Strangers at the Gate: Social Disorder in South China, 1839–1861* (Berkeley: University of California Press, 1966), pp. 11–21. The significance of the Sanyuanli incident in Canton is underscored by Wakeman as follows: "The San-yuan-li incident was a vital prelude to so many of the problems that inflamed South China during the following twenty years: the militia movement, the Taiping revolt, secret societies, clan wars, and the antiforeign movement. Unless San-yuan-li is clearly understood, what came after will seem meaningless" (p. 21). For published literary sources from this period, see A Ying (Qian Xingcun), *Yapian zhangeng wenxue ji* (A literary collection on the Opium War), 2 vols. (Beijing: zhonghua shuju, 1957).

91. *Chinese Repository* 11, no. 6 (June 1842): 325.

92. Ibid.

93. Ibid., p. 326.

94. Ibid.

95. I thank James Hevia for drawing my attention to Rennie's journal.

96. D. F. Rennie, *Peking and the Pekingese: During the First Year of the British Embassy at Peking,* 2 vols. (London: John Murray, 1865), 1:71–72. Rennie was also the author of *British Arms in North China and Japan: Peking 1860; Kagosima 1862* (London: John Murray, 1864).

97. Wade took offense at the term *gui* but did not object to the word *fan.* In light of Liu Fenglu's explication of the official Qing distinction between *fan* and *yi* discussed in Chapter 2, it makes little sense that the British translated *fan* as "foreign" and *yi* as "barbarian."

98. See *Treaties, Conventions, etc., between China and Foreign States,* 2nd ed., 2 vols. (Shanghai: Statistical Department of the Inspectorate General of Customs, 1917), 1:408.

99. Fang Jianchang, "Chao shan diqu zhong ying jiaoshe shu shi" (Episodes in

Sino-British diplomatic affairs in Chaozhou-Shantou), *Shantou daxue xuebao* 3 (2000): 82.

100. Ibid., p. 83.

101. Fang Jianchang's research shows that many lives were lost in numerous skirmishes between the Chaozhou people on the one hand and the British and the Qing regime on the other during the consulate's existence in Chaozhou. Three villages were completely wiped out in a single incident in 1869.

102. This took place on November 1, 1865. Ibid., p. 84.

103. Williams, *The Middle Kingdom*, 2:461.

104. Rennie, *Peking and the Pekingese*, pp. 72–73.

105. Jacques Derrida, *Specters of Marx: The State of the Debt, the Work of Mourning, and the New International,* trans. Peggy Kamuf (New York: Routledge, 1994), p. 116.

106. John Thomson, *Illustrations of China and Its People* (London: S. Low, Marston, Low, and Searle, 1873–74), preface.

107. Thomson's account forms a striking contrast to some of the early Chinese accounts of photography and other technological inventions of the time. The Princess Der Ling's memoir of the Empress Dowager notes that the latter enjoyed having her picture taken by the court photographer, Yu Ling, and expressed a keen interest in the new technology by visiting the photographer's darkroom to observe the processing and printing of the pictures. When the wife of the American minister, Mrs. Conger, arranged to have the Paris-trained artist Katherine Carl paint Her Majesty's likeness, the Empress Dowager seemed less impressed with the art of oil painting (in comparison with traditional Chinese painting) than with the marvels of Western photography. As I will show in Chapter 5, the Empress Dowager manipulated the art of photography by casting herself in the image of a Buddhist bodhisattva to make a statement about her imperial authority. See Der Ling, *Two Years in the Forbidden City* (New York: Moffat, Yard and Company, 1912), pp. 217–226. Der Ling also mentions that the Empress Dowager had a gramophone in her bedroom and owned a large number of recordings of Chinese songs and some Western music.

108. Derrida, *Specters of Marx,* p. 161.

4. Translating International Law

1. See Immanuel C. Y. Hsü, *China's Entrance into the Family of Nations: The Diplomatic Phase, 1858–1880* (Cambridge, Mass.: Harvard University Press, 1960). Hsü's study, though informative, was steeped in the shadow of Fairbank's work on Sino-British trade and diplomacy which, until recently, has long dominated the study of international relations in the field of East Asia. See John King Fairbank, *Trade and Diplomacy on the China Coast: The Opening of the Treaty Ports, 1842–1854* (Cambridge, Mass.: Harvard University Press, 1953), and John King Fairbank, ed., *The Chinese World Order: Traditional Chinese Foreign Relations* (Cambridge, Mass.: Harvard University Press, 1964).

2. See Alexis Dudden, "Japan's Engagement with International Terms," in *Tokens*

of Exchange in Global Circulations, ed. Lydia Liu (Durham: Duke University Press, 1999), pp. 165–191. Also see Dudden's "International Terms: Japan's Engagement with Colonial Control" (Ph.D. diss., University of Chicago, 1998); and John Peter Stern, *The Japanese Interpretation of the "Law of Nations," 1854–1874* (Princeton: Princeton University Press, 1979).

3. Lydia H. Liu, *Translingual Practice: Literature, National Culture, and Translated Modernity—China, 1900–1937* (Stanford: Stanford University Press, 1995), p. 40.

4. For a critique of this linear notion of time informing national histories, see Prasenjit Duara, *Rescuing History from the Nation* (Chicago: University of Chicago Press, 1996).

5. For a critique of the myth of China's rejection of Western science and technology, see Joanna Waley-Cohen, "China and Western Technology in the Late Eighteenth Century," *American Historical Review* 98, no. 5 (December 1993): 1525–44.

6. See the Marxist historian Hu Sheng, *Cong yapian zhanzheng dao wusi yundong* (From the Opium war to the May Fourth movement), 2 vols. (Beijing: Renmin Chubanshe, 1981).

7. The ability to use foreign-language sources does not imply that one automatically engages the issue of translation affecting those sources.

8. *Chinese Repository* 3, no. 6 (October 1834): 287.

9. J. Y. Wong, *Anglo-Chinese Relations, 1839–1860: A Calendar of Chinese Documents in the British Foreign Office Records* (Oxford: Oxford University Press, 1983), pp. 7–8. Commissioner Lin's active recruitment of his own translation team was probably the only exception, which terminated with his exile in October 1840. A systematic comparison between the English and Chinese documents would shed fascinating light on the diplomatic exchange of this period of crisis. The Chinese-language archives from the Chinese secretary's office between 1839 and 1860 are deposited in the Public Record Office in London under F.O. 682. The British Foreign Office records in English are classified as F.O. 17.

10. The Zongli yamen was established in 1861, the first centralized modern institution to handle foreign affairs. See Masataka Banno, *China and the West, 1858–1861: The Origins of the Tsungli Yamen* (Cambridge, Mass.: Harvard University Press, 1964).

11. The Imperial College, or the Tongwen guan, was one of the first innovations to follow the Zongli yamen. It was one of two main institutions attached to the Zongli yamen, the other being the Inspectorate General of Customs (Zong shuiwu si). The Tongwen guan was established in 1862 to train diplomatic interpreters. It soon expanded to include Western sciences taught by Western instructors. The first instructor in the English department was John Burdon, an Anglican who later became bishop of Hong Kong. Burdon was followed by John Fryer, who soon made a name for himself as a translator of scientific books in Shanghai. When Fryer resigned, the post was offered to Martin at the recommendation of Anson Burlingame and Thomas Wade. See W. A. P. Martin, *A Cycle of Cathay: or, China, South and North* (New York: Fleming H. Revel,

1900), p. 296. This college was funded by foreign customs revenue. When Robert Hart became the customs inspector-general, he gave strong financial support to the Zongli yamen and its college and acted as political adviser to Prince Gong.

12. Ralph Covell, *W. A. P. Martin: Pioneer of Progress in China* (Washington, D.C.: Christian University Press, 1978), p. 27.

13. The Protestants began, however, by associating primarily with the lower class, unlike the Jesuits, who conversed with high-ranking scholar-officials and were admitted into the emperor's court. According to Patrick Hanan, Robert Thom (1807–1847), who was a student of Chinese in Guangzhou in the 1830s, complained that he was much worse off than the Jesuits in seventeenth-century Beijing: "*We* are not surrounded by the *gens de lettres* as were the missionaries at Peking, *we* have not access to their stores of knowledge as these able men had, nor are *we* looked up to with that profound respect, which they, for a season at least, extracted from the Throne itself. Oh no, *Our* Chinese associates are Hong merchants, Linguists, Compradores, and Coolies, people who make no pretensions to literary merit, people who cannot if they would, and who dare not if they could, convey to us any literary instruction—and who, while they eat our bread, most commonly hate and despise us! Such is the case *more or less* of every foreigner who sets foot in China! The writer during a residence of nearly five years, has only three times (and that by mere accident) conversed with persons who can properly be called *literary men (lettrés Chinois).*" Quoted in Patrick Hanan, "Chinese Christian Literature: The Writing Process," in *Treasures of the Yenching: Seventy-fifth Anniversary of the Harvard-Yenching Library,* ed. Patrick Hanan (Cambridge, Mass.: Harvard-Yenching Library, Harvard University, 2003), p. 270.

14. Covell, *W. A. P. Martin,* p. 114.

15. Chinese Letters of the Board of Foreign Missions of the Presbyterian Church in the United States of America, vol. 7, Peking, Martin to Board, no. 44, October 1, 1863.

16. Covell quotes this letter (*W. A. P. Martin,* p. 146) but does not tell us that the American minister Ward also had a hand in this matter from the very beginning.

17. Martin, *Cycle of Cathay,* pp. 221–222.

18. Reed's reference to this detail is contained in a letter dated December 31, 1857, which he sent from Macao to Secretary of State Lewis Cass. It reads, "The copy of Wheaton's International Law was purchased to supply the place of the one which was sent from the Department in 1855, but did not reach China." Diplomatic Despatches, China Despatches, United States National Archives and Records Administration (hereafter NARA), vol. 15, Reed to Cass, December 31, 1857.

19. W. A. P. Martin, translator's preface (in English) to *Wanguo gongfa* (Public law of all nations, a translation of *Elements of International Law*), (Beijing: Tongwen guan, 1864), p. 3.

20. W. A. P. Martin, preface (in English) to *Gongfa bianlan* (An overview of public law, a translation of Theodore Dwight Woolsey, *Introduction to the Study of International Law*) (Beijing: Tongwen guan, 1878), p. 2.

21. W. A. P. Martin, preface (in English) to *Gongfa xinbian* (A new compilation of public law, translation of W. E. Hall's *Treatise on International Law*) (Shanghai: Guangxue hui, 1903), p. 1.

22. *Chinese Repository* 8, no. 12 (April 1840): 634–635. For a new study of Parker's commissioning of racialized medical portraiture in Guangzhou, see Larissa Heinrich, "The Pathological Body: Science, Race, and Literary Realism in China" (Ph.D. diss., University of California at Berkeley, 2001).

23. *Haiguo tuzhi* was originally published in 50 *juan* in 1844. The edition in 60 *juan* appeared in 1849, and a third in 100 *juan* in 1852. Wei Yuan was also the author of *Shengyu ji* (Record of imperial military exploits), completed in 1842.

24. See Hsü's comparative analysis of the translated text and the original, *China's Entrance into the Family of Nations*, pp. 123–124.

25. See Chang Hsi-tung, "The Earliest Phase of the Introduction of Western Political Science into China (1820–1852)," *Yenching Journal of Social Studies* 5, no. 1 (July 1950): 14. See also my discussion of Yuan Dehui and other members of Commissioner Lin's translation team in 1839 in Chapter 5.

26. Emmerich de Vattel, *The Laws of Nations* (New York, 1796), p. 97; quoted in Hsü, *China's Entrance into the Family of Nations*, p. 123.

27. The irony is that James Matheson of Jardine and Matheson—the foremost among opium-trading companies—evoked Vattel in the interest of his imperialist trade policy. Citing Vattel on the eve of the Opium War, Matheson, then a member of Parliament, argued that the arrogant Chinese people and their government must be made to follow the terms of free trade, by which he meant that "all men ought to find on earth the things they stand in need of," by force if necessary. See James Matheson, *The Present Position and Prospect of Our Trade with China* (London, 1836), pp. 7–20.

28. Martin, *Cycle of Cathay*, p. 234.

29. These and other complex circumstances do not support Hsü's argument that Martin made the translation because he "was in sympathy with the Chinese need for a translation of a work on international law." See Hsü, *China's Entrance into the Family of Nations*, p. 126.

30. Diplomatic Despatches, China Despatches, NARA vol. 21, Burlingame to William Seward, October 30, 1863. Also see Martin, translator's preface to *Wanguo gongfa*, p. 2.

31. Martin, *Cycle of Cathay*, p. 222.

32. Ibid.

33. Covell, *W. A. P. Martin*, p. 146. The date given is based on Martin's "Peking News," *New York Times*, January 8, 1864. Hsü gives a slightly different date, September 11, 1863, on the basis of Martin's "Journal of Removal to Peking," *Foreign Mission*, no. 22 (February 1864): 228. See Hsü, *China's Entrance into the*

Family of Nations, pp. 128 and 238n28. For a discussion of the discrepancies among the sources, see Covell, *W. A. P. Martin,* p. 164n102. Also see China Letters of the Board of Foreign Missions of the Presbyterian Church in the United States of America, vol. 7, Peking, Martin to Board, no. 44, October 1, 1863, and no. 71, July 19, 1864.

34. Martin, *Cycle of Cathay,* p. 233.

35. Ibid., pp. 233–234. Also see Hsü, *China's Entrance into the Family of Nations,* pp. 237–238n16. On Hart's translation, see Robert Hart, "Note on Chinese Matters," in an appendix to Frederick W. Williams, *Anson Burlingame and the First Chinese Mission to Foreign Powers* (New York: Charles Scribner's Sons, 1912), p. 285. Hart's translation can no longer be found.

36. Martin, *Cycle of Cathay,* p. 234.

37. The four were He Shimeng, Li Dawen, Zhang Wei, and Cao Jingrong.

38. Covell, *W. A. P. Martin,* p. 146. Also see China Letters of the Board of Foreign Missions of the Presbyterian Church in the United States of America, vol. 7, Peking, Martin to Board, no. 44, October 1, 1863, and no. 71, July 19, 1864.

39. When Martin first arrived in Beijing, Robert Hart was out of town, but he soon wrote to Martin from Tianjin, expressing pleasure at learning of his intention to translate Wheaton. See Martin, *Cycle of Cathay,* p. 234.

40. Ibid., p. 235.

41. Diplomatic Despatches, China Despatches, NARA, vol. 21, Burlingame to William Seward, October 30, 1863.

42. Martin, *Cycle of Cathay,* p. 234.

43. Diplomatic Despatches, China Despatches, NARA, vol. 22, S. Wells Williams to William Seward, November 23, 1865.

44. This suspicion was not groundless. Martin did ask for an official decoration during his meeting with the four members of the Zongli yamen on September 10, 1863. Later he recalled in his memoir, "They paid me in due time with substantial appointments, much better than empty honors, and titles and decorations were not forgotten" (*Cycle of Cathay,* p. 234). His biographer Covell comments in a footnote that Martin's request for a decoration was less blunt than it sounds in English and yet is indicative of "Martin's increasing passion for official recognition." Covell, *W. A. P. Martin,* p. 164n104.

45. Martin, *Cycle of Cathay,* p. 235.

46. *Chouban yiwu shimo* (A complete Account of the management of foreign affairs) (Beijing: Gugong bowuguan, 1930), Tongzhi period, 27:25b–26; the translation used here is by T. F. Tsiang, with minor modification, in "Bismarck and the Introduction of International Law into China," *Chinese Social and Political Science Review* 15 (April 1931): 100. John King Fairbank had worked closely with T. F. Tsiang (Jiang Tingfu) in the 1930s, and the latter may have influenced his views on China's foreign relations.

47. For a detailed description of this incident, see Hsü, *China's Entrance into the Family of Nations,* pp. 132–133. T. F. Tsiang suggests that the Zongli yamen did not

explicitly cite Wheaton's text in handling the case because the ministers were afraid that Wheaton might be a double-edged sword. This gift from the West could have been a Greek gift. Tsiang, "Bismarck," p. 100.

48. *Chouban yiwu shimo*, 27:26, quoted in Hsü, *China's Entrance into the Family of Nations*, p. 128.

49. See Martin et al., translators' headnote to *Gongfa bianlan*.

50. Yan Fu's formal training in Western science began in 1866 at the naval school of the Foochow Shipyard. In 1877–1879 he was sent to England to study naval sciences, first at Portsmouth and then at Greenwich. The Sino-Japanese War marked a turning point in his career after his return from Europe, when he began the enterprise of translating eighteenth- and nineteenth-century European thinkers. *Tianyan lun* (On evolution) was his first translation (of T. H. Huxley's 1893 Romanes lectures on "Evolution and Ethics"), published in 1898. It was followed by his rendering of Adam Smith's classic text *An Inquiry into the Nature and Causes of the Wealth of Nations (Yuanfu)*, John Stuart Mill's *On Liberty (Qunji quanjie lun)* and *A System of Logic (Mule mingxue)*, Herbert Spencer's *Study of Sociology (Qunxue yiyan)*, Montesquieu's *Spirit of the Laws (Fayi)*, and other works. Nationalists and social reformers such as Liang Qichao, Cai Yuanpei, Lu Xun, Hu Shi, and Mao Zedong were all avid readers of his translations. Although Lu Xun and the others would later criticize Yan Fu's "conservative" politics in the Republican era, almost all of them grew up reading his translations. As Benjamin Schwartz has pointed out, in undertaking those translations Yan Fu was deeply concerned with the secrets of Western military, economic, and political power, but unlike some of his predecessors and contemporaries, he was also interested in what Western thinkers had thought about these matters. "He is the first Chinese literatus who relates himself seriously, rigorously, and in a sustained fashion to modern Western thought." See Benjamin Schwartz, *In Search of Wealth and Power* (Cambridge, Mass.: Harvard University Press, 1964), p. 3.

51. See "Zhongxi zimu hebi" (Terms and phrases), in Martin et al., *Gongfa xinbian*.

52. Immanuel Kant, "Toward Perpetual Peace," in *Kant's Political Writings*, ed. Hans Reiss (Cambridge: Cambridge University Press, 1970), p. 108.

53. Jürgen Habermas, "Kant's Idea of Perpetual Peace, with the Benefit of Two Hundred Years' Hindsight," in *Perpetual Peace: Essays on Kant's Cosmopolitan Ideal* ed. James Bohman and Matthias Lutz-Bachmann (Cambridge, Mass.: MIT Press, 1997), p. 124.

54. The standard German term for "international law" is *Völkerrecht*. The ambiguity of this word is interesting because *Völker* also means "peoples," and *Recht* can be taken to mean either "law" or "right." In his own writing, however, Kant glosses *Recht* as a German translation of the Latin *ius* and often puts the Latin in parentheses after the German term. Martha Nussbaum argues that *ius* is best translated as "law" in the eighteenth-century context. See Martha C. Nussbaum, "Kant and Cosmopolitanism," in Bohman and Lutz-Bachmann, *Perpetual Peace*, p. 51n1.

55. August Wilhelm Heffter, *Das Europäische Völkerrecht der Gegenwart*, quoted in

Henry Wheaton, *Elements of International Law* (Boston: Little, Brown, 1866), p. 16. This edition is based on a post-1846 edition, which Martin adapted for his Chinese translation.

56. Martin et al., *Wanguo gongfa,* 1:9.
57. Jacques Derrida, *Specters of Marx: The State of the Debt, the Work of Mourning, and the New International,* trans. Peggy Kamuf (New York: Routledge, 1994), p. 85.
58. Martin, translator's preface to *Wanguo gongfa,* 1:1.
59. Montesquieu, *Persian Letters,* trans. C. J. Betts (London: Penguin, 1973), p. 176.
60. Wheaton, *Elements of International Law* (1866), p. 23.
61. See Jessie G. Lutz, "Karl F. A. Gützlaff: Missionary Entrepreneur," in *Christianity in China: Early Protestant Missionary Writings,* ed. Suzanne Wilson Barnett and John King Fairbank (Cambridge, Mass.: Harvard University Press, 1984), p. 62.
62. Wheaton, *Elements of International Law* (1866), p. 23.
63. Ibid., pp. 21–22.
64. Ibid., p. 22. The Chinese translation of this passage replaces the words "to abandon its inveterate anti-commercial and anti-social principles" with the phrase "loosen up its previous bans to have intercourse with the other nations." The phrase "the former has been compelled" is rendered as "China and the Christian nations of Europe and America have reached agreements . . ." See Martin et al., *Wanguo gongfa,* 1:12.
65. Wheaton, *Elements of International Law* (1866), p. 22n8.
66. Henry Wheaton, *Elements of International Law* (Oxford: Clarendon Press, 1936), p. 16a.
67. Quoted ibid. Fung Sun is probably a misprint for Dong Xun.
68. Li Hongzhang, preface to *Gongfa xinbian* (1903). The English translation used here is included in the original edition of *Gongfa xinbian.*

5. The Secret of Her Greatness

1. The Tongzhi emperor first ascended the throne as a child in 1862. This was when the Empress Dowager began to assist the regency by running the affairs of the empire from behind a screen. She continued to be the most powerful woman in China through the year 1901, when Queen Victoria died.
2. Benedict Anderson, *The Spectre of Comparisons: Nationalism, Southeast Asia and the World* (London: Verso, 1999), pp. 58–74.
3. Adrienne Munich's study shows that the annual Orangemen's parade in Ireland continues to replay the iconicity of the queen's presentation as contemporary Protestants figure the Catholics as "the blacks" of Ireland. See Adrienne Munich, *Queen Victoria's Secret* (New York: Columbia University Press, 1996), p. 147.
4. Interestingly, the clause concerning the freedom to purchase land and property did not appear in the French version of the treaty. The original text reads: "Conformément à l'édit impérial rendu le vingt mars mil huit cent quarante-six par l'auguste Empereur TAO-KOUANG, les étalissements religieux et de bien-faisance qui ont été confisqués aux Chrétiens pendant les persécutions dont ils

ont été les victimes seront rendus à leurs propriétaires par l'entremise du
Ministre de France en Chine, auquel le Gouvernement Impérial les fera
délivrer avec les cimetiéres et les autres édifices qui en dépendaient." *Treaties,
Conventions, Etc. between China and Foreign States.* 2nd ed., 2 vols. (Shanghai: Statistical Department of the Inspectorate General of Customs, 1917), 1:888. In
the Chinese version of the treaty, the French missionary interpreter inserted a
sentence to the effect "that French missionaries be permitted to rent and purchase land and construct buildings thereupon at pleasure." Paul Cohen notes
the disastrous effect of the discrepancy between the Chinese and French versions of the treaty on the escalation of Chinese hostility toward the missionaries and their converts in the second half of the nineteenth century. See Paul A.
Cohen, *China and Christianity: The Missionary Movement and the Growth of Chinese
Antiforeignism, 1860–1870* (Cambridge, Mass.: Harvard University Press, 1963),
p. 69.

5. See Cohen, *China and Christianity.*

6. This much-anticipated occasion coincided with the defeat of the Chinese navy
by the Japanese. The *North China Herald* published an editorial to mark the significance of both events: "It is generally believed that to her sagacity and foresight, aided by the executive skill of her friend Li Hung-chang [Li Hongzhang],
the present Emperor owes his throne, and the Empire its long period of comparative peace. Now, unfortunately, the observation of a day which had been
anticipated for some time by the whole of China, will be shorn of much of its
ostentation and magnificence. With an exasperatingly pernicious enemy lop-
ping off an appendage of the empire, and almost within striking distance of the
home of the dynasty, even official China cannot remain in blissful uncon-
sciousness, so that treasuries which would have been called upon to supply the
outward and visible signs of rejoicing, are now depleted to afford protection
against the invader." *North China Herald,* November 9. 1894, p. 766. This paper,
founded on August 3, 1850, in Shanghai, was published weekly. It became a
daily newspaper after July 1, 1864, under the name *North China Daily News,* but
the old name was retained for the weekly supplement to the daily paper. The
"treasuries" mentioned in the editorial refer to the extravagant expenses associated with the court's preparations for the approaching birthday ceremony.
The Empress Dowager's extravagance outraged many, who charged that the
court was taking money out of the navy's budget and wasting it on ostenta-
tious display. William Scott Ament of the North China Mission wrote from
Beijing on August 1, 1894: "The Empress-Dowager is a lady of large abilities,
commands the respect of the Chinese statesmen and without doubt is the most
influential personage in the empire. The Emperor is preparing to celebrate her
birth-day with truly royal magnificence. The Peking Gazette reports that already a sum equal to about $25,000,000 U.S. gold has been appropriated for
the purpose. The road from her summer palace, about ten miles from the city
to the west, to her city residence has been parceled out among the twenty-two
provinces of the empire, proportioned to their wealth, and every foot of space
is to be occupied with ornamental arches, silk pavilions, theatres and spectacu-

lar shows of all descriptions. Not only are all the officials in the empire as-
sessed, but in Peking all forms of business, even down to the peddling huckster
and donkey-drivers, are compelled to assist in a show which they all pro-
nounce to be unnecessary and wasteful." Letter on record, Beijing, August 1,
1894, China Correspondence, ABS (American Bible Society) Archives, New
York, Reel no. 74A.

7. Apparently there is no surviving copy of this edition of the Presentation New
Testament. The verbal description is in the ABS Archives, Reel no. 74A.

8. In his letter, dated November 5, 1894 (ABS Archives, Reel no. 74A), Hykes
wrote: "We have had three facsimile copies of the book made, and I hope to
send them to you as soon as we can get the introduction written. You will understand this book was not printed by the Bible Societies, nor at their expenses—but Mr. Dyer and I were on the Committee which published it and we
saw it through the press. We read all the proofs, and had general supervision of
the work." Whatever has happened to the copies Hykes sent to New York, they
are now missing. The only surviving copy of the Imperial edition of the New
Testament in the ABS bears a later date.

9. A list of the societies represented among the contributors to the Presentation
New Testament was included in one of Hykes's letters to the American Bible
Society. The list shows a broad spectrum of participating Protestant organiza-
tions as well as women who had no official affiliations: the American Presbyterian Church North, the American Presbyterian Church South, the Canadian
Presbyterian, English Presbyterian, Irish Presbyterian, Scotch United Presbyte-
rian, and Protestant Episcopal churches, the Rhenish Mission, Scandinavian
Free Mission, Swedish Mission, and Wesleyan Mission, the Woman's Union,
American Board of Commissioners on Foreign Mission (ABCFM), the American Reformed, American Baptist North, American Baptist South, English Baptist, Baptist Missionary Union, and Seventh Day Baptist churches, the Basel
Mission, China Inland Mission, Church Missionary Society, Free Methodist
Church Friends' Mission, Honolulu Chinese Mission, London Missionary Soci-
ety, the Methodist Episcopal North and Methodist Episcopal South churches,
the National Baptist Church of Scotland, the Norwegian Mission, Junior Christian Endeavor of Shanghai, and non-missionary foreign ladies from
Chongqing, Shanghai, and the United States. See Rev. John R. Hykes to Rev.
Edward W. Gilman, Shanghai, November 21, 1894, China Correspondence,
ABS Archives, Reel no. 74A.

10. In another letter, Hykes ascertains the total number of subscribers to be
10,900. See Rev. John R. Hykes to Rev. Edward W. Gilman (corresponding secretary of the American Bible Society), Shanghai, November 30, 1894, China
Correspondence, ABS Archives, Reel no. 74A.

11. Rev. John R. Hykes to Rev. Edward W. Gilman, Shanghai, November 21, 1894,
ibid.

12. Ibid.

13. "Presentation to the Empress-Dowager," Shanghai, March 26, 1894, China
Correspondence, ABS Archives, Reel no. 74A. The signatory in the Chinese

version of the memorial was identified as "missionaries," not Chinese converts.

14. Rev. John R. Hykes to Rev. Edward W. Gilman, Shanghai, November 10, 1894, ibid.

15. For an account of the missionary translations of the Bible in classical Chinese, see Patrick Hanan's essay "Chinese Christian Literature: The Writing Process," in *Treasures of the Yenching: Seventy-fifth Anniversary of the Harvard-Yenching Library,* ed. Patrick Hanan (Cambridge, Mass.: Harvard-Yenching Library, 2003), pp. 261–283.

16. Memorial to the Empress Dowager, Shanghai, November 21, 1894, China Correspondence, ABS Archives, Reel no. 74A.

17. Munich, *Queen Victoria's Secret,* p. 145.

18. Quoted ibid., p. 145.

19. Ibid.

20. Ibid.

21. Ibid., p. 231.

22. Quoted ibid., pp. 146–147.

23. James Hevia provides a detailed analysis of the technology of photography in the British and the Allies' conquest of the Qing. See his *English Lessons: The Pedagogy of Imperialism in Nineteenth-Century China* (Durham: Duk University Press, 2003), pp. 195–208; 259–281.

24. Munich, *Queen Victoria's Secret,* p. 147.

25. Rev. John R. Hykes to Rev. Edward W. Gilman, Shanghai, September 20, 1894, China Correspondence, ABS Archives, Reel no. 74A.

26. Memorial to the Empress Dowager, Shanghai, November 21, 1894.

27. Hanan, "Chinese Christian Literature," pp. 272–278. According to Hanan, Medhurst's first Chinese assistant was Jiang Yongzhi (Tseng Yung-che in Medhurst's transcription) and the second known assistant was Wang Changgui, father of Wang Tao. After Wang Changui's death, Wang Tao was invited to continue the translation and was responsible for the latter part of the New Testament and for preparing draft translations of the whole of the Old Testament.

28. Der Ling, *Two Years in the Forbidden City* (New York: Moffat, Yard and Company, 1912), p. 68.

29. *Ye* also means "grandpa," among its many connotations. One of Der Ling's memoirs about Cixi is titled *Old Buddha.*

30. The emasculination of the Guangxu emperor is a theme of nearly all popular narratives and cinematic representations of Cixi's tyranny and cruelty.

31. The Princes and Ministers of the Zongli yamen to Mr. O'Conor, Beijing, December 15, 1894, copy of the translation on file, China Correspondence, ABS Archives, Reel no. 74A.

32. Rev. John R. Hykes to Rev. Edward W. Gilman, Shanghai, December 21, 1894, ibid.

33. "Correspondence," *North China Herald,* December 21, 1894.

34. See Jane Hunter, *The Gospel of Gentility: American Women Missionaries in Turn-of-*

the-Century China (New Haven: Yale University Press, 1984), pp. 1–16. For related studies, see also Patricia R. Hill, *The World Their Household: The American Women's Foreign Mission Movement and Cultural Transformation, 1870–1920* (Ann Arbor: University of Michigan Press, 1985).

35. See Dale Spender, intro. to Elizabeth Cady Stanton, *The Woman's Bible: The Original Feminist Attack on the Bible* (New York: Arno Press, 1972), pp. iii–iv.

36. Elizabeth Cady Stanton, *The Woman's Bible* (Boston: Northwestern University Press, 1993), pp. 125–126.

37. Mary D. Pellauer, *Toward a Tradition of Feminist Theology: The Religious Social Thought of Elizabeth Cady Stanton, Susan B. Anthony, and Anna Howard Shaw* (New York: Carlson Publishing, 1991), p. 22. See also Elizabeth Cady Stanton, *Eighty Years and More: Reminiscences, 1815–1897* (New York: Schocken Books, 1971), pp. 390–393.

38. Elizabeth Cady Stanton, "Collected Papers," in Beth M. Waggenspack, *The Search for Self-Sovereignty: The Oratory of Elizabeth Cady Stanton* (New York: Greenwood Press, 1989), p. 122.

39. Ibid., p. 159.

40. Ann Stoler's reading of Michel Foucault's *History of Sexuality* suggests that the discourse of sexuality in modern Europe must be examined in light of how that discourse has been historically embedded in Europe's colonial experience of the other and in its articulation of race. See Ann Stoler, *Race and the Education of Desire* (Durham: Duke University Press, 1995), pp. 55–94.

41. Margaret Homans, *Royal Representations: Queen Victoria and British Culture, 1837–1976* (Chicago: University of Chicago Press, 1998), p. 72.

42. In her "Address to the Joint Judiciary Committee, New York Legislature," on February 14, 1854, for example, Stanton demanded "the full recognition of all our rights as citizens of the Empire State. We are persons; native, freeborn citizens; property-holders, tax payers; yet are we denied the exercise of our right to the elective franchise. We support ourselves and, in part, your schools, colleges, churches, your poor-houses, jails, prisons, the army, and navy, the whole machinery of government, and yet we have no voice in your councils. We have every qualification required by the Constitution, necessary to the legal voter, but the one of sex. We are moral, virtuous, and intelligent, and yet by your laws we are classed with idiots, lunatics, and negroes." Stanton, "Collected Speeches," p. 97.

43. Ibid., p. 115.

44. This situation continued well into World War II. Jessie Lutz's research on the careers of Minnie Vautrin and Matilda Thurston as educators in China shows that American missionary women in the early twentieth century were able to attain positions of influence and pursue professional careers in China that were not readily accessible to women in America. See Jessie G. Lutz, "The Chinese Education of Minnie Vautrin and Matilda Thurston: Variants that Converged," paper delivered at the 2003 Annual Conference of the Association for Asian Studies (AAS), New York, April 2003.

45. Stanton, "Collected Speeches," p. 135.

46. Elizabeth Stanton, Susan B. Anthony, and Matilda Jocelyn Gage, eds., *History of Woman Suffrage*, 6 vols. (New York: Fowler and Wells, 1881–1922), 3:iv.

47. Murray A. Rubinstein, "The Wars They Wanted: American Missionaries' Use of *The Chinese Repository* before the Opium War, *American Neptune* 48, no. 4 (Fall 1988): 271.

48. Ibid., p. 272.

49. Charles (Karl) Gützlaff, *The Journal of Two Voyages along the Coast of China in 1831 and 1832* (New York: John P. Haven, 1833), pp. 123–124.

50. Elizabeth Cady Stanton, "Speech on the Anniversary of the American Anti-Slavery Society," in *The Elizabeth Cady Stanton–Susan B. Anthony Reader*, ed. Ellen Carol Dubois (Boston: Northeastern University Press, 1992), pp. 83–84. For a superb analysis of Catherine Beecher's use of Victoria, see Amy Kaplan, "Manifest Domesticity," *American Literature* 70, no. 3 (Sept. 1998): 586.

51. See Homans, *Royal Representations*, pp. 100–156. For an analysis of Victoria's own thoughts on being a female sovereign, see the piece by Gail Turley Houston, "Reading and Writing Victoria: The Conduct Book and the Legal Constitution of Female Sovereignty," in *Remaking Queen Victoria*, ed. Margaret Homans and Adrienne Munich (Cambridge: Cambridge University Press, 1997), pp. 159–181.

52. Homans, *Royal Representations*, p. 147.

53. Ibid., p. xxv.

54. Quoted ibid., p. 149.

55. Hunter, *Gospel of Gentility*, p. 14.

56. Ibid., p. 84. A major source of inequities in the field lay within the structure of the home church. Hunter writes: "The Presbyterian denominations, as late as 1927, denied women lay privileges at home, a restriction that also limited the participation of women in the church polity in China. The Methodist conferences barred those who were not ordained and automatically barred women who were ineligible for ordination."

57. Ibid., p. 96.

58. Pearl Buck, *The Exile* (New York: John Day, 1936), p. 107.

59. Hunter, *Gospel of Gentility*, p. 95.

60. Rev. John R. Hykes to Rev. Edward W. Gilman, Shanghai, December 21, 1894.

61. The Empress Dowager left few verbal records of her sentiments with regard to Christianity during this volatile period of Qing history, although we know that she detested the missionaries. She was quoted as saying: "I may be conservative in saying that I admire our custom and will not change it as long as I live. You see our people are taught to be polite from their earliest childhood, and just look back at the oldest teachings and compare them with the new. People seem to like the latter the best. I mean that the new idea is to be Christians, to chop up their Ancestral Tablets and burn them. I know many families here who have broken up because of the missionaries, who are always influencing the young people to believe their religion." Der Ling, *Two Years in the Forbidden City*, p. 175.

62. Ibid., p. 225.
63. Chün-fang Yü's study *Kuan-yin: The Chinese Transformation of Avalokiteśvara* (New York: Columbia University Press, 2001), p. 294, suggests that the feminine transformation of Guanyin has scriptural roots in the "Universal Gateway" chapter of the Lotus Sūtra, where Avalokiteśvara appears in as many as thirty-three different forms in order to save different types of people. Among these forms, seven are feminine: nun, laywoman, wife of an elder, householder, official, Brahmin, and girl.
64. Der Ling's memoir gives a detailed description of the elaborate staging of Buddhist plays in the Summer Palace, as well as the Empress Dowager's interest in modern stage design (*Two Years in the Forbidden City*, pp. 24–35). These photographs, taken by Der Ling's brother, the court photographer Yu Ling, were not intended for public release. The journalistic potential of photography, however, was not lost on the Empress Dowager, since she had seen and complained about some of the 1,900 pictures taken by the Allied Forces, one of which showed an officer sitting on the imperial throne. See Figure 15.
65. Rev. John R. Hykes to Rev. Edward W. Gilman, Shanghai, December 21, 1894.
66. Rev. John R. Hykes to Rev. Edward W. Gilman, Shanghai, November 21, 1894.
67. A surviving copy of the imperial edition of the New Testament is owned by the American Bible Society. This book had passed from the imperial house to the hands of a Christian Guomindang official, who gave it to Pastor Shen Yu-shu, formerly of the city of Nanjing, in return for some service. Shen then emigrated to California and was persuaded by a retired Methodist missionary, Edward James, to sell the book to the American Bible Society, which he did for $110 in 1944.
68. See *China Mission Year Book,* app. IX (1911), 2:xxxii–xxxiii; *Chinese Recorder* (1909): 587–588 (beginning of the project), and (1910): 758 (editorial comment).
69. For the report and the financial statement of the Presentation Committee, See *Chinese Recorder* (1911): 134 and 184–186.
70. BFBS report for 1911, cited in China Correspondence, ABS Archives, Reed no. 74A.
71. *China Mission Year Book,* app. IX (1911), 2:xxxiii.
72. Ibid., 2:xxxii.
73. Ku Hung-ming is the romanized spelling of the Chinese name under which the author published all his writings in English. The romanization Ku used to matriculate at the University of Edinburgh was Hong Beng Kaw. The commonly adopted spelling of his family name in Penang, however, is Koh. According to the Pinyin romanization that is the standard system used today in the PRC and elsewhere, Ku's name should be spelled Gu Hongming. To avoid confusion, I use his publishing name, Ku Hung-ming.
74. For a detailed account of Joshua Marshman's work as translator in Serampore, see Hanan, "Chinese Christian Literature," pp. 266–267.
75. It appears that Rong Hong was not the first student to study in the United

States. Ya Lin had been there twenty years before him. See Lin Yongyu, "Lun Lin Zexu zuzhi de yiyi gongzuo" (A study of Lin Zexu's organizing of the work of translation), in *Lin Zexu yu ya pian zhan zheng yanjiu lunwen ji* (Collected essays in the study of Lin Zexu and the Opium War), History Institute of the Fujian Academy of Social Sciences (Fuzhou: Fujian renmin chubanshe, 1985), p. 123.

76. See Jonathan Spence, *God's Chinese Son: The Taiping Heavenly Kingdom of Hong Xiuguan* (New York: W. W. Norton, 1996), pp. 16–18.

77. See Lin Yongyu, "Lun Lin Zexu zuzhi de yiyi gongzuo."

78. Somerset Maugham, *On a Chinese Screen* (London: William Heinemann, 1922), pp. 147–148.

79. Ibid., pp. 149–150. Ku had ignored Maugham's previous informal request to see him until the author wrote a polite letter asking for permission to visit. Ibid., p. 148.

80. Ibid., pp. 153–154.

81. Ibid., pp. 154–155.

82. G. Lowes Dickinson (1862–1932), a Cambridge professor, adopted Ku's persona and his words without actually naming him in his best-selling book *Letters from John Chinaman*, published in 1901. In this book, Dickinson invented the character of John Chinaman to criticize European imperialism in the manner of Ku, who had signed himself "a Chinaman" in articles he published before 1901. Thus John Chinaman and Ku merge into one as we read:

"'They [the Chinese] believe in right,' says Sir Robert Hart—let me quote it once more 'they believe in right so firmly that they scorn to think it requires to be supported or enforced by might.' Yes, it is we who do not accept it that practise the Gospel of peace; it is you who accept it that trample it underfoot. And—irony of ironies!—it is the nation of Christendom who have come to us to teach us by sword and fire that Right in this world is powerless unless it by [sic] supported by Might! Oh do not doubt that we shall learn the lesson! And woe to Europe when we have acquired it! You are arming a nation of four hundred millions! a nation which, until you came, had no better wish than to live at peace with themselves and all the world. In the name of Christ you have sounded the call to arms! In the name of Confucius, we respond!" G. Lowes Dickinson, *Letters from John Chinaman* (London: George Allen & Unwin, 1901), p. 40.

A similar view was expressed in Ku's essay "For the Cause of Good Government in China," published in January 1901. Ku alludes to the prophetic words of Sir Robert Hart, who warned about a future of "Boxerdom" in China, and argues that the literati can learn the art of war just as quickly as they unlearned it in the past, but "the question of whether the Chinese nation will have to fight or not, is a very grave question for the cause of civilization in the world." Ku Hung-ming, *Papers from a Viceroy's Yamen: Chinese Plea for the Cause of Good Government and True Civilization of China* (Shanghai: Shanghai Mercury,

1901), p. 78. There is no need to highlight every technical detail that blurs the textual boundaries between Ku and Dickinson. Suffice it to say that Maugham's portrait of Ku in "The Philosopher" may be a fascinating collage of all three images of the invented persona of a Chinese critic: Ku, the author of *Papers from a Viceroy's Yamen;* Dickinson's John Chinaman; and Maugham's own response to Ku's reaction to his visit.

83. Ku's ethnicity is by no means settled. While the majority of my sources indicate that he was an ethnic Chinese, a few suggest, on the basis of firsthand physiognomic evidence, that he was probably a Creole with Caucasian or other blood from his mother's line.

84. Huang Xingtao, *Wenhua guaijie Gu Hongming* (Ku Hung-ming the cultural eccentric) (Beijing: Zhonghua shuju, 1995). Conflicting information exists as to when Ku began to grow his queue and wear Chinese clothes. See note 86.

85. As the author of the first systematic grammar of classical Chinese prose written in Chinese, Ma Jianzhong initiated comparative linguistic studies in China. He retired from diplomatic service in the last years of the nineteenth century and devoted himself to writing his grammar book as well as working for business firms. See Chapter 6.

86. See Huang Xingtao, *Wenhua guaijie Gu Hongming,* pp. 18–19. Huang suggests that Ku had had a queue as a child but cut it off sometime after he arrived in Scotland. Ku was apparently without a queue and wore a Western suit when he met Ma Jianzhong in Singapore.

87. For the meaning of the Qing haircutting code for the native men, see Chapter 3.

88. Maugham, *On a Chinese Screen,* p. 154.

89. For other contemporary accounts of Ku, see Alfons Paquet's forword to Ku Hung-ming, *Chinasverteidigung gegen Europäische Ideen* (Jena: Eugen Diederichs Verla, 1921), p. viii.

90. Likewise, identity politics in an immigrant society such as the United States has always been about the sovereign rights of those groups that are construed negatively by the racial, gender, or sexual categories of the state and society. The argument of essentialism or constructivism in the contemporary discussions of identity is hardly meaningful if one neglects to address the fundamental issue of sovereign subjectivity in the processes of social struggle.

91. Ku, *Papers from a Viceroy's Yamen,* pp. 20–21.

92. Ibid., p. 17. The conflict over the name *Yihe Tuan* and the Western portrayal of "the Boxers" has continued to this day. Chinese scholars always use *Yihe Tuan,* a name that was used by members of the organization themselves. To the best of my knowledge, there is no equivalent of "the Boxer Rebellion" in any serious Chinese-language studies of the Yihi Tuan. It is the Western-language scholarship that insists on calling the members of that society "the Boxers," whose equivalent is *quan fei* (Boxer thug), not *Yihe Quan. Quan fei* also appeared in the Qing official condemnation of the uprising.

93. Ibid., p. 82. Attempts to discredit Ku also include casting doubt on his author-

ship because of his race. When Ku's article "Defensio Populi ad Populos" first appeared in English, signed "a Chinaman," in the *North China Daily News*, the *Times* of London is said to have responded with a lead article suggesting that the essay probably could not have been written by a Chinese author because the language would not have "had that repose which stamped the caste of Vere de Vere." This reaction was typical of the kind of colonial inscription of racial difference that Henry Louis Gates Jr. discusses in connection with the first African American poet in English, Phillis Wheatley. The slave girl was made to undergo an oral examination in the courthouse of Boston in 1772 to obtain a formal document attesting to the authenticity of her authorship and, therefore, secure a publisher for her poetry. See Henry Louis Gates Jr., "Editor's Introduction: Writing 'Race' and the Difference It Makes," in *"Race," Writing, and Difference*, ed. Henry Louis Gates Jr. (Chicago: University of Chicago Press, 1985), pp. 7–8. Anticipating further attempts to discredit his writing because of his race, Ku posted an introductory letter to the editor of the *Japan Mail* to be printed along with his treatise "Moriamur pro Rege, Regina!" in 1900:

"Now, as an unknown Chinaman appearing to speak publicly for the first time in his own name and on his own responsibility, I think the civilized world has a right to ask my qualifications to speak on this great and important question. I think it therefore necessary to say that the present writer is a Chinaman who has spent ten years of his life in Europe in studying the language, literature, history and institutions of Europe, and twenty years in studying those of his own country. As for his character, I will only say this much: although the present writer cannot boast to be *chevalier san peur et sans réproche*, yet, I think those foreigners in China who have known me personally and come in contact with me in any relation will bear me out when I say, that the present writer has never, by any unworthy act, sought the favour or deserved the disfavour of the foreigners in China." Ku, *Papers from a Viceroy's Yamen*, p. 32.

94. The southern viceroys Zhang Zhidong and Liu Kunyi had issued a declaration of independence of the provinces south of the Yangzi River in order to distance themselves from the 1900 movement and contain the encroachment of the Western fleets from the North. This was known as the *Jiangnan huzhu* (mutual protection movement in the southern provinces). For a discussion of Ku's role in this incident, see Huang Xingtao, *Wenhua guaijie Gu Hongming*, pp. 108–133.

95. Ku, *Papers from a Viceroy's Yamen*, pp. 25–26 (emphasis added).

96. It has been suggested that Ku's articles in the *Japan Mail* and *North China Daily News* did have some influence on public opinion and helped soften the Allies' attitude toward the Empress Dowager, if not toward the princes, in the aftermath of the 1900 movement. See Shen Laiqiu, "Luetan Ku Hung-ming" (Some thoughts on Ku Hung-ming), in *Wentan guaijie Ku Hung-ming* (Ku Hung-ming the strange literary genius), ed. Wu Guoqing (Changsha: Yuelu shushe, 1988), pp. 172–184. Two highly embellished versions of Ku's role in the 1900 crisis also exist. One of them, written by his student Zhao Wenjun,

gives a dramatized account of Ku's story told in Ku's own voice, and the other is found in the late Qing novel *Niehai hua* (The flowers in the sea of evil). Chapters 31 and 32 of that novel recount Ku's adventures in the pleasure quarters of Beijing and his relationship with Sai Jinhua, the famous courtesan, who is said to have had an affair with the German army commander. Ku's name in the novel is given as Ku Ming-hung instead of Ku Hung-ming.

97. Ku, preface to *Papers from a Viceroy's Yamen*, p. iii. For a detailed examination of the Allies' acts of revenge and punishment, see Hevia, *English Lessons*, pp. 195–240.

98. Ibid., pp. 22–23.

99. To this day, Western scholarship continues to draw on missionaries' accounts and Western journalism as reliable sources of information and does not mention Ku's writing in English or Chinese on the subject, although we know that Ku's published writing exerted pressure on the Allies' decisions in the aftermath of the 1900 movement and their plans for punishing the Manchu princes. James Hevia was one of the first to draw attention to the imperial value of the writings of Smith and Brown in their documentation of the Allies' attacks on Beijing, see his *English Lessons*, pp. 282–291.

100. Anderson, *Spectre of Comparisons*, p. 41.

101. Ku, *Papers from a Viceroy's Yamen*, p. 27.

102. See Nigel Cameron, *Barbarians and Mandarins: Thirteen Centuries of Western Travelers in China* (Chicago: University of Chicago Press, 1976), p. 353n. Looty's image appeared in a drawing printed in *Illustrated London News*, June 15, 1861. See Hevia, *English Lessons*, p. 88.

103. See Munich, *Queen Victoria's Secrets*, pp. 127–143.

104. There had been an eighteenth-century precedent to the adoption of oriental dogs by the British royal house. Craig Clunas shows that one such dog, the King Charles spaniel, was memorialized in porcelain figurines commissioned and reproduced in China and sent back to England. See Craig Clunas, *Chinese Export Art and Design* (London: Victoria and Albert Museum, 1987), pp. 48–50.

105. Der Ling, *Two Years in the Forbidden City*, p. 356.

106. Ibid., pp. 356–357. A miniature portrait of Queen Victoria is said to have stood by Cixi's bed, a detail I have not been able to verify. See Marina Warner, *The Dragon Empress: Life and Times of Tz'u-hsi, Empress Dowager of China, 1835–1908* (New York: Macmillan, 1972), p. 158.

107. Ku, *Papers from a Viceroy's Yamen*, p. 71.

108. For a study of the relationship between positivism and colonialism, see Anthony Anghie, "Finding the Peripheries: Sovereignty and Colonialism in Nineteenth-Century International Law," *Harvard International Law Journal* 40 (Winter 1999): 1–80.

109. Henry Wheaton, *Elements of International Law*, (Oxford: Clarendon Press, 1936), pp. 28–29.

110. W. E. Hall, *A Treatise of International Law*, 2nd ed. (Oxford: Clarendon Press, 1884), p. 40. The book was translated into Chinese in 1903.

6. The Sovereign Subject of Grammar

1. William Dwight Whitney, *Language and the Study of Language: Twelve Lectures on the Principles of Linguistic Science* (New York: Charles Scribner & Company, 1870), p. 14 (emphasis added).

2. Ferdinand de Saussure, *Course in General Linguistics*, trans. Roy Harris (La Salle: Open Court, 1983), p. 5.

3. See Hans Aarsleff, *From Locke to Saussure: Essays on the Study of Language and Intellectual History* (Minneapolis: University of Minnesota Press, 1982), p. 393.

4. See John E. Joseph, "Saussure's Meeting with Whitney, Berlin, 1879," *Cahiers Ferdinand de Saussure* 42 (1988): 205–214.

5. Roman Jakobson, "The World's Response to Whitney's Principles of Linguistic Science," in *Whitney on Language: Selected Writings of William Dwight Whitney*, ed. Michael Silverstein (Cambridge, Mass.: MIT Press, 1971), pp. xxxiii–xxxiv.

6. For a detailed study of the schools, individuals, and their theories of a universal language, see Umberto Eco, *The Search for the Perfect Language*, trans. James Fentress (Oxford: Blackwell, 1997).

7. See Thomas R. Trautmann, *Aryans and British India* (Berkeley: University of California Press, 1997), pp. 13 and 28. This is a very different Aryan story from the sinister Nazi or neo-Nazi uses of the name with which most of us are familiar. Trautmann's genealogy of Aryan learning greatly helps clarify some of the common misunderstandings of the nature of colonial rule and orientalism in British India.

8. Sir William Jones, who promoted the study of Indo-European languages as the first president of the Asiatic Society at Calcutta in the 1780s, has somehow been credited with the invention of comparative philology. But as Roy Harris has pointed out, Jones was hailed as the founder of comparative grammar in the nineteenth century because the British considered it a national honor to be foremost in establishing Aryan linguistic credentials, although they were actually lagging behind the German scholars (Bopp, Grimm, Pott, and Humboldt) whose rigorous *indogermanisch* studies were making waves in Europe. See Roy Harris, "Comparative Philology: A 'Science' in Search of Foundations," intro. to Franz Bobb, *Über das Conjugationssystem der Sanskritsprache* (London: Routledge, 1999), p. 10. For a discussion of the burgeoning of a proto–Indo-European hypothesis that goes as far back as the seventeenth century, see George van Driam, *Languages of the Himalayas: An Ethnolinguistic Handbook of the Greater Himalayan Region*, 2 vols. (Leiden: Brill, 2001), 2: 1039–51.

9. Quoted in Harris, "Comparative Philology," p. 10.

10. For a discussion of how Chinese was conceived and debated by the Europeans as the original primitive language of the world in seventeenth-century theological and scientific writings, see David Porter, *Ideographia* (Stanford: Stanford University Press, 2001), pp. 15–77.

11. Carl Wilhelm Friedrich von Schlegel, *On the Language and Wisdom of the Indians*, trans. E. J. Millington (London: Ganesha Publishing, 2001), p. 447. (1808)

12. Whitney, *Language and the Study of Language*, p. 233.
13. Ibid., p. 257.
14. Ibid., p. 331.
15. James Legge, trans., *The Chinese Classics*, vol. 2 (Hong Kong: Hong Kong University Press, 1960), p. 125. See "Wang yue" in the Glossary, p. 299.
16. See Haun Saussy, "Always Multiple Translation, or How the Chinese Language Lost Its Grammar," in *Tokens of Exchange in Global Circulations*, ed Lydia H. Liu (Durham: Duke University Press, 1992), p. 122n5.
17. Ibid., p. 111.
18. Whitney, *Language and the Study of Language*, p. 265. For Whitney's argument with Renan, see ibid., pp. 279–286.
19. See August Schleicher, *Die Sprachen Europas in Systematischer Übersicht* (European languages in systematic overview), new ed. with introductory article by Konrad Koerner (Amsterdam: John Benjamins Publishing Company, 1983), pp. 50–54.
20. I have examined a litany of retranslations in this book, from Roboert Morrison's auto-correction of his earlier translation of the character *yi*, to the anonymous English translation of the Latin version of Su Shi (see Chapter 2), to Ssu-yü Teng and John King Fairbank's retranslation of Lin Zexu's letter (see Appendix) and Dikötte's racializing of James Legge's translation of *zulei* (see Chapter 3).
21. Roger Hart, "Translating the Untranslatable: From Copula to Incommensurable Worlds," in Liu, *Tokens of Exchange*, p. 54.
22. See my essay "The Question of Meaning-Value in the Political Economy of the Sign," ibid., pp. 13–41.
23. Whitney, *Language and the Study of Language*, p. 8.
24. Ibid., p. 232.
25. Ibid.
26. William Dwight Whitney, "Phusei or Thesei—Natural or Conventional?" in Silverstein, *Whitney on Language*, p. 115; originally published in *Transactions of the American Philological Association for 1874* (1875): 95–116.
27. Ibid., pp. 131–132
28. Whitney, *Language and the Study of Language*, p. 38.
29. Daniele Gambarara, "The Convention of Geneva: History of Linguistic Ideas and History of Communicative Practices," in *Historical Roots of Linguistic Theories*, ed. Lia Formigari and Daniele Gambarara (Amsterdam: John Benjamins Publishing Company, 1995). See Chapter 1 for my discussion.
30. See Yen-lu Tang, "The Crumbling of Tradition: Ma Chien-chung and China's Entrance into the Family of Nations" (Ph.D. diss., New York University, 1987), pp. 64–123.
31. Ma Xiangbo, *Ma Xiangbo wenji* (Collected essays of Ma Xiangbo), ed. Fang Hao (Beiping: Shangzhi bianyiguan, 1947), p. 404.
32. W. South Coblin and Joseph A. Levi, *Francisco Varo's Grammar of the Mandarin Language (1703): An English Translation of "Arte de la Lengua Mandarina"* (Amsterdam: John Benjamins Publishing Company, 2000), p. x.

33. Ma Jianzhong, *Mashi wentong* (Ma's universal principles of classical Chinese) (Beijing: Commercial Press, 1998), pp. 361–362.

34. Ibid., p. 323.

35. In a short essay on Ma Jianzhong, Victor Mair continues to evoke this line of argument by comparing Sinitic and Sanskrit grammar as follows: "One might speculate why the Indians were so well disposed to grammar and why the Chinese were so ill disposed to it. My own interpretation would be that it has something to do with the fact that Sanskrit is one of the most highly inflected languages known to have existed whereas Sinitic (especially in its Classical Chinese form which was the basis for all but the tiniest portion of language studies in premodern China) is perhaps the least inflected language on earth." See Victor Mair, "Ma Jianzhong and the Invention of Chinese Grammar," *Journal of Chinese Linguistics,* monograph series "Studies on the History of Chinese Syntax," ed. Chaofen Sun, no. 10 (1997): 9.

36. Ma Jianzhong, *Mashi wentong,* p. 285.

37. Ibid., pp. 178–179.

38. Ibid., p. 43.

39. See Zhang Ruogu, *Ma Xiangbo xiansheng nianpu* (A chronological biography of Ma Xiangbo) (Taipei: Wenxing Shudian, 1965), p. 4.

40. Ma Jiangzhong is said to have contemplated becoming a priest himself but decided against it after witnessing the unfair treatment of Chinese priests at the ecclesiastic monastery where his brother received his training. See Yen-lu Tang, "Crumbling of Tradition," p. 12.

41. See Alain Peyraube, "Sur les Sources du *Ma Shi Wen Tong*" (On the sources of *Ma's Universal Principles of Classical Chinese*), *Histoire, Épistémologie, Langage* 21, no. 2 (1999): 74–75.

42. Peyraube argues that Ma was familiar with Prémare and Abel-Rémusat and followed some of Prémare's methods, but he also departed from them, and especially from Abel-Rémusat's approach to Chinese grammar. Ibid., p. 74.

43. Noam Chomsky, *Cartesian Linguistics* (New York: Harper and Row, 1966), p. 45; quoted in David Herman, *Universal Grammar and Narrative Form* (Durham: Duke University Press, 1995), pp. 12–13.

44. Otto Jespersen, *The Philosophy of Grammar* (1924; reprint, New York: Haskell House, 1965), p. 46; quoted in Herman, *Universal Grammar,* p. 13. Likewise, Umberto Eco argues that the novelty of *La Grammaire générale et raisonnée* was "simply the decision of taking as a model a modern language—French." See Eco, *Search for the Perfect Language,* p. 314.

45. Ma Jianzhong, *Mashi wentong,* p. 9.

46. Ma Jianzhong, *Shikezhai jiyan* (Essays from the Shike studio) (Beijing: Zhonghua shuju, 1960), p. 91.

47. Ma Xiangbo, also known as Ma Liang, was four years older than his brother. He was a scholar, Jesuit priest, educator, and diplomat. He joined the Society of Jesus in the early 1860s, completing his probationary term in 1864 and being ordained in 1870. In 1871 he was sent by the Jesuits to work as a missionary in

Nanjing. He disliked the work, however, and returned to Shanghai to become the principal of the College of St. Ignatius in 1872. In 1881 he joined the foreign service and was appointed consul in Osaka in the same year. Thereafter, he became an adviser to Li Shuzhang, newly appointed minister to Japan, and accompanied Li to Tokyo as councillor of the mission early in 1882. He devoted his later life to education and was one of the founders of Aurora University in Shanghai. After the birth of the new Republic, he served as interim president of National Peking University. He died in 1939 at the age of one hundred. See Yen-lu Tang, "Crumbling of Tradition," p. 10.

48. Ma Jianzhong, *Mashi wentong,* p. 13.

49. Ibid., p. 15.

50. Ibid., p. 12.

51. Ding Wenjiang, *Liang Rengong xiansheng nianpu changbian chugao* (A preliminary draft of the chronological biography of Liang Qichao) (Taipei, 1972), 1:33; quoted in Yen-lu Tang, "Crumbling of Tradition," p. 136.

52. Liang Qichao, "Zhongguo jin sanbainian xueshushi" (Chinese scholarship in the past three hundred years), in *Yinbing shi heji (zhuanji)* (Collected essays from the ice-drinker's studio (Shanghai: Zhonghua shuju, 1936), 17:214. Wang and Yu were prominent Qing scholars.

53. Ma Jianzhong, *Mashi wentong,* p. 7.

54. Liang Qichao, "Bianfa tongyi" (General discourse on reform), in *Yinbing shi heji (wenji),* (Shanghai: Zhonghua shuju, 1936), 1:52.

55. Liang Qichao, "Lun Zhongguo xueshu sixiang bianqian zhi dashi" (Changing directions in Chinese thoughts and scholarship), in *Yinbing shi heji (wenji),* 3:93.

56. Sun Zhongshan (Sun Yat-sen), *Jianguo fanglue* (Blueprint for nation building), (Beijing, Renmin chubanshe, 1956), 1:128–129.

57. Ma Jianzhong, *Mashi wentong,* p. 68.

58. See Peyraube, "Sur les Sources du *Ma Shi Wen Tong,*" p. 74.

59. See Porter, *Ideographia,* pp. 69–72.

60. I have borrowed the term "brush talk" from H. T. Douglas; see chap. 2 of his book *Borders of Civilization* (Durham: Duke University Press, 1996).

61. See Zhang Shizhao, *Zhongdeng guowen dian* (An intermediary grammar of Mandarin) (Shanghai: Shangwu yinshuguan, 1928); Liu Bannong, *Zhongguo wenfa tonglun* (A comprehensive grammar of Chinese) (Shanghai: Qunyi shushe, 1920) and *Zhongguo wenfa jianghua* (Lectures on Chinese grammar) (Shanghai: Beixin shuju, 1932); Jin Zhaozi, *Guowen fa zhi yanjiu* (A study of Mandarin grammar) (Shanghai: Zhonghua shuju, 1922). Other influential grammarians who proposed revisionary systems in the first three decades after Ma include Chen Chengze, *Guowenfa caochuang* (A preliminary grammar of Mandarin) (Shanghai: Shangwu chubanshe, 1922); Li Jinxi, *Guoyu wenfa* (A grammar of Mandarin) (Shanghai: Shangwu chubanshe, 1924), and *Bijiao wenfa* (Comparative grammar) (Shanghai: Kexue chubanshe, 1957); and Yang Shuda, *Gaodeng guowenfa* (Advanced grammar of Mandarin) (Shanghai: Shangwu chubanshe, 1930), who also published an annotated edition of *Ma's Universal*

Principles of Classical Chinese (Shanghai: Shangwu chubanshe, 1931). Zhang, Li, and Yang, in particular, helped popularize the substitution of *ci* for Ma's *zi*.

Conclusion

1. Frantz Fanon, *Black Skin, White Masks,* trans. Charles Lam Markmann (New York: Grove Press, 1967), p. 91. In the latter quotation, Fanon is echoing the words of Francis Jeanson.
2. I thank one of my anonymous reviewers for suggesting the term "inter-imperiality" to better characterize the focus of my study.
3. See Terry Castle, "Phantasmagoria: Spectral Technology and the Metaphysics of Modern Reverie," *Critical Inquiry* 15, no. 3 (Autumn 1988): 64.
4. Henry Fox-Talbot, who patented the first negative-positive process, the calotype, in 1841, saw the principle of photography as that of chemically and permanently "fixing the shadow" of images thrown by the sun itself. Before the invention of the neologism in mid-century by Sir John Herschel, who combined the Greek *photos* (light) and *graphos* (drawing), an early cognomen for photography was "sun pictures." See Alan Thomas, *The Expanding Eye: Photography and the Nineteenth-Century Mind* (London: Croom Helm, 1978), p. 7.
5. Peter Pollack, *The Farther Shore: A Natural History of Perception, 1798–1984* (New York: Atlantic Monthly Press, 1990), p. 23.
6. H. G. Wells, "The Time Machine," in *Complete Short Stories* (London: Ernest Benn, 1948), p. 90; quoted in Joss Lutz Marsh, "In a Glass Darkly," in *Prehistories of the Future: The Primitivist Project and the Culture of Modernism,* ed. Elazar Barkan and Ronald Bush (Stanford: Stanford University Press, 1995), p. 168. I find Marsh's discussion of the late Victorian fantastic and primitivism insightful, especially his analysis of Wells and Bram Stoker's *Dracula* in light of photography.
7. See Taussig's analysis of the documentary film *Nanook,* in particular, Robert Flaherty's staging of the scene in which the Eskimo chief Nanook tries to bite the gramophone record. Michael Taussig, *Mimesis and Alterity: A Particular History of the Senses* (New York: Routledge, 1993). For a study of the gramophone and colonial modernity in China, see Andrew F. Jones, *Yellow Music: Media Culture and Colonial Modernity in the Chinese Jazz Age* (Durham: Duke University Press, 2001).
8. The photographic taxonomy of consumptives, maniacs, criminals, social outcasts, prostitutes, and primitives became one of the first tasks of the new technology in the empire building of nineteenth-century Europe. Between 1883 and 1893, Alphonse Bertillon used his camera to document a hundred thousand criminals for the Paris police in one of the most systematic criminological uses of the camera in his time. The Englishman Francis Galton's *Inquiries into Human Faculty and Its Development* (1883) used "composite photographs made by precisely aligned multiple exposures" to construct and classify abnormal physiognomic types. See Sarah Greenough, "The Curious Contagion of the

Camera," in *On the Art of Fixing a Shadow: One Hundred and Fifty Years of Photography,* ed. Sarah Greenough et al. (Washington, D.C.: National Gallery of Art, 1989), p. 140.

9. Nancy Perloff, "Gauguin's French Baggage: Decadence and Colonialism in Tahiti," in Barkan and Bush, *Prehistories of the Future,* pp. 226–269.

10. Craig Clunas, "Oriental Antiques/Far Eastern Art," *Positions: East Asia Cultures Critique* 2, no. 2 (Fall 1994): 318.

11. Ibid. See also Craig Clunas, "Whose Throne Is It Anyway? The Qianlong Throne in the T. T. Tsui Gallery," *Orientations* 22, no. 7 (July 1991): 44–50.

12. Richard H. Davis, "Three Styles of Looting in India," *History and Anthropology* 6, no. 4 (1994): 293.

13. For a discussion of the discrepancies in the naming of the *Yihe Tuan,* or "Boxers," in Chinese and Western historiographies, see Chapter 5.

14. Nominal File: J. P. Swift, Victoria and Albert Registry, quoted in Clunas, "Whose Throne Is It Anyway?" pp. 48–49.

15. Clunas, "Whose Throne is It Anyway?" p. 50.

16. For a new departure in the interpretation of the Opium War and the Arrow War based on a comprehensive examination of archival material, see J. Y. Wong, *Deadly Dreams* (Cambridge: Cambridge University Press, 1997).

17. James Hevia, *English Lessons: The Pedagogy of Imperialism in Nineteenth-Century China* (Durham: Duke University Press, 2003), p. 88.

18. The behavior of the British overlaps with, but is not the same as, the more familiar ethnographic interest of Europeans when they take possession of native objects. Margaret J. Wiener discovered in her research on the Dutch looting of the royal regalia of Klungkung in Bali in 1908 that, after the Dutch military sacked the royal palace of the Klungkung king, they found a silver tea service, a gift from the governor-general, as well as a number of other European objects. "Significantly, there is no record of what became of the European artifacts discovered in the palace—the saddle, the tea service, the portraits of the Queen, and ammunition. Such things may have caught the eyes of journalists, but they could have no ethnological value since they failed to encode the necessary distance between European selves and Balinese others." There is no evidence, though, that the Europeans did not repossess those objects. See Margaret J. Wiener, "Object Lessons: Dutch Colonialism and the Looting of Bali," *History and Anthropology* 6, no. 4 (1994): 353.

19. The story of the disappearance and restoration of the original throne chair is recounted in Zhu Jiajin, *Gugong tuishi lu* (My story of the Palace Museum in retirement), 2 vols. (Beijing: Bejing chubanshe, 1999).

20. Zhu looked mildly intrigued when I described the imperial thrones I had seen at the Victoria and Albert in London and the Asian Art Museum in Edinburgh.

21. See "Preface," in *Photographs of Palace Buildings of Peking, Compiled by the Imperial Museum of Tokyo* (Tokyo, 1906).

22. Der Ling, *Two Years in the Forbidden City* (New York: Moffat, Yard and Company, 1912), p. 184. In a photograph somewhat similar to the one shown in Figure

16, Marina Warner identifies the foreigner sitting on the imperial throne as the French minister M. Pinchon. See Marina Warner, *The Dragon Empress: Life and Times of Tz'u-hsi, Empress Dowager of China, 1835–1908* (New York: Macmillan, 1972), p. 250.

23. Zhu Jiajin, *Gugong tuishi lu*, 2:8.

24. See Marsh, "In a Glass Darkly," p. 169.

25. For an analysis of Lu Xun's exposure to war journalism and photography while he was a medical student in Japan, see my *Tranlingual Practice: Literature, National Culture, and Translated Modernity* (Stanford: Stanford University Press, 1995), pp. 60–64.

26. Rey Chow described a similar experience of watching the film in *Woman and Chinese Modernity* (Minneapolis: University of Minnesota Press, 1991) but was no more successful than I was in my earlier attempt to understand the peculiar magic of *The Last Emperor*. The experience she related was meaningful in light of the situation of colonial Hong Kong, which formed the background of her analysis; but Bertolucci's cinematography, which had probably moved her to write about the film in the first place, such as the representation of royal regalia and so on that create the visual impact of the film, also deserves close attention.

27. For recent studies on the Western museum as a social institution, see Tony Bennett, *The Birth of the Museum: History, Theory, Politics* (London: Routledge, 1995); Ivan Karp and Steven D. Lavine, eds., *Exhibiting Cultures: The Poetics and Politics of Museum Display* (Washington, D.C.: Smithsonian Institution Press, 1991).

28. The setting where Pu Yi meets his English teacher Sir Reginald Fleming Johnston appears to be the Hall of Mental Cultivation (Yangxin dian).

29. Interestingly, the Japanese-language edition of *The Last Emperor* censors some of the scenes relating to the film's portrayal of the Japanese in World War II that were perceived as unfavorable. I thank Philip Hallman for alerting me to the existence of this edition and locating a copy for me.

Glossary of Selected
Chinese Characters

bing ming	稟明
Chang Lin	長麟
chuanyi zhu zi	傳疑助字
ci	詞
da ban	大班
Da Qin	大秦
Da Qin Brahman	大秦婆羅門
Daoguang yangsou zhengfu ji	道光洋艘征撫記
Dayi juemi lu	大義覺迷錄
di	狄
di²	敵
er	而
Er ya	爾雅
fan gui	番鬼
Fei wo zulei qixin bi yi	非我族類其心必異
Feng Chengjun	馮承鈞
fu	夫
geshi gongwen	各式公文
giu zi	鬼子
Gu shu yiyi juli	古書疑義舉例
guomu	國母
He Ao	何鰲
hu	乎
Hu Yuanrui	胡元瑞
Hua	華
Huangchao wenxian tongkao	皇朝文獻通考
hulu	胡虜
jian min	姦民
jian yi	姦夷
Jiangnan huzhu	江南互助
jiao min	教民
jiao shi	教士

Jing zhuan shi ci	經傳釋詞
jun zhu	君主
Kong Yuxun	孔毓珣
Ku Hung-Ming (Gu Hongming)	辜鴻銘
Li Hongzhang	李鴻章
Li Zhenhua	李珍華
Li Zhiying	李質穎
liang yi	良夷
Liu Bannong	劉半農
Lu	虜
Lu²	鹵
Lü Liuliang	呂留良
Ma Jianzhong	馬建忠
Ma Xiangbo	馬相伯
man-mo	蠻貊
Mayu	媽嶼
min	民
Ming (dynasty)	明
Mojiatuo	摩伽陀
Ni Hongwen	倪宏文
Nie hai hua	孽海花
Ouyang Yongshu	歐陽永叔
pian pang	偏旁
Pu Yi	溥儀
qi ci	起詞
qie	切
Qianlong	乾隆
Qin	秦
Qin ding siku quanshu	欽定四庫全書
Qing (dynasty)	清
qiu zi	龜茲
quan fei	拳匪
quan li	權利
Shanyang	山陽
shen chen	申陳
Shen Fuwei	沈福偉
shi yi changji yi zhi yi	師夷長技以制夷
shi yi zhi	師夷智
Shuo wen jie zi	說文解字
Song Lian	宋濂
Sun Yan	孫炎
Tian Shu	天書
wailai zhi jun	外來之君
Wan guo gong fa	萬國公法

Wang yue: sou bu yuan qianli er lai, yi jiang you yi li wuguo hu	王曰：叟不遠千里而來，亦將有以利吾國乎
Wang Zhichun	王之春
Wei Yuan	魏源
Wu Jingfu	吳敬甫
xi	檄
xi yu	西域
Xian Songpu	咸松圃
Xu Jiyu	徐繼畬
Xu Shen	許慎
xun gu	訓詁
ye	耶
yi	夷
yi²	彝
yi-di	夷狄
Yihe Tuan	義和團
Yihe yuan	頤和園
yin yun	音韻
Yinghuan zhilue	瀛環志略
Yong Zheng	雍正
yu	與
Yu Qian	裕謙
Yuanming Yuan	圓明園
Yue Zhongqi	岳鐘琪
zai	哉
Zeng Jing	曾靜
zha xing	劄行
Zhang Shizhao	章士釗
Zhang Xi	張熙
Zhang Xi (author of *Fuyi Riji*)	張喜
Zhang Zhidong	張之洞
zhao hui	照會
Zheng Xuan	鄭玄
zhongwai yijia	中外一家
zhu	諸
zhu quan	主權
Zhuiman yesou	贅漫野叟
zi	字
zi shu	字書
zun wang rang yi	尊王攘夷

Index